With considerable affection and admiration, this book is dedicated to Evelyn Brooks Higginbotham, Harry A. Blackmun, Curtis Bok, William J. Brennan, Jr., Richardson Dilworth, John P. Frank, William Henry Hastie, Bessie Hill, Charles Hamilton Houston, Nelson Mandela, Thurgood Marshall, Bernice Munce, J. Austin Norris, Jessie Treichler, and Earl Warren. In different ways, they have profoundly and positively influenced my life. They have given me the encouragement to seek institutional changes that move from shades of freedom to the fuller sunlight of justice, freedom and equity.

PREFACE

IT HAS BEEN eighteen years since my first book, *In the Matter of Color*, was published. It is twelve years since I gave the Du Bois Lectures at Harvard University, when I first publicly summarized my tentative thoughts on the issues that now comprise the core of this Race and the American Legal Process series.

In many ways, some of the intervening years since I delivered those lectures have been painful for me. Progress toward racial equality has been halting, at best. Instead, the nation often seems to be retreating from the values of a time in which there existed substantial consensus on the need for racial pluralism in positions of power and for the opportunity of upward mobility. We have lost one of the nation's most effective civil rights lawyers and wisest Justices—Thurgood Marshall—and he has been replaced by a person of considerably less compassion for minorities, the weak, the poor, and the powerless.*

My disenchantment has been shared by others. In 1989, concerned about a seemingly consistent majority of five Supreme Court Justices making very conservative decisions on key civil rights and race relations cases, Justice Blackmun wrote, "[s]adly, . . . [o]ne wonders whether the majority [of the Supreme Court Justices] still believes that . . . race discrimination against nonwhites is a problem in our society, or even remembers that it ever was."** In 1993, in response to the majority's opinion in *Shaw v. Reno*, one of the key congressional redistricting cases that invoked a new standard that could cause the elimination of ten to seventeen African-American and Latino Mem-

---

*See A. Leon Higginbotham, Jr., *Justice Clarence Thomas in Retrospect*, 45 HASTINGS L.J. 1405 (1994); A. Leon Higginbotham, Jr., *Open Letter to Justice Clarence Thomas From a Federal Judicial Colleague*, 140 U. PA. L. REV. 1005 (1992); A. Leon Higginbotham, Jr., *A Tribute to Justice Thurgood Marshall*, 105 HARV. L. REV. 55 (1991).

**See Wards Cove Packing Co. v. Atonio, 490 U.S. 642, 662 (1989) (Blackmun, J., dissenting) (citing City of Richmond v. J.A. Croson Co., 488 U.S. 469 (1989)).

bers in the United States House of Representatives, Justice White observed in a dissent that even under North Carolina's new redistricting plan, "whites remain a voting majority in a disproportionate number of congressional districts." He stressed that it was "both a fiction and a departure from settled equal protection principles" for the majority to void a redistricting plan whereby North Carolina "sent its *first* black representatives since Reconstruction to the United States Congress."*

After the high-profile launching of the rhetorical "Contract with America" in 1995, the House of Representatives brought in sixty-five new pages—high school or college students who deliver messages and perform other functions in the House. Of the new pages, sixty-four were white and one was Asian American. According to a former Clerk of the House, in past years, fifteen to twenty pages were Latino, African-American, or from other minorities. As Congressperson Cynthia McKinney observed: "I suppose they couldn't find any Latino or African-American youngsters qualified enough to carry flags."** This exclusion of minorities occurred at the same time that many of these very political leaders were condemning affirmative action concepts. Concurrently, innumerable substantive programs that would have aided the poor and the powerless were being eliminated or modified. Since a disproportionate number of the poor are from minorities, African Americans sustained significant setbacks.

The retreat from pluralism within the federal judiciary was perhaps the most heartbreaking development for me. From 1980 to 1992, there was an intentional reduction of the number of African-American judges on the federal courts. From 1980 to September 1992, of the 115 persons appointed to the U.S. Courts of Appeals, only two were African-American.*** More than fifty judges were appointed to the federal courts of the Sixth Circuit, a region comprising the states of Michigan, Ohio, Kentucky, and Tennessee, and not one was African-American. Four African-American judges in the Southern District of New York went on senior judge status and all were replaced by white judges. One could fairly say that under twelve years of Republican administrations, African-American judges were becoming an endangered species, soon to be extinct.**** Fortunately, we have begun to see a reversal in

---

*Shaw v. Reno, 113 S. Ct. 2816, 2834 (1993) (White, J., dissenting).

**See Juliet Eilperin, *New Page Class Is Virtually All-White*, ROLL CALL, Sept. 25, 1995, at 1.

***Of the two, one was Larry Pierce, whose age made it evident that he would be retiring in a few years; the other was Clarence Thomas, appointed to the U.S. Court of Appeals for the District of Columbia.

****See A. Leon Higginbotham, Jr., *The Case of the Missing Black Judges*, N.Y. TIMES, July 29, 1992, at A21.

the trend to an appointment policy that considers racial and gender pluralism as desirable accomplishments.*

Finishing this second volume has taken far longer than I had contemplated. One of my acerbic colleagues reminded me that at this pace of finishing a volume every eighteen years, I will be 140 years old when the last volume is completed. With my resignation from the court in March 1993, I finally had a sufficient amount of time to continue this intellectual journey.

While this volume focuses almost exclusively on the precept of inferiority, I have also finished most of my writing on the precepts of property, powerlessness, racial purity, manumission, and free blacks. I expect to publish the next volume within two years, and it is my hope that several of my younger colleagues who are now active academicians will continue this series with far greater expedition.

Many of the chapters in this volume are excerpts of my articles published in the last fifteen years. A comprehensive bibliography is noted after the Appendix. While there may have been some significant developments after the publication of my original articles, I will leave it to other scholars to update those issues.

This volume is not intended to be an encyclopedia covering all of the racial legal incidents of the last few centuries—to do that would require many more volumes. I comment on some aspects of race and the American legal process during the twentieth century; however, the more comprehensive details of the twentieth-century history will also be grist for later volumes and for other authors. As an example, I do not discuss in full context *Brown v. Board of Education* and the desegregation cases. I do not explore the allegedly controversial issues of affirmative action, "set asides," the racial implications of capital punishment, or federal habeas corpus law. I also do not address in full the congressional redistricting cases. There is a plethora of books and articles on all of these issues. My purpose in this book has been to highlight significant legal issues that exemplify the precept of racial inferiority.

With the passage of the years, it has become an increasing distraction as to what should be the preferable terminology when referring to "African Americans." When my first major article was published in 1973, the term

---

Compare Democratic President William Jefferson Clinton's judicial appointments with those of Republican Presidents Ronald Reagan and George Bush. In the first *three* years of the Clinton administration, thirty-six African Americans were appointed to the federal judiciary. In contrast, during the previous *twelve* years under the Reagan and Bush administrations, eighteen African Americans were appointed. *See* ALLIANCE FOR JUSTICE, JUDICIAL SELECTION PROJECT: ANNUAL REPORT 8 (1995). *See also* Sheldon Goldman and Matthew D. Saronson, *Clinton's Nontraditional Judges: Creating a More Representative Bench,* 78 JUDICATURE 68 (Sept. 1994).

"Negro" was the standard. Since then, there have been many modifications of the "proper" terminology. In this volume, I have used the terms "Negro," "colored," "black," and "African American" interchangeably. My major mentor, John Hope Franklin, in the early editions of his classic treatise, *From Slavery to Freedom*, used the subtitle "A History of American Negroes." In the latest edition, he and his new co-author, Professor Alfred A. Moss, Jr., used "A History of African Americans" as the subtitle. They explain the progression in the Preface to the Seventh Edition:

> While African American is increasing in current usage, there is no reason to believe that this is a final designation; for the political and cultural winds that produced it continue to blow, perhaps sweeping before them earlier designations and bringing forth at some later time a designation as yet unknown.*

I started my introduction to *In the Matter of Color* by making reference to the tragic assassinations of the foremost leaders of our time: President John F. Kennedy, Robert Kennedy, and Martin Luther King, Jr. Fortunately, in this country today, physical violence against national leaders seems to have ceased.

Despite other despair, I have seen some signs of hope, the most dramatic of which occurred in South Africa.** I finished this Preface on the day the new South African Constitution was adopted. Two years ago in Pretoria, on a bright, sunny day, I witnessed a miraculous transition of power. Former President F.W. deKlerk became the Executive Deputy President, and the African National Congress leader, Nelson Rolihlahla Mandela, became President of the Republic of South Africa. They took their oaths, shook hands, and renewed their pledge to become a fair multiracial society that would "be faithful to" a constitution that will "do justice to all." Many barriers in the United States and even more in South Africa must be overcome. Nevertheless, the South African experience boosts my spirits. I keep my fervent belief in the possibility of substantial equality and significant equity in the United States, despite the conservative winds that sometimes delay the journey.

Upon reflection, in the eighteen years since my first volume was published, nothing has occurred to cause me to believe that the role of the law

---

*JOHN HOPE FRANKLIN AND ALFRED A. MOSS, JR., FROM SLAVERY TO FREEDOM: A HISTORY OF AFRICAN AMERICANS xix (7th ed. 1994).

**In 1994, Nelson Mandela of the African National Congress and Mangosuthu Buthelezi of the Inkatha Freedom Party asked me and six other persons to go to South Africa as international mediators to attempt to resolve some differences on the proposed Constitution. The other six persons were Dr. Henry Kissinger of the United States, Lord Carrington of England, Professor Antonio LaPergola of Italy, Justice H.K. Bhagwati of India, Professor Paul Kevenhorster of Germany, and Professor Antoine Laponce of Canada.

may have less of an impact than I envisioned then, in either perpetuating or eradicating racial injustice. Today, I am even more convinced of the pervasive impact and potential of the American legal process.

Harvard University   A. LEON HIGGINBOTHAM, JR.
Cambridge, Massachusetts
May 8, 1996

ACKNOWLEDGMENTS

A FTER MORE than three decades of intensive research, reading, and writing on the subject of race and the American legal process, my list of indebtedness is endless. I have had thousands of dialogues with law clerks, professorial colleagues, judges, insightful critics, students, and research associates. They have offered invaluable commentary. They have inspired and challenged me, causing revisions of some of my views. I apologize to the hundreds whose names are not noted here.

Over the last fifteen years, eight research associates or law clerks have spent more than two years working with me on discrete aspects of this project. Their wisdom is reflected in some of the chapters in this volume. They are Colleen Adams, Laura B. Farmelo, Aderson B. Francois, Stephanie Franklin-Suber, F. Michael Higginbotham, Rubin M. Sinins, William C. Smith, and Linda Y. Yueh. Several colleagues have spent considerable time on research projects that will be included in future volumes. They are Greer C. Bosworth, Alice Brown, Kathleen Cleaver, Mitchell Duneier, Susan Ginsberg, Farrah Griffin, Anne Jacobs, Cassandra Havard Jones, Robert Kaczorowski, Barbara K. Kopytoff, Susan B. Mann, Sarah W. Mitchell, Stephanie Y. Moore, S. Sandile Ngcobo, Ronald K. Noble, and Marguerite Stricklin. Secretaries have been far more than typists. They have been editors, proofreaders, and often thoughtful critics. They are Kathryn Clark Crawford, Carol Derby, Paulette Didion, Bettie C. Lee, and Martha Rosso.

Families pay a high price when one of their members is driven excessively to use almost every weekend, vacation, and spare evening to pursue a project that seems as if it will never end. Thus, for their patience and for their general understanding, I am profoundly indebted to Evelyn, Stephen, Karen, Kenneth, Nia, Jeanne, and "Jazz." 1 hope that this series of books will be worth the many times lost and events cancelled.

I thank the foundations that have provided the support to the University of Pennsylvania, New York University, and Harvard University over the years—particularly the Ford, Rockefeller, William Penn, Mellon, and Potamkin foundations. Without their generous support, this project would still be a dream that would never have been fulfilled.

Librarians and libraries have been the lifeblood of this project. I am pleased to acknowledge the extraordinary assistance of the library staffs at the University of Pennsylvania, the University of Pennsylvania Law School, Harvard University, Harvard Law School, Northeastern University School of Law, the Library of Congress, the Curator's Office of the United States Supreme Court, and Culver Pictures. I am also appreciative of the publishers who have granted permission to take excerpts from some of my previous articles, which are noted in the appendix. I am personally indebted to Sheldon Meyer of Oxford University Press for his exceptional encouragement and support for this Race and the American Legal Process series. For two generations of academicians, he has been a vigorous advocate for hundreds of scholars who have something to say.

I was again privileged to have a great editor from Oxford, Leona Capeless, the recently retired Vice President who, for more than forty years, exemplified the best of the Oxford University Press tradition. And I want to thank Joellyn Ausanka for her superb copyediting and her considerable patience in accepting many revisions. I was also fortunate to again have Bernice Colt prepare the index.

A special thanks is due Karen Watson, who understands the mission and captured the spirit of the book in her magnificent collage on the cover.

It is now twelve years since I gave the Du Bois Lectures at Harvard, when I first summarized publicly my tentative thoughts on what I now call the Ten Precepts of American Slavery Jurisprudence. I am grateful for the coveted invitation from the late Professor Nathan I. Huggins to give the lectures and for having the opportunity to attempt, in an exhilarating academic environment, to put my concepts in a more systematic order. In 1984, I never contemplated that I would someday return to Harvard and become the Public Service Professor of Jurisprudence at the John F. Kennedy School of Government and be a part of the Law School and the exciting Afro-American Studies Department now so superbly led by Dr. Henry Louis Gates, Jr., the W.E.B. Du Bois Professor of the Humanities.

More than twenty-five years ago, Marvin E. Wolfgang, Renée Fox, and Bernard Wolfman invited me to teach in their respective departments at the University of Pennsylvania. Along with my mentor, John Hope Franklin, then at the University of Chicago, they were my earliest supporters. Dean John Sexton of New York University School of Law, Dean Colin S. Diver of the University of Pennsylvania Law School, Dean Robert C. Clark of the Harvard Law School, Provost Albert Carnesale of Harvard University, Dean Joseph

Nye of the John F. Kennedy School of Government, and Dr. Henry Louis Gates, Jr., of the Afro-American Studies Department at Harvard University, have always been supportive of all my academic projects.

I am also grateful for the year at the National Humanities Center in North Carolina, where I had the opportunity to more precisely formulate my thoughts in the very room where my primary mentor, John Hope Franklin, had written and reflected as a Fellow some years earlier.

I particularly want to thank the extraordinary firm of Paul, Weiss, Rifkind, Wharton & Garrison for creating the exciting, intellectual milieu that made my finishing this book compatible with my association with the law firm. My partners have given me and our other colleagues considerable latitude to retreat, write and reflect on some of the many critical policy issues of our century and also to do substantial *pro bono publico* work. I thank all of them, and particularly Arthur Liman and Ernest Rubenstein for their supportive friendship.

I know that the tradition is to lavishly state appreciation for the contributions an author has received from colleagues and to note that the errors or omissions are solely those of the author. After sharing ideas for more than thirty years with so many scholars on my research and on theirs, I will not let them off the hook. They have influenced me, just as, on some occasions, I may have influenced them. So, some of the errors are collective, and I only wish that I and "we" had been wise enough to catch them.

CONTENTS

Contents xix

INTRODUCTION:
FROM TOTAL RACIAL OPPRESSION
TO SHADES OF FREEDOM

[T]here was a day, and not really a very distant day, when Americans were scarcely Americans at all but discontented Europeans, facing a great unconquered continent and strolling, say, into a marketplace and seeing black men for the first time. The shock this spectacle afforded is suggested, surely, by the promptness with which they decided that these black men were not really men but cattle.—James Baldwin [1]

F ROM the first encounter on the American continent between Africans and Europeans, the journey from total racial oppression toward the goal of true racial equality has been long and tortuous. For blacks, the journey began with total racial oppression in the dark of night on slave ships or on plantations. It moved toward the glimmer of an early dawn with its elusive shades of freedom. The words, "We the People of the United States," as they appear in the Preamble of the United States Constitution were to prove to be truly ambiguous. The process of establishing who would be included in "We the People" exposed the contradiction between Abraham Lincoln's elegant description at Gettysburg of a nation "conceived in Liberty, and dedicated to the proposition that all men are created equal," [2] and James Baldwin's imaginary first encounter when white men decided that "black men were not really men but cattle." [3]

In 1671, the General Assembly of Virginia declared "that sheep, horses, cattle should be delivered in kind to an orphan when he comes of age, to which some have desired that Negroes be added." [4] In 1831, Mr. Gholson of the Virginia legislature said: "I lately purchased *four women* and *ten children* in whom I thought I obtained a great bargain, for I really supposed they were *my property*, as were my *brood mares*." [5] Thus, for at least 160 years, in the eyes of some Virginia legislators, Negroes were not differentiated from "sheep, horses, cattle," or "mares."

At the Constitutional Convention, there was intense debate on whether slaves should be counted in calculating the number of persons that would be included as a basis for determining the number of representatives each state would have in the House of Representatives. The founding fathers also had to determine whether slaves were to be perceived of primarily as property or as human beings. Concerned with maximizing Northern representation, William Paterson of New Jersey asserted on July 9, 1787:

> [Negroes] are no free agents, have no personal liberty, no faculty of acquiring property, but on the contrary are themselves property, and like other property entirely at the will of the master . . . and if Negroes are not represented in the States to which they belong, why should they be [counted as a basis for representation].[6]

Elbridge Gerry of Massachusetts stated that if slaves were to be a basis for Congressional representation for the South, then for the non-slave states of the North, "Horses and Cattle ought to have the Right of Represent[atio]n."[7]

This book will attempt to delineate the law's contribution to the frequent dehumanization of many African Americans and its impact on the journey from the midnight of total oppression to some early dawns, where there were occasional glitters of light and muted shades of freedom.

The Scope of This Volume

This volume continues the search I began over three decades ago and formulated into the series "Race and the American Legal Process." In 1978, in the first book of the series, *In the Matter of Color,*[8] I examined the colonial period. Here, I continue that journey, tracing the kaleidoscopic events of the years of the seventeenth to the twentieth century. These have been centuries of racial oppression, and for many—but not all—African Americans, there have been recent decades of progress. Our nation has moved from total oppression to varying shades of freedom. Rays of liberty and equality have penetrated the darkness, thereby diminishing somewhat the scope of racial injustice.

In 1903, W.E.B. Du Bois wrote: "The problem of the twentieth century is the problem of the color line,—the relation of the darker to the lighter races of men in Asia and Africa, in America and the islands of the sea." He eloquently characterizes these events as "this tale of the dawn of Freedom."[9]

In their extracurricular writings, even some conservative Supreme Court Justices recognize the reasons for the impatience of many African Americans along this journey toward the "dawn of freedom." In official judicial opinions, Justices of the Supreme Court generally use a careful protocol, which masks their inner feelings about what they know to be the egregiously unfair treatment of African Americans. Thus, the Justices' most revealing insights are often to be found made in comments other than those made in their formal opinions. In a tribute to Justice Thurgood Marshall published in the *Stanford Law Review*, Chief Justice Warren Burger wrote:

> [I]t took the Civil War to put an end to slavery, which had been given legal sanction in the Supreme Court's decision in *Dred Scott v. Sandford*. In 1896, the promises of the Declaration of Independence, the Emancipation Proclamation, and the Civil War Amendments were *"put on hold"* when, in *Plessy v. Ferguson*, the Supreme Court approved the *pernicious "separate but equal"* doctrine. [10]

This volume traces what Chief Justice Burger described as the "agonizingly slow . . . progress of the civil rights movement." [11] It also looks at, to again use Chief Justice Burger's telling phrase, the "pernicious" role that the Supreme Court and other whites in power played when "the promises of the Declaration of Independence, the Emancipation Proclamation and the Civil War amendments were 'put on hold.' " [12]

When evaluating the promises "put on hold," I have concluded that the legal process maintained the system of slavery, by using what I call the "Ten Precepts of American Slavery Jurisprudence." These precepts are defined in the Appendix. The dominant perspective within this volume is the role of the American legal process in substantiating, perpetuating, and legitimizing the precept of inferiority.

I define the precept of inferiority as: *presume, protect, and defend the ideal of superiority of whites and the inferiority of blacks.* In application, this precept has not remained fixed and unchanged. Nonetheless, it has persisted even to recent times, when many of the formal, overt barriers of racism have been delegitimized. However, it is probably still helpful to note contemporary incidents of the last decade that will illustrate the continuum up to today of the precept of inferiority that began in an era of slavery centuries ago.

"A Black Man Did It": Commonalities of Perception

To put into historical perspective the challenges of this nation, I start by looking at six relatively recent events. In each of these cases, a white person made false accusations that an African-American man had committed a terrible crime.

These highly publicized incidents reveal that, even in the late twentieth century, some persons will espouse false allegations that attribute the most egregious conduct to African Americans because they believe the public will unhesitatingly accept such stories. The public perception of African Americans as inferior and venal beings provides the basis of acceptability for the most outrageous of lies. I begin with these events because I believe that there is a direct and tragic nexus between the false allegations and perceptions of today, as we approach the end of the twentieth century, and some of the perceptions of black inferiority that have endured from the colonial period to the present.

Lockhart, Florida, 1995—Matthew Gayle told detectives that a black man shot and killed his twenty-year-old wife in their car as they were returning from a prayer service.[13] The day after the shooting, the police were informed that Gayle had long been seeking help to kill his wife. Three months later, Gayle was charged with the murder,[14] along with another white man.[15] Gayle's brother was charged with threatening to kill a witness in the case.[16]

Union, South Carolina, 1994—Susan Smith claimed that an armed black man perpetrated a carjacking, kidnapped her children who were in the vehicle, and left her on the side of the road.[17] Smith made emotional appeals for the safe return of her sons. She denied any part in the alleged kidnapping: "I don't think that any parent could love their children more than I do, and I would never even think about doing anything that would harm them."[18] Television networks gave her prime time coverage, but her story turned out to be a total fabrication. Smith was later arrested for murdering her own children. She confessed that she shoved the vehicle, with her sons strapped in the back seat, into a lake.[19] A South Carolina jury convicted Smith,[20] but spared her from the death penalty.[21]

Valley Stream, New York, 1994—Maryrose Posner claimed that she was robbed by a black man with a gun while she and her two-year-old daughter stood at a Chemical Bank cash machine. She claimed: "The man who did it put a gun to my child's head, while he laughed."[22] She alleged that the black assailant then sped away, with three other black men.[23] Posner later admitted in court that her story was a total lie, fabricated to gain attention from her busy doctor-husband.[24] Although she subsequently recanted her confession, claiming that police had coerced it by throwing lit cigarettes and hot water at her,[25] Posner ultimately pled guilty to a second-degree charge of filing a false instrument.[26]

Albany, New York, 1994—Kendra Gillis claimed that a black man attacked her with a razor in her dormitory at the State University of New York at Albany. A bizarre series of revelations and allegations followed. A police investigation revealed that Gillis tore her own clothing and scratched herself in an effort to show that she had been attacked.[27] Gillis admitted that the allegations were false and stated that she had actually been beaten by her abusive father, David Gillis, who was arrested for the assault.[28] Her mother, however, later reported another alleged incident: Kendra Gillis stated that a black man had shoved her against a wall and beaten her three weeks before her father's assault. Campus police had no record of this incident.[29] Kendra Gillis later refused to sign a statement implicating her father in her assault and would not cooperate with prosecutors.[30]

Three weeks later, three teenagers also in the Albany area admitted they had fabricated a story that a black man, armed with a semi-automatic handgun, demanded the receipts from the car wash where two of them worked. The three teenagers themselves had taken $3,559 from the car wash.[31]

Milwaukee, Wisconsin, 1992—Jesse Anderson claimed that two young black men attacked him and his wife. He claimed the black men fatally stabbed his wife in the face and stabbed him in the chest when he went to assist his wife.[32] The story was a lie, and Mr. Anderson was convicted of his wife's murder.[33]

Boston, Massachusetts, 1989—Charles Stuart claimed that he and his pregnant wife had been driving from a hospital childbirth class when a black man burst into the back seat of his car. Wielding a revolver, the "assailant" demanded cash and jewelry before fatally shooting Stuart's seven-months pregnant wife and shooting Stuart in the abdomen.[34]

Matthew Stuart, Charles Stuart's brother, later "went to authorities to expose his brother's hoax and incriminated himself."[35] The following day, Charles Stuart "apparently committed suicide by jumping from the Tobin Bridge."[36] Although he never confessed and was not tried, Charles Stuart remains the prime suspect in the killing of his wife and has been implicated by his brother, who has confessed to "taking the murder weapon from [Charles Stuart] the night of the killing and tossing it into a river. But he said he believed he was only helping Charles stage a fake robbery, and did not realize at the time that he had shot his wife."[37]

One must ask: Is there a commonality in these six cases spanning 1989 to 1995 with racial perceptions that existed during the slavery era? I submit that the centuries-old precept of inferiority in American slavery jurisprudence and the contemporary events I have cited are part of a continuum that still has an unfair impact on African Americans, even at the present time. The perception of inferiority that motivated these false accusations against blacks in the 1990s is not unrelated to the perception of inferiority that legitimized slavery. Thus, by analyzing the legal process of two centuries ago, this volume will also provide some insight into our present challenges.

"It's a Long Road"

From the arrival on this continent in 1619 of the first shipment of African slaves, there have been many roads intersecting freedom, indentured servitude, and slavery. Crossroads involved choices between equality and white supremacy, and between democracy and perceptions of black inferiority. Bessie Smith used to sing,

> It's a long road, but it's got to find an end.
> I picked up my bags baby, and I tried it again.[38]

After so many setbacks at so many intersections, African Americans have picked up their bags and tried, again and again, to go down the road in search of their rights as human beings. The struggle has always been to become equal citizens, to be included within the majesty of the phrase "We the People." African Americans and their allies have been at that pursuit for centuries and are still at it today.

Although a slaveholder, Thomas Jefferson recognized the tragic discrepancy between the American promise and the American reality. He found that it could not be categorized as anything less than hypocrisy and that it could not persist forever. When speaking of slavery, he wrote:

> And can the liberties of a nation be thought secure when we have removed their only firm basis, a conviction in the minds of the people that these liberties are of the gift of God? That they are not to be violated but with his wrath? *Indeed, I tremble for my country when I reflect that God is just; that his justice cannot sleep forever.* . . . . The Almighty has no attribute which can take side with us in such a contest.[39]

The heightened anger and "long road" for blacks during the nineteenth century were conveyed most eloquently by Frederick Douglass. Born a slave, Frederick Douglass became a leading abolitionist. In 1852, he described Independence Day from the perspective of blacks and slaves, rather than whites and slaveholders:

> This Fourth of July is *yours*, not mine. You may rejoice, I must mourn. . . . I say it with a sad sense of the disparity between us. I am not included within the pale of this glorious anniversary. . . . The blessings in which you, this day, rejoice, are not enjoyed in common. The rich inheritance of justice, liberty, prosperity and independence, bequeathed by your fathers, is shared by you, not by me. The sunlight that brought light and healing to you, has brought stripes and death to me.[40]

Three years later, in 1855, Abraham Lincoln recognized the same duality. Lincoln wrote:

When we were the political slaves of King George, and wanted to be free, we called the maxim that "all men are created equal" a self-evident truth; but now when we have grown fat, and have lost all dread of being slaves ourselves, we have become so greedy to be masters that we call the same maxim *"a self-evident lie."* The Fourth of July has not quite dwindled away; it is still a great day for burning fire-crackers![41]

America has long struggled with the tension between the "self-evident truth" and the "self-evident lie"—the contradiction between ideal and practice, what Gunnar Myrdal called the American Dilemma.[42]

Along that road traveled by those who sought the full sunlight of freedom, the American legal process has provided signposts in the form of constitutions, amendments to constitutions, legislative enactments, and judicial decisions, not all of which have pointed the nation toward the hoped-for destination of blacks as free, full, and equal participants in the whole of American society. Rather, these signposts have sometimes led African Americans down a circuitous path, starting from when they were perceived as not different from cattle. Moving up from the status of being considered less than human, African Americans were later viewed as lower caste, untouchables, second-class "persons"; then as civil rights crusaders and challengers in the federal courts, which in turn became more supportive during the second half of this century to enforce the Thirteenth, Fourteenth, and Fifteenth Amendments. Now, African Americans constitute a multifaceted minority. It is irrational to proffer a monolithic description of their status. They occupy a vast continuum. At one end, some, such as the author of this volume, now have the benefits of substantial equality and have been upwardly mobile. In contrast, at the other end, there continues to be pervasive and unfathomable inequality for many African Americans.

In 1993, 28.9 percent of African-American households earned under $10,000 per year, while 12.2 percent of white households earned under $10,000 annually. Disparities are, perhaps, the most striking when we witness the plight of America's children. In 1989, almost half (46.1 percent) of all African-American children lived in poverty, compared with 17.8 percent of white children. In 1993, in contrast, 1.9 percent of African-American households earned over $100,000 annually, as did 6.3 percent of white households.[43] The courts, legislators, and other public officials have played a powerful role in shaping this uneven economic legacy. At various times they have contributed to the legitimization of institutional racism, but at other times they have fostered policies for the eradication of some of the roots of racial injustice.

The Role of the Supreme Court

In all official pictures of the Supreme Court, there is an image suggested, by their very setting, that the nine Justices in black robes are exceptional individuals who ensure "equal justice under law," the phrase chiseled on the portals of the Supreme Court. But in the long corridor of history, from an African-American perspective, at times these saintly appearing Justices, by their unnecessary legitimization of racism, have caused far more systematic cruelty and grief to African Americans than the hooded vigilantes wearing white sheets and the emblem of the Ku Klux Klan. Many more millions of African Americans were denied the benefits of first-class citizenship by the Supreme Court's opinions in *Plessy v. Ferguson* and other related pivotal cases than by all of the machinations of the Ku Klux Klan.

To emphasize the extraordinary impact the Justices have had on American race relations, I have included pictures of six separate sittings of Supreme Court Justices; with one exception, they presided during significantly different eras. In five chapters of this volume, I have described the Supreme Court's role in at least one of the most critical cases of each respective era.

The first picture is of the Justices of the United States Supreme Court who, in 1857, in *Dred Scott v. Sandford,* [44] declared that "at the time of the Declaration of Independence, and when the Constitution of the United States was framed and adopted . . . [blacks] had no rights which the white man was bound to respect." [45] Two Justices, John McLean and Benjamin Curtis, dissented.

The second picture is of the Justices who decided *Plessy v. Ferguson* [46] in 1896, in which seven Justices of the Supreme Court legitimized under federal law the concept of treating black people differently and more adversely than everyone else—a concept they described as "separate but equal," but which in practice ultimately became a racist system that was almost always separate and always unequal. One Justice, John Marshall Harlan, filed a profoundly significant dissent.

The third picture is of the Justices in *Gaines v. Canada,* [47] which was the starting point on the "road to *Brown,*" [48] where the heretofore pervasive impact of *Plessy v. Ferguson* was restrained. The Court, under the leadership of Chief Justice Charles Evans Hughes, made clear that it was unconstitutional for Missouri to refuse to admit a qualified African American to the only school funded by the state. Again, two Justices dissented.

The fourth picture is of the Justices in *Brown v. Board of Education,* [49] who, in 1954, in the most historic civil rights case of this century, declared a doctrine that, if fully and promptly implemented, would have eradicated most of the roots of slavery jurisprudence that had persisted long after the passage of the Thirteenth, Fourteenth, and Fifteenth Amendments. Judge Louis Pollak was correct when he said that, except for the winning of the Civil War and the two World Wars, the *Brown v. Board of Education* case was "probably the most important American governmental act of any kind since the Emancipation Proclamation."[50]

The fifth picture is of the Justices who, in 1993, in *Shaw v. Reno,*[51] announced a new voting rights rationale that could cause a dramatic reduction of pluralism in the United States Congress through the elimination of ten to seventeen African-American and Latino Members.

The sixth picture is of the current Justices, who will have, as has every Supreme Court, an impact on American race relations for decades.

In most of these cases, the Supreme Court was at critical crossroads whereby, with some semblance of rationality, it could have decided the case either way. Two cases, *Dred Scott* and *Plessy,* were devastating defeats for African Americans and, in the long run, significant setbacks for all Americans. *Gaines* and particularly *Brown* were profound victories for African Americans. As for *Shaw v. Reno,* decided in 1993, it is uncertain as to what its ultimate impact will be, but in Chapter Thirteen, I describe it as a very significant retrogressive case that, like *Plessy v. Ferguson,* was "wrong[ly] decided."[52] I am not certain how far the pendulum of the current Supreme Court will swing, but I am confident that the Supreme Court, the President, and the Congress will have an extraordinary impact in determining whether our nation has significantly more or significantly less racial justice in the twenty-first century.

The Road Ahead: Still Many "Miles to Go"

Six months before he died, Justice Thurgood Marshall spoke from Independence Hall in Philadelphia, when he received the Liberty Bell Award on July 4, 1992. He described the unfinished journey as follows:

> I wish I could say that racism and prejudice were only distant memories . . . and that liberty and equality were just around the bend. I wish I could say that America has come to appreciate diversity and to see and accept similarity. But as I look around, I see not a nation of unity but of division— Afro and white, indigenous and immigrant, rich and poor, educated and illiterate. . . . But there is a price to be paid for division and isolation.[53]
>
>   *   *   *
>
> We cannot play ostrich. Democracy cannot flourish amid fear. Liberty cannot bloom amid hate. Justice cannot take root amid rage. We must go against the prevailing wind. We must dissent from the indifference. We

must dissent from the apathy. We must dissent from the fear, the hatred and the mistrust. We must dissent from a government that has left its young without jobs, education or hope. We must dissent from the poverty of vision and the absence of moral leadership. We must dissent because America can do better, because America has no choice but to do better. . . . Take a chance, won't you? Knock down the fences that divide. Tear apart the walls that imprison. Reach out; freedom lies just on the other side.[54]

I began this chapter by stating that ever since the first Africans were brought to this country, African Americans have been on a journey to take their place within "We the People," a journey that has taken us down what Bessie Smith called a "long road." We have not stood still and we have made some progress down that road. We have left behind the midnight hour of slavery, traveled through the gray dawn of segregation, and we are now in a cloudy divide, poised between freedom and inequality. As Justice Marshall poignantly suggested, "racism and prejudice [are not] distant memories," and the journey is far from over. The poet Robert Frost once wrote about another, though not dissimilar, journey:

> The woods are lovely, dark and deep,
> But I have promises to keep,
> And miles to go before I sleep,
> And miles to go before I sleep.[55]

As a nation, we too have promises to keep, and we too have miles to go before we sleep. For, in the centuries between 1619 and 1996, we have only gone from total oppression to SHADES OF FREEDOM.

Shades of Freedom

1

MY FORTY-YEAR JOURNEY IN FORMULATING THE PRECEPTS

FOR MORE than forty years, I have had a keen interest in the evolution of American colonial and antebellum slavery and the related race relations law.[1] I believe that I have read every published appellate case and statute on this subject from 1630 to 1865. After reflecting on those thousands of statutes and cases and on innumerable related articles and books, I have concluded that, for those Americans in power, there were several premises, goals, and implicit agreements concerning the institution of slavery that at once defined the nature of American slavery and directed how it was to be administered with the imprimatur of the legal process. Sometimes these premises and goals were articulated precisely in statutes, judicial opinions, and executive orders. At other times, they were implicit; since most in power understood and agreed with these pernicious propositions, it would have been superfluous to announce or codify the common understanding. But whether or not articulated as formal rules of law, there was a general consensus on principles or premises that led to the legitimization of slavery and of racism.

In this book and in the remaining volumes of this series, I attempt to distill the essence of these assumptions or premises into what I now call the "Ten Precepts of American Slavery Jurisprudence." These are the precepts that were the foundation for American slavery jurisprudence and early race relations law. These precepts also provide a framework in which to analyze the underlying premises of the institution of slavery and its legitimization by the American legal system.

The term "precept" has at least two possible meanings: one as a broad analytical concept, and a second in a more restrictive legal sense. The first, "a command or principle intended as a *general rule of action*,"[2] denotes the *implicit* understanding of racial differences. In this context, the inferiority of African Americans was given the standing of a natural principle embodied through the existing moral and social climate of the time that was not to be

3

questioned. In a legal sense, there is the alternative definition of "precept," as suggested by my wise former judical colleague, Ruggero J. Aldisert, which covers three concepts: a rule of law, a legal principle, and a legal doctrine.[3] Used in this manner, the term "precept" encompasses the legal mandates explicitly written in the law and legal orders, which established, legitimized, and enforced the inferior position of African Americans before the law.[4]

These precepts concerning slavery and race relations exemplify the premises and perceptions that Justice Oliver Wendell Holmes described, in a somewhat different context, as the "prevalent moral and political theories, intuitions of public policy, avowed or unconscious, *even the prejudices which judges* [and other public officials] *share with their fellow-men.*"[5]

Orlando Patterson has observed:

> There is nothing notably peculiar about the institution of slavery. It has existed from before the dawn of human history right down to the twentieth century, in the most primitive of human societies and in the most civilized. There is no region on earth that has not at some time harbored the institution. Probably there is no group of people whose ancestors were not at one time slaves or slaveholders.[6]

Nevertheless, there *were* different precepts in different slaveholding societies. This book attempts to delineate the precepts in American slavery jurisprudence. Although I note legal precedents from several states in this and succeeding volumes, I believe it is better to provide a more comprehensive view of the evolution of slavery jurisprudence and race relations law in a single state. I focus primarily on Virginia instead of any other state, to ascertain whether each of the precepts can be supported by actual cases, statutes, and events. Virginia, because it provided significant leadership for all the colonies, is an excellent choice as a starting point.

Virginians played a major role in leading the American Revolution and in shaping the destiny of the new nation after 1776. Yet, tragically, Virginia was also a leader in the debasement of African Americans by pioneering a legal process that perpetuated racial injustice. Virginia was the birthplace of American slavery.[7] Just as the other colonies emulated other aspects of Virginia's policies, many followed Virginia's leadership in slavery law.[8]

From my own experience as a federal judge for more than twenty-nine years, I am convinced that Charles Warren was on target when he said:

> The [Supreme] Court is not an organism dissociated from the conditions and history of the times in which it exists. It does not formulate and deliver its opinions in a legal vacuum. Its Judges are not abstract and impersonal oracles, but are men whose views are necessarily, though by no conscious intent, affected by inheritance, education and environment and by the impact of history past and present . . . .[9]

By reason of shared economic interest and political views, the legislators and judges often had a *common understanding* of the issues of race and slavery. This common understanding created what Holmes might have called a "simple universality of the rules."[10] Once established, these rules permeated American slavery culture for more than 200 years. It is this "universality of the rules" that the Ten Precepts of American Slavery Jurisprudence embody. The precepts pertaining to inferiority and powerlessness[11] continue to haunt America even today, although it is now more than one hundred and thirty years after the Thirteenth Amendment abolished slavery.

These precepts summarize the operational perceptions that underlay the maintenance of the slave system to 1865.[12] The voice of these precepts is that of those white men who implemented and perpetuated slavery in American society. The history of American slavery shows that, although the consensus developed incrementally, by the time slavery had "matured," what began as mere notions had become guiding principles.[13]

These precepts were most solidly embedded in the antebellum period from 1820 to 1865. It was during that time that slaveholders made their most zealous doctrinal arguments in defense of slavery and most firmly solidified the ten precepts as the underlying basis of the system of law and governance. Historians who have highlighted the geographic and chronological spread of pro-slavery advocacy recognize the unique character of the era following the Missouri Compromise in 1820. As Professor Drew G. Faust has observed: "Although proslavery thought demonstrated remarkable consistency from the seventeenth century on, it became in the South of the 1830s, forties, and fifties more systematic and self-conscious; *it took on the characteristics of a formal ideology with its resulting social movement.*"[14]

These Ten Precepts of American Slavery Jurisprudence represent the institutionalized values, standards, or assumptions for which there was a broad acceptance, at least on the part of those who wrote and interpreted the laws. Nevertheless, as with most generalizations of social phenomena, there were individuals who deviated from the precepts and even some who repudiated them. There were a few humanitarian groups, such as the Quakers and the German Mennonites, who rejected slavery and who thereby caused "[t]he chains of slavery" to be "loosened by degrees."[15] But they were unable to develop anything close to a national consensus for its abolition. So, while the precepts were cast almost as absolutes, their application was not uniform. Individual adherence to them varied to some extent within the slave system from state to state, community to community, and master to master.

The tone of the precepts is in the imperative, to convey the sense of law and near-holy writ attached to them. Although the totality of the precepts was never codified in one comprehensive legal document, together these precepts, nevertheless, operated as the basic legal premises of this slaveholding land.[16]

Paralleling our written governing documents, they wielded the same authority; they were, in effect, the Shadow Constitution, the Bill of Non-Rights for African Americans, the Anti-Preamble justifying a bifurcation of the society between "We the People" and "We, the *Other* People." [17]

2

THE PRECEPT OF INFERIORITY

They had for more than a century before been regarded as **beings of an inferior order,** *and altogether unfit to associate with the white race . . . and* **so far inferior, that they had no rights which the white man was bound to respect;** *and that the negro might justly and lawfully be reduced to slavery for his benefit. He was bought and sold, and treated as an ordinary article of merchandise and traffic. . . . This opinion was at that time fixed and universal in the civilized portion of the white race. It was regarded as an axiom in morals as well as in politics, which no one thought of disputing, or supposed to be open to dispute; and men in every grade and position in society daily and habitually acted upon it in their private pursuits, as well as in matters of public concern, without doubting for a moment the correctness of this opinion.—Dred Scott v. Sandford (1857).*[1]

The Most Enduring Precept

CHIEF Justice Roger Brooke Taney's opinion in the *Dred Scott* case did not reflect a unique perception about African Americans in that era. In 1857 it probably represented the views of the vast majority of whites in American society. Even in 1996, it might be argued that the belief that African Americans are of an "inferior order" is an idea some find difficult to abandon. Admittedly, this is a terrible accusation to make, and one that many people will challenge and find downright insulting.

When the majority of white Americans consider the history of this nation, they are apt to conclude that the blood of the Civil War washed clean the sins of slavery and that the marches of the civil rights movement erased the remaining vestiges of segregation and racial oppression. Others not given to excessive historical introspection believe—almost equally sincerely—that they personally have nothing whatever to do with slavery, segregation, or racial oppression because neither they nor—as far as they know—their ancestors ever enslaved anyone, ever burned a cross in the night in front of anyone's house, or ever denied anyone a seat at the front of a bus. And so, between the self-absolving denial of the latter group and the self-congratulation—which is a deeper form of self-absolution—of the former, it becomes nearly impossible to have an honest discussion about what used to be called "the Negro Problem."[2]

Indeed, we do not even agree whether we still have a "Negro problem" or, if we do have a "problem," what exactly it might be. Some scholars, like Derrick Bell, argue quite eloquently that any discussion of race must acknowledge that America is still at its core the racist country it has always been and that this racism affects life chances for African Americans.[3] Others, like Shelby Steele, claim that, considering all the progress made in the last century, that at least in the past thirty years, African Americans' shortcomings and not racism may have become their own worst problems.[4] This chapter will not settle the debate concerning the persistence and present-day consequences of racism, but it will try to explore its origins.

Alexis de Tocqueville once observed that, as in the lives of individuals, the circumstances of the birth of nations deeply affect their development.[5] When this nation was being born, one important circumstance of its birth—if the Declaration of Independence and the Constitution are to be taken seriously—was its theoretical commitment to the principles of human freedom and equality. But another equally significant circumstance—as evidenced by the genocide of Native Americans and the enslavement of African Americans—was its dedication to the doctrine of white supremacy.

That doctrine, much as it contradicted the theoretical principles of the Declaration of Independence and the Preamble of the Constitution, deeply and unalterably affected how America has developed as a nation. It gained us the land on which Native Americans and Mexicans used to live; it produced prosperity for the generations who directly and indirectly profited from the free labor of slaves; it resulted in generations of American apartheid; it allowed us to pretend that we were truly a white European nation; it saddled us with what W.E.B. Du Bois called "the problem of the color-line."[6] In other words, the doctrine of white supremacy and its corollary precept of black inferiority made us who we were a very short time ago and, inevitably, who in part we still are today.

In 1953, during oral arguments before the Supreme Court in the case of *Brown v. Board of Education,*[7] challenging as unconstitutional the intentional segregation of African-American children in public schools, Thurgood Marshall posed the following challenge to the assembled justices: "[T]he only way that this Court can decide this case in opposition to our position . . . is to find that for some reason Negroes are *inferior* to all other human beings."[8] In response to Thurgood Marshall's challenge, the Court ruled that the intentional segregation of African-American children in public schools was a violation of the Equal Protection Clause of the United States Constitution. In the justices' words: "To separate them [African-American children] from others of similar age and qualifications solely because of their race generates a feeling of inferiority as to their status in the community that may affect their hearts and minds in a way unlikely ever to be undone."[9]

Thurgood Marshall, by posing the challenge as he did, and the justices, by responding as they did, would seem to have taken for granted that no one in their right mind would ever imagine, and no court under the rule of law could possibly determine, that African Americans were inferior to other human beings. Yet Thurgood Marshall and the justices knew perfectly well that such a brilliant statesman as Thomas Jefferson[10] and such a "respected" Supreme Court jurist as Roger Taney[11] had argued that blacks were indeed inferior to whites. Thurgood Marshall, for reasons of legal strategy, and the justices, for reasons known only to them, may have sealed between them this unspoken understanding of convenient myth.

But the truth was that our nation was founded explicitly, prospered implicitly, and still often lives uneasily on the precept of black inferiority and white superiority. Indeed, that precept helped to legitimize slavery in America and served to justify the segregation of African Americans in this nation long after slavery had been abolished. To this day, the premise of black inferiority and white superiority remains an essential element of the "American identity," mesmerized as we still are by race and color.[12]

The dominance of the precept of inferiority has to do with the fact that "inferiority" is fundamentally different from all the other precepts. Most of the other precepts, in one way or another, defined or enforced certain tangible rights of the slave master or obligations of the slaves. For example, the precept of property described a right of the master. According to that precept, the master owned the slave much in the same way he owned his horse. Once the law abolished slavery, the original precept of property ceased to exist. This is because the precept of property owed its existence to the legal process. The law created it and, with the help of the Civil War and the Thirteenth Amendment, the law eliminated it.

By contrast, the precept of inferiority did not define any specific right or obligation. Instead, "inferiority" spoke to the state of the mind and the logic of the heart. It posed as an article of faith that African Americans were not quite altogether human. What's more, "inferiority" did not owe its existence to the legal process. Although the law came to enforce the precept, it did not create it. From the time the Africans first disembarked here in America, the colonists were prepared to regard them as inferior.[13] When the Thirteenth Amendment abolished slavery and, presumably, all its attendant conditions,[14] it did not eliminate the precept of inferiority. Even much later, when the law abolished state-enforced racial segregation, it still did not eliminate the precept.

Today we have come to a time when whites may not own African Americans as property (Precept Two of American Slavery), when African Americans are not totally powerless to control their fate (Precept Three), when whites and African Americans may marry whomever they wish (Precept Four), when whites may no longer completely control where African Americans live and the status they have in the community (Precept Five), when white control is not a predominant worry of the African-American family (Precept Six), when African Americans are free to get an education if they wish (Precept Seven), when the African-American church can chart its own destiny (Precept Eight), when the Bill of Rights theoretically applies equally to African Americans and whites (Precept Nine), and when overt racism in the public sphere is far less tolerated (Precept Ten). But still we cannot say that we have reached a time when the belief that African Americans are inferior has disappeared without a trace from the American heart. That is why inferiority remains the most enduring—and perhaps most important—precept.

The Object of Hate

During colonial times in America, the ruling class of English colonists had "difficulties in fostering a sense of community in colonies populated by Portuguese, Spanish, French, Turks, Dutch, blacks, and Indians."[15] For example, cases reported between 1640 and 1669 in Virginia reveal that white indentured servants, along with African-American slaves, had rebelled against the English colonists by running away and stealing from their masters.[16] In addition to facing rebellion by whites and African Americans, the English colonies also had to withstand attacks from the Native American population that the colonists were doing their best to subjugate. "Indians and whites conducted guerrilla raids against each other's settlements with ever increasing ruthlessness."[17]

Faced with rebellion from within and attacks from without, the colonists needed to foster a common identity in order to quell the restless stirrings of their own less-happy members, who had no desire to serve their masters indefinitely, and in order to repel the not-unjustified attacks of the Native Americans, who had no intention of being subjugated quietly. The colonists discovered soon enough that nothing makes better friends of former enemies than a new common enemy. Give a people someone to hate and fear and they will have a reason to live with one another. To say this is not to indulge in any form of romantic despair. It is simply to admit that, even though love and its object may be what redeem our spirit in the next world, hate and its object seem to drive us in this world to conquer the land, build the bridges, raise the armies, and fight the common enemy. For the white colonists, the common object of fear and hate became the Africans in their midst.

Scholars have over the years offered different theories about why the Africans became the object of hate and fear that united the white colonists. Some have suggested that the doctrine of black inferiority was developed subsequent to slavery in order to accommodate the economic necessity of slavery. Thus, in 1944, Eric Williams wrote: "Slavery in the Caribbean has been too narrowly identified with the Negro. A racial twist has thereby been given to what is basically an economic phenomenon. Slavery was not born of racism: rather, racism was the consequence of slavery."[18] In contrast, other scholars have argued that in the Caribbean and in other parts of the Americas, blacks were enslaved precisely because, from the earliest of times, whites had perceived them to be inferior. Winthrop Jordan, in a careful canvass of fifteenth-, sixteenth-, and seventeenth-century literature noted:

> Long before they found that some men were black, Englishmen found in the idea of blackness a way of expressing some of their most ingrained values. No other color except white conveyed so much emotional impact. As described by the *Oxford English Dictionary*, the meaning of *black* before the sixteenth century included, 'Deeply stained with dirt, soiled, dirty, foul. . . . Having dark or deadly purposes, malignant; pertaining to or involving death, deadly; baneful, disastrous, sinister. . . . Foul, iniquitous, atrocious, horrible, wicked. . . . Indicating disgrace, censure, liability to punishment, etc.' Black was an emotionally partisan color, the handmaid and symbol of baseness and evil, a sign of danger and repulsion. . . . White and black connoted purity and filthiness, virginity and sin, virtue and baseness, beauty and ugliness, beneficence and evil, God and the devil.[19]

Both theories, although certainly helpful to the general debate on the root causes of slavery in America, fail to settle convincingly the question of whether the precept of black inferiority preceded or followed the institution of slavery. As to the first theory, even if slavery was purely an "economic phenomenon," it does not explain why in America after the seventeenth century, slavery came to be predicated exclusively on race, whereas at other times, in other places, slaves had come from all races. As to the second theory, even if from time immemorial Englishmen had used the color black as a symbol of everything base and evil, it does not explain why, upon coming in contact with Africans, Englishmen should immediately conclude that their concept of the color black was embodied in the Africans who, in all seriousness, were after all never *literally* the color black.

In any event, it may very well be pointless to argue whether the precept of black inferiority was a cause or a consequence of the institution of slavery.

To argue about such an intractable distinction is to insist upon finding reasoned nuances within the precept of black inferiority.[20] That precept, at bottom, was and is based on hate. Hate does not always choose its object with logic. Certainly, there is no logical explanation for the white colonists branding the Africans as inferior to all other human beings. But once they were so branded, the Africans gave the white colonists an indelible marker to fear, a common object of hate, which provided a bond more solid than love. The precept that African Americans were, in some immutable way, inferior became a powerful principle around which all white colonists, even those who did not own slaves, could begin to foster a common identity and forge a united community.

Contrary to some of our most cherished myths, not all of the white colonists who settled in America came here because they wanted to be "free." Some came because they were poor, some because they were convicts, some because they were greedy, some because they were religious zealots, and some because they had no place else to go. For the most part they had little in common, other than the fact that they were all suddenly here, and whatever America had to offer them was probably better than what they had left, and what still might await them back in Europe. So, trapped between the very real memory of the limitations of the Old World and the still unfulfilled hope of the possibilities of the New World, the white colonists may not have understood at the time who and what they were as a people. They were, however, at least able to say who and what they were not: they were not blacks; they were not inferior.

The idea that notions of black inferiority and white superiority serve as a rallying marker for American society is not a new one. Writers with greater imagination have expressed it far more elegantly than this chapter pretends to. For example:

Derrick Bell:

> Black people are the magical faces at the bottom of society's well. Even the poorest whites, those who must live their lives only a few levels above, gain their self-esteem by gazing down on us. Surely, they must know that their deliverance depends on letting down their ropes. Only by working together is escape possible. Over time, many reach out, but most simply watch, mesmerized into maintaining their unspoken commitment to keeping us where we are, at whatever cost to them or to us.[21]

Richard Wright:

> We black folk, our history and our present being, are a mirror of all the

manifold experiences of America. What we want, what we represent, what we endure is what America *is*. If we black folk perish, America will perish. If America has forgotten her past, then let her look into the mirror of our consciousness and she will see the *living* past living in the present, for our memories go back, through our black folk of today, through the recollections of our black parents, and through the tales of slavery told by our black grandparents, to the time when none of us, black or white, lived in this fertile land.

The differences between black folk and white folk are not blood or color, and the ties that bind us are deeper than those that separate us.[22]

Ralph Ellison:

Since the beginning of this nation, white Americans have suffered from a deep inner uncertainty as to who they really are. One of the ways that has been used to simplify the answer has been to seize upon the presence of black Americans and use them as a marker, a symbol of limits, a metaphor for the "outsider." Many whites could look at the social position of blacks and feel that color formed an easy and reliable gauge for determining to what extent one was or was not American. Perhaps that is why one of the first epithets that many European immigrants learned when they got off the boat was the term "nigger"—it made them feel instantly American.[23]

James Baldwin:

[In America], [i]n a way, the Negro tells us where the bottom is: *because he is there*, and *where* he is, beneath us, we know where the limits are and how far we must not fall. We must not fall beneath him. We must never allow ourselves to fall that low. . . .[24]

Toni Morrison:

Africanism is the vehicle by which the American self knows itself as not enslaved, but free; not repulsive, but desirable; not helpless, but licensed and powerful; not history-less, but historical; not damned, but innocent; not a blind accident of evolution, but a progressive fulfillment of destiny.[25]

By the latter part of the seventeenth century, the colonists would have in place a sort of "social and color ladder," occupied at the top rungs by propertied whites, in the middle by the poor and servant whites, and at the bottom rungs by Native Americans and African-American slaves.[26] Through the operation of this social and color ladder, the ruling class of whites was assured the loyalty of the poor and servant whites, upon whose loyalty the fate of the colony depended, without the ruling class having to share its wealth and power with the servant class. For the poor and servant whites, the rewards for their loyalty were the somewhat illusory promise that they too could ascend to the top rungs of the ladder occupied by the propertied whites, and, much more important, the eternal guarantee that they could never fall to the lower rungs occupied by the Native Americans, or to the lowest rungs occupied by the African Americans.

Throughout the eighteenth and nineteenth centuries until 1865, the social and color ladder was reinforced by slaveholders, legislators, and judges who articulated and perfected the rationale of black inferiority and white superiority. As South Carolina Senator James Henry Hammond ruminated in 1861:

> In all social systems there must be a class to do the menial duties, to perform the drudgery of life. That is, a class requiring but a low order of intellect and but little skill. Its requisites are vigor, docility, fidelity. Such a class you must have, or you would not have that other class which leads progress, civilization, and refinement. It constitutes the very mudsill of society and of political government. . . . Fortunately for the South, she has found a race adapted to that purpose at her hand. A race *inferior* to her own, but eminently qualified in temper, in vigor, in docility, in capacity to stand the climate, to answer all her purposes. We use them for our purpose, and we call them slaves.[27]

The rationale for the precept of inferiority was this: blacks, for reasons of physiology, culture, behavior and even religion, were something less than fully human and were therefore inferior to whites. As such, blacks could be enslaved by whites, not only because of the economic benefits that the raw physical attributes of blacks would bring whites in their efforts to turn the primitive American land into a civilized nation, but also because of the moral benefits that dominance by whites would bring blacks in soothing their heathen instincts. If, however, the civilizing restraints of slavery were to be removed and they were free,[28] then blacks had to be segregated from whites because, left entirely to their own devices, free blacks would tend to corrupt the moral virtue and physical purity of white society,[29] and because the two races, one a blessed fulfillment of divine destiny, the other a cursed accident of blind evolution, could not possibly live together peacefully in society without the beneficent controlling hand of the superior race upon the inferior one.

Eventually the precept of black inferiority and white superiority worked itself into the fabric of the American legal process. The social and color ladder became a legal one as well. Looking for evidence of the precept of inferiority in the American legal process, however, is very much like looking for evidence of slavery in the United States Constitution as originally ratified.

The Constitution accommodated the institution of slavery without ever *explicitly* using—prior to 1865—in any article or clause the word "slavery." But the drafters' coyness about using the word "slavery" did not necessarily reveal an aversion to the institution of slavery.[30] Rather, it suggests a reluc-

tance to sully the great document with a word that most of the founders realized, despite their protestations to the contrary, denoted a fundamentally evil
institution.[31]

Similarly, the legal process institutionalized the premise of black inferiority without ever specifically delineating in any one case or statute the entire
rationale for the precept of black inferiority. There are, of course, exceptions.
Some judges and legislators bluntly stated their reasons for believing that
blacks were inferior to whites. But the legal process as a whole was more
subtle in assimilating and perpetuating an ideology in which whiteness was
the nimbus of superiority, and blackness the stigma of inferiority.

The Stages of Development of the Precept of Inferiority

In America, the legal process developed the precept of black inferiority and
white superiority in four distinct stages. This volume analyzes the four stages
of the development of the precept of black inferiority by focusing first on
cases and statutes of Virginia. As such, this work is not an exhaustive historical review of slavery in every American jurisdiction. Rather, it is an attempt
at understanding how the American legal process developed the precept of
black inferiority and white superiority.

In the first stage, lasting approximately from 1619 to 1662, the legal
process presumed, without defining, the precept of black inferiority. During
this stage, even though blacks were considered to be inferior to all other
individuals in colonial society, the law did not succeed in articulating a clear
rationale of, or in providing rigid enforcement for, the precept of black inferiority. This was the laissez-faire stage of the development of the precept of
black inferiority, when the legal process struggled even to articulate a consistent jurisprudence for racial subordination. Whites during that time seemed to
suspect that blacks were inferior, but they did not always articulate precisely
how or why.

In the second stage, lasting from 1662 to the 1830s, the legal process
carefully defined and, when necessary, ruthlessly enforced a precept which
before then it had taken for granted. It was the stage when the rationale for
American slavery was formed with cunning and without pity, when both
blacks and whites became most conscious of and most dependent on the precept of black inferiority and white superiority. As a nation, we crossed the
Rubicon of mere racial distinction, entered the oblivion of chattel slavery,
and wandered lost in the labyrinth of racial oppression.

During the third stage, from the 1830s to the end of the Civil War, the
legal process defended and protected from attacks the crumbling institution of

slavery and the precept of black inferiority. It was the stage during which the abolitionists launched a crusade against slavery and when the Supreme Court, with the disastrous decision in *Dred Scott v. Sandford*,[32] contributed to the outbreak of the Civil War.[33]

During the fourth stage, beginning at the Reconstruction period, the legal process attempted unsuccessfully to break free from the legacy of the precept of black inferiority. It was the stage when the nation generally seemed unable or unwilling to totally erase the vestiges of slavery, despite the significant constitutional amendments. The Supreme Court in several cases effectively nullified the Reconstruction legal changes, and in *Plessy v. Ferguson*[34] announced the "separate but equal" doctrine that formally legitimized segregation.

Just as racial subordination did not stop with the abolition of slavery and the end of the Civil War, the precept of black inferiority did not die during the post-Reconstruction stage. With the help of *Plessy v. Ferguson* and the "separate but equal" doctrine, the precept hid in what Justice Cardozo called the "interstitial" spaces of the law.[35] The Supreme Court decision in *Brown v. Board of Education*[36] was, as much as anything, the start of an effort to reach into these interstitial spaces and to cleanse the legal process of the precept of black inferiority and white superiority.

The four chronological stages described are analytical signposts that can be useful in tracking the development of the precept in the law. They are, however, not meant to be definitive historical categories. It is nearly impossible to determine precisely when this nation moved from one stage of the precept of inferiority to another. Certain judicial decisions such as *Dred Scott v. Sandford*, *Plessy v. Ferguson*, and *Brown v. Board of Education* were indeed critical to the development or the diminution of the precept. But judicial decisions and legislative enactments are unclear and imperfect signposts in the development of the precept of inferiority.

As stated earlier, the inferiority precept is the one precept that did not owe its existence to the legal process. More than any other precept, inferiority was a matter of belief and an article of faith. Thus, to take *Plessy v. Ferguson* as an example, the decision did not *create* state-enforced racial segregation; it merely gave it the imprimatur of the Supreme Court. But long before the decision was issued, whites, both in the South and in the North, practiced racial apartheid. To take *Brown v. Board of Education* as another example, the decision merely struck down state-enforced segregation in public schools. It did not, however, convince a great many white parents in either the North or the South to send their children to school with black children. Nor, in the final analysis, did *Brown* completely succeed in its ultimate goal of assuring to black children in public schools the same educational opportunities available to white children. There are many reasons why some black children continue to attend schools in conditions almost as wretched as during the era when Charles Hamilton Houston began to document the deplorable state of southern black schools. One of these reasons has to do with the precept of inferiority and how it has developed from 1619 to 1996.

This volume is mostly a record of the past. Perhaps it is also in some way a lesson for our own time. Between 1989 and 1991, the collapse of Communism in Eastern Europe and the break-up of the former Soviet Union brought about a rapid and public resurgence of anti-Semitism in Russia. All sorts of deceptive arguments, from the supposed inordinate wealth of the Jews, to their mythical religious depravity, were used to explain the shambles in which the country found itself. Once again Jews became the common object of hate around which other Russians tried to rebuild a common identity that had withered under Communism, and that had now all but died with the fall of the Soviet state. Thousands of Jews left Russia during that period because life there for them was unbearable.

The night before she was to leave Russia with her family, a Jewish woman wrote an anonymous letter to a Moscow weekly. She warned Russians not to suppose that the moral and economic devastation wrought upon their society by so many years of totalitarian government could ever be erased simply by expelling Jews from the country. Russia, she predicted, would not find peace and redemption by hating Jews because "[h]atred that rages in souls and suddenly loses its immediate object does not disappear without a trace."[37]

The precept of black inferiority is the hate that raged in the American soul through over 240 years of slavery and nearly ninety years of segregation. Once slavery was abolished, and once the more oppressive forms of segregation were eliminated, many whites' hate still had not lost its immediate object. The ashes of that hate have, over the course of so many generations, accumulated at the bottom of our memory. There they lie uneasily, like a heavy secret which whites can never quite confess, which blacks can never quite forgive, and which, for both blacks and whites, forestalls until a distant day any hope of peace and redemption.[38]

3

THE ANCESTRY OF INFERIORITY
(1619–1662)

Last Among Equals

WHEN the first Africans arrived at Virginia in August 1619,[1] they were initially accorded an indentured servant status similar to that of most Virginia colonists. In two letters, John Rolfe, Secretary and Recorder of the Virginia colony, reported on the arrival of the Africans. One letter stated that a Dutch man-of-war "brought not any thing but 20. and odd Negroes, which the Governor and Cape Marchant bought for victualles."[2] The other letter, describing the same event, stated: "[A]bout the last of August, came in a dutch man of warre that sold us twenty Negars."[3] The references in the letters to "buying" and "selling" do not necessarily mean that these Africans were being sold into chattel slavery. During that period, the majority of the population in Virginia consisted of servants.[4] It was common practice to refer to the transaction of acquiring a servant as "buying" a person. Buying in that sense simply meant buying the person's services and not actually buying the person's body.[5] Thus, it would appear that, in 1619, the first Africans became one more group in a majority servant class made up of whites and Native Americans.[6]

There are two reasons, however, why the Africans probably did not join this servant class as full equals. First, most but not all white servants came to the colony voluntarily and engaged in service with a written contract of indenture for a specific period.[7] At the expiration of the period of their indenture, whites were released into freedom. The master of a white indentured servant could not, at his sole desire and discretion, prolong the period of servitude. In fact, court approval was necessary for masters and servants to extend the original indenture.[8] Only if the white servant had broken the contract of indenture, or if the servant had in some way violated the laws of the colony, could the period of servitude be extended, either as compensation to the master for the servant breaking the contract or as punishment by society for the servant violating the law.[9] By contrast, as far as we know, the Africans came involuntarily or under duress,[10] and presumably were sold into service *without* a written contract of indenture for a specific period. So, in theory, their period of servitude may have been for as long as the purchaser desired, or even for life.

The second reason why the new Africans probably did not occupy the exact same socioeconomic position as other white servants is that—as Winthrop Jordan has demonstrated—since the fifteenth century, Englishmen had regarded blackness as "the handmaid and symbol of baseness and evil, a sign of danger and repulsion."[11] There is no reason to suppose that, in August 1619, the English colonists of Virginia would have immediately abandoned their historical tendency of associating blackness with inferiority in favor of a more enlightened view of seeing these particular black Africans as fully human. It is more likely that, in the eyes of the English colonists, the Africans represented a dark and inferior quantity. As members of the servant class they probably were last among equals.

Blackness As Sin

Notwithstanding the colonists' predilection for seeing Africans as less than human, from 1619 and for approximately two decades thereafter, the legal system did not appear to actively promote rigid, invidious distinctions between the new African settlers and their European counterparts.[12] The first reference to a black person in a judicial proceeding occurred in 1624, when the Council and General Court of Virginia mentioned, in the case of *Re Tuchinge,* in sum: "John Phillip A negro Christened in England 12 yeers since, sworne and exam sayeth, that beinge in a ship with Sir Henry Maneringe, they tooke A spanish shipp aboute Cape Sct Mary, and Caryed her to mamora."[13]

The case apparently involved the trial of a white man, Symon Tuchinge, for the illegal seizure of a Spanish ship and the kidnapping of various persons. Given that Phillip was referred to specifically by the court as black, it is logical to assume that the defendant, whose race was not similarly specified, was white. This conclusion is supported by the fact that other witnesses were not identified by race.[14]

Phillip's testimony against the white man was accepted presumably because, as the court explained, Phillip had been "Christened in England." Prior to 1680, the colonies would often follow the Spanish and English practice that blacks who had been baptized into the Christian religion were to be accorded the privileges of a free person.

Had the legal process in 1624 in Virginia not yet begun to institutionalize the precept of black inferiority, however, one would have expected the case to have been reported quite differently from the way it was actually reported. Specifically, had Virginia law been free of any theory of racial subordination, the case would have been reported as follows: "John Phillip sworne and exam sayeth, that beinge in a ship with Sir Henry Maneringe, they tooke A spanish shipp aboute Cape Sct Mary, and Caryed her to mamora." There would have been no description of Phillip as a "Negro" and having been "Christened," just as there had been no mention of the white defendant's race or his religion. In a jurisdiction where black did *not* carry the stigma of inferiority, Phillip's race and religion would *not* be material to the determination of whether his testimony was admissible in court because the blemish of his race would *not* need to be washed clean by the grace of his Christian religion. In a jurisdiction such as Virginia, however, where black was already the stigma of inferiority, Phillip's race and religion *were* material to the determination of whether his testimony was to be admitted, because in a real sense, his race was a sin for which he could obtain forgiveness only by becoming a Christian.

By explicitly describing Phillip's race and religion, the court implicitly revealed that, in 1624 Virginia, the legal process was ready to perceive and to treat blacks, by reason of the color of their skin, as different from white colonists. Granted, at first, the consequences of that difference were not immutable. If blackness was a sin, at least it could be absolved by Christianity. But the sinner who obtains Christian forgiveness for his sin always pays a price for that forgiveness. The price is that he has to admit that his sin caused him to be, in some way, a less perfect or inferior image of God. For the African, the sin that caused him to be a less perfect or inferior image of God was his race. So, to the African, Christian forgiveness *and all its attendant legal rights and privileges here on earth* came only at the price of admitting to himself and to society that he was inferior. What's more, the legal process, supported by public opinion and cloaked with the mysticism of Christian religion, reinforced this sense of black inferiority by the identification of the black race in judicial decisions and in legislative enactments. In short, by 1624, the legal process had begun to lay the foundation for the precept of black inferiority and white superiority; the process had "crossed," in the words of historian Lerone Bennett, Jr., "a great divide," and had placed white colonists on one side and Africans on the other side.[15]

The case of *Re Davis,* decided in 1630, illustrates that great divide in very stark terms. The full official court report reads as follows: "Sept. 17. 1630 *Hugh Davis* to be soundly whipt before an assembly of negroes & others for abusing himself to the dishon[o]r of God and shame of Christianity by defiling his body in lying with a negro. w[hi]ch fault he is to actk next *Sabbath* day."[16]

This case demonstrates the evolution of the precept of inferiority in at least three ways. First, though the court did not state that Hugh Davis was white, his race may be inferred from the fact that he is not identified as a "Negro," whereas the person with whom he presumably "defiled" his body was specifically identified as a "negro." The very statement that Davis "abused himself," and that "he defiled his body by lying with a negro," means that he engaged in sexual relations with someone inferior, someone less than human. In short, Davis's crime was not fornication, but bestiality. Second, the statement of the court that Davis had abused himself "to the dishon[o]r of God and shame of Christianity" means that the blacks' inferiority was not simply a custom of society, but also a tenet of Christianity. Finally, the court ordered Davis to be "whipt before an assembly of *negroes & others.*" One must assume that the "others" referred to most probably were white colonists. Therefore, the only reason why the court specified that the assembly was also to include "negroes" was because generally white colonists were not whipped in front of blacks. For Davis, a white colonist, to be whipped in front of blacks would have been especially humiliating, because he would have been debased in front of individuals who were his legal inferiors.

The *Davis* case, decided a mere six years after the *Tuchinge* case, marked an important step in the development of the precept of black inferiority in the common law of Virginia. In *Tuchinge*, the court had remarked upon Phillip's "otherness" by simply identifying him as a "Negro Christened." The precept that Phillip's race marked him as inferior was not stated, but instead remained implicit in the fact that his race alone was identified. By contrast, in *Davis*, the precept of black inferiority was no longer implied, but stated explicitly in the fact that a white colonist "defiled" his body by engaging in sexual relations with an African. In *Tuchinge*, the court recognized that Phillip's inferiority was not so immutable that it could not be mitigated by his Christianity. Phillip, having become a Christian, was permitted to give testimony in court against a white man. God was the African's savior from inferiority. In *Davis*, however, Christianity, instead of supplying a balm for the injury of black inferiority, provided the very instrument which confirmed its existence. Davis's crime of engaging in sexual relations with a black was a crime against Christianity. God now became witness to the African's inferiority. But in *Tuchinge*, the black man's relative equality was measured by his presence in court as a witness against the white man's transgression. By contrast, in *Davis*, the black person's irredeemable inferiority was measured by his presence as the reason for the white man's punishment.

Ten years later, in 1640, the courts in Virginia took the next step in the development of the precept of black inferiority. In *Re Sweat*, the court considered the case of Robert Sweat, a white colonist who had impregnated a black woman servant belonging to a Lieutenant Sheppard.[17] As punishment for Sweat and the unnamed black woman, the court ruled: "[T]he said negro woman shall be whipt at the whipping post and the said *Sweat* shall tomorrow in the forenoon do public penance for his offence at *James city* church in the time of devine service according to the laws of *England* in that case p[ro]-vided."[18]

Sweat, at one level, can be interpreted simply as a case about the invasion of property rights. The black woman servant belonged not to Sweat, but to Lieutenant Sheppard. Sweat impregnated her. During her pregnancy and post-childbirth period, she probably became less valuable to Sheppard.[19] Therefore, Sweat had to pay a price for diminishing the value of Sheppard's property, and the woman servant had to pay a price for allowing her value to Sheppard to be diminished. If the case was, however, only about the invasion of Sheppard's property rights, then Sweat and the woman servant would have been made to pay compensation to Sheppard: Sweat would have had to pay monetary damages to Sheppard, and the woman servant would have had to increase the period of servitude she owed to Sheppard. Instead, Sweat and the woman servant were administered respective forms of punishment, as if this were a criminal prosecution and not a property rights dispute.

That the woman was punished and not made to increase her period of servitude can be explained simply by the fact that she "belonged" to Sheppard and was probably already a servant for life. That Sweat was also not made to pay some form of compensation to Sheppard cannot be easily explained by interpreting the case solely in the context of property rights. Instead, a more complete explanation suggests itself if the case is viewed also as an expression of the precept of black inferiority. By engaging in sexual relations, Sweat and the black woman did much more than diminish Sheppard's property rights. Sweat "defiled his body" and shamed God by sleeping with someone less than human. For that, he needed to be punished by doing public penance in church in order to mortify him and to require him to ask God's forgiveness. The black woman, in turn, defied society and rejected her inferiority by sleeping with her superior.[20] For that, she needed to be punished at the whipping post, so that the mark of her inferiority that she had failed to imprint in her mind would now be whipped into her skin.

For blacks, the lesson of their inferiority was one that was written not only on their own bodies, but also on the bodies of their children. *In Re Graweere* in 1641 described how John Graweere, a black servant belonging to a white colonist named William Evans purchased the freedom of his young child from a Lieutenant Sheppard, the owner of the child's mother.[21] After Graweere purchased his child from Sheppard, it seems that a question arose as to whether the child belonged to him or to Evans, his master.[22] Graweere argued that the child should be freed, so that he would "be made a christian and be taught and exercised in the church of *England.*"[23] The court ruled in Graweere's favor and ordered: "that the child shall be free from the said *Evans* or his assigns and to be and remain at the disposing and education of the said *Graweere* and the child's godfather who undertaketh to see it brought up in the christian religion as aforesaid."[24]

This case is correctly interpreted as significant evidence that, by 1641, the legal process had not contemplated the institution of hereditary slavery. Graweere, himself, may have been a servant for life, but he was able to break the grip of servitude on his posterity by purchasing his child's freedom. Moreover, the facts of the case reveal that Graweere enjoyed certain benefits not usually afforded to slaves. Evans, Graweere's master, permitted him to own and raise hogs under an arrangement whereby Graweere paid half of the profits from his hog business to Evans and kept the other half for himself.[25] However, this case presents more than mere evidence of the ambiguous socio-economic position of black servants in 1641 Virginia.

In Re Graweere also offers an illustration of how the precept of black inferiority operates. The court sided with Graweere's position, by freeing his child, so that he could be raised as a Christian. But nowhere in the opinion was it stated that Graweere himself was a Christian. A close reading of the opinion reveals that Graweere was probably *not* a Christian. There are two reasons for this conclusion. First, Graweere is described only as "a negro servant unto *William Evans.*"[26] During that period, it was common practice to distinguish between "negroes" and "Christian negroes," since certain rights and privileges flowed from a black person being a Christian.[27] Recall the *Tuchinge* case in which the court accepted a black witness's testimony, because he had been baptized a Christian himself. Yet in this case, which turned almost entirely on the very issue of religion, Graweere's own faith was not explicitly mentioned. Surely, Graweere's position to raise his child as a free Christian would have been strengthened in the mind of the court had he been a Christian. Additionally, the court's decision to free the child would have been even more rational had the court stated that Graweere was a "Christian negro." Graweere presumably did not claim that he was a Christian, and the court did not so state in its opinion.

The second reason for that conclusion is: If Graweere was a Christian, or if he desired to convert to the Christian religion, one would assume that he could have petitioned the court to purchase *his own* freedom from Evans, because the court permitted him to purchase the freedom of his child on the promise the child was to be raised as a Christian. In other words, if, as the opinion clearly suggests, religion was the decisive argument that convinced the court to free the child, the same argument would also presumably be convincing in gaining Graweere his own freedom. The most probable reason why that argument did not apply to Graweere's situation was because, even though he wanted his child raised as a Christian, he himself was *not* a Christian.

If this argument is correct, then it inevitably raises a critical question: Why did the court permit a non-Christian black servant to gain the freedom of his child on the promise that the child would be raised and educated as a Christian? Put more simply, how could the court expect a non-Christian parent to educate a Christian child? The answer is suggested by the cryptic last statement in the court's opinion. The court wrote that the child was to "remain at the disposing and education of the said *Graweere and the child's godfather* who undertaketh to see it brought up in the christian religion as aforesaid." [28] The godfather to whom the court refers was a Christian to be sure, either a black Christian or a white Christian. It is unlikely that the godfather was black, because that would have presented a much too obvious way for black servants to achieve their freedom in 1641. Blacks could have petitioned the court, *en masse,* for freedom by getting themselves baptized with black Christian godfathers and promising to follow in the ways of Christianity. The system of non-indentured black servants could not have possibly survived and flourished for as long as it did had the legal process permitted blacks and their children to gain freedom merely with the help of fellow blacks who were Christians.

The only remaining possibility was that the godfather of Graweere's child was white. As implausible as it may at first sound, this does more completely explain the court's willingness to free the child. After all, if the precept of black inferiority meant anything, it certainly meant that, in the court's estimation, the child's Christian education would have been better safeguarded if entrusted to the care of a white colonist than if placed in the hands of a black servant, Christian or otherwise.

In short, this case exemplifies how the legal process, in a subtle but pernicious manner, reinforced the precept of black inferiority and white superiority in the minds and hearts of the colonists. The black parent was not completely denied dominion over his child, but he was made to understand that, alone, he was too inferior to protect the freedom and save the soul of his child. The white godfather, in turn, was given control over the child, not because of any parental rights, but because of the superiority of his race.

The cases of *Tuchinge, Davis, Sweat,* and *Graweere* were not the only judicial decisions in Virginia involving blacks during the first stage in the

development of the precept of black inferiority.[29] Moreover, as was characteristic of the first stage, these four decisions were relatively benign in their
treatment of blacks in comparison with later developments in Virginia law.[30]
While these cases exemplify how the legal process began to recognize the
precept of black inferiority, it should also be noted that the common law at
that time had not yet evolved a seamless rationale for the principles of racial
subordination that would permit judges in successive decisions to apply the
precept of black inferiority to different factual scenarios in a consistent fashion. In other words, the legal process had not yet merged the precept of black
inferiority with the doctrine of *stare decisis*.

These qualifications notwithstanding, reviewing the decisions in *Tuchinge, Davis, Sweat,* and *Graweere* is crucial to a proper understanding of the
precept of black inferiority and white superiority. Taken together, these cases
reveal four essential steps that were taken in the first stage of development of
the precept of black inferiority and white superiority: establish white superiority; establish black inferiority; enforce the notions publicly; and enforce the
notions by way of theology.

*First: convince the white colonists, regardless of their social or eco-
nomic status, that they are superior to the black colonists.* In that way, white
servants, who may in reality have more in common with black servants, will
identify with propertied whites, with whom they may have little in common
other than race. For example, in *Davis* and in *Sweat,* the white colonists who
engaged in sexual relations with black women were made to understand that
they had defiled their own bodies. Had the defendants been propertied whites,
it is difficult to imagine that they would have been punished for sleeping with
their black servants or their slaves. During the antebellum period, when slavery was certainly firmly rooted in Virginia, a white master had the right to
demand sexual compliance from his female slaves, just as surely as he had
the right to ride his mares. This practice, encouraged *openly* as a matter of
right in 1831 Virginia was, to be sure, already tolerated secretly as a matter
of privilege in 1630. This was precisely the position advanced on the floor of
the Virginia legislature in 1831 by a Mr. Gholson, in response to statements
proposing abolition: "Why, I really have been under the impression that I
owned my slaves. I lately purchased *four women* and ten children, in whom I
thought I obtained a great bargain, for I really supposed they were *my property,* as were my *brood mares.*"[31] The only logical conclusion to be drawn
from *Davis* and *Sweat,* then, is that the defendants were probably poor whites
or servants who had managed to sleep with black women belonging to others.
In spite of their relatively modest socioeconomic positions, the legal process
sought to convince these whites that they were superior to blacks.

Second: convince blacks that they are inferior to all others. In that way, they will feel hopeless about their fate, they will become submissive to the propertied whites, and they will not hope to form alliances with white servants. For example, in *Davis*, the simple act of a white man's sleeping with a black woman was described in the space of a single-sentence judicial opinion as the white man abusing himself, dishonoring God, shaming Christianity, and defiling his body. For blacks, the lesson must have been clear: If there was only shame and dishonor and, therefore, no joy or trust in the secret sexual bonding of black and white, then there would have been even more shame and dishonor and, therefore, even less joy or trust in these two groups forging an open political, social, or economic bond.

Third: enforce the inferiority of blacks and the superiority of whites in the most open and public manner. In that way, both blacks and whites will understand the precept as clear evidence of societal custom. For example, in *Davis*, the white defendant was condemned to be whipped "before an assembly of negroes & others." Similarly, in *Sweat* the black woman was sentenced to be whipped "at the whipping post," and the white defendant, to do public penance in church. These forms of public punishment were not only designed to exact retribution from the offenders, but also to deter others from engaging in similar behavior. It must be remembered that, at the time, Virginia had already begun to erect the social and color ladder, with propertied whites at the top, poor and servant whites in the middle, and Native Americans and Africans at the bottom. For a white man to engage in sexual relations with a black woman constituted a private slip down to the bottom-most rung of the ladder. For a white man to be punished publicly for his private fall was society's way of reminding one and all of the terrible cost in status that would accompany any failure to observe the precept of black inferiority.

Fourth: explain the inferiority of blacks and the superiority of whites by reference to Christianity. In that way, both blacks and whites will respect the precept as the natural expression of divine will. For example, in *Tuchinge*, the black witness avoided a disability of inferiority only by the grace of Christianity. In *Davis*, the white colonist was said to have dishonored God and shamed Christianity by his sexual relations with a black. In *Sweat*, the white offender was sentenced to public penance in church. In *Graweere*, the black child was saved from servitude only by the intervention of a white Christian godfather. The colonists realized that, while a foolish few might be tempted to sacrifice their public status in the service of private desires, almost no one would be willing to set his face against God for the sake of a people whose black color was itself a sin.

In one passage in his *Notes on the State of Virginia*, Thomas Jefferson explained in great detail the various physical and mental differences between blacks and whites that he believed rendered blacks inferior and whites superior. After listing those differences, Jefferson concluded: "I advance it therefore as a suspicion only, that the blacks, whether originally a distinct race, or made distinct by time and circumstances, are inferior to the whites in the endowments both of body and mind." [32] That passage, though written in 1782, best sums up the first stage in the legal development of the precept of black inferiority in Virginia between 1619 and 1662.

During that stage, the colonists seemed to believe, "as suspicion only," that blacks were inferior to whites. Their ambivalence was reflected in the uncertain socioeconomic status of the black servants in the colony, and in the relatively benign manner in which the legal process defined and enforced their condition of servitude. By 1662, however, the legal process would begin to put in place the components of lifetime and hereditary slavery for blacks. With that, Virginia would move into the second stage in the development of the precept of black inferiority.

4

THE IDEOLOGY OF INFERIORITY

(1662–1830)

RIOR to the 1660s, the Virginia legal process vacillated between implicit recognition of the relative equality of the new Africans and explicit determination of their irredeemable inferiority, as evidenced by *Re Sweat* in 1640.[1] The implicit recognition of equality was exemplified by *Re Tuchinge* in 1624[2] and *Re Graweere* in 1641.[3] The ambivalence of Virginia law at that time was reflected not only in the substance of its norms concerning African Americans, but also in the way Virginia legal principles developed. Most of the early legal principles espousing black inferiority were contained in isolated judicial opinions, rather than the later, more comprehensive legislative enactments.[4] That the law took root in this manner is significant because the process of judicial decision-making does not lend itself particularly well to the development of the precept of black inferiority.

Developing a racist precept is very much like colonizing a nation or, perhaps more to the point, enslaving its people. One needs to go about these tasks with the enthusiastic devotion and single-minded determination of a zealot. One must hear only the call of one's crusade and not the cries of one's victims. In short, one needs to be totally convinced of the righteousness of one's task, while not being too troubled by one's own conscience or the reasoning of those who disagree.

The tasks require a persistence of belief on the part of the "colonizers" that their actions are justified and even righteous. A racist ideology can—and was—woven into the law that was handed down by the courts and legislatures. Additionally, the ideology was made a part of everyday thought, which was crucial because precepts could not be developed without the dissemination of the "truth." Every man, woman, and child in white Virginia had to learn about the "natural law." Such "truth" was not an esoteric subject that required legal knowledge.

With this goal in mind, Virginia whites set out to develop a gospel of black inferiority. The missionaries of this white-dominant vision explained this ideology and justified it using the legal developments as reinforcement. This powerful symbiosis was self-perpetuating.

White Virginians understood that ideology must be accompanied by action. The African Americans themselves must come to realize their wretched status; black youngsters must be "educated" as to their place and limitations. Only then would African Americans "lose[] all just ideas of [their] natural position."[5] When African Americans believed in their inferiority, the precept would become both a part of law and a part of life.

But these patently zealot attributes are only rarely characteristic of the institution of the judiciary or of the process of judicial decision-making. As Justice Benjamin Cardozo explained, the process of judicial decision-making is one whereby "the judge is under a duty, within the limits of his power of innovation, to maintain a relation between law and morals, between the precepts of jurisprudence and those of reason and good conscience."[6] Limited powers of innovation and the duty to balance jurisprudence with conscience are not usually helpful in developing a racist precept. Rather, the precept of black inferiority is one which requires almost inexhaustible powers of innovation and a seemingly complete abandonment of reason and good conscience. Such powers of innovation were and continue to be available to judges only to a limited extent. Reading judicial decisions such as *Tuchinge* and *Graweere*, one detects a halting attempt by the judges to strike a balance between the central precept of race relations jurisprudence, which mandated that African Americans be deemed inferior, and those tenets of good conscience which, in the words of James Baldwin, make it "impossible to look on a man and pretend that this man is a mule."[7]

If the process of judicial decision-making is fraught with doubts, balancing, and questioning, the process of legislative decision-making suffers from no comparable ambivalence. The legislative process can very easily become hostage to the will of small interest groups, and the resulting laws sometimes owe very little to good jurisprudence and even less to good conscience. In short, whereas ideally the process of judicial decision-making is reflective and ambivalent, the process of legislative decision-making is often shortsighted and overzealous—the perfect attributes for the development of a racist precept. Thus, during the second and most active stage in the development of the precept of black inferiority, the Virginia legislature, in a far more rigorous fashion than did the courts, enacted the fundamental components of the precept of black inferiority and erased all traces of ambivalence concerning African Americans in the Virginia legal process.[8]

The shift from isolated judicial opinions to more comprehensive legislative enactments regarding the precept of black inferiority can be placed around 1662. This statement is not meant to imply that the colonists had undertaken a codification of slave law by 1662. In 1662, there was very little legislation concerning blacks that could be codified or compiled. "The first major slave codes were dated 1680–1682."[9] The earliest comprehensive slave codes would not be drafted until approximately 1705.[10] But from 1662 until approximately 1691, the Virginia legislature passed a series of slave statutes that accomplished what the courts had failed to do: articulate a clear rationale for the precept of black inferiority and white superiority.[11]

From 1705 until the end of legalized slavery in 1865, the slave statutes were compiled into codes that varied in their breadth and scope. The codes were both substantive and procedural. The substantive statutes defined the parameters of slavery, regulated the behavior of slaves, and regulated the behavior of free people interacting with slaves. Procedurally, they set up a separate judicial system for slaves, defined their punishment for various crimes, and turned them into a commodity in the economic system. No aspect of the lives of slaves and free African Americans was too sacred or mundane not to be regulated by the codes.[12] From the time slaves were born, until their death, the codes directly or indirectly regulated where they lived, how and where they worked, what God they worshipped, to whom or whether they "married," with whom they had children and whether they were able to raise them, what sort of clothes they wore, and what kind of foods they ate.[13]

The slave codes are more than the repealed legal instruments of the dead institution of slavery. They are also a detailed catalogue of the oppression that African Americans faced here in America. The codes represent the ultimate expression of this country's belief that African Americans are inferior. This belief manifested itself time and again in the utter contempt in which whites held black life.

Perhaps no more damning example of that contempt can be offered than that of a statute first enacted in 1669, and subsequently re-enacted in 1705 with minor amendments. The statute provided that it was not a felony for a master to kill a recalcitrant black slave, because the slave was the master's property, and a master presumably could not have the requisite malice to "destroy his own estate."[14] The 1705 draft neatly disposed of any potential legal problems surrounding the killing, by stating that if a master killed his slave, the "accident" would be treated as if it "had never happened."[15] The statute appeared in various guises in the slave codes of Virginia and in the codes of several other colonies. It is by no means the only example of the brutality and fear under which African Americans lived in the colonies day in and day out.

Many more examples could be unearthed and spread out on this page.

But to do so would be to succumb to the sweet and awful temptation of turning a study of the precept of black inferiority into another anguished recital of how downtrodden and wretched was the life of African-American slaves, and how evil and mercenary were the ambitions of white masters. There is no point in doing so. There is no point in reviewing the roster of the dead, the tortured, the lynched, and the raped. If, as bell hooks cautions, one is to succeed in excavating the past (and future) of African Americans from the "rubble and debris of American history," [16] one needs to try to understand how and why white Americans developed the precept of inferiority. This sort of understanding will certainly not come with a retelling of the story of the slaves as helpless victims and the masters as mad oppressors.

Even though the Virginia slave codes, written between 1705 and 1792,[17] became more and more deplorable as the years went by, it would be misleading to view the development of slavery and the precept of inferiority as a process whereby whites devised increasingly cruel and elaborate humiliations to heap on slaves. The slave masters were not irrational sadists. There was a method to their madness. There was a method to their development of a precept of black inferiority. This development was driven in part by two considerations that seemed to haunt the lives of the colonists: sex and religion.[18]

From the time the Africans first disembarked in Virginia, the colonists seized upon two obvious characteristics as the basis for distinguishing whites from blacks: physiological attributes and culure. African Americans were "different," because physiologically they were different: the color of their skin was different, the texture of their hair was different, and the shape of their facial features was different. African Americans were also different spiritually. They worshipped different gods, and they cultivated a different relationship with life and with death.

African Americans, in their appearance and in their behavior, must have challenged the colonists' way of life. Many colonists—who, it must be remembered, had taken great risks to make a life for themselves in America—must have interpreted the challenge represented by African Americans as a threat. One way to defeat that threat was to cast African Americans and their way of life as savage and inferior. Thus, to the colonists, the Africans came to be seen as savages because, looking black, they looked like savages and, not living as the colonists lived, they lived like savages.[19]

In defining black inferiority in terms of the way African Americans looked and the way they led their lives, the colonists had painted themselves into a corner. African Americans may have "looked black," but when they began to enter into sexual relations with whites, their children eventually started to look less black and, thus, to use the logic of the colonists—less inferior. What's more, African Americans may have lived like "savages," but when they began to convert to Christianity, they started to live less like "savages" and more like the colonists themselves. Whites had staked the precept of black inferiority on the superiority of white physiology and on the civilizing power of the Christian God. Once the Africans began to assume the very characteristics upon which white superiority was founded—when many began to look "near" white and when many of them started to behave as devoutly as any Christian—the colonists found themselves in the predicament of determining how and whether to consider the Africans inferior. The way out of their predicament was to attach negative connotations to certain aspects of interracial sex and to eliminate any beneficial consequences flowing from Christian conversion.

Accordingly, beginning in 1662, the Virginia colonists adopted two simple principles that formed additional cornerstones of the precept of black inferiority. The first principle was that black inferiority was an indelible condition that children inherited from the blood of their parents. The fact that one of the parents may have been white did not make the child any less inferior. In the language of one statute, the mixture of black and white was "abominable" and produced a "spurious" child.[20] The second principle was that blacks were inferior, not because they failed to recognize God, but because God had made them inferior. Becoming a Christian might reconcile blacks to the inevitability of their condition, but it would not make them any less inferior.[21] These two principles were institutionalized in the legal process in the form of the slave codes.

Indeed, the codes, for all their regulation of the minutiae of the lives of the slaves, seem to have been overly concerned with the two areas of sex and religion. To state this assertion is not to accuse the colonists of having been sexually repressed religious fanatics. Sex and religion represented the foundation of the precept of inferiority because, as has been recounted by so many authors, these two considerations were at the heart of the settling of the New World by many of the Europeans. Toni Morrison eloquently describes the motive for this movement:

> The flight from the Old World to the New is generally seen to be a flight from oppression and limitation to freedom and possibility. Although, in fact, the escape was sometimes an escape from license—from a society perceived to be unacceptably permissive, ungodly, and undisciplined—for those fleeing for reasons other than religious ones, constraint and limitation impelled the journey. All the Old World offered these immigrants was poverty, prison, social ostracism, and, not infrequently, death. There was of course a clerical, scholarly group of immigrants who came seeking the adventure possible in founding a colony for, rather than against, one or another mother country or fatherland. And of course there were the merchants, who came for the cash.

Whatever the reasons, the attraction was of the "clean slate" variety, a once-in-a-lifetime opportunity not only to be born again but to be born again in new clothes, as it were. The new setting would provide new raiments of self. This second chance could even benefit from the mistakes of the first. In the New World there was the vision of a limitless future, made more gleaming by the constraint, dissatisfaction, and turmoil left behind. It was a promise genuinely promising. With luck and endurance one could discover freedom; find a way to make God's law manifest; or end up rich as a prince. The desire for freedom is preceded by oppression; a yearning for God's law is born of the detestation of human license and corruption; the glamor of riches is in thrall to poverty, hunger, and debt.[22]

Many of the colonists had left the Old World, rejecting a society that to them was "unacceptably permissive, ungodly, and undisciplined."[23] They had arrived in the New World, finding an unformed land that promised them "God's law [] born of the detestation of human license and corruption."[24] In the colonists' eyes, the Africans embodied all they had tried to leave behind. Yet, as threatened as they may have been by the presence of the Africans, the Europeans could not have afforded to send them back to Africa or to assimilate them fully into the new society they were trying to build.

The dark, savage, ungodly, and licentious Africans were the perfect image against which the Europeans could favorably contrast the pure, godly, and prosperous selves they dreamed of creating in America. The colonial concept of freedom did not exist in a vacuum. Rather, freedom existed only as it could be highlighted by and contrasted to slavery. The colonists knew they were free because the slaves were not. They knew they were pure and godly because African Americans were licentious and ungodly. Thomas Jefferson described the Africans in this way:

> They are more ardent after their female; but love seems with them to be more an eager desire than a tender delicate mixture of sentiment and sensation. Their griefs are transient. Those numberless afflictions, which render it doubtful whether Heaven has given life to us in mercy or in wrath, are less felt, and sooner forgotten with them.[25]

The aforementioned is intended to show that the scholars Cornel West and James Baldwin are correct in their evaluations of the role of sex and religion in the development of American racism. Cornel West observes that:

> White supremacist ideology is based first and foremost on the degradation of black bodies in order to control them. . . . [T]his white dehumanizing endeavor has left its toll in the psychic scars and personal wounds now inscribed in the souls of black folk. These scars and wounds are clearly etched on the canvass of black sexuality.[26]

James Baldwin describes his own religious experience:

> In my own mind, and in fact, I was told by Christians what I could do and what I could become and what my life was worth. Now, this means that one's concept of human freedom is in a sense frozen or strangled at the root. This has to do, of course, with the fact that though he was born in Nazareth under a very hot sun, and though we know that he spent his life beneath that sun, the Christ I was presented with was presented to me with blue eyes and blond hair, and all the virtues to which I, as a black man, was expected to aspire had, by definition, to be white. . . . [W]hat it did was make me very early, make us, the blacks, very early distrust our own experience and refuse, in effect, to articulate that experience to the Christians who were our oppressors.[27]

These two writers are suggesting that sex (licentious for the Africans, pure for the Europeans) and religion (ungodly for the Africans, godly for the Europeans) became the symbolic representations of the inferiority of the slaves and the superiority of their masters. To understand that—to understand how sex and religion were at the core of white supremacist ideology—is to see clearly how the legal process articulated and enforced the precept of black inferiority and white superiority.

Determining Status by Sex, Marriage, and Racial "Purity"

The first statute enacted by the Virginia legislature relating to sex and inferiority was passed in 1662. The statute read: "Children got by an Englishman upon a Negro woman shall be bond or free according to the condition of the mother, and if any Christian shall commit fornication with a Negro man or woman, he shall pay double the fines of a former act."[28] In considering this statute from the Virginia legislature, one might be led to believe that the purpose was to discourage interracial sex. The legislature seemed to attempt to accomplish this task by taking away what each of the participants presumably wanted from the sex act: freedom for the slave woman, money for the white master. By making the child a slave, the 1662 statute theoretically discouraged black female slaves from seducing their masters in the hope of obtaining their children's freedom and possibly their own freedom as well.[29] By imposing a fine on the white masters, the legislature supposedly discouraged them from raping their female slaves as a means of producing, at a cheap price, a ready supply of home-grown slaves.

But of course we know—if only from the faces of today's African Americans—that the 1662 Virginia statute and similar statutes in the other colonies were far from successful in accomplishing their *stated* goal of discouraging interracial sex. Indeed, the means by which the 1662 Virginia legislature chose to achieve its task were so ineffective as to make one question the legislature's true intent. As drafted, the statute merely imposed a fine on the master, but allowed him to keep the child as his own slave. In the long run, the fine was more than offset by the economic benefits the master reaped from the labor of the slave he had fathered. The master produced a slave who would work in his house and his fields for free, and who would take care of him in his old age, just in case love and gratitude failed to convince his white children to sacrifice themselves to that honor.

Had the legislature really intended to discourage interracial sex between the male master and the female slave, it would have imposed a far more costly punishment on the white master, the one participant who entered into sex willingly. The statute could have been drafted to state that any child born of the union of a white male and a black female would not belong to the father, but instead would be forfeited to the service of the colony.

This sanction is precisely what the legislature decreed in instances in which the child was born of a white woman and a black man. In a 1691 statute, the Virginia legislature provided: "[I]f any English woman being free shall have a bastard child by a Negro. . . . [t]he child shall be bound out by the church wardens until he is thirty years of age."[30] "By 1705, the Virginia General Assembly had clarified all ambiguities and insured that *all* mulatto children would be servants at least until they were thirty-one years old."[31]

These provisions seemed to flatly contradict the 1662 statute. That act had provided that children of interracial unions became free persons or servants according to the condition of their mothers. Thus, logically, a child born of a free Christian white woman and a black man should have been free, because the mother was free. Instead, the child became a servant, simply because the child's father was black. The child's condition was therefore determined by the condition of the father, in apparent contradiction to the 1662 statute.

The 1691 addition to the 1662 statute was one that applied only to the scenario of a child born of a white mother and a black father. Indeed, the legislature made it perfectly clear when it decreed in 1723 that children born to female mulatto or Indian servants who were to serve until age thirty-one were also required to serve his or her mother's master for thirty-one years.[32] So, whenever a white woman had a child with a black man, the child was taken away from the parents and sold by the colony as a servant until he or she reached thirty-one years of age. If the child was female and, as an adult, delivered a baby before her period of servitude expired, the baby also belonged to the mother's master until thirty-one years of age.

When one considers the combined effect of the 1662, 1705, and 1723 statutes, it is possible to imagine the following scenario. A black female slave gives birth to a male child. The father is a white man, the slave's master. According to the 1662 statute, the child becomes a slave. *He is black because his mother is black.* The child grows to adulthood and, somehow, impregnates a free white woman. That woman gives birth to a female child. According to the 1705 statute, that child becomes a servant. *She is black because her father is black.* She, herself, grows into adulthood and gives birth to a male child from a white father. According to the 1723 statute, he becomes a servant. *He is black because his mother is black.*

This scenario is similar to what occurred in two cases, one in 1769, the other in 1770. In *Gwinn v. Bugg,* a black male slave sued for his freedom on the ground, among other things, that his master did not have the right to own him. The facts of the case were as follows:

> A Christian white woman between the years 1723 and 1765, had a daughter, Betty Bugg, by a negro man. This daughter was by deed indented, bound by the churchwardens to serve till thirty-one. Before the expiration of her servitude, she was delivered of the defendant Bugg, who never was bound by the churchwardens, and was sold by his master to the plaintiff.[33]

In *Howell v. Netherland,* the court recounted facts so akin to *Gwinn* as to suggest that the situation was not uncommon:

> [T]he plaintiff's grandmother was a mulatto, begotten on a white woman by a negro man, after the year 1705, and bound by the churchwardens, under the law of that date, to serve to the age of thirty-one. That after the year 1723, but during her servitude, she was delivered of the plaintiff's mother, who, during her servitude, to wit, in 1742, was delivered of the plaintiff, and he again was sold by the person to whom his grandmother was bound, to the defendant, who now claims his service till he shall be thirty-one years of age.[34]

Both cases demonstrate that, under the 1662, 1705, and 1723 statutes, black blood was so indelibly inferior that no amount of white blood could make it any less so. As a component of the precept of black inferiority, the concept of the taint of black blood would become a powerful argument in favor of slavery. The 1662, 1705, and 1723 statutes codified into law, long before the scientific theories had been dreamed up, the idea that black blood was a corrupting agent and that the purity of white blood needed to be protected from its corrosive effects. The statutes created a scheme whereby black blood was the source of both real and symbolic inferiority. To have black blood meant that one would occupy an inferior social and economic position. One would either be a slave, a servant, or one of those belonging to that schizophrenic description, free blacks.[35] On a symbolic level, it meant that once one's skin displayed African heritage, one was marked with the t̲ inferiority, which passed on to one's descendants forever.

Toni Morrison has written that, in our century, "race has become metaphorical—a way of referring to and disguising forces, events, classes, and expressions of social decay and economic division far more threatening to the body politic than biological 'race' ever was."[36] This passage simply means that the precept of inferiority, which was invented at the dawn of slavery, still rules many, if not most, of our social institutions, political decisions, and personal interactions. A child born of interracial parents in 1996 is considered African-American if the color of her skin and her features makes it evident that she is from mixed parentage. From a biological standpoint, she is as much white as she is black. Yet for all practical purposes, very few people will consider her to be white; African-American, yes; mixed, maybe; white, almost certainly not.

During the debates over the confirmation of Supreme Court Justice Clarence Thomas, it was said many times that no matter how unpalatable Justice Thomas's views were to many African Americans, the African-American community still had to claim him as one of its own because, after all, no one else would. In a somewhat similar fashion, ever since the first time Africans set foot in this country, African Americans have always had to claim everyone born here who can be said to have had *any* black blood in them, because the white community certainly would not claim them.

With a far more comprehensive analysis in an article entitled "Racial Purity and Interracial Sex in the Law of Colonial and Antebellum Virginia," Professor Barbara K. Kopytoff and I traced the evolution of Virginia jurisprudence in defining who is colored, who is mulatto, and who is white. Initially, there was no need for statutory definitions of race and there were no problems of racial identity to be solved by legislative fiat. However, as soon as the races began to mingle and reproduce, problems of racial identity arose. How should mixed-race offspring be classified?

Strictly in terms of genetic contribution, the child of one white parent and one black parent had the same claim to being classified as white as he did to being classified as black. He was neither, or either, or both. One could decide to call such half/half mixtures mulattoes, but that merely raised the question of classification again in the next generation. Was the child of a mulatto and a white to be deemed a mulatto or a white? Or should another name, like quadroon, be devised for such a person?

Of course, the important point was not the name but the set of rights and privileges that accompanied the classification. In Virginia, there were only three racial classifications of any legal significance, though there were far more combinations and permutations of racial mixture. Those three were "white," "Indian," and "Negro and mulatto."[37] Mulattoes of mixed black and white ancestry had the same legal position as Negroes, although their social position may have been somewhat different.[38] These legal classifications, then, gave rise to the need for a legal definition of race. As Winthrop Jordan notes, "if mulattoes were to be considered Negroes, logic required some definition of mulattoes, some demarcation between them and white men."[39] Virginia was one of the only two colonies to bow to the demands of logic by creating a precise statutory definition in the colonial period.[40]

As was noted above, slave status was legally independent of race. Slaves who looked white had no special legal privileges until the nineteenth century, and then their only advantage was that they were relieved of the burden of proof in freedom suits.[41] Race did, however, make a considerable difference for free people. Thus, the first legal definition of "mulatto" appeared in a statute dealing with the rights of free persons.[42]

In 1705, the Virginia legislature barred mulattoes, along with blacks, Indians, and criminals, from holding "any office, ecclesiasticall, civill or military, or be[ing] in any place of public trust or power."[43] The mixed-race individuals defined as mulatto under the statute were "the child of an Indian, or the child, grandchild, or great grandchild of a Negro."[44] Whites had distinct legal advantages, but mulattoes had no greater rights than blacks. Thus, the important dividing line was the white/mulatto boundary, not the mulatto/black boundary. The fact that some people were classified as mulatto rather than as Negroes seems to have been simply a recognition of their visible differences.[45]

One notes in the statute's definition of "mulatto" the different treatment of those whose non-white ancestors were Native Americans as opposed to black. A person with one Native American parent and one white parent was a mulatto. Someone with one Native American grandparent and three white grandparents was, by implication, legally white and not barred from public office under the statute. For black-white mixtures, it took two additional generations to "wash out the taint" of black blood to the point that it was legally insignificant. A person with a single black grandparent or even a single black great-grandparent was still considered a mulatto.

Why was there a difference in the legal treatment of white-Indian and white-black mixtures? Perhaps it was related to the degree to which a mixed-race individual looked white to eighteenth-century white Virginians. Perhaps it was also because Europeans tended to see Indians as higher on the scale of creation than blacks, though still lower than themselves.[46]

Note that these definitions of race state the rule in theory; we do not suppose that they were rigidly followed in practice. We have found no case from this period in which a claim to being legally white was based on the exact proportion of white blood. At the time of the statute, in 1705, some eighty-five years after the first blacks had arrived in Virginia, there would barely have been time for four generations of offspring necessary to "dilute the taint" of black blood to the point that it did not count under law. Thus, few if any white/black mixtures would have qualified as white, though it is likely there were some white/Indian mixtures who did.

The Virginia legislature, meeting in 1785, changed the legal definition of mulatto to those with "one-fourth part of more of Negro blood."[47] Thus, by implication, those of one-eighth black ancestry (one black great-grandparent), who by the 1705 statute had been mulattoes, were now legally white.[48] There is no mention in the statute of Indian ancestry.[49] Interestingly, while the definition of mulatto in 1705 excluded from the category of white virtually all of those with any black ancestry at the time, the 1785 definition, some four generations later, did not attempt to do the same. Instead, under the 1785 act, a number of mixed-race people who previously would have been classified as mulatto could be considered white. This was the only time Virginia law was changed to allow persons with a greater proportion of black ancestry to be deemed white. All subsequent changes were in the opposite direction—making a smaller proportion of black blood bar one from being considered white.

Was this statute, as James Hugo Johnston suggests, an effort to bring the law into line with social practice? He says, "[i]t would appear that the lawmakers of the early national period feared that a declaration to the effect that the possession of any Negro ancestry, however remote, made a man a mulatto might bring embarrassment on certain supposedly white citizens."[50] He notes that before the Civil War, in no state did the law provide that a person having less than one-eighth black blood should be deemed a mulatto.[51]

Johnston also says that it was no doubt believed to be exceedingly difficult, if not impossible, to enforce a more drastic law of racial identity.[52] Yet in fact, Virginia did enact more drastic laws in the twentieth century. Under a 1910 statute, as small a proportion as one-sixteenth black ancestry made one "colored."[53] Then, in 1924 and 1930, *any* Negro blood at all meant that one was not legally white.[54]

Another possible explanation for the 1785 statute is that it reflected strategic considerations. If supposedly white men of power and position were declared to be mulatto and thus deprived of civil and political rights, they might have formed a dangerous alliance with other "less white" free mulattoes and blacks whose rights were similarly denied. Their combined forces would have threatened the social control over the society of the remaining smaller number still classified as white. Georgia, to encourage the immigration of free mixed-race persons into the colony, provided in 1765 that free mulatto and "mustee"[55] immigrants might be declared "whites," with "all the Rights,

Privileges, Powers and Immunities whatsoever which any person born of British parents" would have, except the rights to vote and sit in the Assembly.[56] Georgia legislators were apparently at that time more concerned about hostile Indians on their southern border than they were about the racial makeup of the colony's "white" population.[57]

These explanations are merely suggestions. We have no satisfactory answer as to why the 1785 Virginia statute allowed racially mixed persons who formerly were classified as mulatto to become legally white. The Act itself gives no clue as to the reason for the change. The percentage of allowable black ancestry in a legally white person was not changed again until the twentieth century, when Indian mulattoes were reintroduced in an 1866 statute making a person who was one-quarter Indian a mulatto, if he was not otherwise "colored."[58]

Objectively, the effect of statutes defining a mulatto as someone with a certain proportion of black or Indian ancestry, and implying that someone with a smaller proportion of non-white ancestry was legally white, was to make "white" into a mixed-race category. By the early twentieth century, when those classified as white had to have "no trace whatsoever"[59] of black "blood," there was indeed a great deal of untraced (and, in some cases, untraceable) black blood in the white population.

We see the notion that black ancestry can be gradually diluted into legal insignificance in the case of *Dean v. Commonwealth.*[60] There, a criminal defendant claimed that two witnesses were incompetent to testify against him because they were mulattoes, and mulattoes could not testify against whites.[61] The court found the witnesses competent, since they had less than one-fourth black blood, the legal dividing line under the statute then in force.[62] The description of legal "lightening" over the generations in the reporting of the case is telling:

> . . . [F]rom the testimony it appeared certainly, that they had less than one fourth of negro blood. Their grandfather, David Ross, who was spoken of as a respectable man, though probably a mulatto, was a soldier in the revolution and died in the service. The evidence as to the grandmother was contradictory; though she was probably white, the mother was so certainly.[63]

The grandfather would have been incompetent to testify because he was a mulatto, but the grandchildren were not.[64] The grandmother was probably white but the mother was certainly so. Thus, in mid-nineteenth-century Virginia, mulatto parents and grandparents could have children and grandchildren who were legally white. That became legally impossible only in the twentieth century, when any trace of black blood would disqualify a person from being considered white under the law.[65]

Whites in pre-Civil War Virginia paid a strategic price to maintain their ideal of white racial purity. Had they declared, for example, that anyone with more than 50 percent white blood was legally white, they would have had less to fear from an alliance of free mulattoes and slaves. Then, however, their racial rationale for slavery would have been undermined because the number of legally white slaves would have increased greatly. It would have been hard to maintain that slavery was justified by the inferiority of the black if large numbers of slaves were classified as white under Virginia law. The white population was in fact racially mixed, but the proportion of non-white ancestry allowable in a white person was so small that it was not very visible. It was so small that, as we shall see, white Virginians could maintain the myth that it was not there at all.

In a later volume in this Race and the American Legal Process series, I will incorporate the writings on racial purity that I have published with Barbara K. Kopytoff. However, for the purposes of this volume, which focuses primarily on the precept of racial inferiority, it is sufficient to note that at various times the legislature assumed that to be white meant that, somehow, one did not have any, or any significant amount of, black blood.

In developing the precept of black inferiority, whites gradually staked out an absolute definition of what it meant to be white and superior. To be white meant that one did not have any black blood. To be black meant that somehow, somewhere, one had acquired some amount of black blood; it did not matter how much. At best, one might be called a mulatto if it strained the imagination to be called black. But no matter how many words were invented to classify the various hues that miscegenation had produced, with almost any amount of black blood, one remained basically black and, therefore, unalterably inferior.

The 1662, 1705, and 1723 Virginia statutes have always been analyzed for their use of race to define who was a free person, who was a slave, and who was a servant. This sort of analysis is certainly crucial to understanding how the form of slavery that the colonists developed in the New World was unique, in that it relied exclusively on race. But the statutes also have another meaning that is equally important. With the legislators' rather compulsive preoccupation with interracial sex, the statutes grounded the precept of inferiority firmly in biology. If black blood was the mark of inferiority, sex became the instrument by which it was transmitted. Since sex for blacks was licentious and savage, there was a certain perverse logic to this theory that anyone born of such an act would inherit the very characteristics of the act itself.

However "logical" the idea of black inferiority being tied to black sexuality might have been, it was not without its complications for the colonists. I stated at the beginning of this discussion that, in engaging in interracial sex, the slave woman might have expected freedom and the white master money. These motives do not exhaust the possibilities. Sex, interracial or otherwise, is a tricky business. It is not always clear exactly what the participants want from the act. In this instance, the black slave may not have been the only one seeking freedom, and the white master may not have been the only one after money. Aside from the problem that the slave woman was often coerced by her master, she must have been smart enough to realize that freedom for her or her children was not about to be obtained for a single sexual act. But, if not freedom, perhaps she hoped for a bigger cabin in which to live and better food to feed her children.

As for the white master, money was not the only thing that led him down to the slave quarters. It was also a wish for freedom: freedom from fear and freedom from desire. James Baldwin has suggested that white Americans used blacks to store the things they most feared and most desired in themselves: the chaos of violence and the dangers of carnality.[66] Sex between the white master and his female slave was a means by which he could tap into the violence and carnality in his own soul, without being consumed by it. To be in actual control of the body of his slave, who embodied his own fears and desires, was to be in symbolic control of those fears and desires in his own heart.

Today it might be argued that whites have not managed to extricate themselves completely from those myths. Cornel West again provides insight into whites' possible motivations:

> Americans are obsessed with sex and fearful of black sexuality. The obsession has to do with a search for stimulation and meaning in a fast-paced, market-driven culture; the fear is rooted in visceral feelings about black bodies fueled by sexual myths of black women and men. The dominant myths draw black women and men either as threatening creatures who have the potential for sexual power over whites, or as harmless, desexed underlings of a white culture. There is Jezebel (the seductive temptress), Sapphire (the evil, manipulative bitch), or Aunt Jemima (the sexless, long-suffering nurturer). There is Bigger Thomas (the mad and mean predatory craver of white women), Jack Johnson (the super performer—be it in athletics, entertainment, or sex—who excels others naturally and prefers women of a lighter hue), or Uncle Tom (the spineless, sexless—or is it impotent?—sidekick of whites). The myths offer distorted, dehumanized creatures whose bodies—color of skin, shape of nose and lips, type of hair, size of hips—are already distinguished from the white norm of beauty and whose feared sexual activities are deemed disgusting, dirty, or funky and considered less acceptable.
>
> Yet the paradox of the sexual politics of race in America is that, behind closed doors, the dirty, disgusting, and funky sex associated with

black people is often perceived to be more intriguing and interesting, while in public spaces talk about black sexuality is virtually taboo.[67]

The bodies of the slaves, although despised and condemned, nonetheless provided the colonists with a rich field upon which to map out their economic future and to live out their secret dreams. In order to plow and harvest that field, whites had to make certain that the bodies of the slaves remained accessible to them without limitations and without consequences. Hence, interracial sex instigated and controlled by the white male master was promoted, while interracial marriage was strictly forbidden. In 1691, the Virginia legislature enacted the following statute, "designed to prevent 'that abominable mixture and spurious issue . . . by, Negroes, mulattoes and Indians intermarrying with English or other white women' " and provided that: "whatsoever English or other white man or woman, bond or free, shall intermarry with a Negro, mulatto, or Indian man or woman, bond or free, he shall within three months be banished from this dominion forever."[68] Later, in the slave code of 1705, the legislature amended the statute to provide: "Whatsoever white man or woman being free shall intermarry with a Negro shall be committed to prison for six months without bail, and pay 10 pounds to the use of the parish. Ministers marrying such persons shall pay 10,000 pounds of tobacco."[69]

It is noteworthy that even though the legislature purported to find the coupling of blacks and whites "abominable," and the children from such couplings "spurious," it did not expressly forbid interracial sex in the 1691 statute or the 1705 amendment. All that the statute did was make interracial marriage illegal. As argued earlier, since interracial sex among white male masters and black female slaves was economically profitable to the master, the effect of the 1691 and 1705 statutes was to make certain that interracial sex would flourish, but that the institution of marriage between the races would not be permitted.

This contention is clearly demonstrated by comparing the punishment imposed by the 1662 statute on the white master for engaging in interracial sex with the punishment imposed by the 1691 statute on the white master for marrying a black person. The 1662 statute imposed only a small fine on the master, while the 1691 statute banished him from the colony for life. Moreover, the 1691 statute provided for the exile of any white who married a black person, but it did *not* provide for the exile of the black person or of the children of the interracial marriage. They would have been far too valuable as slaves to be sent into exile. Thus, a white person who married a black would lose not only his home but also his family.

The fact that the 1691 statute imposed such a severe punishment on the white master strongly suggests that the legislature intended to discourage interracial marriage. By contrast, the fact that the 1662 statute imposed a relatively mild form of punishment means that the legislature was not truly concerned with discouraging interracial sex. Interracial marriages represented a potentially grave threat to the fledgling institution of slavery. Had blacks and whites intermarried, the legal process would have been hard pressed to recognize the union while keeping blacks in slavery. Interracial sex, by contrast, far from represented a threat to slavery. Rather, it served as its life blood. Blacks were cheaper to produce than to import.

Beyond guaranteeing that black slaves would not gain their freedom by marrying whites, the 1691 and 1705 statutes served an additional purpose. The statutes prohibited whites from marrying "bond or free" blacks. The prohibition against whites' marrying "bonded" or slave blacks may be explained by the need to prevent the indirect undermining of the institution of slavery. A similar concern about not undermining the institution of slavery explains the prohibition against whites' marrying free blacks, even though blacks who were already "free" did not gain freedom by marrying whites. Indeed, the children of such marriages would have been mulattoes. And, mulattoes were held in almost as much contempt as blacks. There may have been an alternative explanation to justify the prohibition against whites' marrying free blacks other than the need to protect the institution of slavery. The one explanation that readily suggests itself is the need to enforce and protect the precept of black inferiority, which itself served as an enforcement mechanism for the institution of slavery.

Recall that, in the 1705 slave code, the legislature had provided that the "bastard" child of a white woman and a black man would be sold into servitude until thirty-one years of age. In the same code, the legislature outlawed any marriage between whites and blacks.[70] Since interracial marriages were not legally recognized, any child born of interracial parents would be immediately labeled a bastard. Furthermore, whites considered blacks inferior in part because they did not respect the social and divine institution of marriage. Yet southern whites generally refused to legitimize under law any marriages entered into among slaves. This hypocrisy turned the precept of black inferiority into a form of self-fulfilling prophecy: blacks were inferior because they did not legally marry; blacks could not marry because they were inferior.

If a white woman had sex with a black man, the myth of the predatory black stud would hold that the white woman had been raped or somehow coerced into the relationship. In the same manner, if a black woman had sex with a white man, the myth of the evil black seductress would hold that the white man had been ensnared into the relationship. Either way, the precept of black inferiority was reinforced. Blacks were rapacious sexual creatures who preyed upon whites. Marriage between whites and blacks served no use. The savage instincts of blacks could not be tamed, even by the supposedly civilizing influence of marriage to whites.

During the 1960s, the question whites often used to end any discussion about integration was: *"Yes, but would you want your daughter or sister to marry one?"* The key as to why the mere posing of this question was always such a powerful argument (to whites) against integration can be found buried in the slave codes. One would not want one's (white) sister to marry a black because her husband would be an inferior being who would subject her to his inferior urges, and would produce inferior children.

Less than two decades ago, a classic example of the anxiety about interracial marriage was revealed in a page-one article in a 1967 *New York Times* news story pertaining to the marriage of the daughter of the then Secretary of State, Dean Rusk, to an African American. Normally, marriages of the children of famous people are restricted solely to the "Society Section," where the couple's photos are surrounded with columns about others who were recently married. It is inconceivable that, if Margaret Elizabeth Rusk had married a white person with credentials similar to those of her African-American husband, that their wedding picture would have been emblazoned on the first page of the *New York Times*.

But, for this couple, in bold type, the headline proclaimed: "Rusk's Daughter, 18, Is Wed to Negro." She was not marrying some ne'er-do-well African American—he was a 22-year-old second lieutenant in the Air Force reserve, and was "awaiting orders to report for active duty and flying instruc-tion[s]," which might lead to an assignment in Vietnam. The second paragraph of the article noted: "In Washington, it was reported that Mr. Rusk had been prepared to resign if his daughter's marriage embarrassed President Johnson politically. But the President apparently saw this as a formal courtesy and gave it no serious consideration.[71]

Redeeming the "Inferior" Through Religion and Civilization?

Traditionally, the justification used by Europeans for enslaving Africans was that Africans were heathens or savages who could be civilized by being converted into Christians. Such a justification drew from long historical roots. Christians almost universally supported slavery if the extension of the Christian faith and civilization was the professed motive. The corollary custom and practice was that the slave became free once converted to Christianity.[72] The slave had become civilized through Christian conversion.

However, as Helen Catterall explains in her treatise on slave law:

The early theory that the enslavement of infidels was justifiable in order to make Christians of them, had for a corollary that, when the purpose of enslavement had been achieved by their conversion, their slavery ceased and they became free. This corollary had become difficult of application. If freedom was a reward of baptism, could any slave resist it, no matter how rudimentary his theology, or could many masters welcome it? And even if slaves had not been baptized, they could easily pretend to have been . . . . It became expedient to require a more "visible" and more permanent "sign" than the water of baptism to differentiate the slave from the free, and a quietus was put on baptism as a method of emancipation, by statutes in the various colonies.[73]

The Africans were not as unenlightened as whites had presumed them to be. If Christianity promised personal redemption *and* freedom, Africans realized very quickly that it was in their best interests to kneel down, bow their heads, and kiss the cross. They may not have heard "God's voice" while plowing the master's fields or seen "Heaven's light" while being whipped at the whipping post, but if that is what it took to free them from pain, then they would make sure they convinced their masters that they had heard "the voice" and seen "the light." Helen Catterall correctly pointed out that granting freedom based on religious conversion posed a real threat to the survival of the institution of slavery.

In addition to being incompatible with the institution of slavery, this theory of religious conversion challenged the precept of inferiority itself. Along with the stereotype of sexual depravity, whites had staked the precept of black inferiority on the idea of the godless nature of the African soul. Once the Africans began to accept the Christian God, it became impossible to insist on their inferiority based on the idea that they did not know God. Instead it became necessary to reinvent their inferiority based on the idea that God did not know *them*.

This reinvention was a simple but terrible turn of the mind. If blacks were inferior because they did not know God, they could eventually be freed from their inferiority once they accepted God. But if they were inferior because God did not know them, they could never be freed from their inferiority by turning their face to God, because God would not turn his face to them.

In a published volume of sermons, Bishop Meade of the Church of England in Virginia recommended to slave masters and mistresses that the following sermon be read to their slaves:

And think within yourselves what a terrible thing it would be, after all your labors and sufferings in this life, to be turned into hell in the next life, and, after wearing out your bodies in service here, to go into a far worse slavery when this is over, and your poor souls be delivered over into the possession of the devil, to become his slaves forever in hell, without any hope of ever getting free from it! If, therefore, you would be God's freemen in heaven, you must strive to be good, and serve him here on earth. Your bodies, you know, are not your own; they are at the disposal of those you belong to . . . And for this you have one general rule, that you ought always to carry in your minds; and that is to do all service for them as if you did it for God himself. . . . And pray do not think that I want to deceive you when I tell you that your masters and mistresses are God's overseers, and that, if you are faulty towards them, God himself will punish you severely for it in the next world, unless you repent of it, and strive to make amends by your faithfulness and diligence for the time to come; for God himself hath declared the same.[74]

Beginning in 1667, the Virginia legislature wrote into law the principle that God himself had rendered the slaves inferior because God was on the side of the master. The first Virginia statute to abandon the principle of freedom based on religious conversion read as follows:

Whereas some doubts have arisen whether children that are slaves by birth, and by the charity and pity of their owners made partakers of the blessed sacrament of baptism, should by virtue of their baptism be made free, it is enacted that *baptism does not alter the condition of the person as to his bondage of freedom; masters freed from this doubt may more carefully propagate Christianity by permitting slaves to be admitted to that sacrament.*[75]

With this 1667 statute, baptism was no longer the sign of freedom. Prior to the passage of this 1667 statute, the terms "Christian," "civilized," and "free" were interchangeable. To be Christian was to be civilized. To be civilized was to be deserving of freedom. The terms "heathen," "savage," and "slave" were also used in a similar manner, but with quite different consequences. To be a heathen was to be a savage. To be a savage was to be fit for slavery. Of course, the key to both sets of reasoning was the question of religious status. In other words, if one were to replace the term "heathen" with "Christian," it would automatically follow that the remaining terms "savage" and "slave" would also change to "civilized" and "free."

What the Virginia legislature accomplished with the 1667 statute was to strip the term "Christian" of its transformative value. With it, it now became possible to be Christian, savage, and slave. Blacks and, at times, Native Americans were the only ones who fit that description. The color of whites' skin alone rendered them civilized, whereas the color of the Africans' skin made them savages.

In 1670, 1682, and again in 1705, the Virginia legislature reinforced this

principle. The 1670 statute provided that: "Negroes or Indians, though baptised and enjoying their own freedom, shall be incapable of purchasing Christians, yet they are not debarred from buying any of their own color."[76]
The 1682 statute read in relevant part:

> It is enacted that all servants, except Turks and Moors, while in amity with his majesty which shall be imported into this country either by sea or by land, whether Negroes, Moors, mulattoes or Indians who and whose parentage and native countries are not Christian at the time of their first purchase by some Christian, although afterward and before their importation into this country they shall be converted to the Christian faith; and all Indians, which shall be sold by our neighboring Indians, or any others trafficing with us for slaves, are hereby adjudged deemed and taken to be slaves to all intents and purposes any law, usage, or custom to the contrary notwithstanding.[77]

The 1705 statute provided:

> That all servants imported and brought into this country, by sea or land, who were not christians in their native country, (except Turks and Moors in amity with her majesty, and others that can make due proof of their being free in England, or any other christian country, before they were shipped, in order to transportation hither) shall be accounted and be slaves, and as such be here bought and sold notwithstanding a conversion to christianity afterwards.[78]

The effect of all these statutes was to make certain that all blacks residing in or coming into the colonies would be subject to slavery, regardless of their religious faith. The 1667 statute declared that blacks who were slaves by birth remained slaves after being converted to Christianity by their masters. The 1682 and 1705 statutes provided that all blacks whose native country or whose ancestry was not Christian were to be considered slaves once imported into the colony, even though they may have been Christian before such importation. These two statutes applied mainly to blacks imported from other slaveholding countries to the colonies. If those blacks had become Christian before entering Virginia, they would still be considered slaves once in Virginia.

Together, the four statutes established a scheme under which all blacks, whether born in Virginia, imported from Africa, or imported from elsewhere, would be subject to slavery. The upshot of the statutes was that blacks were slaves notwithstanding any present status as "Christian." The legal process vindicated the principle that Christianity would best be used to help the slaves accept their condition of servitude. Blacks had been made inferior by God. Therefore, to convert them into Christians was to help them understand their condition, not to change it.

These statutes were, in that way, perfect companions for the 1662 and

1691 legislation regulating interracial sex and marriage. Whereas the latter had maintained that the intervention of human biology was not sufficient to raise blacks from their inferior status, the former went one step further in stating that even God would not intervene to make blacks any less inferior. In addition to being tainted by their blood, blacks were now marked by God. They were inferior in body and in spirit.

In the end, the colonists imposed religion on the slaves without love, the same way they forced children on slave women. I am not saying that the slaves themselves did not find redemption in the religion they had been given. I am also not saying that the slaves did not love the children born of what would later be called—for the sake of historical convenience—miscegenation. They loved their children, fed them, and tried to protect them the best way they knew. No one else would. In that same way, they took the religion they had been offered, infused it with their spirit, and tried to find in it something that would testify to their humanity. No one else would.

The slaves used to sing: "Wash me Jesus, and I shall be whiter, whiter than snow." Perhaps, in the end, only the God or Gods they were really praying to will ever know what they truly meant when they asked to be made "whiter, whiter than snow." But, one thing is certain. Their prayer did not mean that they had mindlessly surrendered to the ancient European conceit of equating black with evil and white with purity. Rather, their plea was a bitter and ironic rejection of the precept of inferiority. After all, the slaves did not ask to be made white. They sang: "I shall be *whiter, whiter than snow.*" It must not have escaped their attention that their *white* masters, by the very fact that they kept slaves, had wholly failed to live up to the Christian piety that was supposed to lead to the kingdom of Heaven. So, they prayed to be made not white, but something more than white, something "whiter than snow." In that prayer, the slaves were speaking to Heaven about the wretchedness of their own condition. But more important, they were also speaking to Heaven about the condition of their masters, which in the end the slaves believed would prove to be even more wretched than their own. By equating salvation to being made "whiter," rather than to being made merely "white," the slaves, at least in the eyes of their own God, had placed the kingdom of Heaven beyond the reach of their merely "white" masters.

Punishment, Murder, Malice, and Inferiority

Once the colonists had grappled with the conundrums of sex and religion to establish clearly that blacks were inferior, slavery, as it would come to be practiced in America, took firm root. When nations go to war, leaders always paint the enemy as ruthless, soulless monsters, because people usually find it difficult to kill others, but easy to destroy monsters. No matter how different and foreign the Africans may have looked to the colonists when they arrived here in America, they still were human beings. They had two eyes, and they walked on two legs. In order for the colonists to assuage their consciences and enslave the Africans, they had to transform them into the godless, sexually twisted monsters that the precept of black inferiority engendered. With the precept in place, whites could humiliate, brutalize, maim, and kill blacks in an attempt to beat back the monsters that they had created as a mirror image of their own dark selves.

One of the corollaries of the precept of inferiority was that blacks were to be made to always feel hopeless, submissive, and docile. This corollary was accomplished by regulating their lives so thoroughly and completely that they would have only the bare minimum of control over their fates. To assure docility and compliance, the slave had to understand that his master knew best, that resistance was futile, and that any attempt to regain control over his life would be met with severe punishment and possibly death. To that end, one of the most striking features of the slave code of 1705 was the amendment to a statute originally enacted by the Virginia legislature in 1669. The 1669 statute provided:

> Whereas the only law in force for the punishment of refractory servants resisting their master, mistress or overseer, cannot be inflicted on negroes [because the punishment was extension of time], Nor the obstinacy of many of them by other than violent meanes supprest. . . . [I]f any slave resist his master . . . and by the extremity of the correction should chance to die, that his death shall not be accompted Felony, but the master (or that other person appointed by the master to punish him) be acquit from molestation, since it cannot be presumed that propensed malice (which alone makes murther Felony) should induce any man to destroy his own estate.[79]

The 1705 amendment read:

> And if any slave resist his master, or owner, or other person, by his or her order, correcting such slave, and shall happen to be killed in such correction, it shall not be accounted felony; but the master, owner, and every such other person so giving correction, shall be free and acquit of all punishment and accusation for the same, as if such accident had never happened.[80]

The Virginia legislature adopted the original 1669 statute to say, in effect, that since blacks were not fully human, to kill one was not murder, as it would be if the victim had been white.

The statute itself requires some background explanation. In 1661 the Virginia legislature had passed an act stating that "christian servants" who ran away from their master with blacks were to be punished by extending their period of servitude.[81] The phrase "christian servants" referred to white indentured servants. The punishment devised for the white servants was ineffectual against blacks who ran away from their masters because, as early as 1661, many blacks were already serving as lifetime slaves.[82] The ostensible purpose of the 1669 statute was to remedy the problem of finding an effective punishment for recalcitrant black slaves. The solution, according to the legislature, was to acknowledge the master's total reign over punishment of the black slave, even to the point of killing the slave.

The statute, however, when read in its entirety, belies its stated purpose of finding an effective punishment for lifetime slaves who ran away or resisted. The statute completely failed to mention what forms of punishment could properly be inflicted on the slaves. The legislature simply assumed that masters already knew how to control their slaves. The statute proceeded to absolve the "person giving correction" of any criminal liability if the slave died as a result of being disciplined. As such, the statute was not directed toward the slaves. It did not seek to deter slaves from running away or resisting by spelling out their punishment if they did. Instead, it is directed toward the master. The statute sought to reinforce the master's right to punish the slave as he saw fit, even if it meant killing the slave because, in the words of the legislature, the slave was part of the master's "estate." He was the master's *property*.

The 1669 statute was the first legislative pronouncement in Virginia that blacks were not fully human. Prior to 1669, legislative enactments and judicial decisions had mainly determined that blacks were inferior to whites and, therefore, deserved to occupy the inferior position of slavery. While even before the advent of the African slave trade, blacks were considered savages, heathens, and uncivilized, up until 1669 the Virginia legal process had not made any determinations that they were "property" in a fashion similar to cattle. Once they were so branded, there remained no doubt that they were indeed inferior.

By 1705 the precept was even more deeply embedded in the minds and laws of white Virginians. The 1705 statute stated that if a master killed his slave, the law would treat the killing "as if such accident had never happened." Whereas the 1669 statute had strained to give some justification for not punishing a master who killed his slave, the 1705 statute offered no such justification. In 1669, the legislature had reasoned that since malice was necessary for murder, it could not be "presumed" that in killing a slave, the master would be driven by malice to destroy his own property. Thus, the master could not be found guilty of murder. In contrast, the 1705 statute made no mention of the master's being *excused* for killing his slave because the slave was the master's property. Such a justification was no longer necessary; Virginia society had fully accepted the idea that blacks were not quite human.

In his *Notes on the State of Virginia,* Thomas Jefferson argued against the emancipation of the slaves by contrasting them with Roman slaves. According to Jefferson, "[a]mong the Romans, emancipation required but one effort. The slave, when made free, might mix with, *without staining the blood of his master.* But with us a second is necessary, unknown to history. When freed, he is to be removed beyond the reach of mixture."[83] Following from the Virginia slave codes excerpted above, as well as Jefferson's apparent sentiments, the black slave should not be freed into the general population because, aside from the fact that his inherent inferiority made him unsuitable for freedom, his inferior black blood might mix with and "stain" the white blood of the master.

Jefferson's words were written during the second stage of the development of the precept of black inferiority. And, while Jefferson admittedly harbored ambivalent feelings about slavery throughout his life, his statement that black blood had the capacity to stain white blood captured the essence of the precept of inferiority. The mark of inferiority, branded into the minds of white Americans during this second stage, contributed to our nation's headlong entry into the darkness of chattel slavery.

5

THE POLITICS OF INFERIORITY
(1830–1865)

Abolition and Uncle Tom: Political Posturing Without Challenging
Notions of Inferiority

URING the second stage in the development of the precept of inferiority, as this nation began to wander into the labyrinth of racial oppression, a few prophetic voices called out, warning of the dangers ahead, and beseeching us to stop and turn back. As early as 1688, fewer than seven decades after the first Africans had arrived in Virginia and many years before slavery would be fully institutionalized into law, a small group of German Mennonites and Quakers gathered near Philadelphia and passed a resolution declaring slavery immoral. That resolution condemned the "traffic of Men-body" and stood as the first recorded official protest against slavery in any of the American colonies.[1] It stated in part:

> [W]e hear that the most part of such negers are brought hither against their will and consent, and that many of them are stolen. Now, though they are black, we cannot conceive there is more liberty to have them slaves, as it is to have other white ones. There is a saying, that we should do to all men like as we will be done ourselves; making no difference of what generation, descent, or colour they are. And those who steal or rob men, and those who buy or purchase them, are they not all alike?[2]

In addition to the Quakers and Mennonites who opposed slavery on religious grounds, others rejected slavery purely on human and civil rights grounds. Thus in 1764, in his revolutionary pamphlet *The Rights of the British Colonies Asserted and Proved,* James Otis condemned slavery as "the most shocking violation of the law of nature," and affirmed African Americans' inalienable right to freedom as colonists.[3] Nathaniel Appleton, of Cambridge,

Massachusetts, followed Otis in 1767 by opposing slavery on the ground that it was every man's "natural right to be free."[4] Thomas Jefferson, himself a slaveowner, proposed to the Virginia Assembly that the slaves be emancipated as early as 1769.[5] Jefferson, in the first draft of the Declaration of Independence, wrote that the slave trade was "a cruel war against human nature itself, violating its most sacred rights of life and liberty."[6] Finally, Thomas Paine published an essay in 1775, *African Slavery in America*, urging Americans to end slavery and comparing its inherent immorality to that of "murder, robbery, lewdness and barbarity."[7]

But these early Jeremiahs, from the Quakers to Thomas Paine, were few and far between. If the nation heard their voices echoing over time and distance, it chose not to heed their messages and instead moved ahead through the wilderness. It was not until the 1830s, with the rise of radical Abolitionism, that the nation can be said to have started tentatively searching for a way back, by then loaded with all of the waste and blood-stained badges of slavery.

In 1852 Harriet Beecher Stowe published *Uncle Tom's Cabin*. Even today, this work is regarded in certain intellectual circles and in most high school history classes as the most passionate antislavery statement ever drafted in America. Mrs. Stowe wrote in the book's Preface that the story was about the life and times

> among a race hitherto ignored by the associations of polite and refined society; an exotic race, whose ancestors, born beneath a tropic sun, brought with them, and perpetuated to their descendants, a character so essentially unlike the hard and dominant Anglo-Saxon race, as for many years to have won from it only misunderstanding and contempt.[8]

Mrs. Stowe, however, insisted that a "better day is dawning" and that the "hand of benevolence is everywhere stretched out, searching into abuses, righting wrongs, alleviating distresses, and bringing to the knowledge and sympathies of the world the lowly, the oppressed, and the forgotten."[9] The lowly and oppressed to which Mrs. Stowe referred was, of course, "unhappy Africa . . . who began the race of civilization and human progress in the dim, gray dawn of early time, but who, for centuries, has lain bound and bleeding at the foot of civilized and Christianized humanity, imploring compassion in vain."[10]

In its day *Uncle Tom's Cabin* was hailed by no less than Frederick Douglass as a powerful and effective blow struck against slavery. Douglass wrote:

> The word of Mrs. Stowe is addressed to the soul of universal humanity. . . . *God bless her for that word!* The slave in his chains shall hear it gladly, and the slaveholder shall hear it; *both* shall rejoice in it, and by its light and love learn lessons of liberty and brotherhood.[11]

Notwithstanding Douglass's praise of the book as a guiding light to the slave and to the master, it is doubtful that many slaves were thumbing through the book during breaks from work in the fields. It is even more doubtful that *Uncle Tom's Cabin* ever convinced a single southern slaveowner to emancipate his slaves. Still, it is also probable that Mrs. Stowe was not merely preaching to the already converted. Her work was addressed to a northern audience that was not necessarily "converted" to the abolitionist cause, but was, at best, indifferent to slavery in the South and often hostile to the free African Americans living in the North. Historian Edgar McManus notes that

> Many whites [in the North] who opposed slavery as an institution were nevertheless unwilling to relinquish their racial prerogatives. Frequently white support of abolition owed more to immediate self-interest than to any concern for the welfare of blacks. Indeed, much of the working-class opposition to slavery was motivated primarily by the desire to eliminate slave competition.[12]

Even Mrs. Stowe's contemporaries noticed that Northerners were not entirely comfortable thinking of African Americans as anything other than slaves. In 1856 Frederick Law Olmsted published a collection of essays based on his travels in the South. He remarked:

> I am struck with the close co-habitation and association of black and white—negro women are carrying black and white babies together in their arms; black and white children are playing together (not going to school together); black and white faces are constantly thrust together out of the doors, to see the train go by.
> . . . Once, to-day, seeing a lady entering the car at a way-station, with a family behind her, and that she was looking about to find a place where they could be seated together, I rose, and offered her my seat, which had several vacancies around it. She accepted it, without thanking me, and immediately installed in it a stout negro woman; took the adjoining seat herself, and seated the rest of her party before her. It consisted of a white girl, probably her daughter, and a bright and very pretty mulatto girl. They all talked and laughed together, and the girls munched confectionery out of the same paper, with a familiarity and closeness of intimacy that would have been noticed with astonishment, if not with manifest displeasure, in almost any chance company at the North. When the negro is definitively a slave, it would seem that the alleged natural antipathy of the white race to associate with him is lost.[13]

Such was the audience to which Mrs. Stowe and her fellow abolitionists preached: one still convinced that nature had made blacks an inferior people, one still unable to associate with whites unless they were reduced to slavery. In a way, Mrs. Stowe's abolitionist message was well-crafted to reach that audience, inasmuch as it concentrated on the *uncharitable* nature of slavery rather than on its *anti-egalitarian* aspects. In Mrs. Stowe's view, as in the view of many prominent abolitionists, slavery was wrong because it was immoral and un-Christian. It exploited an "exotic" creature whose gentle and loyal character was unlike that of the "hard and dominant Anglo-Saxon race." It destroyed the family and corrupted the character. It promoted laziness on the part of the slave, and brutishness on the part of the master. And, in the end, it denied blacks what their heathen hearts needed most: the civilizing effects of Christianity.

Viewed in that light, Mrs. Stowe's abolitionist message was effective because it did not challenge the beliefs of her audience. It allowed them to rail against the horrors of slavery without owning up to their own wretched treatment of free African Americans living in the North. It allowed them to extend their Christian charity to the slaves without for one moment imagining that slaves might not be grateful for the sort of charity that only gave back what should never have been taken away in the first place. It allowed them the luxury of thinking they could eventually give freedom to the slaves without fearing that one day the slaves would become tired of waiting, rise up, cut their masters' throats, burn their houses, and take their own freedom. It spoke of Christian charity and human decency without mentioning civil rights and political self-determination. It made a place in the popular imagination for a fictional character such as the kindly and loyal Uncle Tom without acknowledging the very real and violent revolutionary ardor of Nat Turner. In short, it managed to ignore what Frederick Douglass knew intimately and expressed so well:

> The whole history of the progress of human liberty shows that all concessions yet made to her august claims, have been born of earnest struggle. The conflict has been exciting, agitating, all-absorbing, and for the time being, putting all other tumults to silence. It must do this or it does nothing. If there is no struggle there is no progress. . . .
>
> This struggle may be a moral one, or it may be a physical one, and it may be both moral and physical, but it must be a struggle. Power concedes nothing without a demand. It never did and it never will. Find out just what any people will quietly submit to and you have found out the exact measure of injustice and wrong which will be imposed on them. . . . The limits of tyrants are prescribed by the endurance of those whom they oppress. In the light of these ideas, Negroes will be hunted at the North, and held and flogged at the South so long as they submit to those devilish outrages, and make no resistance, either moral or physical.[14]

Indeed, it was precisely Douglass's insistence that freedom would come to the slaves only after they actively resisted their masters, and his urging that citizens use their *political* as well as their moral power to end slavery, that eventually led to a bitter separation between Douglass and the abolitionists led by William Lloyd Garrison.[15] Garrison was perhaps the most influential of the white abolitionist leaders. As advocated by Garrison, the philosophy of the abolitionist movement was based on the principle of moral suasion.[16] That principle had as its fundamental tenet the belief that slavery would be abolished not by resistance but by moral example. Garrisonian abolitionists saw as their mission to establish "in the hearts of men a deep and wide-spreading conviction of *the brotherhood of the human race*; that God hath indeed made of one blood all nations of men for to dwell on all the face of the earth."[17] They sincerely believed slavery was evil but, to them, so was resistance to slavery with physical weapons or political pressure. In their view, to fight evil with evil was itself a greater evil.[18] In 1844, William Lloyd Garrison thus articulated his abolitionist position:

> Politically, the American Anti-Slavery Society has "passed the Rubicon" in regard to this blood-cemented Union; and on its banner is inscribed the motto, 'No Union with Slaveholders.' No step has yet been taken in our cause, so trying to those who profess to be abolitionists, or that is destined to make such a commotion in Church and State. It will alienate many from our ranks, but their defection will be our gain. "The battle is the Lord's," not man's, and victory will be achieved not by numerical superiority—not by physical might or power—but by the Spirit of Truth, and the omnipotence of Love.[19]

Frederick Douglass, for his part, while at first accepting the Garrisonian philosophy of "the Spirit of Truth, and the omnipotence of Love," would later challenge it. In 1849, he addressed an antislavery audience in Boston with the following words: "I should welcome the intelligence tomorrow, should it come, that the slaves had risen in the South, and that the sable arms which had been engaged in beautifying and adorning the South, were engaged in spreading death and devastation."[20]

Then in 1860, on the eve of the Civil War, Douglass would finally reject Garrison's philosophy by writing the following editorial in *The North Star:*

> I have little hope of the freedom of the slave by peaceful means. . . . A long course of peaceful slaveholding has placed the slaveholders beyond the reach of moral and humane considerations. They have neither ears nor hearts for the appeals of justice and humanity. While the slave will tamely submit his neck to the yoke, his back to the lash, and his ankle to the fetter and chain, the Bible will be quoted, and learning invoked to justify slavery. The only penetrable point of a tyrant is the *fear of death.*[21]

Perhaps the seeming inability of Garrison, Mrs. Stowe, and other abolitionists to harden their antislavery message was based on nothing more than their belief that the abolitionist movement would lose its moral and religious center the moment it ventured into national political discourse. Garrison seemed to believe that, even though political action may jeopardize the abolitionists' integrity, inherent flaws in the American Constitution would render political action—for their purpose—useless.[22]

Yet one reads a book such as *Uncle Tom's Cabin*, or other antislavery articles and speeches of the time, with the nagging suspicion that the sweet-tasting flesh of the fruit of the abolitionists' good works was wrapped around a hard and bitter seed of contempt for the very group they were trying so hard to free. This nagging suspicion comes at a price. One forever feels like a loathsome ingrate for ascribing less than pure motives to the abolitionists who, after all, made an incalculable contribution in the struggle to free the slaves. In the case of the abolitionists, however, the cup of charity and brotherhood they fed to the slaves was often laced with more than a touch of condescension and high-handedness.

For example, Garrison once observed: "[T]he Anti-Slavery cause, both religiously and politically, has transcended the ability of the sufferers from American Slavery and prejudice, *as a class,* to keep pace with it, or to perceive what are its demands, or to understand the philosophy of its operations."[23] To which Douglass replied:

> The colored people ought to feel profoundly grateful for this magnificent compliment (which does not emanate from a Colonizationist) to their high, moral worth, and breadth of comprehension so generously bestowed by William Lloyd Garrison!—Who will doubt, hereafter, *the natural inferiority of the Negro,* when the great champion of the Negroes' rights, thus broadly concedes all that is claimed respecting the *Negro's inferiority* by the bitterest despisers of the Negro race.[24]

For another example, consider that in its day *Uncle Tom's Cabin* was thought to be a "revolutionary achievement" in its depiction of African Americans. It is quite instructive to realize that there is not a single truly human, African-American character in the story. Every African-American character fits neatly into a particular stereotype, and every scene featuring an African-American character is rendered in the sort of hushed and reverential tone in which the African Americans are poor but noble, ignorant but kind, oppressed but forgiving. The only time any African-American character dares to express any emotion as messy as anger or, God forbid, hatred, is in response to such a grave personal injustice that the anger or hatred ceases to be human. It becomes almost divine. It is no wonder Garrison himself said: "The battle [against slavery] is the Lord's, not man's."

Admittedly, the abolitionists' perception of African Americans as simpleminded was to be expected. During that same period, while the colonists were busy trying to exterminate the Native Americans, the few who considered themselves "friends" of the Native Americans never managed to think of them as anything more than "noble savages"; noble yes, but savages still. On the social and color ladder erected by the colonists, African Americans ranked one rung below the Native Americans. So, there is no reason to suppose that the abolitionists, who although "friends" of African Americans, were after all as much a product of their times as the slaveowners, would be any different. They would never consider African Americans to be their equals.

As for Mrs. Stowe, her portrayal of the African-American slaves was not that much different from Charles Dickens's depiction of the poor of London or Honoré de Balzac's rendering of the underclass of Paris.[25] Dickens and Balzac too tended to portray the wretched of England and France as pure and simple folk who suffered bravely and beautifully. Of course, this is all a lot of nonsense. Those who are oppressed may have the capacity to be brave and noble like everyone else, but the oppression itself is probably not what makes them brave and noble. Those who are oppressed may be in possession of certain absolute and simple truths beyond the knowledge of others, but chief among those truths is that freedom is preferable to oppression. Yet those who insist on seeing beauty in oppression often do so in order to assuage their guilt for contributing to that oppression. That is why the temptation to find beauty and nobility in suffering and oppression has a long and distinguished history. As for Mrs. Stowe, she probably should not be judged too harshly for being guilty of the sort of lapse to which many other writers have also succumbed.

Is it too much to expect Mrs. Stowe to have depicted Uncle Tom with the character traits and political beliefs of, say, Malcolm X? Whatever their view of African Americans, Mrs. Stowe and the abolitionists were at least willing to fight for what the slaves wanted most: freedom from slavery. And, in the context of history, is it not that achievement which should be remembered and honored?

Perhaps. In the context of the precept of inferiority, however, how the abolitionists perceived African Americans matters and should be remembered. For southern slaveholders were not the only ones who looked upon African Americans as not fully human. Neither did the abolitionists grant African Americans the full and complex humanity granted to whites. If William Lloyd Garrison could maintain that the slaves did not have the mental faculties to understand the "philosophy" of the antislavery movement, it is because, to the abolitionists, African Americans represented "an exotic race," gentle, good, misunderstood, despised, sweet, and, of course, simpleminded.

In other words, if southern slaveholders looked into the mirror that African Americans represented for them and saw the reflection of what they feared was their own *worst* selves, northern abolitionists looked into the same African mirror and found the reflection of what they thought was their own *best* selves. To southern slaveholders, African Americans represented what they assumed they themselves once were but were never going to be again: ignorant, savage, God-less, unable to want and long for anything other than food, sex, and shelter. To northern abolitionists, African Americans represented what they believed they themselves had lost and wanted to find again: the close communion with nature, the ability to suffer humbly and forgive easily, the gift to find happiness in the simple joys of life. To southern slaveholders, African Americans represented violence, carnality, and chaos—in a word, Hell. To northern abolitionists, they represented innocence, purity, and nature—in a word, Heaven. Neither representation was based on reality, and each was rooted in the precept of inferiority.

The precept of inferiority presumes, preserves, protects, and defends the ideal of the superiority of whites and the inferiority of blacks. For southern slaveholders who saw in the Africans their own vision of Hell, this simply meant they must presume that blacks were demons who had to be tamed and civilized within the confines of slavery. For northern abolitionists, who found in blacks their own dreams of Heaven, this meant they should presume that blacks were infantile saints who needed to be protected and who could not even understand their own need for freedom and equality.

Thus, abundant good intentions aside, the abolitionists' view of African Americans served to sustain the precept of inferiority. For in the end, the precept of racial inferiority is really the process of removing a race from human consideration by ascribing to that race either negative or positive attributes as a way of contrasting those attributes to one's own human virtues *and* frailties. The fact of the matter is that Africans were no more saints than they were demons. They no more existed to serve as the abolitionists' dream of Paradise Lost than they existed to represent the slaveholders' vision of Hell. They deserved to be free, not because they were good and gentle, or because they were "innocent," but because they were human. They were members of this nation who should have enjoyed the same civil liberties and political rights as others. The abolitionists' perception of African Americans as saintly savages, however benign, was but a mirror image of the slaveholders' perception of African Americans as demonic workhorses.

Again, none of this is to imply that the brand of inferiority practiced by northern abolitionists was as destructive as that practiced by southern slaveholders. To do so would be historically inaccurate and morally indefensible. During the years preceding the Civil War, many abolitionists, at great risk to reputations and their lives, mounted a relentless attack against slavery. William Lloyd Garrison himself wrote of his crusade in the inaugural issue of his antislavery newspaper *The Liberator:* "I will be as harsh as truth and as uncompromising as justice. . . . I will not equivocate—I will not excuse—I will not retreat a single inch—and I will be heard."[26] The efforts of the abolitionists in no small part placed slavery in the flow of national political discourse. As Don Fehrenbacher writes in his classic treatise, *The Dred Scott Case: Its Significance in American Law and Politics:*

> The most striking development [in the years prior to the Civil War], of course, was the rise of radical abolitionism as exemplified in the person of William Lloyd Garrison and signalized by his launching of *The Liberator* in Boston on New Year's Day, 1831.
>
> . . .
>
> . . . Except among the Quakers, earlier antislavery activity had often been a secondary concern of busy men of affairs and therefore not entirely free of dilettantism. The new, Garrisonian breed made the war on slavery the central factor in their lives. They thus professionalized the movement, and, in spite of their alleged anti-institutional bias, they institutionalized it. Opposition to slavery for the first time became . . . an interest as well as a sentiment, and the slaveholding interest felt the difference immediately.[27]

Not only did the "slaveholding interest" feel the difference in the rise of radical abolitionism, it quickly rose to offer a two-sided response to it. This two-sided response is what characterizes the third stage in the development of the precept of inferiority. On one side the legal process defended and protected from all attacks the crumbling institution of slavery and the precept of black inferiority, culminating in the disastrous decision in *Dred Scott v. Sandford*.[28] On the other side, slaveholders and southern politicians began to view any attack on slavery as a personal attack on their virtue and patriotism.

Dred Scott v. Sandford: The Legal Defense of Inferiority

Dred Scott v. Sandford is by far the most articulate and authoritative defense of the precept of black inferiority ever mounted by the American legal process. The Supreme Court decision represented, at the time it was decided in 1857, the apogee of more than two hundred years of racial oppression and slavery. The opinion of the Court, while clothed in the usual garments of legal theory, was in effect nothing more than a southern manifesto on the institution of slavery. As Fehrenbacher writes: "[*Dred Scott v. Sandford*] is not only a statement of southern assumptions and arguments but also an expression of the southern mood—fearful, angry, and defiant—in the late stages of national crisis."[29]

Dred Scott was a slave born in Virginia in the early 1800s. He had "very dark skin and may have been no more than five feet tall." A newspaper article that appeared to be based on a personal interview with Dred Scott described him as "illiterate but not ignorant," with "a strong common sense."[30] Dred Scott originally belonged to the proprietor of a St. Louis boarding house named Peter Blow. Either before or after Blow's death in 1832, Dred Scott was sold to Dr. John Emerson of St. Louis.[31] After receiving his appointment as an assistant surgeon in the United States Army, Emerson reported to duty at Fort Armstrong in Illinois and took Dred Scott with him.[32] At the time, Illinois was a free state. Dred Scott lived with Emerson in Illinois for more than two years, from December 1833 to the middle of 1836. In 1836, Emerson was transferred to Fort Snelling, located on the west bank of the upper Mississippi River, in what was the Wisconsin Territory.[33] Once again Emerson took Dred Scott with him.[34] At the time, slavery was forbidden in the Wisconsin Territory under the Missouri Compromise.

While at Fort Snelling, Dred Scott met and married a slave woman named Harriet Robinson.[35] In 1838 Emerson traveled without his slaves to Louisiana and, while there, married a woman named Eliza Irene Sanford.[36] In the spring of 1838, Dred Scott and his wife Harriet traveled from Fort Snelling to join Emerson and his wife in Louisiana. Their stay in Louisiana was brief. They returned to Fort Snelling in the fall of 1838. During that trip, one of their daughters was born in free territory.[37] They remained there until 1840.[38] In the fall of 1842, Emerson received his discharge from the army.[39] In the spring of 1843, he moved to Davenport, a town located in the Iowa Territory,[40] where slavery was also forbidden. Soon after moving to Davenport, Emerson's health began to deteriorate and he died in December 1843, leaving nearly his entire estate to his wife Irene for her life, and then to their daughter, Henrietta.[41]

From around the time of Emerson's stay in Davenport, or after his death until possibly the early part of 1846, Dred and Harriet Scott were apparently lent out to the brother-in-law of Irene Emerson, Captain Bainbridge. If in his service at that time, Dred Scott traveled with Bainbridge to Louisiana in 1844, and to Texas in 1845. It is unclear if Harriet or Eliza accompanied them.[42] In February 1846, Captain Bainbridge apparently sent Dred Scott back to Irene Emerson, who at the time was living in St. Louis, Missouri.[43] Upon the Scotts' arrival in St. Louis, Irene Emerson hired them out to a Samuel Russell.[44]

On April 6, 1846, Dred and Harriet Scott filed petitions in the Missouri circuit court in St. Louis, seeking permission to sue Irene Emerson to establish that she was illegally holding them in slavery.[45] On the same day that the judge granted them permission to bring suit, they "filed declarations initiating actions of trespass for assault and false imprisonment."[46] Filing separate petitions, the Scotts each claimed, inter alia, ten dollars as damages for their wrongful enslavement.[47] And so began the case of *Dred Scott v. Sandford.*

The Scotts' petitions originally went to trial in Missouri circuit court under two separate captions: *Scott v. Emerson* and *Harriet v. Emerson.* The cases described the same basic facts and presented the same legal issues.[48] Basically the Scotts argued that they had become free when they had resided on free soil.[49] In Dred Scott's case, he had lived in Illinois, a free state, for more than two years, between 1833 and 1836, while his master was posted at Fort Armstrong. Moreover, between 1836 and 1842, Dred Scott had also lived intermittently at Fort Snelling in the Wisconsin Territory where slavery was prohibited. As for Harriet Scott, at the time she married Dred Scott in 1838, she was already living at Fort Snelling in the free Wisconsin Territory.

By all expectations, the Scotts' petitions for freedom should have been granted fairly quickly. In 1847, it was a settled tenet of Missouri law that a slave became emancipated the moment his master took him to reside in a state or territory where slavery was prohibited.[50] Even if the master was required to travel to a free state or territory, the slave would still become emancipated. Thus in *Rachel v. Walker,* a case particularly relevant to the Scotts' petitions, the Missouri Supreme Court had held that Rachel, a slave, had become emancipated when her master, a military officer, had taken her to live at his post at Fort Snelling and at Prairie du Chien.[51] The court found that even though Rachel's master was required to be at Fort Snelling, "No authority of law or the government compelled him to keep the plaintiff there as a slave."[52]

Yet, in spite of settled Missouri law, the jury in the Missouri circuit court returned a verdict denying the Scotts' petitions for freedom. The verdict was based on the technicality that the Scotts did not prove that they were owned by Mrs. Emerson.[53] The Scotts' counsel requested and was granted a new trial.[54] Mrs. Emerson's counsel appealed the order for a new trial and the case was transferred on writ of error to the Supreme Court of Missouri.[55] In April 1848 that court remanded the case back to the circuit court for a new trial.[56]

In January 1850, the Scotts' petitions came to retrial.[57] The trial ended with a jury verdict granting the Scotts their freedom. Mrs. Emerson immediately appealed to the Missouri Supreme Court.[58] There, in 1852, the court reversed the jury verdict and found that the Scotts were still slaves.[59] The court based its reversal of the jury verdict on a doctrine of conflict of laws. The court reasoned that the fact that the Scotts had been taken to a free state or territory did *not* make them free because the laws of that state or territory could not trump the laws of the slave state that had made them slaves. Whether to give effect to another state's laws was a matter of "judicial discretion," to be "controlled by circumstances."[60]

As a preview of the pro-slavery policy statements that would dominate the United States Supreme Court's opinion, the Missouri Supreme Court wrote that slavery was a "civilizing force that had raised the American Negro far above the 'miserable' African." As such, the court concluded, "[T]he introduction of slavery amongst us was, in the providence of God, who makes the evil passions of men subservient to His own glory, a means of placing that unhappy race within the pale of civilized nations."[61]

Toward the end of 1853, Irene Emerson apparently sold Dred Scott and his family to her brother, John Sanford.[62] The case thus became *Dred Scott v. Sandford*. And under that caption, it was submitted to the United States Supreme Court in December 1854. Oral arguments before the Court began on February 11, 1856, and lasted over four days.[63] Reargument on the case took place in December of that same year.[64] Ostensibly, the *Dred Scott* case, by the time it reached the United States Supreme Court, involved legal questions concerning the limits of congressional power under the Constitution and the meaning of judicial review in a federalist system of government. However, at bottom, *Dred Scott v. Sandford* was all about the correctness of slavery—an institution that would last, in the words of counsel for Sanford, "for all time."[65] Indeed, if there was any doubt that the case was meant to settle once and for all the "preferred" status of African Americans in America, Chief Justice Taney's opinion for a majority of the Court quickly put those doubts to rest.

Chief Justice Taney began his opinion by defining the question presented to the Court as follows:

> The question is simply this: Can a negro, whose ancestors were imported into this country, and sold as slaves, become a member of the political community formed and brought into existence by the Constitution of the United States, and as such become entitled to all the rights, and privileges, and immunities, guarantied by that instrument to the citizen?[66]

Chief Justice Taney answered that, during the founding of this nation, African Americans were never meant to be "constituent members" of society, but that

> [o]n the contrary, they were at that time considered as a subordinate and inferior class of beings, who had been subjugated by the dominant race, and, whether emancipated or not, yet remained subject to their authority, and had no rights or privileges but such as those who held the power and the Government might choose to grant them.[67]

Thus, in Chief Justice Taney's view, African Americans were "a subordinate and inferior class" that, whether slave or free, remained "subject to [the] authority" of the "dominant" and superior white race.[68] Taney then proceeded to review the inferior status of African Americans throughout American history. First he stated:

They had for more than a century before [the Declaration of Independence and the Constitution of the United States] been regarded as beings of an *inferior order*, and altogether unfit to associate with the white race, either in social or political relations; and so far *inferior*, that they had *no rights which the white man was bound to respect*; and that the negro might justly and lawfully be reduced to slavery for his benefit. He was bought and sold, and treated as an ordinary article of merchandise and traffic, whenever a profit could be made by it. This opinion was at that time fixed and universal in the civilized portion of the white race. It was regarded as an axiom in morals as well as in politics, which no one thought of disputing, or supposed to be open to dispute; and men in every grade and position in society daily and habitually acted upon it in their private pursuits, as well as in matters of public concern, without doubting for a moment the correctness of this opinion.[69]

As far as the statement in the Declaration of Independence that "We hold these truths to be self-evident: that all men are created equal," Chief Justice Taney reasoned that it was "too clear for dispute, that the enslaved African race were not intended to be included."[70] Turning to the Constitution, Chief Justice Taney concluded that African Americans "were not regarded as a portion of the people or citizens of the Government then formed."[71] Indeed, as Chief Justice Taney reasoned, during the Constitutional Convention, the slaveholding states would not have accepted the Constitution if African Americans had been recognized as citizens:

For if they were . . . entitled to the privileges and immunities of citizens, it would exempt them from the operation of the special laws and from the police regulations which they considered to be necessary for their own safety. It would give to persons of the negro race . . . the right to enter every other State whenever they pleased . . . to go where they pleased at every hour of the day or night without molestation . . . and it would give them the full liberty of speech in public and in private upon all subjects upon which its own citizens might speak; to hold public meetings upon political affairs, and to keep and carry arms wherever they went. And all of this would be done in the face of the subject race of the same color, both free and slaves, and inevitably producing discontent and insubordination among them, and endangering the peace and safety of the State.[72]

In the opinion, Chief Justice Taney made twenty-one references to African Americans as inferior and to whites as dominant or superior. Chief Justice Taney referred to African Americans as an "inferior class of beings,"[73] an "unfortunate race,"[74] a "degraded" and "unhappy" race,[75] "unfit to associate with the white race,"[76] "excluded from civilized Governments and the family of nations,"[77] "far below [whites] in the scale of created beings,"[78] "held in subjection and slavery, and governed [by the dominant race] at their own pleasure,"[79] "separated from white[s] by indelible marks,"[80] "impressed [with] deep and enduring marks of inferiority and degradation,"[81] and "separated and rejected."[82] In the context of the precept of inferiority, the most significant aspect of Chief Justice Taney's opinion was its insistence that "no distinction in this respect was made between the free negro or mulatto and the slave, but [the] stigma, of the deepest degradation, was fixed upon the whole race."[83] This meant that the stigma of degradation and mark of inferiority were impressed on African Americans not because they were or had been slaves, but because they were African-American. Thus, slavery did not render African Americans inferior. Rather, African Americans, by their very nature, were inferior. Slavery was merely the natural place for such an "unnatural" race.

If the opinion of the Supreme Court in *Dred Scott v. Sandford* was intended to settle once and for all the question of slavery, it produced the exact opposite effect. Southerners read the opinion as a vindication of their beliefs, and some northern newspaper editors, such as those of the *New York Times*, suggested:

> [T]he circumstances attending the present decision have done much to divest it of moral influence and to impair the confidence of the country. . . . Among jurists, it is not considered to settle anything more than the denial of jurisdiction. . . . But it exhibited the eagerness of the majority of that tribunal to force an opinion upon the country and to thrust itself into the political contests.[84]

The Constitutionalist, a Georgia newspaper, editorialized: "Southern opinion upon the subject of southern slavery . . . is now the supreme law of the land . . . and opposition to southern opinion upon this subject is now opposition to the Constitution, and morally treason against the Government."[85] Another commentator hailed Chief Justice Taney as "the very incarnation of judicial purity, integrity, science, and wisdom."[86] Chief Justice Taney, himself, in reference to the *Dred Scott* opinion, would later describe blacks as a "weak and credulous race," who enjoyed a "usually cheerful and contented" life in slavery.[87] To Taney, "sudden emancipation [of African-American slaves] would mean 'absolute ruin.' "[88]

When speaking of the majority's opinion in *Dred Scott*, Abraham Lincoln suggested that he supported the dissenting opinions of Justices McLean and Curtis,[89] and summarized the brewing political controversy over the propriety of slavery and the colonization of African Americans:

> How differently the respective courses of the Democratic and Republican parties incidentally bear on the question of forming a will—a public

sentiment—for colonization, is easy to see. The Republicans inculcate, with whatever of ability they can, that the negro is a man, that his bondage is cruelly wrong, and that the field of his oppression ought not to be enlarged. The Democrats deny his manhood; deny, or dwarf to insignificance, the wrong of his bondage; so far as possible, crush all sympathy for him, and cultivate and excite hatred and disgust against him; compliment themselves as Union-savers for doing so; and call the indefinite outspreading of his bondage "a sacred right of self government."[90]

Even having asserted the humanity of African Americans, Lincoln nevertheless stressed the potential need for separation of the races, perhaps by colonization of African Americans.[91] He declared that there was a "natural disgust in the minds of nearly all white people at the idea of an indiscriminate amalgamation of the white and black races,"[92] and that "[a] separation of the races is the only perfect preventive of amalgamation; but as an immediate separation is impossible, the next best thing is to keep them apart where they are not already together."[93]

Lincoln's position suggested that, in 1857, most whites were unwilling to live alongside African Americans as equal citizens. In effect, the Supreme Court's majority opinion in *Dred Scott* codified into law, at the highest level of the American legal process, the precept of black inferiority.

6

THE CONSTITUTIONAL
LANGUAGE OF SLAVERY

From Non-disclosure to Abolition, 1787–1866

The Framers' Intentional Non-disclosure of Their Legitimization of
Slavery and Their Implementation of the Precept of Black Inferiority

IT IS indeed ironic that the first time the word "slavery" appeared in the
United States Constitution was when the institution of slavery was abolished by ratification of the Thirteenth Amendment in December 1865.
The founding fathers' refusal to use the word "slavery" in the Constitution of
1787 reveals that they did not want to acknowledge to the world their legitimization of slavery and their persistent implementation and legitimization of the
precept of black inferiority.

Although slavery offered some commercial advantages to most northern
states, it was obvious that the financial viability of southern states was primarily
dependent upon slave power. The southern representatives had made it abun-
dantly clear that they would not agree to a federal union that would have the
national power to tamper with any state's maintenance of domestic slavery.
Thus, to assure creation of a national union, there was an overwhelming consensus that the new federal government would sanction slavery as it had in the past.

The framers sought the most artful method of not disclosing, on the face
of the document, their maintenance and sanctioning of the venal institution of
slavery. They were concerned that the document's words not blatantly reveal
their sanctioning of an institution the morality of which was increasingly questioned throughout the world. In 1841, John Quincy Adams, a former President of the United States, arguing before the United States Supreme Court on
behalf of a slave in the *Amistad* case, put the matter of non-disclosure in its
historic perspective, when he noted:

The words slave and slavery are studiously excluded from the Constitution.
Circumlocutions are the fig-leaves under which these parts of the body politic are decently concealed.[1]

Justice McLean, dissenting in *Dred Scott,* gave a different explanation as to why the word "slavery" was not originally included in the enacted Constitution:

[W]e know as a historical fact, that James Madison, that great and good man, a leading member in the Federal Convention, was solicitous to guard the language of that instrument so as not to convey the idea that there could be property in man.[2]

It was relatively easy to attack the international slave trade as a nefarious institution and to place the blame on the British merchants, as George Mason of Virginia had done.[3] It was much more difficult to condemn domestic slavery. Such an attack would have been a direct assault by non-slave delegates on their fellow delegates because most, if not all, representatives from the slave states owned slaves. Thus, almost everyone at the Constitutional Convention was anxious to avoid discussing the morality of slavery or noting on the public record their legitimization of slavery.

Despite their seeming innocuousness as written, there were several key provisions included in the Constitution in order to assure to each state the option of perpetuating slavery and that ultimately maximized the political power of southern slaveholders. Among these provisions were Article 1, section 2, clause 3, the "three fifths of all other *Persons*" standard for representation and direct taxes;[4] Article 1, section 9, clause 1, the guarantee that "The Migration or Importation of such *Persons* . . . shall not be prohibited by the Congress prior to . . . [1808]";[5] Article 4, section two, clause 3, stating that "No *Person* held to Service or Labour in one State . . . escaping into another, shall . . . be discharged from such Service or Labour, but shall be delivered up on Claim of the Party to whom such Service or Labour may be due";[6] and Article 5, which prohibits the amendment of the Constitution prior to 1808 as to the Article 1, section nine, clauses 1 and 4 provisions.[7] In these clauses some references to "Persons" meant slaves, but the provisions were drafted so that only the most sophisticated would know that the term "Persons" had such a malevolent meaning in the Constitution.

In his message to the Maryland legislature, Luther Martin commented on the Article 1, section nine, clause 1 language as follows: "The design of this clause is to prevent the general government from prohibiting the importation of slaves. . . ."[8] Yet although the importation clause, when in draft form, originally referred to slaves, the word "slaves" was struck out and the word "Persons" was substituted.[9] "They anxiously sought to avoid the admission of expressions [i.e., "slavery"] which might be odious in the ears of Americans, although they were willing to admit into their system those *things* which the *expressions* signified."[10]

Twenty-one years after the Constitutional Convention, Abraham Baldwin of Georgia in a speech before the House of Representatives said:

> [I]t was found expedient to make this provision [Article 1, section 9] in the Constitution; there was an objection to the use of the word slaves, as Congress by none of their acts had ever acknowledged the existence of such a condition. It was at length settled on the words as they now stand, "that the migration or importation of such *persons* as the several States shall think proper to admit, should not be prohibited till the year 1808." It was observed by some gentlemen present that this expression would extend to other persons besides slaves, which was not denied, but this did not produce any alteration of it.[11]

In 1819, James Madison commented on the Constitutional Convention as follows:

> They had scruples against admitting the term "Slaves" into the Instrument. Hence the descriptive phrase "migration or importation of persons"; the term migration allowing those who were scrupulous of acknowledging expressly a property in human beings, to view *imported* persons as a species of emigrants, whilst others might apply the term to foreign malefactors sent or coming into the country. It is possible tho' not recollected, that some might have had an eye to the case of freed blacks, as well as malefactors.[12]

Since most at the Convention were not willing to challenge frontally the basic premise of slavery, that an African-American human being could be the exclusive property of another, and because the Constitution implicitly accepted this doctrine, one could argue that Madison guarded the language not for humanitarian purposes, but solely for the sake of politics and linguistic sensitivity to the larger moral problem. As Justice Story noted in his classic *Commentaries on the Constitution of the United States,* the Constitution referred to servitude and the slave trade only in vague terms as "things the existence of which under a free constitution was to be overlooked rather than recognized."[13] Others, though probably the minority, thought as did Oliver Ellsworth of Connecticut, that slavery would gradually come to a halt—presumably without violence or even the need for federal governmental pressures.[14] Dean Kelly Miller of Howard University suggests that: "Somehow, the fathers and fashioners of this basic document of liberty hoped that the reprobated institution would in time pass away when there should be no verbal survival as a memorial of its previous existence."[15] Thus, unlike the Articles of Confederation, which had phrases that clearly implied that African Americans were excluded from the protection of that Constitution (the Articles of Confederation used the terms "free inhabitants" in Article 4 and "white inhabitants" in Article 9), the Constitution of 1787 had no such recognizable phrases. It was not until 1865, with the passage of the Thirteenth Amendment and slavery's abolition, that the word "slavery" was mentioned in the United States Constitution. "To hide the evil one may hide its name. To expunge it, bring its name to light."[16]

Conflicting Assessments of a Constitution that Sanctioned Slavery: Was the Constitution a Document "near to perfection"[17] Or Was It "conceived in sin and shapen in iniquity"[18]—"a covenant with death, and an agreement with hell"[19]

On Monday, September 17, 1787, the forty-one delegates[20] assembled at Philadelphia finished their task when they unanimously voted in favor of the Constitution. On that day, prior to its adoption, a statement of Dr. Benjamin Franklin was presented to the weary assembly:

> I doubt too whether any other Convention we can obtain may be able to make a better Constitution. For when you assemble a number of men to have the advantage of their joint wisdom, you inevitably assemble with those men, all their prejudices, their passions, their errors of opinion, their local interests, and their selfish views. From such an Assembly can a perfect production be expected? It therefore astonishes me, Sir, to find this system *approaching so near to perfection as it does* . . . .[21]

The abolitionist Franklin of course did not believe that for African Americans the Constitution was anywhere "near to perfection"; so his conclusion referred to a "near to perfection" for *whites only.*

The same day, another antislavery advocate, Gouverneur Morris of Pennsylvania, asserted that:

> he too had objections, but considering the present plan as the best that was to be attained, he should take it with all its faults. . . . [T]he great question will be, shall there be a national Government or not? and this must take place or a general anarchy will be the alternative.[22]

From a racial perspective, Morris's remarks meant that it was far preferable to have a national union than to risk its viability with dissension on slavery issues. Viewing the Constitution in a nonracial context, it was an extraordinary achievement for all except for African Americans. As Alexis de Tocqueville wrote:

> It is a novelty in the history of a society to see a calm and scrutinizing eye turned upon itself, when apprised by the legislature that the wheels of government are stopped; to see it carefully examine the extent of the field and patiently wait for two years until a remedy was discovered, which it voluntarily adopted, without having ever wrung a tear or a drop of blood from mankind.[23]

Still, the issue of slavery versus freedom could neither be hidden by careful rhetoric nor permanently compromised even by the other national priorities. Recognizing the inevitability of the clash, Thomas Jefferson commented near the time the Constitution was ratified: "Indeed I tremble for my country when I reflect that God is just: that his justice cannot sleep for ever. . . ."[24]

Less than three years after Benjamin Franklin's statement was presented on the "near to perfection" of the Constitution, Franklin, as president of the Pennsylvania Society for Promoting the Abolition of Slavery, signed a memorial petitioning the First Congress for "the restoration of liberty to those unhappy men who alone, in this land of freedom, are degraded into perpetual bondage, and who amidst the general joy of surrounding freemen, are groaning in a servile subjection."[25]

Perhaps the most pointed critique of the inclusion of slavery in the Constitution was made by Frederick Douglass many years after the Constitution's adoption. Douglass said:

> Liberty and Slavery—opposite as Heaven and Hell—are both in the Constitution; and the oath to support the latter, is an oath to perform that which God has made impossible. . . . If we adopt the preamble, with Liberty and Justice, we must repudiate the enacting clauses, with Kidnapping and Slaveholding.[26]

On another occasion, Douglass said:

> The Constitution of the United States.—What is it? Who made it? For whom and for what was it made? Is it from heaven or from men? . . . [W]e hold it to be a most cunningly-devised and wicked compact, demanding the most constant and earnest efforts of the friends of righteous freedom for its complete overthrow. It was "conceived in sin, and shapen in iniquity."[27]

Echoing Frederick Douglass's earlier remark, and in a seeming point of agreement, abolitionist William Lloyd Garrison said of the Constitution:

> It assumes that to be practicable which is impossible, namely, that there can be freedom with slavery, union with injustice, and safety with bloodguiltiness. A union of virtue with pollution is the triumph of licentiousness.

The Constitutional Language of Slavery

A partnership between right and wrong is wholly wrong. A compromise the principles of justice is the deification of crime. . . .

* * *

. . . The truth is, our fathers were intent on securing liberty to themselves, without being very scrupulous as to the means they used to accomplish their purpose. . . . [A]nd though in words they recognised occasionally the brotherhood of the human race, in practice they continually denied it. They did not blush to enslave a portion of their fellow-men, and to buy and sell them as cattle in the market, while they were fighting against the oppression of the mother country, and boasting of their regard for the rights of man. . . .

* * *

Three millions of the American people are crushed under the American Union! They are held as slaves, trafficked as merchandise, registered as goods and chattels! The government gives them no protection—the government is their enemy, the government keeps them in chains! . . . The Constitution which subjects them to hopeless bondage is one that we cannot swear to support.[28]

William Lloyd Garrison branded the Constitution as "a covenant with death, and an agreement with hell."[29]

The Emancipation Proclamation and the Thirteenth Amendment: Neither Rejections of the Precept of Black Inferiority Nor an Implied Assurance of Equality Under Law

Almost every nation desires to depict some of its past leaders as bona fide heroes, and in the process it is not surprising that even those persons, such as Abraham Lincoln, who are entitled to hero status may be lauded for some acts that they did not perform or some tasks that they did not finish completely. The lore on the Emancipation Proclamation reflects that revisionist history.

Almost every school student is taught that "Abraham Lincoln freed the slaves." But the Emancipation Proclamation was a somewhat more restrictive document. It did not free *all* of the slaves. It provided that, as of January 1, 1863, "all persons held as slaves within any state or designated part of a state" where the people were *"in rebellion against the United States"* shall be free.[30] As President Lincoln noted, he issued this proclamation in accordance with the power "in me vested as commander-in-chief of the army and navy of the United States, in time of actual armed rebellion against the authority and Government of the United States, and as a fit and necessary war measure for suppressing said rebellion."[31]

The language of the Emancipation Proclamation notes its limited, though significant, scope and notes its non-applicability to those slave counties or geographic areas within any state that was not in rebellion. Thus, as to Louisiana he "exempted" the parishes of St. Bernard, Plaquemines, Jefferson, St. John, St. Charles, St. James, Ascension, Assumption, Terre Bonne, Lafourche, St. Mary, St. Martin, and Orleans, including the city of New Orleans, and in Virginia he exempted the forty-eight counties designated as West Virginia, and also the counties of Berkeley, Accomac, Northhampton, Elizabeth City, York, Princess Ann, and Norfolk, including the cities of Norfolk and Portsmouth.[32] He noted that those "excepted parts are for the present left precisely as if this proclamation were not issued."[33] Probably under the applicable constitutional law, Lincoln could have done no more than the significant proclamation that he issued, but the document reveals that all slaves were not freed. Furthermore, slavery was not abolished even in the rebellious states because of any primary concern that the rebellious states' perceptions of racial inferiority were erroneous.

In December 1865, the Thirteenth Amendment was ratified. The Constitution, which Garrison had called "a covenant with death, and an agreement with hell,"[34] because of its sanction of slavery, had been profoundly changed. In rather bland language, the Amendment provided that:

> Section 1. Neither slavery nor involuntary servitude, except as a punishment for crime whereof the party shall have been duly convicted, shall exist within the United States, or any place subject to their jurisdiction.
> Section 2. Congress shall have power to enforce this article by appropriate legislation.[35]

By its precise language slavery was prohibited, as was involuntary servitude. But did the Amendment, by the second section, authorize Congress to grant African Americans any indicia of citizenship? Could the federal government define the civil rights of African Americans in the states, as the states formerly had done during slavery? Could an unemployed or idle African American now be required by state law to work for his or her former owner?[36] Would it make a difference if the former owner now paid the former slave such a token wage that it was inadequate to feed the freedperson or his or her family? In short, was the slave merely freed from the chains of slavery, but in all other respects as powerless or even worse off than during slavery?

In his opinion in the *Slaughter-House Cases*,[37] Justice Samuel Miller put into perspective the issue of the scope of liberty and freedom granted by the Thirteenth Amendment. He noted that those states that had "sided with the rebellion" had at the conclusion of the Civil War passed a series of laws whereby "the condition of the slave race would, without further protection of the Federal government, be almost as bad as it was before."[38] As the Court noted, these "black codes"

> imposed upon the colored race onerous disabilities and burdens, and curtailed their rights in the pursuit of life, liberty, and property to such an extent that their freedom was of little value, while they had lost the protection which they had received from their former owners from motives both of interest and humanity.[39]

These questions, about citizenship and federal and states' rights, raised by the passage of the Thirteenth Amendment were inextricably related to the precept of inferiority. For more than a century since 1865, Americans have struggled to define the scope of civil rights guaranteed by the Thirteenth Amendment. In short, did the Thirteenth Amendment and the civil rights statutes passed exclusively in reliance on the Thirteenth Amendment implement the dream of freedom as envisioned by Frederick Douglass and William Lloyd Garrison, so that the revised Constitution should no longer be viewed as a "covenant with death, and an agreement with hell"?

The Civil Rights Act of 1866

An analysis of the scope and vitality of the Thirteenth Amendment should start with the 1866 Civil Rights Act, passed just months after the Thirteenth Amendment was ratified. This statute exemplifies the goals of the Reconstruction period and the original efforts to eradicate many of the vestiges of former racial oppression.[40]

Following the passage of the Thirteenth Amendment, it became clear to national legislators that the Amendment alone would not guarantee equality under law for the freedpersons. The Amendment merely stated that slavery and involuntary servitude shall not "exist within the United States." It did not explicitly state whether African Americans could become citizens and enjoy equal rights. If a legislature wanted to eradicate all or most of the shades of racial oppression that existed during slavery, what language should they use to make their intent clear? What standard of fairness should be established so that judges could determine whether African Americans were being treated fairly? In 1866, Congress met the challenge and did not mute their words. The language of the statute and its title could not have been more precise as to intention: "An Act to protect *all* Persons in the United States in their Civil Rights, and furnish the Means of their Vindication."[41] By using the phrase "all Persons," African Americans implicitly were included. But the legislators did not use ambiguous language in stating their concerns and purposes. The Act first specified the prerequisites to becoming a citizen of the United States:

"That all persons born in the United States and not subject to any foreign power, excluding Indians not taxed, are hereby declared to be citizens of the United States."[42]

Since the Act endowed African Americans with many of the rights of United States citizenship, it was a repudiation of the *Dred Scott v. Sandford*[43] decision, in which the Court had held that African Americans "had no rights which the white man was bound to respect."[44] The 1866 civil rights statute applied to *all citizens*, regardless of race, color, or previous condition of servitude. Thus the fact that a person was African-American or a former slave became irrelevant.

The title of the statute also spoke of "means of . . . Vindication" for civil rights—and the Act declared that:

> citizens, of every race and color, without regard to any previous condition
> of slavery . . . shall have the same right, in every State and Territory in
> the United States, to make and enforce contracts, to sue, be parties, and
> give evidence, to inherit, purchase, lease, sell, hold, and convey real and
> personal property, and to full and equal benefit of all laws and proceedings
> for the security of person and property, as is enjoyed by white citizens.
> . . .[45]

The statute also had an "equal protection" core with declarations that all citizens: "shall be subject to like punishment, pains, and penalties, and to none other, any law, statute, ordinance, regulation, or custom, to the contrary notwithstanding."[46]

In many respects, the statute was a direct assault on the precept of racial inferiority. The most decisive line and criteria were that, as to the rights guaranteed, African Americans would have the "full and equal benefit of all laws and proceedings for the security of person or property, *as is enjoyed by white citizens.*" It was a full elevation of African Americans to the equivalent and identical status of whites in many aspects of citizenship.

The Civil Rights Act of 1866 was an exemplification of what was thought to be the authority of Congress to define civil rights. Not only did the Act give African Americans certain citizenship rights, it also provided that federal courts could punish persons for various violations of the rights of African-American citizens. The statute gave jurisdiction to the district courts and the circuit courts of the United States which shall "have, exclusively of the courts of the several States, cognizance of all crimes and offences committed against the provisions of this act."[47] The statute protects persons "who are denied or cannot enforce in the courts or judicial tribunals of the State or locality where they may be any of the rights secured to them by the first section of [the Civil Rights] act."[48] It also provided that if any suit or prosecution, civil or criminal, has been or shall be commenced in any State court against any such person, for any cause whatsoever . . . such defendant shall have the right to remove such cause for trial to the proper district or circuit court in the manner prescribed by the Act relating to habeas corpus and regulating judicial proceedings in certain cases. . . .[49]

Early prosecutions under the Civil Rights Act of 1866 established that Congress did have the power to define these rights. No one has written more thoughtfully on legal developments in this era than has Professor Robert Kaczorowski, and this chapter and the one that follows rely on much of his path-breaking research as noted in his seminal treatise, *The Politics of Judicial Interpretation: The Federal Courts, Department of Justice and Civil Rights, 1866–1876.*

United States v. Rhodes,[50] a case prosecuted in the federal courts in Kentucky, reveals the breadth of the 1866 civil rights statute and its clash with the prior precepts of slavery jurisprudence. In 1866, the United States Attorney prosecuted three whites in federal court for the burglary of the home of an African American, Nancy Talbot. The indictment charged that, on May 1866, Rhodes "did break and enter the dwelling house . . . of Nancy Talbot, a citizen of the United States of the African race . . . who was then and there, and is now, denied the right to testify against the said defendants, in the courts of the state of Kentucky."[51] A Kentucky statute enacted in 1852, and still enforced in 1866—even after the Civil War—provided: "That a slave, negro, or Indian shall be a competent witness in a case of the commonwealth for or against a slave, negro, or Indian, or in a civil case to which only negroes or Indians are parties, *but in no other case.*"[52] The case was brought to federal court because the United States Attorney believed the defendants could not possibly have been "brought to justice" in the state courts in part because, by reason of the Kentucky statute, the victim, Nancy Talbot, was unable to testify against whites because she was black.[53]

Justice Noah Swayne, who heard the case while sitting as Circuit Justice for Kentucky, explained the former legal order and rules when the precepts of slavery jurisprudence prevailed:

> The difficulty was that where a white man was sued by a colored man, or was prosecuted for a crime against a colored man, colored witnesses were excluded. This in many cases involved a denial of justice. Crimes of the deepest dye were committed by white men with impunity. Courts and juries were frequently hostile to the colored man, and administered justice, both civil and criminal, in a corresponding spirit.[54]

He noted that Congress met these evils by giving to African Americans everywhere the same right to testify "as is enjoyed by white citizens," thereby abolishing the distinction between white and colored witnesses, and by "giving to the courts of the United States jurisdiction of all causes, civil and criminal, *wherever the right to testify as if he were white*" was denied or could not be enforced in state courts.[55]

The malevolent defendants wrapped themselves in the "states' rights" garb, a concept which in the future would give immunity to thousands of vigilantes. They argued that the Civil Rights Act of 1866 was unconstitutional and that, even if it were valid, the rights secured were only an equality of rights provided by the Act's first section, not to be infringed upon by *state* actors. There was no allegation of a denial of equal rights and there could have been no state deprivation, argued the defense, because the state courts were not allowed to hear the matter.[56]

The opinion by Justice Swayne is remarkable because it provides a contemporaneous construction of the Thirteenth Amendment, which had recently been enacted.[57] Justice Swayne wrote:

> They [proponents of the Thirteenth Amendment] felt that much was due to the African race for the part it had borne during the war. They were also impelled by a sense of right and by a strong sense of justice to an unoffending and long-suffering people. These considerations must not be lost sight of when we come to examine the amendment in order to ascertain its proper construction.[58]

He upheld the Civil Rights Act and, in effect, found that Talbot was denied a civil right of national citizenship provided for by the Thirteenth Amendment and Civil Rights Act of 1866 by reason of her not being able to testify under the Kentucky statute. "It would be a remarkable anomaly," Justice Swayne wrote,

> if the national government, without this amendment [the Thirteenth], could confer citizenship on aliens of every race or color . . . and can not, with the help of the amendment, confer on those of the African race, who have been born and always lived within the United States, all that this law seeks to give them.[59]

Such a result would have been paradoxical, and the practical effect of voiding this type of enforcement of the Act's protections would have been extremely troubling. Had Justice Swayne voided the Civil Rights Act of 1866 or severely limited jurisdiction in the federal courts, the effect would have been to relegate African Americans to the whim of racist oppressors, just as they had been during the times of slavery. The whites in effect would have immunity from any prosecution where the only witnesses—apart from their co-conspirators—could not testify against them. As Justice Swayne noted the situation before the passage of the Civil Rights Act of 1866: "Crimes of the deepest dye were committed by white men with impunity."[60]

In 1872, six years after Justice Swayne's decision as a circuit justice in *United States v. Rhodes*, the U.S. Supreme Court in *Blyew v. United States*[61] had the opportunity either to affirm or to reject his thoughtful opinion that gave vitality to the 1866 Civil Rights Act and some modicum of federal protection for African Americans. The *Blyew* case was the sequel to Kentucky's slavery jurisprudence.

In 1868, two whites, John Blyew and John Kennard, killed and mutilated several members of an African-American family in Kentucky.[62] The evidence showed that Kennard had said to Blyew: "that he (Kennard) thought there would soon be another war about the niggers; that when it did come he intended to go to killing niggers, and he was not sure that he would not begin his work of killing them before the war should actually commence."[63] Shortly thereafter, Jack Foster and his wife were found dead in their cabin, along with Mrs. Foster's over 90-year-old mother, Lucy Armstrong, who had been blind.[64] Armstrong's head had been hacked open as with a broad-axe. Jack and Sallie Foster were "cut in several places, almost to pieces."[65] Richard Foster, Jack's son, who was a teenager, was also cut as with a broad-axe, but managed to crawl to a neighbor's home about 200 yards away, where, before he died from his wounds, he "made a dying declaration tending to fix the crime on Blyew and Kennard."[66]

Under Kentucky law, statements or testimony of the African-American witnesses, including Richard Foster and Laura Foster, a thirteen-year-old girl, were kept from being presented against the defendants because the witnesses were African-American. The prosecution for the murder of Lucy Armstrong was brought to federal court in Louisville. Kennard and Blyew were found guilty and sentenced to death.[67]

The U.S. Supreme Court, after deliberating for more than a year,[68] decided that the federal court lacked jurisdiction to prosecute the defendants. The Civil Rights Act of 1866 provided for federal causes "affecting persons who are denied or cannot enforce in the courts . . . any of the rights secured to them by the first section of this act."[69] Because the only persons "affected" by the criminal prosecution were the defendants and *not*, said the Court, the African-American witnesses—the crime's *victims* among them—the jurisdictional basis for the prosecution was absent.[70] The Court repudiated the rationale that Justice Swayne had articulated in *Rhodes*, that the African-American victims were indeed affected parties under the Civil Rights Act, and that where justice was not to be had in state courts, the action could be brought in federal court.[71] Justice Joseph Bradley, joined by Justice Swayne dissented, and Chief Justice Salmon Chase did not participate.[72]

By the Supreme Court's judgment the convictions were set aside, and the slavery jurisprudence precepts that African Americans were inferior and should remain powerless were reincarnated. The Court implicitly reaffirmed

the validity of the Kentucky statute enacted in 1852, but still enforced following the Civil War and passage of the Thirteenth Amendment, and passage of
the Civil Rights Act of 1866. The Kentucky statute precluded African Americans from testifying that they had witnessed whites hack their relatives to
death.

This decision by the Supreme Court in 1872 could have been the final
blow to the aspirations of African Americans—if their future status would
have been forever predicated on the scope of the Thirteenth Amendment. The
Court in *Blyew* was relying on that Amendment and the 1866 civil rights
statute. Fortunately, Congress enacted future laws, and two potent constitutional amendments were ratified, one in 1868 and another in 1870. With legislation based on the broader constitutional authority of the Fourteenth and Fifteenth Amendments, one could argue that the tragedy of the *Blyew* case was
eradicated and should not be repeated, just as the Amendments themselves
obliterated the racist rationale of the *Dred Scott* case.

7

THE DREAM OF FREEDOM
AND ITS DEMISE

Had "The long sickness . . . come to end"?[1]

TO UNDERSTAND the health or pathology of America's race relations law, one must always scrutinize the calendar year in which important statements were made, and the dates when constitutional amendments or statutes were enacted. This provides the historical context and circumstance of the legal development. What at one time may have been prophetic statements or warnings by individuals, courts, or legislative bodies later may become irrelevant because of intervening legal events.

Prior to the passage of the Fourteenth and Fifteenth Amendments, Justice Noah Swayne made it clear in *United States v. Rhodes* that he "entertain[ed] no doubt of the constitutionality of the [1866 civil rights] act in all its provisions."[2] He noted, however, that the statute "gives only certain civil rights. Whether it was competent for congress to confer political rights also, involves a different inquiry. We have not found it necessary to consider the subject."[3]

By 1868 the American people had become concerned about the "inquiry" that Swayne had raised. In response they ratified the Fourteenth Amendment in 1868 and the Fifteenth Amendment in 1870. Additionally, by 1875, Congress had enacted several related and comprehensive civil rights acts, which presumably ensured equal justice under the law for African Americans. As to the past pathology of slavery, many believed, as Loren Miller explains, that "[t]he long sickness had come to [an] end."[4] Those persons asserted that slavery and its total pathology had been excised, and that "the majestic rhetoric of the Declaration of Independence had full meaning: '*All* men are created equal [and] are endowed by their Creator with certain unalienable Rights, that among these are Life, *Liberty* and the pursuit of Happiness.' "[5] They thought that the Preamble of the Constitution had become more inclusive, so that its phrase "We the People" now meant *all* of the people, and thus included African Americans, for whom the government was now obligated to "secure the Blessing of Liberty." It was believed that the United States was ready to commit itself, for the first time, to the safeguarding of African Americans "against the aggressions of individuals, of the states, and of their agents and servants."[6] In sum, the vision of the times was infused with the idea that: *"[i]n spirit, 'in all of our legislation,' there was 'no such word as black or white . . . only . . . citizens.' "*[7]

In the excerpts above from his seminal book *The Petitioners: The Story of the Supreme Court of the United States and the Negro*, Loren Miller captured the idealists' dreams and, I submit, much of the intent of most of the early political leadership that lobbied vigorously for the enactment of the Thirteenth, Fourteenth, and Fifteenth Amendments, and the related civil rights statutes passed from 1866 to 1875. Yet sadly, despite the dreams and intent of the political leadership, the implementation of these Amendments and statutes came to a screeching halt in the late 1870s and the early 1880s. In less than two decades after their enactment, there was a pervasive reluctance and often a total hostility toward implementing the goal of full and equal justice for African Americans.

Thus, in 1953, *eighty-five* years after the enactment of the Fourteenth Amendment, Thurgood Marshall stood before the Supreme Court in *Brown v. Board of Education*[8] and asserted that the precept of inferiority established in slavery jurisprudence still existed. In fact, he argued that it was being ruthlessly implemented to the profound and incalculable detriment of African Americans, as exemplified in the statutes that the plaintiffs were challenging. Marshall, in his closing argument, framed the issue as follows:

So whichever way it is done, the only way that this Court can decide this case in opposition to our position, is that there must be some reason which gives the state the right to make a classification that they can make in regard to nothing else in regard to Negroes, and we submit the only way to arrive at this decision is to find that for some reason Negroes are *inferior* to all other human beings.

Nobody will stand in the Court and urge that, and in order to arrive at the decision that they want us to arrive at, there would have to be some recognition of a reason why of all of the multitudinous groups of people in this country you have to single out Negroes and give them this separate treatment.

It can't be because of slavery in the past, because there are very few groups in this country that haven't had slavery some place back in the history of their groups. It can't be color because there are Negroes as white as the drifted snow, with blue eyes, and they are just as segregated as the colored man.

The only thing can be is an inherent determination that the people who were formerly in slavery, regardless of anything else, shall be kept as near that stage as is possible, and now is the time, we submit, that this Court should make it clear that that is not what our Constitution stands for.
Thank you, sir.[9]

Thurgood Marshall's advocacy explained that in the post-Reconstruction period the slavery precept of inferiority had been reincarnated by state legislatures and the federal and state judiciaries. In the post-Reconstruction era, legislatures and courts disingenuously affixed labels to their enactments and pronouncements that suggested compliance with the Fourteenth Amendment's requirements: labels such as "equal protection," "due process," and "privileges and immunities." Nevertheless, their conduct, rulings, and declarations were most often associated with black inferiority and powerlessness. Their actions were directly linked to the old plantation owners' machinations for keeping African Americans "as near . . . as is possible" to the state of oppression that existed in African Americans' former racial enslavement.

This chapter traces the momentary hopes and the ultimate demise of the dreams of freedom as the Fourteenth and Fifteenth Amendments were born and later partially nullified. In the nullification process, the political and other governmental actors denied power to those African Americans who were seeking a role in the governance of this nation and demanding racial equality. This nullification disempowered the relatively few African Americans who had sufficient status to protect their communities and to help their people prosper.

The One Pervading Purpose

[T]he one pervading purpose found in them all [the Thirteenth, Fourteenth, and Fifteenth Amendments], lying at the foundation of each, and without which none of them would have been even suggested . . . the freedom of the slave race, the security and firm establishment of that freedom, and the protection of the newly-made freeman and citizen from the oppressions of those who had formerly exercised unlimited dominion over him. [*Slaughter-House Cases* (1873)[10]]

It is indeed ironic that the *Slaughter-House Cases,* the first major cases before the Supreme Court construing the Reconstruction Amendments, did *not* involve any "newly-made freeman" or person of color. The plaintiffs in the *Slaughter-House Cases* of 1873 were white butchers who sought the broadest possible construction of the Thirteenth and Fourteenth Amendments so that they could maximize their business profits.

The cast of characters in this litigation would be prime candidates for a historical novel or a documentary film. The plaintiff butchers were represented by John C. Campbell, who, in 1861, had resigned as a justice of the United States Supreme Court and who had subsequently become Confederate Assistant Secretary of War.[11] At the end of the war, he was jailed for four months at Fort Pulaski, Georgia, and was ultimately released by order of President Andrew Johnson.[12] The lawyer for Louisiana was Matthew Carpenter, a distinguished Supreme Court advocate[13] and also a senator from Wisconsin.[14]

The butchers were challenging an 1869 Louisiana statute that granted to one private corporation, which was statutorily created, the "*sole and exclusive privilege*" of conducting the "live-stock landing" and operating the slaughterhouses in the City of New Orleans.[15] The plaintiffs alleged that the slaughterhouse statute created an "involuntary servitude" forbidden by the Thirteenth Amendment.[16] As to the Fourteenth Amendment, they claimed that the statute abridged their "privileges and immunities" as citizens of the United States, denied them the "equal protection of the laws," and deprived them of their property "without due process of law."[17]

The *Slaughter-House Cases* put into historic perspective the purpose of the Thirteenth, Fourteenth, and Fifteenth Amendments and the related civil rights acts from 1866 to 1875. In many ways the *Slaughter-House Cases* may also be considered seminal. The Court's extensive analysis of the slavery jurisprudence that had incorporated the precept of black inferiority, its description of the post-Civil War black codes, and its commentary on the constitutional amendments are of profound significance for understanding how the precept of inferiority could be embedded into law and then extracted. This chapter therefore extensively quotes portions of the majority's opinion.[18]

The justices had been keen observers of the national scene during the antebellum period, the Civil War, and the time when these critical constitutional amendments were passed. Thus, the significance of their observations, such as the following, cannot be overemphasized:

> We repeat, then, in the light of this recapitulation of events, almost too recent to be called history, but which are familiar to us all; and on the most casual examination of the language of these amendments, no one can fail to be impressed with the *one pervading purpose* found in them all, lying at the foundation of each, and without which none of them would have been even suggested; we mean the *freedom of the slave race, the security and firm establishment of that freedom, and the protection of the newly-made freeman and citizen from the oppressions of those who had formerly exercised unlimited dominion over him.* It is true that only the fifteenth amendment, in terms, mentions the negro by speaking of his color

and his slavery. But it is just as true that each of the other articles was addressed to the grievances of that race, and designed to remedy them as the fifteenth.[19]

In their majority opinion, the Supreme Court described vividly the environment immediately following the Civil War, the era when black codes were being enacted. They noted that the states of the former Confederacy had, after the Civil War, passed laws ("black codes") so that "the condition of the slave race would, without further protection of the Federal government, be almost as bad as it was before."[20] Legislation adopted by several of the southern states immediately after the Civil War were laws that

> imposed upon the colored race onerous disabilities and burdens, and curtailed their rights in the pursuit of life, liberty, and property to such an extent that their freedom was of little value, while they had lost the protection which they had received from their former owners from motives both of interest and humanity.[21]

The Court summarized the plight of the recently freed slaves:

> They were in some States forbidden to appear in the towns in any other character than menial servants. They were required to reside on and cultivate the soil without the right to purchase or own it. They were excluded from many occupations of gain, and were not permitted to give testimony in the courts in any case where a white man was a party. It was said that their lives were at the mercy of bad men, either because the laws for their protection were insufficient or were not enforced.
>
> These circumstances . . . [created] the conviction that something more was necessary in the way of constitutional protection to the unfortunate race who had suffered so much. They accordingly passed through Congress the proposition for the fourteenth amendment, and they declined to treat as restored to their full participation in the government of the Union the States which had been in insurrection, until they ratified that article by a formal vote of their legislative bodies.
>
> . . . A few years' experience satisfied the thoughtful men who had been the authors of the other two amendments that, notwithstanding the restraints of those articles on the States, and the laws passed under the additional powers granted to Congress, these were inadequate for the protection of life, liberty, and property, without which freedom to the slave was no boon. They were in all those States denied the right of suffrage. The laws were administered by the white man alone. It was urged that a race of men distinctively marked as was the negro, living in the midst of another and dominant race, could never be fully secured in their person and their property without the right of suffrage.
>
> Hence the fifteenth amendment, which declares that "the right of a

citizen of the United States to vote shall not be denied or abridged by any
State on account of race, color, or previous condition of servitude." The
negro having, by the fourteenth amendment, been declared to be a citizen
of the United States, is thus made a voter in every State of the Union.[22]

Arguing before the Supreme Court in *Brown v. Board of Education*
(eighty years after the *Slaughter-House Cases*), Thurgood Marshall stressed
the relevance of the black codes in much the same fashion as the Supreme
Court had done in their 1873 opinion. He asserted:

> They can't take race out of this case. . . . [N]obody has in any form
> or fashion, despite the fact I made it clear in the opening argument that I
> was relying on it, done anything to distinguish this [school segregation]
> statute from the Black Codes. . . . [T]he Fourteenth Amendment was in-
> tended to deprive the states of power to enforce Black Codes or anything
> else like it.
> We charge that they are Black Codes. They obviously are Black Codes
> if you read them. They haven't denied that they are Black Codes, so if
> the Court wants to very narrowly decide this case, they can decide it on
> that point.[23]

Although the justices in the *Slaughter-House Cases* and Thurgood Marshall in *Brown* did not use the term "precept of inferiority," it is clear that
both the Court and Thurgood Marshall recognized that the major foundation
and enduring legacy of slavery was a notion or presumption of black inferiority. The Court recognized that all or most of the badges and incidents of
slavery were meant to be eradicated by the Thirteenth, Fourteenth, and Fifteenth Amendments. By their language in the *Slaughter-House Cases,* the
Supreme Court *seemed* to demonstrate an understanding similar to that of
Senator Jacob Howard, a member of the committee that framed the Fourteenth
Amendment, who said:

> I look upon the first section [of the Amendment] as very important. It will,
> if adopted by the States, forever disable everyone of them from passing
> laws trenching on those fundamental rights which pertain to citizens of the
> United States and to all persons who may happen to be within their jurisdic-
> tion. *It establishes equality before the law, and it gives to the humblest, the
> poorest, the most despised of the race the same rights and the same protec-
> tion before the law as it gives the most powerful, the most wealthy, or the
> most haughty.*[24]

For my present study, it is not necessary to ponder the issue of whether
the Supreme Court in the *Slaughter-House Cases* construed the Thirteenth and
Fourteenth Amendments too narrowly. The factor I wish to focus on is that
the Court recognized that "slavery, as a legalized social relation, perished"

with the wartime events and later passage of the Thirteenth Amendment.[25] They declared that the Thirteenth Amendment was a "simple declaration of the personal freedom of all the human race within the jurisdiction of this government—a declaration designed to establish the freedom of four millions of slaves."[26]

The basic egalitarian perspective of the Supreme Court of 1873 as revealed above in the language of the *Slaughter-House Cases* was not inconsistent with the rationale that it had articulated in another case decided the same year. In *Railroad Company v. Brown*,[27] the issue was, what was meant by the District of Columbia charter for the Georgetown Railroad, which provided that "no person shall be excluded from the cars on account of color." The Supreme Court rejected the railroad company's argument that segregating African Americans did not amount to their "exclusion" from the railroad cars so that this was not discrimination which Congress had prohibited.[28] The Court found that it was "the discrimination in the use of the cars on account of color, where slavery obtained, which was the subject of discussion at the time, and . . . Congress, in the belief that this discrimination was unjust, acted."[29] Thus, long before *Plessy v. Ferguson*[30] legitimized the "separate but equal" concept, the Supreme Court of 1873 had refused to give the Court's imprimatur to the pernicious concept that "separate but equal" was *not* discrimination under the law.

Rather, the *Railroad Company v. Brown* Court held that a District of Columbia charter for the Georgetown Railroad, which provided that "no person shall be excluded from the cars on account of color,"[31] meant that persons of color could not be segregated. The unanimous Court ruled that persons of color could travel in the *same* car as whites and that the railroad's offering of a "separate but equal" car assigned exclusively to people of color was in contravention of the legislative mandate in the charter, even though the cars assigned to African Americans were "alike comfortable."[32] In 1873 the Supreme Court seemed to be signaling that it was prepared to repudiate the judicial doctrines that sanctioned the precept of racial inferiority.

The Beginning of the Judicial Betrayal of African Americans

While *Blyew v. United States*[33] of 1872 was a setback for African Americans, it could be easily explained as a decision that was limited merely to defining the scope of congressional power authorized by the Thirteenth Amendment. The *Slaughter-House Cases* had *mixed* messages, some that were favorable— for example, holding that the pervading purposes of the recent constitutional amendments were to aid African Americans—and others that were troublesome—such as the portion of the ruling that unduly bifurcated the "privileges and immunities" one has as a citizen of the United States and as a citizen of a state.[34] By 1875, however, there were no longer mixed or muted messages from the Court as to the scope of protection Congress could give African Americans. In 1876, the Supreme Court started to sink the boat of African-American constitutional aspirations. They left no life preservers to offer any hope of a sustained federal effort to ensure African Americans' rights. The hope that the Fourteenth and Fifteenth Amendments' vitality would be recognized by the Supreme Court appeared to vanish three years after the *Slaughter-House* opinion.

Following a disputed gubernatorial election in Louisiana, both the incumbent governor, Conservative Henry C. Warmoth, and the challenger, Republican William P. Kellogg, claimed victory, and each attempted to gain control of the Grant Parish courthouse.[35] Historian Robert Kaczorowski relates what then transpired:

> On Easter morning, April 13, 1873, a "veritable army" of "old time Ku Klux Klan" led by the Conservatives [Alphonse] Cazabat [Warmoth-appointed judge of Grant Parish] and [Christopher Columbus] Nash [Warmoth-appointed sheriff of Grant Parish] stormed the courthouse. . . . At least 60 freedmen were killed after they had surrendered, and their bodies were mutilated and left to rot in the parching sun. . . . Federal investigators reported that the Conservatives viewed the conflict over the local political offices as a "test of white supremacy," and they were joined by men from surrounding parishes in a determined effort to restore white rule. Government investigators put the onus of blame for the violence on the white Conservatives. They concluded that the Conservatives had massacred the black Republicans in a political vendetta motivated by racial hatred.[36]

A federal grand jury indicted ninety-seven of the attackers for multiple violations of the Enforcement Act of 1870.[37] In *United States v. Cruikshank*, the defendants were charged with, among other things, conspiring to deprive African Americans of various constitutional rights, including their rights to peaceably assemble and to vote, and with murder pursuant to the conspiracy.[38] Following a two-month trial and six weeks of jury deliberations, the jury acquitted one of the nine defendants brought to trial and could not reach a verdict as to the other defendants.[39] On retrial, only three defendants were convicted of conspiracy, and *all eight* remaining defendants were acquitted of the murder charges.[40]

The convicted defendants brought a motion in arrest of judgment, which alleged that the statute on which the prosecution was based, the Enforcement Act of 1870, was unconstitutional.[41] Justice Bradley of the United States Supreme Court, sitting at the lower court level in this case, granted the defendants' motion and dismissed the indictment.[42] Bradley claimed that, for federal jurisdiction, the offenses must have been race-based, and therefore relied on the point that the indictment *did not allege a racial motivation* for the conspiracy.[43] This point seems a little ironic, given the overtly racial bias exhibited in the attack. No person familiar with the history of the times could possibly believe that a brutal attack by an "army" of the Ku Klux Klan on a group of African-American Republicans, who were meeting for a political purpose, was motivated by anything other than racial hostility and the desire to prevent the exercise of political rights.

Consequently, despite Bradley's discussion of the significant expansion of federal authority established by the Reconstruction amendments, he nevertheless dismissed the indictment in the case of an obviously race-based massacre of African Americans. In the words of Professor Kaczorowski: "Southern Republicans were understandably demoralized. . . . Louisiana Conservatives, however, were delighted."[44]

The full Supreme Court ruled on the case in 1876 and struck another blow to federal civil-rights enforcement. The Court, in an opinion by Chief Justice Morrison Waite, shrouded the gruesome events that led to the indictments in abstract constitutional theory. The counts in the indictment alleged a conspiracy to deprive African Americans "of their respective several lives and liberty of person without due process of law." Chief Justice Waite asserted that: "[s]overeignty, for this purpose, rests alone with the States. It is no more the duty or within the power of the United States to punish for a conspiracy to falsely imprison or murder within a State, than it would be to punish for false imprisonment or murder itself."[45]

The reason for the enactment of the Enforcement Act, however, was in part that states were *unwilling or unable* to accomplish this goal, so that the *only* real protection African Americans could receive would come directly through federal intervention. Thus, over twenty years after the Civil War, the Supreme Court nullified the dramatic impact the recent constitutional amendments and federal laws were supposed to have on civil rights enforcement.

Many years later, Justice Felix Frankfurter pointed out that "there comes a point where this Court should not be ignorant as judges of what we know as men."[46] In reviewing these cases, there comes a point where it is obvious that the justices deliberately disregarded the facts they knew as men about the violence that led to the cases, as well as about the events surrounding the Civil War and the passage of the Reconstruction amendments and federal laws, which were meant to assure the protection of African Americans.[47]

The undiluted message to hoodlums and other vigilante groups was that they would be free to keep African Americans "in their place." Any prosecution that could still take place under a Reconstruction amendment or statute

would have to scale the barriers erected by the Court: technical pleading requirements must be met, and then the Court's apparent hostility to federal
enforcement efforts would have to be countered. Certainly during the Reconstruction era, there was no more effective way to preclude African Americans
from legal equality or even fair treatment than by denying or severely diluting
federal enforcement power. By denying to African Americans access to justice in the federal courts, the Supreme Court had effectively disabled the
federal government's ability to prosecute those who could or would not be
effectively prosecuted in state courts. Unburdened by any real threat of penalty, these white supremacists were free to revive and enforce the discredited
legal and social notion that African Americans were inferior.

Given the harm that would be inflicted on African Americans deprived
of their most basic citizenship rights—including the rights of voting or holding public office—one might assume that there was an uproar at the death
knell for rights enforcement in the South. But such protests, if any, were
drowned out by a public sentiment that the time was at hand to end federal
intervention on behalf of African Americans. Professor Kaczorowski summa-
rizes the public's response to these decisions:

> The public reacted to *Reese* and *Cruikshank* as welcome correctives to
> the centralization of power that was brought about by Congressional Recon-
> struction. Republican and Democratic Conservative newspapers applauded
> the *Reese* and *Cruikshank* decisions for their alleged judiciousness, impar-
> tiality and wisdom. The Supreme Court was lauded for restoring the pub-
> lic's confidence in the national judiciary by correcting the imbalance in
> federal powers created by a misguided Congress striving to maintain unwor-
> thy and corrupt politicians in public office. The obviously devastating con-
> sequences for desperately needed national civil rights protection in the
> South were rationalized away by a cynical justification of the decisions.
> The opportunity for renewed terrorism in the South was characterized as
> merely an apparent injurious effect of the decisions. The Court's reaffirma-
> tion of the "traditional" division of federal powers was more important be-
> cause it was in the best interests of all Americans. Equally remarkable was
> the press's acceptance of the Supreme Court's interpretation of the statutes
> and Amendments that differed so fundamentally from the meaning that uni-
> formly had been attributed to them by federal, and most state, judges.[48]

Without using the explicit terms of slavery jurisprudence, the Supreme
Court nevertheless gave those slavery precepts renewed vitality in the post-
Civil War era. African Americans were being killed because white citizens
wanted to maintain white supremacy and to preclude African Americans from
having any political power. These white supremacists received the imprimatur
of the Supreme Court whose interpretation of the constitutional amendments

and statutes, as Professor Kaczorowski establishes, "differed so fundamentally from the meaning that uniformly had been attributed to them by federal, and most state, judges."[49]

The Political Betrayal: The 1877 Hayes-Tilden Election Compromise—"[N]iggers take care of yourselves"[50]

Hostile Supreme Court decisions abandoned the prior thoughtful jurisprudence that had established that the Constitution sanctioned federal protection of the citizenship rights of African Americans. Yet despite this judicial abandonment, the Reconstruction era was not completely over. In some southern states, federal troops were still present in significant numbers, and therefore, the possibility of renewed federal effort remained as a possible deterrent to white supremacists.

As African Americans were killed, mutilated, and oppressed for exercising their rights of citizenship, the courts denied redress for African Americans by drawing—for them—meaningless distinctions. The courts wore blinders to the realities of the South.

"States' rights" often prevailed over African-American victims' rights, and this result was often affirmed in the Supreme Court,[51] while vigilante and state repression of African Americans simultaneously occurred. Still, white supremacists could not hope to resurrect the precept of black inferiority as effectively as it had existed during the antebellum period, at least until their desires controlled the actions of all branches of the government: the judiciary, the legislature, the governorships, and the presidency. Unfortunately, this time was close at hand.

The disputed presidential election of 1876 resulted in a political betrayal of African Americans and an effective end to the federal presence in the South. Following the presidential election, the Republican candidate, Rutherford B. Hayes, had 166 electoral votes, and his opponent, Democrat Samuel J. Tilden, had secured 184, just one vote short of the number necessary for election. The rulings on disputed electoral votes from Louisiana, Florida, Oregon, and South Carolina would determine the election: if Hayes obtained all the votes, he would gain the presidency; otherwise, Tilden would win.[52]

The result was of the utmost significance for African Americans in the South. The Democratic party, which controlled all but three southern states (South Carolina, Florida, and Louisiana),[53] was committed to the annihilation of the Republican Reconstruction program in the South and to the restoration of "Home-Rule."[54] The Democrats thereby hoped to reinstate laws and policies that returned African Americans to a condition not unlike slavery. African Americans would be precluded from voting or holding public office even more completely than had been recently accomplished with terrorist violence.

Hayes's Republican platform offered more promise for African Americans. Hayes had initially supported African Americans.[55] The day after the 1876 election, Hayes expressed little confidence in his chances, or those for African Americans if Tilden were elected, as he wrote in his diary:

> I don't care for myself; and the party, yes, and the country, too, can stand it; but I do care for the poor colored men of the South. . . . The result will be that the Southern people will practically treat the constitutional amendments as nullities, and then the colored man's fate will be worse than when he was in slavery.[56]

Hayes's apparent sympathy for the plight of southern African Americans seemingly vanished when he was later confronted with the opportunity to secure the presidency. In an effort to garner the remaining electoral votes, he abandoned his concern for the protection of African Americans' citizenship rights. Some weeks after the election, Hayes expressed a desire to meet with prominent Southerners to work a deal.[57] Hayes made clear he would "require absolute justice and fair play to the negro, but . . . he was convinced that this could be got best and almost surely by trusting the honorable and influential southern whites."[58]

Hayes must have known that without the federal government's presence, and without any fear of federal prosecution, the "honorable" southern whites would deny African Americans even their most basic civil rights. Indeed, he had recognized this potential in his diary entry two weeks earlier. Nevertheless, Hayes assured the southern Democrats in this deal that he would support "Home-Rule" and would require their support of his candidacy. This faustian pact was sealed and Hayes became "the principal presidential architect of the consolidation of white supremacy in the South, during the post-Reconstruction period."[59]

Reconstruction effectively ended with Hayes's inauguration. During the weeks of secret bargaining with southern Democrats, Hayes had promised, among other things, that he would withdraw the remaining federal troops from South Carolina and Louisiana.[60] During his inaugural address, Hayes asserted the primacy of the "honest and efficient *local* government as the true resources of these [i.e., Southern] states for the promotion of the contentment and prosperity of their citizens."[61] Thus, the very same southern whites who had exhibited the consistent use of fraud, violence, and intimidation to prevent African Americans from taking part in government would now somehow be responsible for enforcing laws *of their own making*, which would provide for the "contentment and prosperity" of African Americans as well as whites.

African Americans were hardly fooled by this rhetoric, and were quite aware of the consequences of Hayes's promise to remove federal troops. Louisianan Henry Adams, an African American, noted that "[t]he whole South—every state in the South—had got into the hands of the very men that held us as slaves."[62] Another African American from South Carolina pointed out the irony of Hayes's actions: "To think that Hayes could go back on us, when we had to wade through blood to help place him where he is now."[63]

The compromise that resulted in Hayes's election marked the final retreat from the federal government's position of protecting African Americans' fundamental rights of citizenship. The tragedy of the compromise was more than the President's moral abdication of the protection of African Americans as citizens. It lay in the political results that followed from the end of Reconstruction. In 1878, Congress prohibited the use of armed forces to monitor elections,[64] and thus removed the only real deterrent to physical intimidation at the polls. In 1894, they stopped appropriations for special federal marshals and supervisors of elections.[65] In 1898, a "final amnesty" removed "the last disabilities laid on disloyal and rebellious Southerners."[66]

The Reconstruction era had great potential for eradicating the precepts of black inferiority and powerlessness. A strong national government issued unequivocal statements that federal law did not recognize different classes of citizens based on skin color. Each citizen was equal before the law. Nonetheless, legal developments threatened and nullified many of the legal gains made by African Americans. By the end of Reconstruction, states were free from the federal control that had urged—though certainly did not convince—southern whites to reject the precept of African Americans' inferiority. The result of Hayes's election was aptly described by the chairman of the Kansas Republican state committee: "As matters look to me now, I think the policy of the new administration will be to conciliate the white men of the South. Carpetbaggers to the rear, and niggers take care of yourselves."[67]

8

THE SUPREME COURT'S SANCTION OF RACIAL HATRED

The 1883 Civil Rights Cases

[T]his bill seeks to coerce an unnatural alliance between the races, unpleasant to them and disgusting to us, in our social relationships . . . . [Y]ou cannot control taste, revolutionize habits, nor change color by legislation. . . . [Y]ou cannot benefit him by dragging the white race down to his degraded level, and enforcing the degradation by the infliction of penalties.—Rep. Hiram P. Bell, Georgia[1]

THE ULTIMATE betrayal of African Americans that ended Reconstruction gave rise to a reappearance of racial patterns, laws, and court decisions in the states that differed little from antebellum slavery jurisprudence. Following Reconstruction, in terms of failing to protect African Americans, the Supreme Court continued to legitimize the resurrection of the inferiority precept and gave sanction to acts of discrimination against African Americans. The Court did so partly by blinding itself to the unequal treatment, and partly by creating unnecessary legal doctrine that had harsh racial consequences.

Whether a society grants or denies equal access rights to minorities reveals whether its government repudiates or sanctions perceptions of inferiority. In the post-Civil War era, racial hostility was often manifested in denials to African Americans of the right to equal and full access to public accommodations. States continued to implement and perpetuate the precept of black inferiority in innumerable ways, through the exclusion of African Americans from equal access to major public accommodations, rampant racial segregation, and all manner of unequal and adverse treatment.

Although there were some early efforts during Reconstruction by state legislators to preclude racial discrimination in public transportation, such discrimination was common. On railroads, for example, even when African Americans had purchased first-class tickets or were willing to do so, they were denied first-class accommodations as a matter of course and consigned to substandard, less desirable areas. Additionally, African Americans were often denied the right to be customers at first-class or even fifth-class hotels, restaurants, theaters, and other places of public accommodation. The unfair and unjust treatment of African Americans in public accommodations during the 1860s, 1870s, and 1880s was not much different from the treatment they received during the antebellum period.[2]

From the birth of this nation to the present day there has been continuous tension among some white Americans as to whether hatred of African Americans is to be sanctioned or whether the state and federal governments must assure to African Americans the full panoply of citizenship rights, including equal access to public accommodations. In the 1870s, this divisive issue was intensely debated in Congress. Debate on the civil rights bill that ultimately became the Civil Rights Act of 1875—which was designed to ensure African Americans equal access to public accommodations—revealed the racial tensions in the Congress and the nation.

The Inferiority Precept and Public Accommodations: Debating the Meaning of the Civil Rights Act of 1875

Senator Charles Sumner of Massachusetts[3] and several other members of Congress had for many years proposed legislation to eradicate the pervasive discrimination in areas of public accommodations and had encountered intense hostility from many of their colleagues. During debate on the 1875 civil rights bill, the unmuted language of many white members of Congress revealed their hatred of African Americans and their determination to keep them in as degraded a position as possible. These members were unwilling to accept African Americans as equals in the public sphere and attempted to justify this opposition to equal treatment as follows:

> [T]his civil-rights bill . . . is trifling. You talk about giving these people (the negroes) the right to go to the theater, when there is not one of them in a hundred who knows what they are. . . . You talk about granting them the right to travel with the white people in the cars, when there is not one of them in five hundred who travels once a year in a train. You talk about giving them the right to go to hotels, when there is not one of them in a thousand who desires the privilege or would avail himself of it if he had it. These people are poor, and these things they care nothing about.—Rep. James H. Blount, Georgia[4]

> The bill implies the hopeless inferiority of the negro race, and proposes to cure this inferiority by an act of Congress. If this inferiority exists, Congress cannot change it by a statute. It may repeal its own laws, but

cannot repeal the laws of God. If this inferiority does not exist . . . there
is no need of this bill. Sir, any legislation to counteract natural principles
or to repeal natural laws or to obliterate natural distinctions, is impotent for
good.—Rep. John M. Glover, Missouri[5]

[T]his bill seeks to coerce an unnatural alliance between the races, unpleasant to them and disgusting to us, in our social relationships. . . . [Y]ou
cannot control taste, revolutionize habits, nor change color by legislation.
. . . [Y]ou cannot benefit him by dragging the white race down to his
degraded level, and enforcing the degradation by the infliction of penalties.—Rep. Hiram P. Bell, Georgia[6]

Fortunately, many in Congress repudiated these assertions premised on
notions of black inferiority. Those who spoke in favor of the civil rights bill
provided insight into the opponents' venal motives and supplied a much
needed corrective by way of explaining the true premise of the proposed civil
rights statute:

The colored citizens ask [for] this legislation, not because they seek to
force themselves into associations with the whites, but because they have
their prides and emulations among themselves, and wish *there* in those
associations to feel that there is no ban upon them, but that they are as
fully enfranchised as any who breathe the air of heaven.—Sen. Frederick
T. Frelinghuysen, New Jersey[7]

There is not a white man at the South that would not associate with the
negro—all that is required by this bill—if that negro were his servant. He
would eat with him, suckle from her, play with her or him as children, be
together with them in every way, provided they were slaves. There never
has been an objection to such an association. But the moment that you
elevate this black man to citizenship from a slave, then immediately he
becomes offensive. That is why I say that this prejudice is foolish, unjust,
illogical, and ungentlemanly.—Rep. Benjamin F. Butler, Massachusetts[8]

Perhaps the most eloquent remarks of the congressional debates were made
by the African-American congressman and lawyer from Mississippi, John R.
Lynch. His remarks effectively repudiated the racist diatribes and misleading
statements made by those who would reject the civil rights bill. Lynch's
thoughtful reasoning also demolished the idea that African Americans should
not take part in politics because they were intellectually inferior to whites and
therefore incapable of such high responsibilities of citizenship:

I will now endeavor to answer the arguments of those who have been
contending that the passage of this bill is an effort to bring about social
equality between the races. . . .
No, Mr. Speaker, it is not social rights that we desire. We have

enough of that already. What we ask is protection in the enjoyment of *public* rights. Rights which are or should be accorded to every citizen alike.

* * *

Mr. Speaker, if this unjust discrimination is to be longer tolerated by the American people, which I do not, cannot, and will not believe until I am forced to do so, then I can only say with sorrow and regret that our boasted civilization is a fraud; our republican institutions a failure; our social system a disgrace; and our religion a complete hypocrisy. But I have an abiding confidence . . . in the patriotism of this people, in their devotion to the cause of human rights, and in the stability of our republican institutions. I hope that I will not be deceived. I love the land that gave me birth; I love the Stars and Stripes. This country is where I intend to live, where I expect to die. To preserve the honor of the national flag and to maintain perpetually the Union of the States hundreds, and I may say thousands, of noble, brave, and true-hearted colored men have fought, bled, and died. And now, Mr. Speaker, I ask, can it be possible that that flag under which they fought is to be a shield and a protection to all races and classes of persons except the colored race? God forbid![9]

Representative Lynch, in demanding that the ideal of democratic equality be secured for African Americans just as it had been secured for white Americans, spoke on behalf of the many African Americans who were denied access to or received unequal treatment in public accommodations.

The supporters of the civil rights bill prevailed, and the Civil Rights Act became law. The first section of the Act read as follows:

That all persons within the jurisdiction of the United States shall be entitled to the full and equal enjoyment of the accommodations, advantages, facilities, and privileges of inns, public conveyances on land or water, theaters, and other places of public amusement; subject only to the conditions and limitations established by law, and applicable alike to citizens of every race and color, regardless of any previous condition of servitude.[10]

Violators of the Act were subject to fines and imprisonment.[11] The Act therefore prohibited unequal treatment of African Americans in places such as theatres, inns, and common carriers.

Despite the passage of this important federal statute, African Americans' access to public accommodations on an equal basis with whites was not secure. For, as Alexis de Tocqueville has written, "[scarcely] any question arises in the United States which does not become, sooner or later, a subject of judicial debate."[12] The judicial conclusion in the Supreme Court would not be announced for another eight years after the passage of the 1875 Civil Rights Act. These cases that became known as the *Civil Rights Cases* had roots that were put down in the treatment of African Americans during slavery. When, in the 1880s, they attempted to seek redress for violations of their right to equal treatment—which was now federally protected—these citizens sometimes even encountered segregation and unequal treatment in the court-rooms where discriminators should have been brought to justice.

The Impact of the Precept of Inferiority in the Supreme Court's Review

As so often occurs, there is an extraordinary gap between the declared national legislative policy and societal reality. Congressional passage of the 1875 Civil Rights Act sounded a rejection by the federal government of the belief that African Americans, who in the past had an inferior legal status, could be denied equal access to public accommodations. The societal reality was that racism and the preclusion of African Americans from public accommodations were common. The record of the *Civil Rights Cases* established that equal accommodations were often denied African Americans solely because of their skin color.

The events that comprised the appeals before the Supreme Court in the *Civil Rights Cases* involved five instances, from different states, in which African Americans were denied equal treatment in public facilities due to their race. The cases arose in Kansas, Missouri, California, New York, and Tennessee. These suits involved the following charges and allegations: the denial of accommodations in inns;[13] the denial of seats in theatres;[14] and the unequal treatment of African Americans who sought the right to ride in the "ladies' car" of a train.[15] I focus on the last case, *Robinson v. Memphis & Charleston Railroad Company*,[16] because it revealed the racial, class, *and* gender prejudices that still existed following slavery's prohibition and the passage of Reconstruction legislation.

The precept of inferiority was embedded in the hearts and the minds of many whites, and thus not merely in the legal codes they developed to perpetuate racial inferiority. The *Civil Rights Cases* made it clear that, for many whites in power, the passage of the Thirteenth, Fourteenth, and Fifteenth Amendments did not eradicate or alter the widely accepted slavery precept that African Americans were presumed to be inferior.

The *Civil Rights Cases* provided the Supreme Court with the opportunity to affirm the national legislative policy and to take a major part in stamping out discrimination contrary to that policy. More basically, the cases provided a setting for the Court to either legitimize or to condemn racism in the area of public accommodations. As described below, the Court's chosen course served to perpetuate racism in public accommodations and thereby to legitimize, yet again, the precept of black inferiority.

It would be a mistake to view the Court's decision in the *Civil Rights Cases*—or in any other case—in a vacuum. By definition, cases are disputes over the legal meaning of events. These events were formed, and may be understood, only by reviewing the history and circumstances that led to the disputed incident. Thus, it is necessary to reflect on the history of slavery jurisprudence as it affected, after the Civil War, later developments in the law of public accommodations. Because of space limitations, I do not in this volume focus on the complete breadth of the public accommodation issues. Instead, I focus on the treatment of African-American slave women under the law, and then compare their abuse during the antebellum era with the lower court's and Supreme Court's treatment of the case of an African-American woman, Sallie Robinson, who sought to vindicate her rights as a national citizen under the Civil Rights Act of 1875.

"Ain't I a Woman?" [17]—*Aren't African-American Women "Ladies?"*

At issue in *Robinson v. Memphis & Charleston Railroad Company* was not just determining whether African Americans must be treated equally on trains; the case also raised the question of how African-American women should be viewed by society and through the eyes of the law.[18] Analysis of the law's treatment of African-American women during slavery, therefore, provides a nexus with how African-American women such as Sallie Robinson were treated by the law following emancipation.

From the time the first African-American woman slave was purchased by her master, the message was clear—the master did not view her as a lady. From the time when the first African-American woman slave was raped by her American master, the message was even clearer—in the eyes of the law, an African-American slave woman was not regarded as a human being and had no rights to control even her own body. Thus under slavery, an African-American woman could not be a "lady." In America the term "lady" was reserved for refined white women.

The case *State of Missouri v. Celia*[19] exemplifies the hostility of the legal process toward African-American women during the antebellum period. Arising out of Missouri, even the caption of the case, "The State of Missouri against Celia, a slave" reveals the law's denigration: Celia had no last name. Celia was an African-American slave girl who in 1850, when she was fourteen years old, was purchased by Robert Newsom, a seventy-year-old farmer. Celia was a mere adolescent; Newson was a grandfather. The record of the case suggests that Newsom forced Celia to have sexual intercourse with him often and always against her will, even on the way home after he had purchased her.[20] Celia said that Newsom was the father of her second child.

While Celia was still a teenager, she was pregnant for the third time and was ill, having been sick since February.[21] One witness at her later trial testified that she threatened to hurt her slavemaster if he continued to force her to have sexual intercourse with him while she was sick.[22] From the summarized testimony,[23] one could find that on June 23, 1855, Celia told Newsom that she would hurt him if he would not stop sexually abusing her.[24] The master had told her that he was "coming down to her cabin that night."[25] She told him not to come and that she would hurt him if he came.[26] Celia then "armed herself with a stick."[27] He came down that night, and she struck him with the stick twice.[28] He apparently died immediately. She then burnt his body in the fireplace and the next morning spread his ashes on the pathway.[29]

Did Celia, as an African-American slave woman, have the right to resist her master's sexual advances, or was she guilty of first-degree murder as charged in the indictment? The instructions given by the court and those requested by her counsel reveal polar opposite perceptions as to the rights of a slave woman. Celia's counsel in substance asked the court to instruct the jury that the rape of a slave woman was not a property right of the master, that the master's economic privileges did not include the right of sexual molestation of his slave, and that the right to force her to work in the fields did not include the right to sleep in her bed and violate her at his whim. Celia's counsel asserted that Celia had the same right of self-defense that was assured all free white women under the Missouri laws.[30] In short, the court was asked to recognize that Celia, despite her involuntary servitude, was a human being entitled to some semblance of dignity and that she had the same right to resist sexual assault as did a white woman. The request was rejected by the court.[31]

Rather than recognizing that Celia, as a woman, was entitled to the statutory right of self-defense, and that it was a crime to defile her by duress or force, the trial judge rejected her lawyer's requests for jury instructions that assumed she was protected by the statutes. Instead, he gave the following instruction submitted by the state:

> If Newsom was in the *habit of having intercourse* with the defendant who was his slave and went to her cabin on the night he was killed to have intercourse with her *or for any other purpose* and while he was standing in [sic] the floor talking to her she struck him with a stick which was a dangerous weapon and knocked him down, and struck him again after he fell, and killed him by either blow, it is murder in the first degree.[32]

What did the trial judge mean by "habit of having intercourse with the defendant who was his slave?" Was he not suggesting that Celia had no right to resist if the master wanted to have sexual intercourse with her? By the very' nature of the master-slave relationship—in which the master had the right to whip her or beat her without provocation, or give her inadequate food or housing—any request by the slave master should have amounted to duress within the meaning of the statute. The master's "habit of having intercourse with his slave" was a habit predicated on the implicit coercive power of his status; it was duress that would have been illegal under the Missouri law had the court understood what Sojourner Truth meant in her plea, "Ain't I a woman?" My reading of the record and the instructions suggests that the trial judge believed that under Missouri law a slave woman had no sexual rights over her own body and thus had to acquiesce to her master's sexual demands.

The jury followed the court's dehumanizing instruction, which made Celia a person without any rights over her body. She was convicted of murder in the first degree, and the court ordered that she be executed by hanging. The Missouri Supreme Court affirmed, stating it saw "no probable cause for [an] appeal," and denied a stay of execution on December 14, 1855.[33]

Celia escaped from the jail but was subsequently returned. Her execution was delayed until she could give birth to her child, who was born dead.[34] The taking of Celia's life was not even of sufficient importance for the clerk of the court to note the day she was hanged. Her death was noted solely by: "Bill of Costs: Executing Death Warrant paid 15.00."[35] Professor Hugh Williamson, in a moving article on Celia, summed up the case as follows:

> Such was the brief life of Celia, the slave girl. She lived in a hard and cruel world, which held her in only slightly higher regard than it did the beasts of the field and forest. Before the law she had no standing, and from it she had no protection simply because the law did not regard her as a human being.[36]

Presumably, after the end of slavery, African-American women should have been accorded a status different from that to which Celia was relegated. African-American women were to be regarded as more than the "beasts of the field and forest." Yet many issues remained: What was to be the status of African-American women? Could they now be considered "ladies"? How should "lady" be defined? It would be naive to think that, after having relegated African-American women to such a degraded position as Celia's, whites would be willing to accept African-American women just as they did other women.

Sallie Robinson's Treatment as an Inferior

The shifting status of women, depending whether they were white or African-American, was acutely described by Congressman John R. Lynch during his forceful advocacy for passage of the Civil Rights Act of 1875. He described starkly the disparity in the treatment of African-American and white women in public accommodations:

> Under our present system of race distinctions a white woman of a questionable social standing, yea, I may say, of an admitted immoral character, can go to any public place or upon any public conveyance and be the recipient of the same treatment, the same courtesy, and the same respect that is usually accorded to the most refined and virtuous; but let an intelligent, modest, refined colored lady present herself and ask that the same privileges be accorded to her that have just been accorded to her social inferior of the white race, and in nine cases out of ten, except in certain portions of the country, she will not only be refused, but insulted for making the request.[37]

The only relevant issue for white women seeking first-class treatment on railroads was whether they could pay for a first-class ticket. African-American women would not receive equal access to first-class accommodations nor would they be treated as "ladies" even when they could pay the full fare. They were presumed to be inferior solely because of the color of their skin.

Four years after Congressman Lynch's eloquent description of the rampant racial and gender discrimination in the nation's public accommodations, African Americans Sallie Robinson and her nephew, Joseph Robinson, presented their first-class tickets to a conductor at Grand Junction, Tennessee. They attempted to enter the "ladies' car" of the train, which was reserved for women and their escorts.[38] The conductor told them they could not enter that car, and then, Sallie Robinson alleged, he grabbed her by the arm and spun her around roughly, injuring her.[39] The conductor blocked the ladies' car entrance and forced them to ride in the smoking car.

Joseph Robinson again approached the conductor to ask a question, presumably to find out the reason for their exclusion. The conductor asked him, "Why do you people try to force yourselves in that [the ladies'] car?"[40] Joseph Robinson responded that he and his aunt had first-class tickets and were entitled to ride in the ladies' car.[41] The conductor then said they could ride in the ladies' car, but that they should wait until the next stop, which was approximately fifteen minutes from Grand Junction.[42]

Sallie Robinson, a former slave,[43] and her husband brought suit against the railroad for violation of the Civil Rights Act of 1875. But access to federal courts did not always guarantee justice, particularly for former slaves and other African Americans. At trial, the conductor asserted that he excluded the Robinsons from the ladies' car because he supposed that Joseph was a white man traveling with an African-American woman.[44] He reasoned that from his experience, when "young white men travelled in company with young colored women it was for illicit purposes" and that they generally acted improperly and bothered other passengers.[45]

The Robinsons' attorney objected to the introduction of this testimony of the conductor as incompetent and irrelevant, as well as not being an excuse or justification. The trial court, however, not only admitted this testimony, but also instructed the jury that, "If you find . . . the conductor in fact and in good faith believed that she [Mrs. Robinson] was a prostitute travelling with her paramour, then, whether such belief was well or ill founded, the [railroad] company is not liable for this penalty."[46]

With this instruction to the jury, the trial judge perpetuated the very negative stereotypes of African-American women suggested by the conductor's actions. Solely because Mrs. Robinson was African-American, the conductor had questioned the propriety of her riding in the ladies' car. The "test" that the conductor used to make that determination was whether she was accompanied by a white or an African-American man. If her escort was a white man, then the conductor presumed her to be a prostitute. The trial court accepted this type of assumption about African-American women by allowing the conductor this discretion.[47]

The court also instructed the jury that if Sallie Robinson was suspected of being a prostitute, and that her exclusion would not have been the corresponding treatment to a white woman "similarly suspected," then the statute was violated.[48] At first glance this instruction may appear to guarantee legal equality for African-American women, but further analysis reveals that the instruction is based on a legal fiction. White women could *never* be "similarly suspected." Sallie Robinson was suspected because she was African-American. What was the equivalent basis to suspect white women of being prostitutes? It is difficult to believe that the judge would have given the conductor as wide a latitude to make this determination with respect to white women.[49]

The trial judge placed the law's imprimatur on racial stereotypes when the judge instructed that there was no civil rights violation when a respectable African-American woman was treated as though she were a prostitute. By permitting the conductor to deny Mrs. Robinson a seat in the "ladies' car," because she was African-American and traveling with a man the conductor supposed to be white, the lower court in effect sanctioned racial discrimination and legitimized the conductor's notions of suitability.

The view of African-American women as inferior was thus continued, albeit more subtly, from Celia to Sallie Robinson. Neither the fact that Mrs. Robinson had purchased a first-class ticket, nor the fact that she and her nephew did not threaten any disturbance, was sufficient to overcome the inferior status that the conductor accorded her. The trial judge placed the law's imprimatur on the precept of black inferiority when it affirmed the relevance of the conductor's observations. Not surprisingly, given the court's instructions, the jury found for the defendant railroad.[50]

The dynamics between the conductor and the Robinsons were significant in terms of the precept of inferiority. Professor Evelyn Brooks Higginbotham has found:

> During the late nineteenth century, segregated railroad trains were emblematic of racial configurations of both class and gender; the first-class railroad car also was called the "ladies car." Indeed, segregation's meaning for gender was exemplified in the trope of "lady." Ladies were not merely women; they represented a class, a differentiated status within the generic category of "women." Nor did society confer such status on all white women. White prostitutes, along with many working-class white women, fell outside its rubric. But no black woman, regardless of income, education, refinement, or character, enjoyed the status of lady.[51]

Even before the formal creation of Jim Crow under *Plessy v. Ferguson's* "separate but equal" doctrine, when separate was not required, the application of law itself perpetuated negative stereotypes about African Americans, and thereby assured the existence of such stereotypes in the minds of the public.

The Supreme Court's Implicit Acceptance of the Precept of Inferiority

The Supreme Court decided the Robinsons' case, as well as the other four, in the *Civil Rights Cases* of 1883. As described above, the cases concerned much more than abstract constitutional theory. The cases were about whether the Supreme Court was willing to assure a level of equal dignity to African Americans in public accommodations. The clear answer that emerged was that the Court was not willing to make this assurance. Presented with the chance to repudiate the slavery jurisprudence inferiority precept, the Supreme Court declined. The Court's reasoning demonstrates that it was unwilling to sanction federal *protection* and guarantees of civil rights for African Americans, whereas previously it had no reluctance to enforce the total *repression* of African Americans.

Common carriers, such as railroads, had always been understood to be businesses for the *public's* benefit. Thus, they had been treated differently under the law than mere *private* businesses.[52] The Supreme Court in 1848 found that common carriers were "in the exercise of a sort of public office, and [have] public duties to perform."[53] The *public* nature of places of amusement and common carriers placed certain restrictions on their business discretion.

The formal legal issue that came before the Supreme Court in the *Civil Rights Cases* was whether Congress had the authority, under the Thirteenth or Fourteenth Amendments, to enact the Civil Rights Act of 1875, prohibiting discrimination in public accommodations. Without a strong message from the Supreme Court that racial discrimination in public accommodations violated the 1875 Civil Rights Act and could not be tolerated, African Americans would be at the mercy of any businessperson's discretion. African Americans would be relegated to second-class citizenship, when businessmen excluded them from various accommodations.

The consequences of allowing such discrimination would ripple throughout the legal system. *Even with* the Civil Rights Act being "enforced," Sallie Robinson was allowed to be subjected, *in a courtroom,* to a witness's estimation of whether she was a prostitute. Without any semblance of federal statutory protection, she would have no way even to effectively challenge and seek redress for the obvious injustice she faced on the railroad car.

The Supreme Court majority, in an opinion written by Justice Bradley, held that Congress could *not* prohibit racial discrimination in these public accommodations. The Court's opinion asserted that: "It [the Fourteenth Amendment] does not invest Congress with power to legislate upon subjects which are within the domain of State legislation. . . . It does not authorize Congress to create a code of municipal law for the regulation of *private rights*. . . ."[54] Justice Bradley advocated, without legal justification, the constitutional fiction that a "social right," rather than a civil right, was involved in these cases. This "social right" fiction was then used to preclude African Americans from equal treatment in public accommodations regardless of their individual character or merit.[55]

According to Justice Bradley, when "the owner of the inn, the public conveyance, or place of amusement" denied to African Americans accommodations, it had *nothing* to do with any "badge" or "incidence" of slavery or servitude prohibited by the Thirteenth Amendment; nor did it involve the privileges and immunities and equal protection guarantees of the Fourteenth Amendment. Bradley said that:

> [I]t would be running the slavery argument into the ground to make it apply to every act of discrimination which a person may see fit to make as to the guest he will entertain, or as to the people he will take into his coach or cab or car or admit to his concert or theatre or deal with in other matters of intercourse or business.[56]

Bradley added unnecessary invective in the Court's opinion by almost admonishing African Americans for expecting or demanding that the federal government assure them the same equality others had. Justice Bradley wrote:

> When a man has emerged from slavery, and by the aid of beneficent legislation has shaken off the inseparable concomitants of that state, there must be some stage in the progress of his elevation when he takes the rank of a mere citizen, and ceases to be the special favorite of the laws, and when his rights as a citizen, or a man, are to be protected in the ordinary modes by which other men's rights are protected.[57]

But of course African Americans were not seeking favoritism, but were merely attempting to secure the equality of rights as citizens which whites of all classes held as inherent rights.

Thus, despite the vigorous dissent of Justice John Harlan,[58] the Court held that racial discrimination by private owners of public places of accommodation was merely a social right that did not involve "those fundamental rights that appertain to the essence of citizenship and [its] enjoyment."[59] Therefore, such discrimination was not violative of the Thirteenth or Fourteenth Amendments; as a result, Congress could not pass legislation to prohibit "private" racial discrimination.[60] Following the Civil War and the significant constitutional amendments of Reconstruction *expanding* federal authority to protect civil rights, the Court implausibly claimed a lack of federal authority to prohibit this discrimination.

The majority's opinion resulted in the unnecessary creation of racially hostile constitutional doctrine. The Court could have found, as Justice Harlan noted in his dissent, that the first sentence of the Fourteenth Amendment, declaring "[a]ll persons born or naturalized in the United States and subject to the jurisdiction thereof are citizens of the United States and of the State wherein they reside," gave Congress power under the Amendment's fifth section to declare through legislation what the civil rights of citizens under the Amendment were.[61] One of these rights was freedom from racial discrimination in public accommodations.[62] The Court's relative disregard of the first sentence of section 1 and its focus solely on the second sentence diluted the vitality of the Amendment as a guarantor of universal civil rights.

The Supreme Court set back the civil rights aspirations of African Americans for more than a century by distorting the definition of social rights. The Court's chosen course perpetuated racism and legitimized, once again, the precept of black inferiority. The Court's decision may be regarded, at best, as merely an obliviousness to the precept of black inferiority and the enforcement mechanisms used by whites to make African Americans powerless. The

Court's decision may, however, be seen as an intentional effort to implement and resurrect their precept of black inferiority. Seven years after the *Civil Rights Cases*, the Court was being told by a Louisiana legislature that the Court's implicit tolerance of unequal treatment in 1883 should be legitimized with an explicit doctrine that would come to be known as "separate but equal."

9

THE SUPREME COURT'S
LEGITIMIZATION OF RACISM

Plessy v. Ferguson: A Case Wrongly Decided

*"[W]e think Plessy was wrong the day [May 18, 1896] it was decided. . . ."—
Justices Kennedy, O'Connor, and Souter (1992)*[1]

O N JUNE 7, 1892, Homer A. Plessy, who had "seven eighths Caucasian and one eighth African blood,"[2] took a seat on a "white" railway car. At the time, he had probably not anticipated that his act
marked the beginning of the most important civil-rights case that would come
down from the Supreme Court in the decades following the Civil War, and
one of the three most important race relations cases ever to be decided by the
Court. He could not have known that it would take sixty-two years before an
enlightened Supreme Court in *Brown v. Board of Education*[3] would modify
the tragic error that would be made in his case. In 1954, during the era of
Chief Justice Earl Warren, a unanimous Supreme Court adopted in substance
the argument Plessy had made in 1896: that the scope of the Equal Protection
Clause of the Fourteenth Amendment prohibited state-imposed racial discrimination. *Brown* implicitly overruled *Plessy v. Ferguson,*[4] but it is shocking to
think of the millions of injustices and tragic consequences that state-imposed
segregation thrust upon African Americans during the interim, between 1896
and 1954, as a result of the decision in Plessy's case in 1896.

Even though Homer Plessy could not have forecast these exact events,
nonetheless, in 1892 he was fully aware that the precept of racial inferiority
was interwoven with the criminal prosecution against him for violation of an
1890 Louisiana statute that required racially segregated facilities on trains.
Plessy's brief to the Supreme Court raised the issue of widespread perceptions
of racial inferiority. Plessy stressed his racial status as "seven eighths Caucasian," and claimed that being ordered to sit in a colored car was a violation
of the Thirteenth Amendment and his Fourteenth Amendment property

rights.[5] He contended that being considered a white man was a valuable property right "which has an actual pecuniary value" that could not be taken without due process of law. The "property" was *the reputation of being white.*"[6] His justification for this argument was a poignant commentary on the racism of that era; he asked:

> How much would it be *worth* to a young man entering upon the practice of law, to be regarded as a *white* man rather than a colored one? . . . Probably most white persons if given a choice, would prefer death to life in the United States *as colored persons.* Under these conditions, is it possible to conclude that the *reputation of being white* is not property? Indeed, is it not the most valuable sort of property, being the master-key that unlocks the golden door of opportunity?[7]

A Circular Journey: Louisiana's Retreat from Its Original Antidiscrimination Laws to Its Subsequent Enactment of Racist Segregation Laws

Some persons view the evolution of the African-American experience as a one track continuum from the eradication of slavery in 1865 to plodding efforts that led to the ultimate adoption of the civil rights acts of the 1960s. They do not recognize that there have been *two* circular journeys leading up to the modern civil rights acts. First, immediately after the Civil War, some states passed significant civil rights statutes. These antidiscrimination laws constructed a new plateau that restrained racist hostility and assured substantial equality of opportunity among the races. If these original state civil rights statutes had been upheld and enforced, much of the militancy and activism that took place in the twentieth century would have been unnecessary. Unfortunately, within two decades after the Civil War, the positive accomplishments of the earlier state civil rights legislation were repudiated. Thus, within twenty years, from approximately 1868 to 1890, the first civil rights circular journey was complete: from non-rights to rights to non-rights again.

The segregation statutes of the 1890s put African Americans "in their place," right back to their ambiguous status that existed immediately after the Civil War. From the 1890s, African Americans had to start once again a second journey to eradicate state-imposed racism. No state reveals those dual circular journeys better than Louisiana.

The Louisiana constitution adopted in 1868 assured an unprecedented measure of legal equality in that state. African Americans were given "the same civil, political, and public rights and privileges," including equal access to public conveyances and "all places of business, or of public resort, or for which a license is required," and equal educational opportunity.[8] An Act of February 23, 1869, prohibited the exclusion of persons of color from public conveyances and accommodations, and even conditioned the granting of licenses on adherence to this non-discrimination requirement.[9] Historian John Blassingame notes that "[o]ne of the most controversial positive laws was the one forbidding discrimination in places of public resort."[10] The opponents in 1869 made the same arguments that white businesses, a century later, would make in opposition to the 1964 Civil Rights Act. The nineteenth-century opponents claimed that "their white customers would desert them because they did not believe in social equality."[11] African-American leaders stressed that "since the law applied to all businesses, where would the whites run? And even if boycotts started, they would be brief; whites simply could not do without the services the businesses provided."[12]

The original statute, passed one year after the Fourteenth Amendment was ratified, was a foundation assuring equal, non-discriminatory treatment in transportation regardless of one's skin color. These provisions were expanded to cover all public accommodations in 1873.[13] But within less than two decades that bulwark of equality was destroyed and replaced with segregation laws that revived the precept of black inferiority inherent in the earlier slavery jurisprudence.

Following Reconstruction's demise, among the actions taken by legislators to re-establish the precept of black inferiority was the enactment of an 1890 statute requiring segregation on railroads.[14] The statute provided that: "[A]ll railway companies carrying passengers in their coaches in this State, shall provide equal but separate accommodations for the white, and colored races, by providing two or more passenger coaches for each passenger train, or by dividing the passenger coaches by a partition so as to secure separate accommodations. . . ."[15]

The legislature made an exception to the segregation requirements so that their children could be attended to. The statute provided that "nothing in this act shall be construed as applying to nurses attending children of the other race."[16] Since whites were not nurses for African-American children, this exception was relevant only to those instances of African-American nurses caring for white children. The legislature knew that African-American nurses caring for their children did not pose a threat to white control and dominance of African Americans.[17] The counsel for Homer Plessy incisively noted: "The exemption of nurses shows that the real evil lies not in the color of the skin but in the relation the colored person sustains to the white. If he is a dependent [integration on railroad coaches] may be endured: if he is not, his presence is insufferable."[18]

This 1890 segregation law was premised on notions of black inferiority.

Interaction with whites on an equal basis challenged these notions and threatened to overthrow the racial thinking that developed during slavery. Consequently, the white-controlled legislature attempted to assure white superiority. Segregation meant enforcement of the concept of black inferiority; anyone breaching this precept could, under the statute, be fined and sent to prison. The true meaning of the segregation statute would become obvious when someone challenged the law as unconstitutional.

Should Someone Seven-eighths White Be Sent to Jail for Sitting in the "Whites Only" Compartment?

In 1892, Louisiana attempted to prosecute Homer Plessy for violating their segregation statute. According to the statement Plessy filed in state court, he "paid for a first class passage on the East Louisiana Railway from New Orleans to Covington." [19] He took a seat in the whites-only compartment, but a conductor ordered him to move. When Plessy refused, the conductor and a police officer "forcibly ejected" him from the train and imprisoned him in the New Orleans parish jail. [20] Thus, Plessy was prosecuted for allegedly violating the 1890 law.

It is instructive to view the background to Plessy's case. This history has been thoughtfully described by Judge John Minor Wisdom of New Orleans, now Senior Judge of the United States Court of Appeals for the Fifth Circuit and one of the great federal judges in the history of America. Professor Jack Bass has described Judge Wisdom as the "scholar of a court that served as the legal battleground for the civil rights movement." [21] On April 18, 1972, Judge Wisdom gave the George Abel Dreyfous Lecture on Civil Liberties at Tulane Law School, and he discussed *Plessy v. Ferguson* in great detail. Judge Wisdom was kind enough to share with me his lecture paper, which has never been published.

Judge Wisdom noted part of the legal strategy employed in bringing suit to challenge the 1890 segregation law:

> The Committee [Comité des Citoyens] also employed a New Orleans attorney, James C. Walker, a white criminal lawyer and one-time Republican, to assist [Albion Winegar] Tourgée. Walker approached the railroads and found them *not* uncooperative for a proposed test case. One railroad could not work with him because it did not enforce the law. The other railroads were sympathetic because of the extra costs of enforcement. [Louis A.] Martinet wrote Tourgée "They want to help us but dread public opinion." Tourgée advised that a "nearly white" person should be chosen for the test case. Martinet objected that in New Orleans "persons of tolera-

bly fair complexion, even if unmistakably colored, enjoy a large degree of immunity from the accursed prejudice."[22]

In the first test case, Daniel Desdunes, "son of Rodolphe Desdunes, an octoroon," was arrested and charged under the "penal clause" of the law, and Judge John Ferguson sustained Desdunes's plea of not guilty "on the ground that the law did not apply to interstate travel." The case did not reach the Supreme Court of Louisiana.[23] A second case, involving Homer Plessy, was then used to test the law. Judge Wisdom described how Plessy's case began:

> Plessy boarded the East Louisiana Railroad. . . . He informed the conductor that he was a Negro as he took his seat in a coach reserved for white passengers. A New Orleans detective, apparently having previous information of the plan, arrested Plessy when he refused to move to the Jim Crow car. The case was assigned to Judge Ferguson's division and to Lionel Adams, Assistant District Attorney for the Parish of Orleans, to try.[24]

Ironic in light of the legal legacy of his case, Homer Plessy alleged that he was "of mixed descent, in the proportion of seven eighths Caucasian and one eighth African blood; that the mixture of colored blood was not discernible in him."[25] He later refused to admit that he was "in any sense or in any proportion a colored man."[26] Counsel for Plessy argued:

> The crime, then, for which he became liable to imprisonment so far as the court can ascertain, was that a person of seven-eighths Caucasian blood insisted on sitting peacefully and quietly in a car the state of Louisiana had commanded the company to set aside exclusively for the white race. Where on earth should he have gone? Will the court hold that a single drop of African blood is sufficient to color a whole ocean of Caucasian whiteness?[27]

Although to some these facts about racial composition and distinctions may seem trivial, they were in fact *vital* to the prosecution and to the constitutional challenge. How Louisiana defined who was black determined whether Plessy could be prosecuted. If he were legally white, not only was he immune from this prosecution but he might have also had a right to collect damages from the railroad for being treated as a black man.[28]

The Majority's Legitimization of Racism

Plessy challenged the Louisiana statute on the grounds that it violated both the Thirteenth and Fourteenth Amendments. The Supreme Court's majority opinion, written by Justice Henry Billings Brown, dismissed Plessy's argument that the statute violated the Thirteenth Amendment. The Court ruled that segregation in public accommodations did not amount to servitude or a state of bondage for African ·Americans.[29] The majority also concluded that the statute's use of a legal distinction "founded in the color of the two races" was not violative of the Constitution.[30] It rejected the idea that the requirement of racial segregation "stamps the colored race with a badge of inferiority," and concluded that "[i]f this be so, it is . . .' solely because the colored race chooses to put that construction upon it."[31]

As one reads neatly printed Supreme Court opinions, there is a tendency to give some presumption of rationality to the writings because of their format and dignified style. Yet on great issues of public policy, some opinions do nothing more than to mask with civil terminology a justice's intention to distort the record or to give an imprimatur of logic that does not exist to those familiar with the evolution of the precedential case law. There can be no more deceptive approach than when a Court *improperly* cites and relies upon cases as having precedential significance in determining the case in issue.

In finding that segregation laws were constitutional and permissive, the Court relied on a number of cases that were decided *prior to* the enactment of the Thirteenth, Fourteenth, and Fifteenth Amendments. The.Court relied on *Roberts v. City of Boston,*[32] an 1850 decision allowing school segregation. Not only was *Roberts* rendered prior to the Civil War and the post-war constitutional amendments, but even before the Court had decided in *Dred Scott v. Sandford*[33] that African Americans could not be citizens and had "no rights which the white man was bound to respect."[34] The majority's use of *Roberts* as a relevant precedent was a nullification of the significant legal advancements which guaranteed a broader base of equality to African Americans through the Thirteenth, Fourteenth, and Fifteenth Amendments.

Another pre-Civil War amendments case the *Plessy* majority relied on was *West Chester & Philadelphia Railroad Company v. Miles,*[35] in which the Pennsylvania Supreme Court used a bizarre mixture of natural law and racial fears to justify racial segregation on trains. In 1867, prior to the passage of the Fourteenth Amendment, the Pennsylvania court asserted:

> Why the Creator made one [race] black and the other white, we know not; but the fact is apparent, and the races distinct, each producing its own kind, and following the peculiar law of its constitution. Conceding equality, with natures as perfect and rights as sacred, yet God has made them dissimilar, with those natural instincts and feelings which He always imparts to His creatures when He intends that they shall not overstep the natural boundaries He has assigned to them. The natural law which forbids their intermarriage and that social amalgamation which leads to a corruption of races, is as clearly divine as that which imparted to them different natures. The tendency of intimate social intermixture is to amalgamation, contrary to the law of races.[36]

The United States Supreme Court's reliance on a pre-Fourteenth Amendment case, which announced that "God has made" African Americans "dissimilar," suggested that, as to the Court, the intent and the meaning of the Civil War and Reconstruction constitutional amendments were irrelevant.

The Reasonableness of Racism

The Court met another of Plessy's arguments with an implicit reincarnation of the precept of inferiority developed in slavery jurisprudence. Plessy asked, if the State of Louisiana were permitted to segregate on the basis of race, then what prevented it from segregating on other grounds, such as hair color?[37] The majority responded that a state's regulation must be "reasonable, and extend only to such laws as are enacted in good faith for the promotion for the public good, and not for the annoyance or oppression of a particular class."[38] But, by what rationale does one determine what is reasonable? There is no litmus test for reasonableness, as when one is distinguishing an acid from a base. The Court held that, in evaluating reasonableness, states could act "with reference to the established usages, customs and traditions of the people."[39]

In ruling that "usages, customs and traditions" were acceptable criteria for determining whether a law was reasonable, the Court did nothing more than to incorporate into constitutional law all of the slavery jurisprudence that had supposedly been washed away with the recent constitutional amendments. Slavery laws and jurisprudence were based on the precept of inferiority. Yet the Court dictated that states, under the guise of "usages, customs and traditions," could revert to the past biases, prejudices, and discrimination that had provided the rationale for slavery.

Was the "Underlying Fallacy" of Plessy's Argument Solely in the Mind-Set of African Americans, Perceiving Themselves as Inferior?

The *Plessy* Court concluded that the Louisiana statute separating the races did not suggest the inferiority of African Americans. "If this be so," the Court argued, "it is not by reason of anything found in the act, but solely because the colored race chooses to put that construction upon it."[40] In his dissent, Justice John Harlan swept aside the distortion by pointing to the true intent of the legislators: to exclude African Americans from compartments occupied by whites. Harlan noted: "Every one knows that the statute in question had its origin in the purpose, not so much to exclude white persons from railroad cars occupied by blacks, as to exclude colored people from coaches occupied by or assigned to white persons."[41]

If the races were in fact on equal terms before the law, then a conductor's improper assignment of a white to a blacks-only car should cause no injury to anyone. But the Court's opinion failed to hold that a state could not allow a damage award to any white for his or her loss of reputation of being white by being misassigned to a "colored" coach. The Court seemed to suggest that, under state law, a white person was entitled to damages when his or her reputation of being white had been denied or disregarded by the conductor.[42] In short, after their earlier deceptive language that any perceptions of inferiority must be in the minds of African Americans, the Court nevertheless protected whites by ruling that Plessy might be entitled to damages from the railroad *if* Plessy were white under Louisiana law *and* he had been treated as if he were African-American.

In the last paragraph of their opinion, the Court noted:

> It is true that the question of the proportion of colored blood necessary to constitute a colored person, as distinguished from a white person, is one upon which there is a difference of opinion in the different States, some holding that any visible admixture of black blood stamps the person as belonging to the colored race; others that it depends upon the preponderance of blood; and still others that the predominance of white blood must only be in the proportion of three fourths. But these are questions to be determined under the laws of each State and are not properly put in issue in this case. Under the allegations of his [Plessy's] petition it may undoubtedly become a question of importance whether, under the laws of Louisiana, the petitioner belongs to the white or colored race.[43]

Justice John Marshall Harlan's Dissent: Was It an Omniscient Egalitarian Pronouncement or Was It a Muted Racist's Statement?

By any fair evaluation of his substantive opinions, Justice John Marshall Harlan was one of the ten or twelve truly great justices to have ever served on the Court. He served on the Supreme Court from 1877 to 1911. When one compares his views with those of his colleagues and contemporaries of the late nineteenth century, Justice Harlan seems omniscient and heroic. There is no doubt that the status and daily lives of African Americans during the twentieth century would have been far better if the majority of the Supreme Court in 1896 had adopted the constitutional views expressed in Justice Harlan's powerful dissent. Nevertheless, for the "purists" who choose to use a twentieth-century lens to examine someone who primarily was a nineteenth-century jurist, flaws can be found in even his most memorable dissent. From my perspective, it is more fair to compare Justice Harlan with his judicial contemporaries of 1896 than to expect of him the more expansive democratic insights that were exemplified decades after his death by luminaries such as Chief Justice Earl Warren, or Justice William Brennan and Justice Thurgood Marshall; these three justices' views reached their maturity many decades after Justice Harlan's dissent.

The tensions as to how one should evaluate Justice Harlan are exemplified in one extraordinary nine-sentence paragraph of his several-paged dissent. For devotees of Justice Harlan, there is a tendency to focus exclusively on the last six sentences of this paragraph:

> But in view of the Constitution, in the eye of the law, there is in this country no superior, dominant, ruling class of citizens. There is no caste here. Our Constitution is color-blind, and neither knows nor tolerates classes among citizens. In respect of civil rights, all citizens are equal before the law. The humblest is the peer of the most powerful. The law regards man as man, and takes no account of his surroundings or of his color when his civil rights as guaranteed by the supreme law of the land are involved.[44]

Harlan's most severe critics would stress the first three sentences of the same paragraph, which may dilute or minimize the egalitarian language which I have just quoted. These pivotal three sentences read as follows:

> The white race deems itself to be the dominant race in this country. And so it is, in prestige, in achievements, in education, in wealth and in power. So, I doubt not, it will continue to be for all time, if it remains true to its great heritage and holds fast to the principles of constitutional liberty.[45]

From my point of view, there is no value in having a prolonged debate on whether Justice Harlan's statement was racist or merely factual, that "The white race deems itself to be the dominant race in this country," or characterizing his apparent opinion that "it will continue to be for all time, if it remains true to its great heritage and holds fast to the principles of constitutional liberty." For me, the more important fact is that, if four other justices had adopted Harlan's view, African Americans would not have suffered from the legitimization of racism that *Plessy* caused. Justice Harlan recognized the consequences of the pernicious doctrine that the majority had approved.

He correctly observed that, in his opinion, "the judgment this day rendered will, in time, prove to be quite as pernicious as the decision made by this tribunal in the *Dred Scott case*."[46] Harlan the former slaveowner recognized the cruelty that this opinion, where a majority of the justices were not Southerners, would impose upon African Americans. There was a pragmatic insight when Harlan commented that: "It is, therefore, to be regretted that this high tribunal, the final expositor of the fundamental law of the land, has reached the conclusion that it is competent for a State to regulate the enjoyment by citizens of their civil rights solely upon the basis of race."[47]

The Consequences of the "Separate But Equal" Doctrine

Although many lower courts had explicitly endorsed "Jim Crow segregation" prior to *Plessy*,[48] the significance of the Supreme Court's affirmation of the doctrine of "separate but equal" in 1896 cannot be overestimated. The Court's approval was the final and most devastating judicial step in the legitimization of racism under state law. In numerous subsequent school cases, state and federal courts continued to approve racial discrimination and segregation; most of the courts or counsel of record in those cases cited or relied upon *Plessy* as support for expansive endorsements of racial subjugation.[49]

From a race-relations standpoint, *Plessy v. Ferguson* was one of the two most venal decisions ever handed down by the United States Supreme Court.[50] It is equalled only by the pernicious *Dred Scott v. Sandford.* Most recent scholars who have carefully studied the *Dred Scott* case have concluded that, as a matter of constitutional law, the *Dred Scott* case was wrongly decided, and that it can be explained solely by recognizing the Court's machinations to issue a political decision rather than principled adjudication.[51] Nevertheless, in many respects, the decision of the seven justices[52] in the majority in *Plessy v. Ferguson* was even less justifiable than the rationale proffered in *Dred Scott.* Viewing the majority opinion in *Dred Scott* in its most favorable light, one could argue that the drafters of the original Constitution had not explicitly guaranteed any citizenship rights for free African Americans and that, therefore, it was not totally irrational for the Court to reach its conclusion that an African-American man could not be a citizen of the United States. But when *Plessy* arose, it was after the Constitution had declared with specificity that African Americans were citizens of the United States and were entitled to the full privileges and immunities of citizenship. Morevoer, the impact of the decision in *Plessy* was even more devastating to African Americans than that of *Dred Scott.*

Because it sanctioned the continuing oppression of African Americans, *Plessy* was one of the most catastrophic racial decisions ever rendered by an American appellate court. After *Plessy* sanctioned the concept of "separate but equal," the system in practice was separate and *un*equal. As Professor Derrick Bell notes:

> In 1915, South Carolina was spending an average of $23.76 on the education of each white child and $2.91 on that of each black child. As late as 1931, six Southern states (Alabama, Arkansas, Florida, Georgia, and North

and South Carolina) spent less than one third as much for black children as [it did] for whites, and ten years later this figure had risen to only 44 percent. At the time of the 1954 decision in Brown v. Board of Education, the South as a whole was spending on the average $165 a year for a white pupil, and $115 for a black.[53]

Although the Court's erroneous construction of the Fourteenth Amendment prevailed for over a half-century, the overwhelming consensus today is that *Plessy* was an untenable statement of the law that set in motion an era of oppression from which our nation still has not fully recovered. The view that *Plessy* was an untenable statement of the law is shared by jurists and lawyers with varying philosophies of federalism. From the 1970s to the 1990s, conservative Supreme Court justices and even Reagan and Bush Administration officials, as well as centrist justices of the Supreme Court declared that this case, *Plessy v. Ferguson,* was "wrong" when it was decided. Dissenting in *Fullilove v. Klutznick,* Justice Potter Stewart, joined by now-Chief Justice William Rehnquist, expressly stated that *"Plessy v. Ferguson* was wrong" and cited with approval Justice Harlan's famous dissent.[54] William Bradford Reynolds, former Assistant Attorney General for Civil Rights and a noted conservative, has asserted that "racial classifications [such as those found in *Plessy*] are wrong—morally wrong—and ought not to be tolerated in any form or for any reason."[55] In a plurality concurring opinion in *Planned Parenthood of Southeastern Pennsylvania v. Casey,* Justices Kennedy, O'Connor, and Souter wrote, "[W]e think *Plessy* was wrong the day it was decided. . . ."[56]

In short, had the majority of the *Plessy* Court realized, as Chief Justice Rehnquist now does, that their decision was wrong, our nation might never have needed a *Brown v. Board of Education,*[57] *Missouri ex rel. Gaines v. Canada,*[58] *Sweatt v. Painter,*[59] or *McLaurin v. Oklahoma State Regents*[60] in the field of education, because state-imposed segregation would not have been sanctioned by federal law. There also might have been no need for some of the other significant civil-rights cases that were initiated solely because the Supreme Court had held in *Plessy* that states could treat African Americans differently from how they treated the majority white population or any of the other major ethnic, religious, or national origin groups in this country. Even though many other racist forces were operating within American society—including the explicitly racist pronouncements by United States presidents, congressmen, and state governmental officials[61]—the historical oppression of African Americans in the United States would have been far less pervasive had, in the Supreme Court, the 1896 views of Justice John Harlan prevailed.

10

TOO INFERIOR TO BE
THEIR NEIGHBOR

It is shown by philosophy, experience, and legal decisions, to say nothing of Divine Writ, that . . . the races of the earth shall preserve their racial integrity by living socially by themselves.—Brief for City of Louisville, Kentucky, as filed in U.S. Supreme Court in Buchanan v. Warley (1917).[1]

ROM the earliest times slavery advocates have justified its cruelty by way of the Bible and reliance on religious doctrine. So too the City of Louisville, Kentucky—fifty-four years after the Emancipation Proclamation and fifty-two years after the Thirteenth Amendment—justified its residential segregation ordinance by calling on Divine Writ and various racist legal precepts.

One could write volumes on the housing issues. Just as in other fields, such as in education and employment, the Ten Precepts of Slavery Jurisprudence in the housing context have particular relevance. The precept of inferiority[2] was used in the housing area for the exclusion of, and or the substantial segregation, of African Americans. Many books or chapters have been written about the re-incorporation of slavery jurisprudence concepts—through the manipulation of the law—into residential legislation and court decisions. In this volume it would be impossible to cover the totality of those racial housing experiences. Nevertheless, I focus here, for illustrative purposes, only on a few aspects of the manipulation of the legislative and judicial concepts. These manipulations were predicated on the assumptions of whites in power that African Americans were too inferior to be their neighbors. These whites in power therefore used the legal process to implement their racial prejudices.

During the early 1900s, most American state courts located in southern and borderline states interpreted the Constitution in a racist manner.[3] Not only did these state courts sanction racial housing segregation under law, but they encouraged its application in the broadest and most pervasive context. Moreover, in upholding such segregation, these courts used judicial reasoning that was analytically inconsistent and philosophically biased. Their reasoning reflected the values and personal prejudices of some judges who viewed African Americans as different from and inferior to whites. Thus, state and city governments could do to African Americans what they could not do to other Americans.

While often the courts were reluctant to state explicitly that they viewed African Americans as inferior, their implicit premise had to be their envisioning African Americans as inferior because racial inferiority was the only justification for separating only African Americans—when no white ethnic, religious, or national origin group was separated so comprehensively by law. There was no statutory or judicial fiat that separated Irish, Italians, Jews, or Catholics into separate neighborhoods. The language in many of the cases reveals that the state courts perceived of African Americans as inferior. As an example, in *Berea College v. Commonwealth*,[4] the Kentucky Court of Appeals concluded that it was a "fair exercise of the police power to prohibit the teaching of the white and negro races together."[5] The court analogized integrated education as creating a danger of "the mingling of the blood of the white and negro races by interbreeding—[and thus] harmful to the welfare of society."[6] Though the court thought that the interbreeding of African Americans and whites was harmful to society, it did not seem to be concerned with the interbreeding of white Christians and white Jews or white persons of different national origins. Its rationale is explainable only on the basis of an assumption that African Americans were inferior and as such the racial intermingling would diminish the qualities of whites.

In 1899, three years after the decision in *Plessy v. Ferguson*, W.E.B. Du Bois published *The Philadelphia Negro*.[7] Du Bois provided the now renowned map of the Seventh Ward in four colors, which illustrated African-American residences dispersed throughout the city, rather than restricted to any one zone. This pattern was typical of most American cities of the period.[8]

In the early twentieth century the legislatures and courts of nearly every southern state, with the full sanction of the state governments and the white power structures, approved racist doctrines in the housing area. These policies authorized a comprehensive ghettoization program for their major urban areas.[9] Municipal segregation zoning ordinances were passed in over a dozen cities. These actions followed Baltimore's passage in 1910 of the first such ordinance directed exclusively at African Americans.[10] In fact, some scholars refer to segregation zoning statutes as the "Baltimore idea."[11] Many other cities in the North and South delayed passage of similar measures until the validity of these ordinances was decided.[12]

A 1911 Baltimore ordinance called for "preserving peace, preventing conflict and ill feeling between white and colored races in Baltimore City, and promoting the general welfare of the city by providing, so far as practicable, for use of separate blocks by white and black people for residences, churches and schools."[13] Members of the Baltimore city council had conceptualized the ordinance with no specific authorization from the state legislature.[14] Its formulation and passage were a direct response to attempts by African Americans to move into neighborhoods that by 1910 had become all white.[15] The plight of George McMechen and his family is a typical example of this pattern, which occurred in other states as well.

In 1910, George McMechen purchased a house in Eutaw Place, a previously all-white section of Baltimore.[16] The family was harassed and required police protection.[17] Shortly after the McMechens moved into their new neighborhood, over 10,000 members of the community petitioned the city council in the hope of preventing future intrusions.[18] In response to this petition, the city council implemented the "Baltimore idea."[19]

The Baltimore ordinance provided for residential segregation by street blocks. African Americans were prohibited from moving into or assembling in residences located on blocks that were occupied by whites, and vice versa.[20] The ordinance, however, was inapplicable to mixed blocks where both African Americans and whites lived.[21] Furthermore, the ordinance prohibited the establishment of African-American schools or churches on blocks where the residents were all white, and vice versa.[22] Domestic servants were exempted from the statute's coverage.[23]

The experiences of John Gurry served as a basis for the legal challenge to the merits of Baltimore's racial housing segregation ordinance. Gurry, an African American, purchased a house on a block then used as residences only by whites. He was indicted for violating the Baltimore housing ordinance.

The trial court held that the ordinance was invalid and unenforceable,[24] finding that enforcement of the ordinance would depopulate the "great many blocks" occupied "in part" by African Americans and whites, by prohibiting both African Americans and whites from residing in these areas.[25] An African American could not, under the ordinance, move into a block occupied in whole *or in part* by whites, and vice versa. "When, then," the court held, "by the definition in the Ordinance a block can be at the same time both a white block and a colored block, it would seem unnecessary to say that the Ordinance is invalid and unenforceable to punish either white or colored persons."[26]

On appeal,[27] on grounds different from those asserted by the trial court, the Maryland Court of Appeals held the ordinance violated the state constitution.[28] Contrary to the lower court, the Court of Appeals reasoned that the ordinance permitted both African Americans and whites to move into mixed blocks.[29] The appeals court, however, concluded that the ordinance was unreasonable on other grounds and found that the ordinance withdrew the vested property rights of white owners who might wish to reside in their property located on all-African-American blocks.[30] In so finding, the court described the potential harm the ordinance could inflict on vested property rights:

> If the traverser, for example, on May 15, 1911, when the ordinance was passed, owned a dwelling in what was made a white block, he could not under the ordinance move into it, although it was perfectly lawful for him to own it when he became owner and to use it as a dwelling. He might be unable to rent it to a white person, and as a colored person was prohibited from moving into it he could not rent it to a colored person, and he could not under the ordinance move into it himself. The result would be that the house would remain idle, unless he could sell it, . . . although when he acquired it he had the right under the Constitution and laws of Maryland to occupy it as his dwelling, or to rent it to any person, white or colored, to be used for legitimate purposes.[31]

Thus the court concluded that such a withdrawal of vested property rights was unreasonable, especially without specific authorization from the state's legislature.[32]

The most despicable aspect of the *Gurry* opinion was that even as it invalidated a racial housing segregation ordinance, the court emphasized that the property rights protected were principally those of whites. The court's language was telling in terms of institutionalizing the inferiority precept. After affirming the police power of the state to protect the welfare of its African-American and white citizens, the court argued that such a statute placed some whites in a position in which it would be difficult to recoup the full value of their homes. The Maryland Court of Appeals explained:

> [I]t might be that a white person had a valuable and attractive house in a "block" which was otherwise occupied by colored people. . . . *To deny him such rights* [to move into it or to rent it to a white person] *would be a practical confiscation of his property, for his house might be of a character he would not rent to a colored person. . . .*[33]

After noting its extensive concern regarding the adverse impact of the ordinance on white persons, the court almost as an afterthought noted that "of course the same conditions might exist when the owner of the one house was colored and the other residents of the block were white, although probably not so likely to happen."[34]

The logic of this decision is based on the idea that African Americans, as inferior beings, are not capable of taking care of property. Even in cases like *Gurry,* in which the municipal segregation statutes were overturned, the courts presumed the inferiority of African Americans in their decisions. The primary concern of the court was that there be no economic diminution of the property rights of white citizens.

The court understood that the neighborhood, composed of individual homes, has traditionally been a center for the expression of public civility. This occurs through the upkeep of the physical structure of the home and lawn. These patterns of civility are understood to distinguish those who dominate from those who "naturally" have no entitlement to power. There are many not too subtle sociological assumptions involved in these implicit judicial premises. The neighborhood is a measure of equal dignity derived from common participation in a public sphere or multiple site accessible to all.[35] Anyone who participates in the setting of residential superiority, the white neighborhood, can—at least in theory—express the values associated with civility.[36] The segregated neighborhood serves as a mechanism by which those who are residentially superior (whites) maintain an exclusive monopoly on vehicles for the proper expression of "civilized" patterns of conduct. The *Gurry* decision affirmed perceptions on the inferiority of the African American by asserting his inability to properly take care of property.

Although the court overturned the statute in *Gurry,* it affirmed the police power of the state to avoid social conflict, and recognized (without challenging) the exception for domestic servants who were permitted to live with or near their employers.[37] Since it was unlikely any whites would be working for African Americans as their domestics, the rule amounted to a recognition of black inferiority. If African Americans could not move onto blocks with whites, then patterns in which the two races would share residential space independent of ties of servitude could not exist. In other words, the only social patterns in which African Americans and whites would be seen residing in close proximity would be those in which African Americans were in the inferior position of servants. The goal of these municipal segregation ordinances, thus similar to *Plessy,* was not simply to separate the races to ensure social cohesion, but rather to brand African Americans with the mark of inferiority through the arm of the law.

The precept of inferiority presumed that African Americans were alien and inferior beings. The dominating white powers wished to avoid incorporating African Americans into their collective self-consciousness by preventing them from moving to blocks that were predominantly white.[38] Although some states voided municipal segregation statutes to protect white property rights, it was not until 1917, in the leading case of *Buchanan v. Warley,* that the Supreme Court construed and struck down these ordinances. The Court declared in *Buchanan* that the state's power to ensure public peace "cannot be accomplished by laws or ordinances which deny rights created or protected by the Federal Constitution."[39]

But what constitutional "rights" were violated by these segregation ordinances? The Court in *Buchanan* was not concerned with the constitutional right of African Americans to choose where they wanted to live. Rather, the Court sought to ensure to white property holders the right to sell their land to whomever they chose. The Court was anxious to assure the nation that it was protecting *"property* rights" not *"social* rights." Thus Justice William Day, for a unanimous Court, concluded that these Kentucky ordinances do "not deal with the *social* rights of men, but with those fundamental rights in *property* which it was intended to secure upon the same terms to citizens of every race and color."[40]

Justice Day stressed that "[t]he right which the ordinance annulled was the civil right of a white man to dispose of his property if he saw fit to do so to a person of color and of a colored person to make such disposition to a white person."[41] The Supreme Court rejected the bugaboos raised by Louisville as to public peace, purity of the races, and depreciation of property because these concerns were not a proper basis for the state to deprive a person of the right to sell property.[42] In characterizing the issue in *Buchanan*, Justice Day reasoned that every landowner possessed the common-law right to occupy his own house, or to sell or lease it to whomever he or she pleased.[43] Counsel for the City of Louisville counterargued that only the rights of African Americans were at issue, and that Buchanan, who was a white man, had no right to assert the claim of constitutional violation.[44]

The decision in *Buchanan* could be construed as one of the most progressive decisions pertaining to segregation before World War I because it voided the racial segregation ordinances. At the time, the decision was greeted with a great deal of enthusiasm by many African-American and liberal white Americans,[45] much the way the decision in *Brown* was applauded decades later.

Although the United States Supreme Court in *Buchanan* held that municipal housing-segregation statutes violated the Constitution, segregationists did not abandon their position. One commentary by a Southerner, writing ten years after *Buchanan*, exemplifies the racial attitudes that continued to motivate this struggle:

> [W]hile the two races should be accorded equal treatment, the public welfare and the highest social interests of both Caucasian and African can best be secured by preserving each people in its racial purity. Commingling of the homes . . . of white men and black men gives unnecessary provocation

for miscegenation, race riots, lynchings, and other forms of social malaise, existent when a child-like, undisciplined, inferior race is living in close contact with a people of more mature civilization.[46]

Many whites with similar attitudes continued attempts to prevent African Americans' integration into predominantly white neighborhoods. The battle over residential segregation was far from over.

One could argue that the *Buchanan* case was of minimal importance because white owners were still able to implement racist policies through restrictive covenants and other private devices that precluded African Americans from moving into "their areas."[47] The restrictive covenant, by which property owners agreed not to sell to African Americans, became the new foundation of what would become the post-World War I ghetto.[48]

In the years prior to World War II, social scientists began to realize that residential segregation would have deleterious effects on the African-American population. Gunnar Myrdal criticized black residential segregation in his classic 1944 study *An American Dilemma.*[49] By the time Drake and Cayton published *Black Metropolis* around World War II, the widely scattered residences that Du Bois described in *The Philadelphia Negro* had been completely transformed: a new map would have revealed areas that were nearly all African-American. The courts had consistently upheld the restrictive covenant to institutionalize black residential inferiority. As a result, almost two-thirds of African Americans lived in communities that were over 90 percent African-American.[50] By 1948, when *Shelley v. Kraemer*[51] established the illegality of restrictive covenants, the great "Black Metropolises" of the United States had already been formed with the sanction of prior cases.

To attempt to comprehend the contemporary social and economic position of African Americans without understanding the importance of residential segregation as a partial cause of the existence of an underclass would be futile. Without taking into account the effects of residential segregation, sociologists and demographers cannot provide adequate reasons for the overrepresentation of African Americans and Puerto Ricans in the ranks of the poor and the confinement of the underclass to older cities of the Northeast and Midwest.[52] Given the trends in residential inferiority since *Plessy*, "the geographic concentration of black poverty was *inevitable.*"[53] Where residential segregation accompanied economic decline, the effects on urban neighborhoods were devastating.[54]

When Kenneth Clark testified in *Brown v. Board of Education* that African-American children found white dolls more attractive than African-American dolls, he firmly believed that if America desegregated its schools, the precept of black inferiority could be eliminated. Indeed, after *Brown,*

Clark and others were optimistic that within a decade, America would be free of its "moral schizophrenia."[55] Decades later, however, despite some educational desegregation, residential inferiority remains a deep-rooted reality in American society.

Some of the earliest victories against segregation overturned residential segregation. Yet, ironically, it was in the lingering existence of residential segregation that the precept of inferiority became firmly imprinted. Who would have thought that the separate sections of cities which African Americans came to inhabit would become almost impossible to dismantle through the legal system?

While substantial de facto racial segregation still exists in the United States,[56] the plight of African Americans today would be *far worse* if the state governments had been able to enforce their original policies requiring racial segregation. In reversing discriminatory state court decisions in *Buchanan v. Warley,* the Supreme Court adopted a more "equalitarian"[57] jurisprudence.

Even after we recognize the devastating impact of racially restrictive covenants and those cases decided after *Buchanan* holding that racially restrictive covenants could be judicially enforced,[58] *Buchanan* was of profound importance in applying a brake to decelerate what would have been run-away racism in the United States. Though it did not come close to assuring open housing in America, at least the decision removed the legislative sword that cities were holding over the heads of African Americans to enclose them in only the most run-down, narrowly confined, and congested areas.[59]

11

UNEQUAL JUSTICE IN THE STATE CRIMINAL JUSTICE SYSTEM

[Can] American justice, American liberty, American civilization, American law, and American Christianity . . . be made to include and protect alike and forever all American citizens in the rights which have been guaranteed to them by the organic and fundamental laws of the land?—Frederick Douglass[1]

Race Matters[2]

CHISELED in marble over the entrance to the United States Supreme Court is the ultimate American aspiration: "Equal Justice Under Law." Also written with careful thought, the Preamble of the United States Constitution reads:

> We the People of the United States, in Order to form a more perfect Union, *establish Justice,* insure domestic Tranquility, provide for the common defence, promote the general Welfare, and secure the Blessings of Liberty to ourselves and our Posterity, do ordain and establish this Constitution for the United States of America.[3]

Thus, after formation of "a more perfect Union," the next national priority was to *"establish Justice."* But the American irony has been that, even after the Civil War, the judicial system has not been one of *"Equal* Justice Under Law." From a racial standpoint the system has been one dominated often by the *un*equal justice imposed upon African Americans.

To use Cornel West's felicitous phrase, "Race [m]atters."[4] In the criminal justice system the fact of one's race sometimes has been a critical factor in determining whether prosecutions are initiated or terminated, whether the jury returns a verdict of guilty or not guilty, whether certain judicial instructions are given to the jury, whether witnesses are or are not believed, and in determining the formulation of ultimate judicial rulings. I do not want to be misunderstood. I am not suggesting that factors of race have been decisive in *all* cases or in the *majority* of cases. I am submitting, however, that during the nineteenth and twentieth centuries, the issue of race has mattered in a substantial number of cases. As we approach the end of the twentieth century, it is to be hoped that there indeed has been a diminution in the number of cases in which the issue of race has been significant. Unfortunately, I remain confident that even today there are many cases whose outcome can be explained only by way of racial considerations. I recognize these statements are serious indictments of the criminal justice system, but nevertheless, I submit that the cases that will be discussed hereafter corroborate my general thesis. In 1996, despite the innumerable words espoused by lawyers, lawyer-politicians, and law professors proclaiming the progress of American law, for many there still persists a nagging doubt as to whether the legacy of legally sanctioned racism will be eradicated in this decade or even in the next century.[5]

This chapter explores efforts to move from the legal order of the colonial and antebellum periods, with its patent racism and unequal justice, to a more neutral system that does not reinforce the values of slavery jurisprudence, including the precept of inferiority, in which African Americans are perceived and treated as inferior. As discussed below, the movement theoretically away from a judicial system marked by unequal justice has nevertheless shown a troubling pattern of racist actions and statements that have diverted the journey from slavery jurisprudence and the precept of black inferiority.

Racial segregation and other forms of discrimination have a long and tragic history in the criminal justice system of many state courts. When one race receives harsher treatment than another, the court is announcing to the world that one group is perceived as superior and the other inferior, the latter not being entitled to the quality of justice that is assured to the dominant group. The entire antebellum period was so infected with racism that it was the remote exception, rather than the rule, when witnesses, defendants, or litigants who were African-American were treated just like everyone else.

Racism in the courts is reflective of significant symptoms, signals, and symbols of racism in the broader society. Many state court cases exemplify the unfair treatment of African-American citizens by courts—both northern and southern—despite the abolition of slavery and the enactment of the Thirteenth, Fourteenth, and Fifteenth Amendments. These cases are an endorsement of the slavery jurisprudence embodied in the precept of inferiority. Post-Civil War history lends itself to the question whether in general the courts have been protectors of or impediments to African Americans' exercise of the right to equal justice.

The Appeal.

"This Fourth of July is yours, not mine. You may rejoice, I must mourn. To drag a man in fetters to the grand illuminated temple of liberty, and call upon him to join you in joyous anthems, were inhuman mockery and sacrilegious irony. . . . I say it with a sad sense of the disparity between us. I am not included within the pale of this glorious anniversary. . . . The blessings in which you, this day, rejoice, are not enjoyed in common. The rich inheritance of justice, liberty, prosperity and independence, bequeathed by your fathers, is shared by you, not by me. The sunlight that brought light and healing to you, has brought stripes and death to me."—Frederick Douglass (July 1852). *(Culver Pictures)*

THE TANEY COURT: (From top left to right, each row) James Wayne, John Catron, Peter Vivian Daniel, John McLean, Roger B. Taney, Samuel Nelson, John Campbell, Benjamin R. Curtis, Robert Grier. "[A]t the time of the Declaration of Independence, and when the Constitution of the United States was framed and adopted . . . [blacks] had no rights which the white man was bound to respect."—*Dred Scott v. Sandford* (1857). *(Photograph by Handy Studios, Collection of the Supreme Court of the United States)*

The First Vote. *(Culver Pictures)*

The First Colored Senator and Representatives (1872).
(Library of Congress)

"[Can] American justice, American liberty, American civilization, American law, and American Christianity . . . be made to include and protect alike and forever *all* American citizens in the rights which have been guaranteed to them by the organic and fundamental laws of the land?"—Frederick Douglass (1891). *(Artwork by Karen Watson)*

Frederick Douglass
(Culver Pictures)

THE FULLER COURT: Edward Douglas White, Henry Billings Brown, Horace Gray, Stephen J. Field, Melville W. Fuller, John Marshall Harlan, David J. Brewer, George Shiras, Jr., Rufus Peckham.

Majority Opinion: "The [plaintiff's] argument also assumes that social prejudices may be overcome by legislation, and that equal rights cannot be secured to the negro except by an enforced commingling of the two races. We cannot accept this proposition."

Dissent by Justice John Marshall Harlan: "The destinies of the two races, in this country, are indissolubly linked together, and the interests of both require that the common government of all shall not permit the seeds of race hate to be planted under the sanction of law." —*Plessy v. Ferguson* (1896). *(Collection of the Supreme Court of the United States)*

IDA B. WELLS.

LEFT: Congressman John R. Lynch. "Mr. Speaker, it is not social rights that we desire. We have enough of that already. What we ask is protection in the enjoyment of public rights. Rights which are or should be accorded to every citizen alike . . . if this unjust discrimination is to be longer tolerated by the American people . . . I can only say with sorrow and regret that our boasted civilization is a fraud; our republican institutions a failure; our social system a disgrace; and our religion a complete hypocrisy. . . . Mr. Speaker, I ask, can it be possible that that flag under which [the colored soldiers] fought is to be a shield and a protection to all races and classes of persons except the colored race? God forbid!" —Congressman John R. Lynch from Mississippi speaking before the United States Congress (1875). (Library of Congress)

RIGHT: Ida B. Wells Barnett. "I [had] firmly believed all along that the law was on our side and would, when we appealed to it, give us justice. I feel shorn of that belief and utterly discouraged, and just now, if it were possible, I would gather my race in my arms and fly away with them. O God, is there no redress, no peace, no justice in this land for us? Thou hast always fought the battles of the weak and oppressed. Come to my aid this moment and teach me what to do, for I am sorely, bitterly disappointed. Show us the way even as thou led the children of Israel out of bondage into the promised land."—Ida B. Wells Barnett. (Library of Congress)

Booker T. Washington. "As we have proved our loyalty to you in the past, in nursing your children, watching by the sickbed of your mothers and fathers, and often following them with tear-dimmed eyes to their graves, so in the future, in our humble way, we shall stand by you with a devotion that no foreigner can approach, ready to lay down our lives, if need be, in defence of yours, interlacing our industrial, commercial, civil, and religious life with yours in a way that shall make the interests of both races one. In all things that are purely social we can be as separate as the fingers, yet one as the hand in all things essential to mutual progress."—Booker T. Washington (1895). (Library of Congress)

James K. Vardaman. "I am just as much opposed to Booker Washington as a voter, with all his Anglo-Saxon reinforcements, . . . as I am to the coconut-headed, chocolate-covered, typical little coon, Andy Dodson, who blacks my shoes every morning. Neither is fit to perform the supreme function of citizenship."
—Senator and former Governor James K. Vardaman of Mississippi. *(Library of Congress)*

W.E.B. Du Bois. "One ever feels his twoness,— an American, a Negro; two souls, two thoughts, two unreconciled strivings; two warring ideals in one dark, whose dogged strength alone keeps it from being torn asunder. . . . He would not Africanize America, for America has too much to teach the world and Africa. He would not bleach his Negro soul in a flood of white Americanism, for he knows that Negro blood has a message for the world. He simply wishes to make it possible for a man to be both a Negro and an American, without being cursed and spit upon by his fellows, without having the doors of Opportunity closed roughly in his face."—W.E.B. Du Bois (1903). *(Painting by Winold Reiss, The National Portrait Gallery, Smithsonian Institution)*

Congressman George White. "I want to enter a plea for the colored man, the colored woman, the colored boy, and the colored girl of this country. . . .This, Mr. Chairman, is perhaps the negroes' temporary farewell to the American Congress; but let me say, Phoenix-like he will rise up some day and come again. These parting words are in behalf of an outraged, heart-broken, bruised, and bleeding, but God-fearing people, faithful, industrious, loyal people—rising people, full of potential force. . . . The only apology that I have to make for the earnestness with which I have spoken is that I am pleading for the life, the liberty, the future happiness, and manhood suffrage for one-eighth of the entire population of the United States."
—Farewell speech of George White of North Carolina as the last African American Member of Congress during the Reconstruction period (1901). *(Library of Congress)*

The burning of William Brown in Omaha, Nebraska (1919). *(Culver Pictures)*

From 1939 to the 1960s and until its final covering in the late 1970s, all persons entering the federal courthouse in Jackson, Mississippi, saw a mural depicting blacks as inferiors, picking cotton, strumming a banjo, and serving a master, while all whites had status and positions of power, including the judgeship. *(Photograph by the General Services Administration)*

"Charles Houston was much more than a good teacher and dean. He was a man possessed by his vision and confident of the nature of his special mission. . . .'A lawyer's either a social engineer or he's a parasite on society,' he told all students. A social engineer was a highly skilled, perceptive, sensitive lawyer who understood the Constitution of the United States and knew how to explore its uses in the solving of 'problems of . . . local communities' and in 'bettering conditions of the underprivileged citizens.' The 'written constitution and inertia against . . . amendment give the lawyer wide room for experimentation and enable [black people] to force reforms where they could have no chance through politics.'" —Genna Rae McNeil, *Groundwork: Charles Hamilton Houston and the Struggle for Civil Rights* (1983). *(Painting by Betsy Graves Reyneau, The National Portrait Gallery, Smithsonian Institution)*

THE HUGHES COURT: (Top row) Bejamin Cardozo, Harlan Fiske Stone, Owen J. Roberts, Hugo L. Black. (Bottom row) George Sutherland, James C. McReynolds, Charles Evans Hughes, Louis D. Brandeis, Pierce Butler. "[T]he seminal civil rights decisions of this era redressed some of the most egregious instances of state-sponsored racism. In so doing, the [Supreme] Court took its first tentative steps away from *Plessy* and toward *Brown.*"—A. Leon Higginbotham, Jr., and William C. Smith, "The Hughes Court and the Beginning of the End of 'Separate But Equal' Doctrine," *Minnesota Law Review* (1992). *(Photograph by Harris and Ewing, Collection of the Supreme Court of the United States)*

William H. Hastie. "Saint Francis of Assisi is said to have prayed: 'God grant me the serenity to accept the things I cannot change, the courage to change the things I can and the wisdom to know the difference.' But at times it may be better for the Omnipotent One to give men the wit and the will to continue to plan purposefully and to struggle as best they know how to change things that seem immutable."—William H. Hastie, "Toward an Equalitarian Legal Order, 1930-1950," *The Annals of the American Academy of Political and Social Science* (1973). *(Courtesy of the Art Collection, Harvard Law School)*

THE WARREN COURT: (Top row) Tom C. Clark, Robert H. Jackson, Harold Burton, Sherman Minton. (Bottom row) Felix Frankfurter, Hugo Black, Earl Warren, Stanley Reed, William O. Douglas. "Except for waging and winning the Civil War and World Wars I and II, the decision in the *School Segregation Cases* was probably the most important American governmental act of any kind since the Emancipation Proclamation."—Louis H. Pollak, *The Constitution and the Supreme Court* (1966). *(Photograph by Bachrach, Collection of the Supreme Court of the United States)*

Part of plaintiffs' legal team in *Brown v. Board of Education:* John Scott, James M. Nabrit, Jr., Spottswood W. Robinson III, Frank D. Reeves, Jack Greenberg, Thurgood Marshall, Louis L. Redding, U. Simpson Tate, and George E. C. Hayes (1954). *(Photograph from the NAACP Legal Defense and Educational Fund, Inc.)*

Constance Baker Motley and James Meredith during a tense recess in the controversial case. Behind Meredith is Medgar Evers, the NAACP leader who was later murdered (1962). Constance Baker Motley filed the lawsuit "for James Meredith, against the University of Mississippi. . . . Thurgood had pondered long and hard before ordering her to proceed. He feared bloodshed and didn't want to proceed without being certain that Meredith really wanted to go to Old Miss. . . . [Later,] Meredith entered the university through tear gas and gunfire that cost several lives."
—Jack Greenberg, *Crusaders in the Courts* (1994). *(Photograph by UPI)*

THE REHNQUIST COURT: (Top row) David Souter, Antonin Scalia, Anthony Kennedy, Clarence Thomas. (Bottom row) John Paul Stevens, Byron White, William Rehnquist, Harry Blackmun, Sandra Day O'Connor. One of the Supreme Court's most retrogressive civil rights cases in the 1990s was *Shaw v. Reno*, where the Justices divided five to four. Justice White in dissent said: ". . . the notion that North Carolina's plan, under which whites remain a voting majority in a disproportionate number of congressional districts, and pursuant to which the State has sent its *first* black representatives since Reconstruction to the United States Congress, might have violated appellants' constitutional rights is both a fiction and a departure from settled equal protection principles." Justice Blackmun in dissent said: "It is particularly ironic that the case in which today's majority chooses to abandon settled law and to recognize for the first time this 'analytically distinct' constitutional claim . . . is a challenge by white voters to the plan under which North Carolina has sent black representatives to Congress for the first time since Reconstruction." *See* A. Leon Higginbotham, Jr., Gregory A. Clarick, and Marcella David, "*Shaw v. Reno*: A Mirage of Good Intentions with Devastating Racial Consequences," *Fordham Law Review* (1994). *(Collection of the Supreme Court of the United States)*

Congressperson Eva Clayton
of North Carolina

Congressperson Melvin Watt
of North Carolina

Congressperson Sanford Bishop
of Georgia

Congressperson Cynthia McKinney
of Georgia

From 1901 to 1993, there were no African Americans in Congress from North Carolina; from 1871 to 1973, there were no African Americans in Congress from Georgia; from 1877 to 1991, there were no African Americans in Congress from Louisiana. Until 1993, there had never been an African American in Congress from Florida, and until 1973, there had never been an African American in Congress from Texas. As a result of a series of U.S. Supreme Court and lower court cases decided since June 1993, some of the Congresspersons whose photographs appear above and on the following page may not be re-

Congressperson Cleo Fields
of Louisiana

Congressperson Corrine Brown
of Florida

Congressperson Eddie Bernice Johnson
of Texas

Congressperson Sheila Lee Jackson
of Texas

elected to Congress, and with the new district boundaries, they may be replaced by whites. In addition to those noted, there is a possible loss of seven seats in other states. *See Shaw v. Reno,* 509 U.S. 630 (1993), *Shaw v. Hunt,* 1996 U.S. LEXIS 3880 (1996), *Miller v. Johnson,* 115 S. Ct. 2475 (1995), *Hays v. Louisiana,* 115 S. Ct. 2431 (1995), *Bush v. Vera,* 1996 U.S. LEXIS 3882 (1996), and *Johnson v. Mortham,* 1996 U.S. Dist. LEXIS 7792 (N.D. Fla. 1996).

Photographs on this page: Trial and appellate counsel and expert witnesses in the voting rights cases (1996). *(Photographs by Melvin Terry)*

Pamela Karlan, Keith Reeves, and David Bositis.

Jacqueline Berrien, Theodore Shaw, A. Leon Higginbotham, Jr., and Maria Valdez.

Arthur Baer, Brenda Wright, Laughlin MacDonald, Penda Hair, and Julius Chambers.

CURRENT SUPREME COURT (1996): (Top row) Ruth Bader Ginsburg, David Souter, Clarence Thomas, Stephen Breyer. (Bottom row) Antonin Scalia, John Paul Stevens, William Rehnquist, Sandra Day O'Connor, Anthony Kennedy.

"The life of the law has not been logic: it has been experience. The felt necessities of the time, the prevalent moral and political theories, intuitions of public policy, avowed or unconscious, even the prejudices which judges share with their fellow-men [and women], have had a good deal more to do than the syllogism in determining the rules by which men [and women] should be governed."—Oliver Wendell Holmes, *The Common Law* (1881). *(Collection of the Supreme Court of the United States)*

Justice Thurgood Marshall at Independence Hall, as he gave one of his last two speeches upon receiving the Liberty Bell Award. He was introduced by Judge A. Leon Higginbotham, Jr. (July 4, 1992). *(Photograph by Delcina Wilson)*

"I wish I could say that racism and prejudice were only distant memories . . . and that liberty and equality were just around the bend. I wish I could say that America has come to appreciate diversity and to see and accept similarity. But as I look around, I see not a nation of unity but of division —Afro and white, indigenous and immigrant, rich and poor, educated and illiterate. . . . But there is a price to be paid for division and isolation.

. . .

We cannot play ostrich. Democracy cannot flourish amid fear. Liberty cannot bloom amid hate. Justice cannot take root amid rage. We must go against the prevailing wind. We must dissent from the indifference. We must dissent from the apathy. We must dissent from the fear, the hatred and the mistrust. We must dissent from a government that has left its young without jobs, education or hope. We must dissent from the poverty of vision and the absence of moral leadership. We must dissent because America can do better, because America has no choice but to do better. . . . Take a chance, won't you? Knock down the fences that divide. Tear apart the walls that imprison. Reach out; freedom lies just on the other side."

*Racism in the Courts as Symptoms, Signals, and Symbols of Racism
in the Broader Society*

From my experience as a United States District Court judge and later as a
Court of Appeals judge, I have always been impressed with the divergence of
views as to how widely the virus of racism infects the justice system. Many
white judges share an underlying belief about the rarity of racist occurrences
in the courtroom; they assume that instances of racism are infrequent, periph-
eral, tangential, and almost irrelevant episodes to the central function and
experiences of adjudicating the cases before them. In contrast, I know of only
one African-American federal judge who minimizes the significance of the
fact that societal racism, even unintentionally, often affects the adjudicatory
and fact-finding process of courts.

My view is that those past and present instances of racism are more than
mere aberrations or isolated blemishes that occasionally crop up and mar the
normally effective dispensation of justice. Rather, they are symptoms, signals, and symbols of racism in the broader society. When racism occurs in
the courts, it is symptomatic of racist attitudes, myths, and assumptions that
constitute the ideology of societal racism. Such instances of courtroom racism
also act as signals, triggering and mobilizing those racist attitudes and stereotypes in the minds of all the courtroom participants, and possibly affecting
the judgment and actions of the judge, jury, and attorneys at this and other
junctures in the case. Finally, racist occurrences in the courts are particularly
powerful symbols, acting to reinforce, legitimate, and perpetuate racism in
the broader society.

Reflecting on the American experience, Professor Charles Lawrence III
has developed a theory of racism as the systemic imputation of stigma onto
African Americans through the courts and through extralegal actions.[6] As he
explains, racism is part of the common cultural heritage of all Americans.[7]
According to Lawrence, racism is a group of assumptions about the world
and its inhabitants that are expressed, often unconsciously, in a "mutually
reinforcing and pervasive pattern of stigmatizing actions that cumulate to
compose an injurious whole that is greater than the sum of its parts."[8] These
assumptions are based on notions, explicit or implicit, of African Americans
as dirty, lazy, oversexed, in poor control of their ids, and otherwise less than
fully human.[9] Indeed, such assumptions give rise to behavior, such as the
establishment of race-segregated housing and bathrooms, that dramatize white
stereotypes of African Americans as impure, contaminating, or untouchable.[10]
Similarly, the use of devices that reduce the number of African-American
policemen or that challenge the competency of African-American professors
and managers, reinforces a cultural message that whites should be in positions

of authority over African Americans.[11] While, as Lawrence's article demonstrates, these cultural messages can be decoded, they are often tacit, or even unconscious.[12]

RACISM IN THE COURTROOM AS A SYMPTOM OF SOCIETAL RACISM

Courts do not dispense justice in sterile isolation, unaffected by the prevailing political, social, and moral attitudes and currents of the broader society in which they operate.[13] Judges, prosecutors, and other lawyers are not immune to the unconscious influence of—indeed they may even consciously subscribe to—the group of negative stigmatizing assumptions that Lawrence describes as characteristic of the ideology of racism. Thus, the broader societal racism may, consciously or unconsciously, infect the attitudes and behavior of judges and lawyers in the courtroom.

RACISM IN THE COURTROOM AS A SIGNAL OF SOCIETAL RACISM

A second important effect of instances of racism in the courtroom is the indication that racial bias affects other courtroom participants besides the judge or lawyer who makes a racist declaration. Instances of racism in the courtroom tap into the ideology of societal racism and are symptomatic of the existence of societal racism. A racist remark or insinuation by a judge or prosecutor acts as a signal, triggering and mobilizing a host of attitudes and assumptions that may be consciously held, or unconsciously harbored, by the judge, jury, and lawyers in the courtroom. The effect of the racist act or statement can be felt beyond its immediate context: it acts to trip additional racist assumptions at other junctures in the proceeding.

In the United States, segregated courthouse restrooms, cafeterias, and spectator seating also acted as signals. In these cases all participants, particularly juries in criminal or civil trials involving an African-American defendant or litigant, were constantly reminded that African Americans were to be accorded inferior status in this society. Every time jurors and spectators walked into a courtroom, they were presented with a ringing affirmation of the assumptions, myths, and attitudes that compose the ideology of racism in the United States.

When a prosecutor or judge appeals to fears of African-American violence directed against whites, elaborate and detailed myths about African Americans are ushered into the conscious and unconscious minds of courtroom participants. Once these racist attitudes and assumptions have been tapped into, the judge, jury, and lawyers are more likely to stimulate and rely on their collective consciousness or unconsciousness, applying related racist myths and stereotypes that African Americans are untrustworthy, dishonest, and shiftless to other issues during the trial or hearing.

When a judge or prosecutor makes a racially disparaging remark during the course of a trial, the comment may affect the judgment and actions of the judge, jury, and attorneys for the duration of the case. Consequently, instances of racism in the courtroom cannot be viewed as isolated incidents, limited in effect to the immediate context in which they occurred, or as "harmless error."

As Professor Anthony Amsterdam has commented:

> [W]hen a prosecutor makes racist comments in closing arguments to a jury, more is going on in the trial than those specific comments. Courts that hold such comments as "harmless error" seem to view the situation as one in which the prosecutor tried, but failed to interject racial prejudice into a case that was otherwise free of racial prejudice. This view is exactly backwards. Unless a case has *already* been infected with racial prejudice, the prosecutor would never venture to make the racist comments in the first place. Prosecutors do not make arguments that they do not expect the jury to buy, and prosecutors particularly do not make arguments that they have any reason to fear that even one juror will actively resent. Before a prosecutor (even a personally bigoted prosecutor) would try to use the defendant's race (or a defense witness's race) against the defendant in a jury argument, the prosecutor would have to be pretty confident that the argument will fall on fertile ground. Thus, the very fact that a racist pitch is made in closing argument almost always means that the prosecutor has read the jury—on the basis of knowledge about the individual jurors or their backgrounds or the community or on the basis of a hundred signs that may be very subtle or very glaring in the atmosphere of the courtroom but are totally undetectable on the cold, written record preserved for appeal—and that the prosecutor has decided that, with *this* jury in *this* case, a racist pitch will *work*. Courts that ignore this reality are willfully blind.[14]

RACISM IN THE COURTROOM AS CULTURAL SYMBOLISM

In addition to acting as signals for those participants in the courtroom, instances of racism in the courts also send signals beyond the confines of any particular courtroom and affect society at large. The judicial system is charged with interpreting, upholding, and enforcing the law. Since most societies claim to offer their citizens equal justice under the law, the courts are the presumed repositories of equality and the solemn fora for the just adjudication of the law without regard to race, creed, color, appearance, or any other categorical distinction. Because of this role, instances of racism in the courtroom are particularly powerful symbols that act to legitimate, reinforce, and perpetuate the culture of racism operating in society as a whole.[15]

Similarly, when courthouses in the southern United States maintained segregated restrooms, cafeterias, and spectator sections in courtrooms—the

solemn fora of equality before the law and equal protection by the law—
they sent a symbolic message that legitimated, reinforced, and perpetuated
the segregation that was a way of life in the post-*Plessy* South and helped to
justify the ideology of racism underlying its existence and enforcement.

Likewise, when judges overruled defense objections to prosecutors' racist actions, the courts symbolically were affirming the racist myths and stereotypes of black untrustworthiness, dishonesty, lack of control, and proclivity
to violence and rape, especially toward whites. By so doing, the courts helped
to perpetuate the racist ideology of which these attitudes were a part.

Acts of racism in the courts are symptomatic of the society's cultural
racism. They trigger other racist assumptions in the minds of courtroom participants and symbolize to society the legitimacy of the ideology of racism.
Even murals in a courthouse can convey racist assumptions that African
Americans instantly recognize and to which whites may be oblivious regarding their implications. Professor Jack Bass describes a Jackson, Mississippi,
courthouse mural as follows:

> A heavy off-white drapery hangs from the ceiling and covers the wall
> that faces spectators in the fourth-floor federal courtroom above the old post
> office in Jackson, Mississippi. Although many façades in today's American
> South hide the harsh, historic reality of an unjust social order that crumbled
> in the civil rights revolution of the 1960s, the curtain in the Jackson court-
> room is a literal mask.
>
> Behind it there is a brightly colored mural, 40 feet across and 20 feet
> high, painted by an artist of Czech extraction, commissioned in 1939 by
> the Works Progress Administration (WPA). The tableau begins at the left
> where a black mammy is picking cotton in a green field. It moves to a
> poorly dressed, graying black man sitting on stone steps, happily strum-
> ming a banjo. As the plantation master moves to dismount, another deferen-
> tial black reaches up to help. A hoopskirted white woman stands in front
> of the columned plantation house with her daughter. A stern-faced judge,
> dressed in black suit and string tie, dominates the foreground. He has a law
> book under his arm.[16]

Apartheid in the Courthouse

Segregated Spectator Seating

In American courtrooms there has never been any formal segregation among the
various white groups. Protestants have not been segregated from Catholics, or
Jews from Gentiles. For those white persons whose ancestors were born, as an
example, in England, France, Germany, Italy, Sweden, or from any other Euro-

pean nation where predominantly the citizens are white, there has never been any segregation in the courtroom on the basis of national origin. Thus one must identify the evolution of these racial segregation policies and how the courts justified this different treatment for African Americans.

In 1948—the same year the Nationalist Party came into power in South Africa to initiate apartheid—the Mississippi Supreme Court, in *Murray v. State*,[17] was asked to reverse the murder conviction of an African-American man tried in a courtroom that segregated African-American spectators, allowing them to sit only in the balcony. The court's language reveals the long tradition and implicit approval of courthouse racial segregation: "It is asserted that the seating arrangement, suggested pursuant to a custom whose immemorial usage and sanction has made routine, resulted in a concentration in the balcony of those of the same race as the defendant."[18] The court's language not only implicitly approved of that "routine" tradition, but its decision permitted its continuance:

> Assuming that this seating arrangement was insisted upon and deemed prejudicial to such as were piqued thereby—as to which there is no showing—such reactions may not be magnified into a fancied denial of constitutional rights and thereupon made assignable to the defendant.[19]

The court affirmed the conviction.

In 1963, fifteen years after the *Murray* case, when the success of the civil rights movement had sensitized the country to the derogatory meaning of segregation, the Supreme Court finally recognized, in *Johnson v. Virginia*,[20] that race-segregated seating in courts constituted a denial of equal protection.

Ford T. Johnson, Jr., an African American, was seated in a section of the Richmond Traffic Court reserved for whites, and when requested by the bailiff to move, refused to do so. The judge then summoned the petitioner to the bench and instructed him to be seated in the right-hand section of the courtroom, the section reserved for African Americans. The petitioner moved back in front of the counsel table and remained standing with his arms folded, stating that he would not comply with the judge's order. Upon refusing to obey the judge's further direction to be seated, he was arrested for contempt. At no time did Johnson behave in a boisterous or abusive manner, and there was no disorder in the courtroom.[21]

The state, in its brief to the Supreme Court, conceded that seating space in the Richmond Traffic Court "is assigned on the basis of racial designation, the seats on one side of the aisle being for use of Negro citizens and the seats on the other side being for the use of white citizens."[22] The Supreme Court reversed the conviction, noting:

It is clear from the totality of circumstances, and particularly the fact
that the petitioner was peaceably seated in the section reserved for whites
before being summoned to the bench, that the arrest and conviction rested
entirely on the refusal to comply with the segregated seating requirements
imposed in this particular courtroom. Such a conviction cannot stand, for it
is no longer open to question that a State may not constitutionally require
segregation of public facilities. State-compelled segregation in a court of
justice is a manifest violation of the State's duty to deny no one the equal
protection of its laws.[23]

The ultimate insight that race-segregated seating in courtrooms denied a spectator "equal" protection doubtless rested on what Professor Lawrence has
characterized as the central insight of *Brown v. Board of Education*: that
equal protection doctrine includes the right to be free from social ostracism
and its stigmatizing effect on the "hearts and minds" of African-American
adult citizens as well as on African-American children.[24]

The Barriers of Standing

Regrettably, *Johnson* was not the end of the matter. As in non-civil rights
areas, some of the Court's contributions to social justice have been curtailed
by rigid enforcement of standing requirements. Just after *Johnson*, an
African-American demonstrator was tried in a racially segregated Louisiana
courtroom. The Louisiana Supreme Court, in considering appellant's claim
that racial segregation in the courtroom had denied him a fair trial in violation
of his due process and equal protection rights, acknowledged that the courtroom in question had been segregated for many years.[25] However, the court
affirmed the conviction, distinguishing *Johnson* on the basis that the African-
American defendant did not have standing to challenge the segregation of
those African-American spectators who came to watch his trial:

[I]n the *Johnson* case the objection to segregation was made by a Negro
who had been arrested for contempt of court for sitting in seats assigned
for white citizens, and the arrest and conviction was for that conduct. In
the case before us, there is no charge against the defendant for having
violated the court-imposed seating arrangement and none of the parties
upon whom the segregation was imposed are before this court in this case.
Hence the Johnson case is not authority for reversing this conviction. It has
not been made to appear that the segregation resulted in a miscarriage of
justice to the defendant . . . . If it were otherwise, it would result that
every Negro convicted in that court in the past would be entitled to have
his conviction set aside.[26]

Thus, the courtroom segregation would be allowed to continue at least until
challenged by the proper party, an African-American spectator.[27] The court

refused to conclude that the racist setting of a courtroom could, in any possible manner, affect the administration of justice.

Whites Only Courthouse Cafeterias: One Court's View of "Separate But Equal" as a Step Forward

Shortly after the decision in *Brown v. Board of Education*, African-American residents of Harris County, Texas, challenged a policy which excluded them from the privately operated cafeteria in the new county courthouse.[28] The court entered a judgment declaring that the county could not constitutionally deny African Americans the right to patronize the only courthouse cafeteria. However, the court did not go beyond the mandate of "separate but equal" in its injunction. Thus, it required the county only to make "specific assurances that facilities will be made available for the use of colored persons under circumstances and conditions substantially equal to those afforded members of the white race," and enjoined the private operator from excluding African Americans "solely by reason of their race or color under the circumstances here prevailing."[29] Apparently, the court was declaring that the county could properly exclude African Americans from the cafeteria as long as it provided African Americans access to "substantially equal" eating facilities.[30] This requirement of "equality" rested on a white judiciary's failure to perceive the stigmatizing—and thus unconstitutional—effects of segregation, especially in official settings, which serve a legitimizing role.

Race-Segregated Restrooms

In 1958, a young African-American lawyer by the name of E. A. Dawley, Jr., filed a suit in federal court against the city of Norfolk, Virginia, for a mandatory injunction to remove the word "colored" from doors to certain restrooms in courthouse buildings occupied and used exclusively by state courts and judges.[31] He alleged that the "presence of these signs conveys the thought that the [state] judges consider Negro attorneys inferior, which, in turn, adversely affects the prestige of Negro attorneys in the eyes of the public and thereby diminishes their earning capacity."[32] Dawley cited and relied on *Brown v. Board of Education* in arguing that such segregation generates a feeling of inferiority among African Americans because of African-American lawyers' lower status in the community. The trial judge called counsel's theory "ingenious," but then belittled it, concluding that:

> there is no more reason to suggest that judges deemed Negro attorneys inferior than there is to say that a white attorney is inferior because he may use a restroom marked "White". . . . To say that there is a loss of earning

power, or a denial of equal protection laws . . . would reduce the law to an absurdity.[33]

By insisting that a policy of courtroom segregation did not carry the stigmatizing message that contact with African Americans in intimate settings, such as restrooms (or swimming pools), is contaminating, the trial judge embraced the formalism of *Plessy v. Ferguson*,[34] which had recently been implicitly rejected by the recognition in *Brown* that segregation stigmatizes African-American school-children.[35] Professor Charles Black, however, in defending *Brown* in the face of formalist attacks, voiced perhaps the most eloquent description by a contemporary Southerner of the real meaning of segregation:

> I am sure it never occurred to anyone, white or colored, to question [segregation's] meaning. The fiction of "equality" is just about on a level with the fiction of "finding" in the action of trover. I think few candid southerners deny this.
> . . . Segregation in the South grew up and is kept going because and only because the white race has wanted it that way. . . .
> Segregation is historically and contemporaneously associated in a *functioning complex* with practices which are indisputably and grossly discriminatory. . . . [Black discusses the exclusion of African Americans from voting and the poor quality of African-American schools.] Then we are solemnly told that segregation is not intended to harm the segregated race, or to stamp it with the mark of inferiority. How long must we keep a straight face?
> The society that has just lost the Negro as a slave, that has just lost out in an attempt to put him under quasi-servile "Codes," the society that views his blood as a contamination and his name as an insult, the society that extralegally imposes on him every humiliating mark of low caste . . . this society, careless of his consent, moves by law . . . to cut him off from mixing in the general public life of the community. The Court that refused to see inequality in this cutting off would be making the only kind of law that can be warranted outrageous in advance—law based on self-induced blindness, on flagrant contradiction of known fact.[36]

It is because segregation was indeed part of "a functioning complex" of discriminatory practices that the marking of racially separate restroom facilities was an official public statement that those in power thought African Americans were inferior. And when, by the use of separate restroom facilities, the state announces in the courthouse that African Americans are inferior, it is not surprising that a potential African-American client, who will be appealing to the discretion of the (white) courts, or seeking the leniency of the (white) sentencing judge, might be leery of having an African-American lawyer as his counsel—one whom the state brands so "inferior" that he cannot even use the same toilets as whites. In finding Dawley's legal theory absurd, both the trial judge and the appellate court were oblivious to the symbolic power of this branding.

Overt Discrimination by Judges in the Courtroom

Failure to Accord Black Witnesses the Civilities Customarily Accorded to White Witnesses

In 1963, an African-American woman was testifying on her own behalf in a habeas corpus proceeding arising out of a civil rights demonstration.[37] The state solicitor persisted in addressing the African-American witnesses by their first names.[38] When the solicitor addressed the petitioner as "Mary," she refused to answer, insisting that the prosecutor address her as "Miss Hamilton."[39] The trial judge directed her to answer, but again she refused. The trial judge then cited her for contempt.[40] On appeal, the Alabama Supreme Court affirmed because, it said, the record showed that the witness's name was "Mary Hamilton," not "Miss Mary Hamilton."[41] Miss Mary Hamilton received a five-day sentence because of her insistence that she be treated with the same dignity accorded to white witnesses in the court.

To justify the contempt citation, the Alabama Supreme Court had to go through analytic contortions. It relied on *Ullmann v. United States*,[42] a McCarthy era case in which a United States Attorney was investigating matters of alleged espionage and membership in the Communist Party. Ullmann, who had been called to testify before a grand jury under a grant of immunity, nevertheless refused to testify on the grounds of his Fifth Amendment right against self-incrimination.[43] The Alabama Supreme Court wrenched the *Ullman* court's comment that every man has a duty to testify and that wide latitude ought to be allowed in the cross-examination of witnesses, out of their factual context. The court upheld the contempt citation of Miss Mary Hamilton.[44] The court thus blithely ignored a crucial difference between the cases: Miss Hamilton was not refusing to testify—she merely wanted to be called "Miss," the way a white woman would have been addressed. In contrast, Ullman presumably would not have testified even if he were called "Sir," "Dr.," "Your Honor," "My Lord," or "Reverend."

Fortunately, the Supreme Court of the United States granted certiorari and summarily reversed the contempt judgment.[45] Some might say that this case exemplifies an unjustifiable waste of legal talent and judicial effort to determine whether the appellation "Miss" should be used in cross-examination. I disagree. At the core of this case stood an individual insistent that a judicial system, which is supposed to dispense justice fairly, treat her with the dignity and sensitivity that Alabama courts automatically accorded to white middle-class men and women.[46]

The Denial of Standing to a Lawyer Seeking to Assert His Client's Right to Be Addressed with the Civilities Accorded to Whites

Again, constitutional victories at the Supreme Court level cannot provide a full solution to overt racial discrimination in the courtroom unless the lower courts are willing to give these decisions practical effect, rather than formalistically limiting them through the doctrine of standing. For example, the *Hamilton* decision did not provide a remedy for the defendants in *Farmer v. Strickland*.[47] *Farmer* involved resentencing hearings for an African-American man convicted of murder in Georgia. Throughout the hearings, the prosecuting attorney continually addressed the defendant by his first name while addressing white witnesses by their titles. The defense attorney, Farmer, explained to the trial judge that the discrepancy was "demeaning. . . . He is not his friend."[48] The trial judge sharply overruled Farmer's objections. When the prosecutor persisted in calling the defendant by his first name and Farmer continued to object, the court held Farmer in contempt and sentenced him to a day in jail.

The Fifth Circuit affirmed the state court's denial of a writ of habeas corpus, rejecting Farmer's argument that *Hamilton* and *Johnson* were controlling and that his objections were "the only way to vindicate effectively and fairly [the defendant's] right to be free of racial discrimination in the courtroom."[49] The circuit court called Farmer's argument "vacuous," distinguishing *Hamilton* and *Johnson* because the decisions in those cases reversed contempt convictions which had been imposed because "*the contemnors* had refused to comply with racially discriminatory orders given to *them* in open court."[50] Here, the trial judge's ruling that Farmer's client could be addressed by his first name, "even though clearly racially discriminatory to the client under the *Johnson* holding, certainly cannot be said to have infringed on any rights of Farmer to be free from racial animus."[51] One lesson, then, of the *Farmer* case is that Supreme Court decisions banning overt race discrimination in the courtroom cannot be relied upon to ensure consistent judicial neutrality. Instead, judges who are unsympathetic to the cause of equal justice will continue to use doctrines, such as standing, that enhance their ability to blunt the impact of the Court's rulings.[52]

*Examples of Racially Discriminatory Courtroom Treatment Resting on
Derogatory Myths About African Americans as a People*

The cases canvassed above are not isolated or unique. Instead, they have
grown from the same root that has spawned hundreds of cases and hundreds
of thousands of actual instances of discriminatory treatment. To begin to grasp
the manifold contours of racism in American courts, one must analyze some
of these additional cases. The racist conduct in these cases has ranged from
outrageously blatant appeals to racial hatred and fear to mere references to
the race of a defendant or witness.[53] These cases reflect the ways in which
courts have directly or indirectly contributed to the maintenance of black subjugation within an interlocking system of discriminatory practices and beliefs:
enforcing the precept of inferiority.

RACIALLY BIASED STATEMENTS BY COUNSEL

In many American cases, counsel have attacked the credibility of African-
American defendants and witnesses by appealing to stereotypical notions of
African Americans as either fools or liars.

One group of cases has seen such racially derogatory prosecutorial appeals reversed by appellate courts, which described them as clearly discriminatory. For instance, the Supreme Court of Mississippi, in *Moseley v. State*,[54]
reversed a conviction where the prosecutor had made numerous racist statements. The defendant was charged with violating prohibition laws. In his
closing argument, the prosecutor told the jury that "[i]t is just a question of
whether or not you believe this negro or [a white witness]."[55] Upon the defense counsel's objection to this statement, the prosecutor retorted: "[s]he is
a negro: look at her skin. If she is not a negro, I don't want you to convict
her."[56] The trial judge did not rule on the defendant's objection, but merely
asked "[w]ell, what is she?"[57] In reversing, the court held that these statements "had nothing to do with the case, except as an appeal to race antipathy
and prejudice."[58] The court also admonished the trial judge, who, "by ignoring the objection of appellant's counsel, seems to have approved the issue
presented by the lawyer for the state."[59]

In a closing argument in another early southern case, a prosecutor told
the jury: "You know the Negro race—how they stick up to [*sic*] each other
when accused of a crime, and that they will always get up an alibi, prove it
by perjured testimony of their own color, and get their accused companion
clear if they can."[60] On appeal, the court held that these statements constituted an appeal to racial prejudice that required reversal.[61]

Another early Alabama case, one that preceded *Brown*, specified that
racially derogatory comments in the courtroom constituted a violation of equal

protection. The Alabama trial court had overruled a defense objection to a prosecutor's assertion that "[y]ou must deal with a negro in the light of the fact that he is a negro, and applying your experience and common sense."[62] The appellate court, reversing the conviction, said that the statement was "improper and calculated to prejudice the defendant before the jury. . . . The fact that the defendant was of the negro race did not deprive him of the equal protection of the law, or necessarily discredit his testimony. . . ."[63]

Such cases are by no means limited to the early part of this century and before, nor to courts in the southern states. A prosecutor in a Texas trial court in the 1950s stated: "I am not criticizing the defendant for bringing a witness of the same race. I just want to let you know for the purpose of the record they try to help their own race."[64] The trial judge denied defendant's motion that the jury be instructed not to consider the prosecutor's statement.[65] The appellate court reversed the conviction, calling the prosecutor's argument "an appeal to racial prejudice. . . . *The implication was clear that state's counsel sought to condemn as a class all testimony coming from members of the colored race.*"[66]

In the 1970s, one Illinois prosecutor remarked in his closing argument:

> First of all, concerning the defendant's witness, you have to remember that they don't live in the same social structure that we do, that you and I do. The witnesses that the defendant brought are street people—simple as that. The society they live in do [sic] not consider the truth a great virtue. The society they live in, they lie every day. It is nothing to them to protect one of their own kind by lying.[67]

The defendant and his witnesses were African-American; the prosecution's witness was white. The appellate court reversed the conviction, stating that "[t]he apparent attempt to depict defendant's witnesses as liars, not on the basis of the evidence, but on the basis that they would perjure themselves to help a member of the same race is clearly prejudicial."[68]

While one might take some comfort that each of these attempts by prosecutors to use racial antipathy to win their cases was reversed, it is worth pondering why similar cases from the same region, at the same time, were *not* reversed. In the following four early southern cases, prosecutors made equally crass appeals to negative stereotypes of African Americans in contests of credibility between African-American and white witnesses, and appellate courts failed to reverse.

The Texas Court of Criminal Appeals in 1910 affirmed the conviction of an African American for carrying a gun, in *Johnson v. State.*[69] Among other disparaging remarks concerning the credibility of African Americans, the prosecutor at trial told the jury: "The negro race is all alike and about the same the world over—they are untruthful and unreliable—they are, as a rule, a set of reprobates and liars. . . ."[70] If anything, this comment is more overtly offensive than any of those in cases that led to a reversal. Yet, the appellate court affirmed the conviction, holding that "the matter is not of sufficient importance to require a reversal."[71]

Similarly, the Supreme Court of Louisiana in 1906 refused to reverse a murder conviction in a case where the prosecutor urged the jury to disregard the testimony of African-American defense witnesses and then told the jury: "[y]ou must believe the testimony of these two white boys, two American citizens."[72] The Louisiana Supreme Court accepted the conclusion of the trial court that the prosecutor's statements were not intended to inject racial prejudice into the proceedings, but merely to distinguish the prosecution and defense witnesses. Without questioning the effect of the comments on the jury, the court refused to reverse the conviction.[73] Equally disturbing as this refusal to reverse is the implicit suggestion that the use of "citizens" could distinguish American-born whites and African Americans.

In *James v. State*,[74] the prosecutor asked the jury, "[a]re you gentlemen going to believe that nigger sitting over there [pointing at the defendant], with a face on him like that, in preference to the testimony of [a white] deput[y]?"[75] The Alabama Court of Appeals upheld the conviction, holding that the trial court did not err in refusing to uphold the defendant's objection to this comment.[76] Finally, in *Allen v. State*,[77] the court held that the trial judge did not err in refusing to exclude, upon defendant's objection, the prosecutor's statement that "[the defendant's lawyers] ask you to believe a couple of Negroes instead of the white girls."[78]

Just as these prosecutorial comments were effective because they appealed to then-common societal prejudices, the courts' curt refusals to reverse were a product of their members' conscious or unconscious internalization of those prejudices. Had these courts viewed African Americans as fully human, they would have seen how stigmatizing each prosecutor's comments were to the individual witnesses. Moreover, they might have reflected on how harmful they were, since failure to reverse legitimized the systemic discrediting of African Americans' testimony. In a society such as ours, where courts wield coercive power on behalf of the state in administering criminal law and in structuring social and individual relations in civil law, to disadvantage a group in the courtroom systematically by allowing them to lose all contests of credibility is to ensure their continued societal disadvantage. To privilege the testimony of whites is to allow the state to abuse its power. To have a southern prosecutor appeal to race hatred when one is on trial for one's life is as terrifying—and as dangerous—as facing the police beatings that we so easily deplore in the early American cases.[79] The unequal protection from the state's use of force once contributed powerfully to the exploitation of African Americans by whites in the South and elsewhere. If we wish to preserve even our limited advances toward equality for African Americans in this century, courts must be vigilant to prevent any such infection of trials by race hatred.

PROSECUTORIAL APPEALS TO FEAR OF VIOLENCE BY AFRICAN AMERICANS

In numerous instances, prosecutors have tried to stimulate white jurors' fears that violent racial minorities would prey upon their families and communities if the defendant and others of his race were not convicted. As Charles Lawrence notes, such comments appeal to the general white stereotype of African Americans as less controlled, and so more violent or more prone to crime than whites, and are on par with a South African judge's comment that blacks kill from a "lust for stabbing."[80] In this manner, prosecutors have both perpetuated and capitalized on racist stereotypes by characterizing African Americans as particularly prone to violence.[81]

In several cases, the appellate courts have recognized these appeals as racist stereotypes and reversed defendants' convictions. For example, in California during the 1970s, a district attorney prosecuting an African-American man for the rape of a black girl reminded the jury that "maybe the next time it won't be a little black girl from the other side of the tracks; maybe it will be somebody that you know; maybe it will be somebody that I know. And maybe next time he'll use the knife. . . ."[82] The United States Court of Appeals for the Ninth Circuit reversed the conviction, holding that the comments constituted a "highly inflammatory and wholly impermissible appeal to racial prejudice."[83]

In another more recent prosecution, also from the North, the prosecutor, as described by the reviewing court:

> talked of black crimes in general . . . and how crimes committed against blacks by blacks are a serious problem in our society. The prosecutor next designated Detroit as the murder capital of the United States . . . . The prosecutor then argued that the defendant and his accomplice wanted to make it in Joliet like it is in Detroit, a city of fear . . . he asked the jurors to think of their own death as the result of a crime, referred to lawlessness ravaging this [Joliet] community, and that an acquittal would be to invite an open season for shooting victims and would encourage "these people" to commit more crimes of violence.[84]

Defendant's counsel made repeated objections to the prosecutor's remarks during trial; the response of the trial judge to those objections is unclear. The appellate court, reversing on other grounds, called the remarks "not only intemperate but prejudicial."[85]

In a case against an African-American man for robbery of another African American, the prosecution remarked that "[i]f you don't stop them now, they will next be robbing white people."[86] The trial judge overruled an objection to this statement, but the Mississippi Supreme Court reversed the conviction.[87]

Although some courts have had the sensitivity to recognize racism when they have seen it, it is equally important to recognize that some appellate courts have permitted prosecutorial appeals to stereotypes of African Americans as violent, by holding that such appeals constitute "harmless error." These only help to perpetuate injustice in the criminal justice system. They have effectively condoned the sheriffs and police that use the legal system as a tool for subjugating African Americans, by allowing African Americans to be convicted simply for being African-American, rather than for the evidence linking them with a particular crime. Indeed, the threat of groundless conviction has always been relied upon as an effective way of enforcing deference in African-American men toward whites. Thus, in a Mississippi rape case, the prosecutor, in closing remarks, stated: "[Y]ou can acquit the defendant on this charge and let him go free, and if you do he may kill another person, and the next time it may not be a colored person."[88] The trial judge sustained an objection to this remark but overruled a motion for a mistrial. The Mississippi Supreme Court found that, because the trial court had sustained the objection, no reversible error had occurred.[89]

In 1962, a California appellate court affirmed the conviction of an African-American man, despite a prosecutor's remark that:

We should not be forced to be in a position where we cannot enjoy ourselves, where our children—we have to be in fear that something might happen to our children.

I am not saying this for the fact that there might be a number of Negroes there. I am saying this strictly from the fact that if this type of activity that you heard of exists, if it keeps going on, no one can be safe to go there, or to even enjoy the facilities that they have in Griffith Park.[90]

The appellate court deemed the remarks not prejudicial, since "any reasonably minded juror" would interpret the statement to mean that "defendants of every race or color should be treated equally under the law."[91]

In *Brown v. State*,[92] the prosecutor remarked in his closing argument that "prejudice against defendant and his race was brought upon themselves by the damnable heinous crimes, such as murder and rape, committed by them."[93] The trial court instructed the jury to disregard the statement, and the appellate court held that in view of the court's instruction, the statement did not constitute reversible error, despite the fact that it was an explicit appeal to racial prejudice.

APPEALS TO THE STEREOTYPE OF AFRICAN AMERICANS AS PRONE TO RAPE WHITE WOMEN

While rape is a form of violence, it differs in the cultural imagination significantly from forms of violence that are not committed specifically against women.[94] Moreover, the myth that African-American men are particularly prone to rape white women was an especially important part of the mythology that sustained the reign of Jim Crow.[95] It is no accident that the lynchings that were used to enforce white dominance were often based upon the allegation that the victim of the lynching had raped a white woman;[96] nor is it coincidence that many of the men on death row in the southern states at that time were African Americans convicted of raping white women.[97] I therefore treat rape cases separately.

The Supreme Court of Alabama affirmed the conviction of an African American who, in the company of eight other African Americans, was charged with raping a white girl on a train.[98] During the trial, the prosecutor asked the jury: "How would you like to have your daughter on that train with nine Negroes in a car?"[99] The Alabama Supreme Court held that the trial judge did not err in overruling the defendant's objection to the statement as inflammatory.[100]

In *Garner v. State*,[101] where an African-American defendant was convicted of raping a white girl, the prosecuting attorney stated in his closing argument that it was "not uncommon to pick up a paper and see where some brute has committed this crime . . . where a brute of his race has committed this fiendish crime."[102] The trial court overruled defendant counsel's objection to this statement, but the appellate court reversed the conviction.[103]

In *Kindle v. State*,[104] the Arkansas Supreme Court upheld the rape conviction of an African-American defendant in which the prosecutor told the jury in his closing argument: "Gentlemen, you don't know that he will rape the same color the next time."[105] The court, in affirming the rape conviction, described the remark as "highly improper," but noted that the prosecutor withdrew the remarks at the suggestion of the court and the defense did not object or raise an exception at the time.[106]

All these remarks both rely on and reinforce the common stereotype of African Americans as prone to rape, and particularly to raping white women.

CLAIMS OF AFRICAN-AMERICAN RACE HATRED TOWARD WHITES

Prosecutors also appeal to the white fear that African Americans harbor a hatred for whites, which they will manifest violently. In a case in which an African-American defendant was convicted of murder, the prosecutor stated: "I am well enough acquainted with this class of niggers to know that they have got it in for the race in their heart, and in their hearts call them all white sons of bitches."[107] The trial judge refused defense counsel's request that he reprimand the prosecutor and admonish him against the use of such language. The appellate court reversed the conviction.[108]

In a prosecution of an African American for killing a white, in which the defendant was convicted of manslaughter, the prosecutor stated that "a member of this defendant's race is ordinarily a peaceful man, but when he does have trouble with a member of the white race, he gets murder in his heart."[109] The trial court sustained the defense counsel's objection, and instructed the jury to disregard the statement.[110] However, the prosecutor continued to remark on the respective races of the defendant and victim, prompting the appellate court to reverse the conviction.

In *Moulton v. State*,[111] the Alabama Supreme Court reversed a conviction in a case where the prosecutor told the jury: "Unless you hang this Negro, our white people living out in the country won't be safe; to let such crimes go unpunished will cause riots in our land."[112] This comment, coming only two generations after the Civil War, when there had in fact been some widely publicized riots by slaves anticipating freedom, appealed to the white fear that African Americans might rise up as a body and shake off their subjugation. As these appellate courts rightly perceived, an African-American defendant cannot have a fair trial where the prosecutor appeals to the white fear that African Americans hate whites and will express that hatred violently.

RACIST CHARACTERIZATIONS OF AFRICAN AMERICANS—FROM "PICKANINNY"
TO "NIGGER"

Because of the various derogatory myths about African Americans, partly canvassed in the cases discussed above, prosecutors could summon up hostile stereotypes of African Americans by simply referring to them by the derogatory names that were part of the system of Jim Crow. The early emphasis in the civil rights movement on exacting courtesy from courts and others—requiring the use of Negro instead of "nigger," last names instead of first names[113]—indicates the importance of such apparently semantic distinctions. Those who refer to African Americans as "niggers" see them as lazy, dirty, or oversexed, while "black man" and "African-American man" carry with them an image of competence and dignity.

Reported cases are replete with instances of counsel making racist statements, ranging from blatantly explicit exclamations to subtly pernicious comments and nearly benign remarks. In some instances, courts have held such comments to be sufficiently prejudicial to require reversal of a conviction. In others, appellate courts have upheld convictions where trial courts struck from the record offensive remarks or instructed the jury to disregard the comments.

But in some cases, even egregious comments that neither have been stricken nor criticized by a trial judge were held not to constitute reversible error.

A number of courts have perceived the implicit appeal to racial prejudice in derogatory comments. During the prosecution of a mulatto man for murder in *Hampton v. State*,[114] the appellate court reversed the conviction where the prosecutor had made the following statements:

> Not a Negro in that great concourse of Negroes who threatened (*sic*) to be respectable has dared to come here and testify in behalf of this mulatto . . . mulattoes should be kicked out by the white race and spurned by the Negroes . . . they [mulattoes] were Negroes as long as one drop of the accursed blood was in their veins they had to bear it . . . these Negroes thought they were better than other Negroes, but in fact they were worse than Negroes; they were Negritoes, a race hated by the white race and despised by the Negroes, accursed by every white man who loves his race, and despised by every Negro who respects his race.[115]

A more blunt espousal of racial prejudice is difficult to imagine.

In *Jones v. State*,[116] the Court of Appeals of Alabama reviewed, among other issues, racist remarks by a prosecutor during the trial of an African American convicted of vehicular homicide. Referring to the defendant's negligent operation of an automobile, the prosecutor told the jury "[h]e was trying to save his own yellow head and that of his black mammy and pickaninny sitting on the back of the car."[117] While the trial court sustained the defendant's objection to this remark, the trial judge denied the defendant's motion that the jury be instructed to disregard it, stating "the court does not think it highly improper."[118] The Court of Appeals reversed and held that the remarks were improper and that the trial court erred in refusing to so instruct the jury.[119]

In *Funches v. State*,[120] the trial court did not rule on an objection by the defendant to the following statement by the prosecutor:

> The defendant in this case has got enough white man's blood in him to make him a man of judgment and sense, and he is a smart fellow indeed, and on the other hand, he has enough African in him to make him as mean as Hades itself.[121]

While the appellate court condemned this statement, it did not reach the issue of whether it constituted reversible error, but reversed the case on other grounds.[122]

In *Cooper v. State*,[123] the appellate court reversed a conviction where the prosecutor made the following comments at trial:

> But, gentlemen, while this is just another Negro killing . . . it is important to you as citizens of this County, because it is your tax dollars that are

being spent to try to keep some semblance of law and order out here in our Negro section. And, gentlemen, it is a far more serious proposition than it may appear to you on its face. Ninety per cent of every tax dollar that is spent in law enforcement in this County is because of the crimes that are committed by Negroes.[124]

In the case of an African-American man charged with the crime of cohabitating with a white woman, the prosecutor remarked in his closing argument: "Since the days of the Carpetbagger colored people have thought, and still think, that they are as good as a white man."[125] The trial judge instructed the jury to disregard the statement, but declined to withdraw the case from the jury. Later in his closing argument, the prosecutor made the following comment: "Down here in the south there are few white people and a great number of colored people, and we should keep the colored man in his place."[126] The trial judge overruled the defendant's objection to that statement. The appellate court reversed the conviction, ruling that these and other remarks by the prosecutor constituted an appeal to racial prejudice.[127] They also make clear the fact that that prejudice is explicitly aimed at subjugation of African Americans by whites.[128]

In *Manning v. State*,[129] the Supreme Court of Tennessee reversed a murder conviction where, at trial, the prosecutor condemned whites for appearing as character witnesses for the African-American defendant. Among the statements made by the prosecutor were the following:

> How can any white man come in here and tell you that he knows the reputation of a colored man in this Community—it was a disgrace for [a white police officer] to come in here and say that man had a good character. I think that's a disgrace to any County.[130]

This was but another way of saying that, because whites dominate African Americans, and in part use the criminal justice system to do so, a white man, especially a white policeman, must never attempt to aid an African-American defendant in the courtroom.

Even though it reversed the conviction, in its opinion the Tennessee Supreme Court displayed a racist, patronizing attitude: "Our judges, court officials, and jurors, are uniformly white men. The white race is dominant and the Negroes are, in a sense, our wards."[131]

In *United States ex. rel. Haynes v. McKendrick*,[132] the United States Court of Appeals for the Second Circuit reversed a 1966 conviction in a New York state case[133] in which the prosecutor had made numerous racist statements at trial, including the following:

> There is something about it, if you have dealt with colored people and have been living with them and see them you begin to be able to discern their

mannerisms and appearances and to discern the different shades and so on . . . .

[Defense attorney for petitioner Haynes] knows [blacks'] weaknesses and inability to do certain things that maybe are commonplace for the ordinary person to do or remember or know certain things. . . . It gets confusing when you talk to some of these black youngsters like that because they don't express themselves as clearly as you and I might possibly be able to do so. . . .[134]

The prosecutor also went on at length about how many African Americans were wearing "exotic" hairstyles and sideburns, and how different such hairstyles were from ordinary (i.e., white) people's conceptions of normal hairstyles.[135] Because whites have negative stereotypes of African Americans, to focus on differences even between white and African-American styles is a covert appeal to racial prejudice, as the appellate court correctly saw.

The preceding cases attest to the importance of the appellate process as the first line of defense against court-sanctioned racism. However, many appellate courts, captives of their own conscious or unconscious racism, have allowed racially derogatory comments in the courtroom to go unchecked. For example, in *Dodson v. State*,[136] the Court of Criminal Appeals of Texas upheld a conviction of an African American for assault with intent to murder. The defendant had been employed by the victim to cut cotton all day for sixty cents. The defendant threw a rock at his employer after the latter threatened the defendant with violence for daring to quit his job at mid-day and then demand part or all of his sixty cent wage.[137] At trial, the prosecutor told the jury that "[i]t is just such impudent and sassy negroes as the defendant is shown by the evidence to be causing trouble in this country."[138] In holding that this remark was not prejudicial, the court noted, among other things, that "we do not see how [the remark] could have injured the appellant."[139] The injury is obvious, however; the suggestion that the African-American defendant be punished for having responded "impudently" to economically exploitive treatment, rather than for what he had actually done, was just the type of reasoning that kept the structures of economic exploitation in place. A legal system that allows such patterns of exploitation, rather than the relevant facts of an incident, to draw the lines between assault with intent to murder and ordinary assault cannot be other than substantively unjust.

The Supreme Court of Alabama, in *Davis v. State*,[140] overturned an appellate court's reversal of a conviction of an African American for assaulting a white who had intervened in a fight between the defendant and another African American. The reversal was based upon a statement by the prosecutor that "the jury should deal harshly with such cattle."[141] Although the trial judge denied a motion for a mistrial based upon this reference to the defendant, he did admonish the jury to ignore the prosecutor's remarks, and to "try this defendant just as you would a white man."[142] In overturning the appellate court's reversal, the Alabama Supreme Court held that "there [wa]s nothing to illustrate the probable effects of the solicitor as prejudicial, when considered in the light of the admonition of the judge."[143]

In many other cases, appellate courts have upheld convictions despite prosecutors' references to African-American defendants and witnesses in such racist terms as "black rascal,"[144] "burr-headed nigger,"[145] "mean negro,"[146] "big nigger,"[147] "pickaninny,"[148] "mean nigger,"[149] "three nigger men,"[150] "nigger,"[151] and "nothing but just a common Negro, [a] black whore."[152] It is inconceivable to me that these same courts would have allowed a prosecutor to make equally repulsive comments directed at other minorities, such as referring to a Jewish witness or defendant as a "kike," or to an Italian as a "wop." Thus, these court rulings are as much a reflection of judicial insensitivity and racism as they are of the racism of the prosecutors who spoke these heinous epithets.

Judicial Conduct

All the instances of prosecutorial misconduct explored above also contain elements of judicial misconduct insofar as the trial judges overruled defense objections, denied motions for mistrials based upon racist statements of the prosecutor, or failed to declare mistrials based on racist comments *sua sponte*. Likewise, we have seen instances where appellate judges have refused to reverse convictions despite egregious injections of racial prejudice, bias, or similar irrelevant, but damaging, considerations into a trial.

While few in number, acts of overt racism on the part of judges also have been reported. In an *en banc* opinion, the Supreme Court of California ordered the public censure of a Superior Court judge named Stevens, who was found by the state's Commission on Judicial Performance ("Commission") to have made repeated racist comments off the bench during his judicial tenure.[153]

In a concurring opinion, Justice Kaus noted the numerous contexts in which the judge had made racist remarks. Judge Stevens had referred to African Americans as "Jig," "dark boy," "colored boy," "nigger," "coon," and "jungle bunny."[154] In a probate case between African-American litigants the judge stated, in the presence of court personnel only, "let's get on with this Amos and Andy show."[155] During an in-chambers discussion, the judge stated that "Filipinos can be good hard-working people and that they are clean, unlike some black animals who come into contact with the court."[156]

Again in chambers, the judge stated that his court clerk was "lazier than a coon."[157] While none of these comments were made while court was in session, it is not difficult to imagine the dispiriting effect on the African-American, Hispanic, and Asian communities of being forced to deal with this judge's racism during in-chambers conferences, and the encouragement that his open racism must have given to more subtly racist lawyers in the community to treat minority lawyers with less than full professional respect and courtesy.

Justice Mosk dissented from the court's order for public censure for Judge Stevens. Noting that the Commission was authorized by statute to discipline judicial conduct, not speech, Justice Mosk claimed that there was no finding of judicial misconduct by the Commission.[158] The Commission did find that, "according to most witnesses . . . Judge Stevens has at all times performed his judicial duties fairly and equitably, and free from actual bias against any person regardless of race."[159] Even in the face of such an outrageous and persistent display of racism, Justice Mosk was satisfied that Judge Stevens's comments bore no relation to the performance of his judicial duties, and could not agree with the Commission that such mere speech was "prejudicial to the administration of justice" or that it "brings the judicial office into disrepute."[160] One is tempted to respond to this artificial speech/conduct distinction with Charles Black's rejoinder to the formalism of those who defended the doctrine of "separate but equal" on the grounds that it did not stigmatize African Americans: "How long must we keep a straight face?"[161]

In his charge to the jury in State v. Belk,[162] the trial judge referred to defendants in a robbery prosecution as "three black cats in a white Buick."[163] The Supreme Court of North Carolina affirmed the lower court's ruling that this reference "unduly influenced the jury" and was an improper expression of judicial opinion.[164] The court did not consider the racist nature of the statement, however, or comment on the fact that the judge specifically identified the defendants as African-American. Instead, the court went into an almost comical analysis of the probability that, by calling the defendants "cats," the judge was not referring to felines, but to the slang term for a "worldly, wise, or hep" man who "dresses in the latest style and pursues women."[165]

Finally, lest one believe that demonstrations of racial bias by judges are reserved exclusively for disenfranchised, poor, African-American criminal defendants, the case of Berry v. United States[166] is instructive. In that case, the rich and famous grandfather of rock 'n' roll, Mr. "Back in the U.S.A." Chuck Berry, was denied a fair trial through the hostile and racially motivated conduct of a United States District Court trial judge. While the United States Court of Appeals for the Eighth Circuit failed to describe any of the racist conduct of the trial judge, the court noted that:

It seems safe to say that . . . a trial judge who, in the presence of a jury, makes remarks reflecting upon a defendant's race or from which an implication can be drawn that racial considerations may have some bearing upon the issue of guilt or innocence, has rendered the trial unfair.[167]

One can take comfort in the appellate court's clear grasp of equal protection doctrine, but it is still discomforting to note that the doctrine had to be enforced by an appellate panel.

The examples above are primarily from reported appellate cases. Many of the criminal justice proceedings at the trial court level were not transcribed when no appeals were filed, and thus those cases are not available for review by scholars. In thousands of cases where racial slights and denigrations occurred, no objections were made and no appeals were taken on racial grounds. It is my hunch that, out of every thousand cases where racial denigration occurred, probably fewer than two were appealed. Nevertheless, among the appellate cases reported, the often openly hostile language and actions on the part of prosecutors, judges, and court officials reveal a jurisprudential culture in which there were much-displayed notions of black inferiority in the state criminal justice system.

12

LIMITING THE SEEDS
OF RACE HATRED

The Charles Evans Hughes Supreme
Court Era (1930–1941)

The destinies of the two races, in this country, are indissolubly linked together, and the interests of both require that the common government of all shall not permit the seeds of race hate to be planted under the sanction of law.—Dissent, Justice John M. Harlan, Plessy v. Ferguson (1896) [1]

IN THE race sensitive milieu of the United States, it is difficult to present a well-balanced view that fairly notes both the deficits and the strengths of the American judicial process. As Justice John Harlan said in his dissent in *Plessy v. Ferguson,* at times the United States Supreme Court has permitted "the seeds of race hate to be planted under the sanction of law." But as a counterbalance, it must also be recognized that at times the Supreme Court has, extracted or destroyed some of the seeds of racial hatred previously planted by those in power.

To discuss only those cases that involved the perpetuation of racism in the American courts would significantly distort one's over-all view of the American judicial process. There were thousands of cases involving African Americans that were decided fairly. Furthermore, at various times, the federal courts did impose restraints on the state courts regarding issues involving state-imposed racism.

In the decades following *Plessy v. Ferguson,* the seeds of race hate planted by the *Plessy* Court decision yielded a bitter harvest of divisiveness, racial degradation, and judicial disrespect for the constitutional guarantees of equal treatment under the law. [2] Still, during the same period, a few opinions handed down by the United States Supreme Court were symbolic lightning bolts that destroyed some barriers and narrowed some gaps between the treatment of African Americans and that of whites.

Many books evaluate what are often called the "Warren" Court,[3] "Burger" Court,[4] and "Rehnquist" Court.[5] Since this volume is primarily focused on a more remote American legal history, I shall not evaluate the last five decades of the Court's history. Those are chapters for future volumes. Instead, in this chapter I write primarily about the Supreme Court's civil rights record under Charles Evans Hughes, who served as Chief Justice from 1930 to 1941. A comprehensive study of this aspect of the Supreme Court during the Hughes era offers much insight into the difficult choices that the Court confronted as well as the tensions within the Court itself. It opens the judicial window into the period that marks the beginning of the end of the separate but equal doctrine, the journey aptly called the "Road to *Brown*."

On February 13, 1930, when Charles Evans Hughes became Chief Justice of the United States Supreme Court, an impartial observer would not have needed to ponder long over whether the United States Supreme Court had in fact been the protector of the rights of African Americans for the past half-century. Clearly, more often the Court had not offered an adequate legal shield of protection. Because the Court failed to uphold their legal rights, African Americans were effectively barred from southern voting booths, relegated to inferior public schools and facilities, excluded from most southern state colleges and universities, and subjected to a hostile criminal justice system. Indeed, the "Road to *Brown*" was a difficult one. "Separate but equal" was more than a theoretical legal doctrine; it was part of the foundation of the precept of black inferiority.

Americans rightly view the Warren Court's 1954 decision in *Brown v. Board of Education*[6] as the critical turning point in the legal battle against racial segregation and the Supreme Court's most promising rejection of the precept of black inferiority to date. *Brown*, however, was not just a revolutionary event; it is more properly viewed also as an evolutionary decision. It was the result of decades of litigation that chipped away at the legal foundation of the "separate but equal" jurisprudence of *Plessy* and its progeny.

The Hughes Court represents the midpoint between the birth of the *Plessy* doctrine and the beginning of the Rehnquist era. It started approximately twenty-five years before the *Brown* Court, and prior to the time when the nation went to war against the Aryanism and racism of Hitler and Hirohito.

The Hughes Court is perhaps best remembered for its decisions in the early 1930s that overturned many of the key statutes of President Roosevelt's New Deal and later sanctioned similar statutes. Many scholars of the Supreme Court give inadequate recognition to the fact that it was during the Hughes era that courageous civil rights lawyers, working in isolation or under the auspices of organizations such as the NAACP, confronted the Supreme Court with cases challenging racism in the courts and the electoral process, as well as challenging racial segregation in public schools, facilities, and transportation. The Court's decisions in these cases present a mixed record of progress. In a number of critical cases, the Court stopped far short of guaranteeing African Americans the full enjoyment of "rights which have been guaranteed to them by the organic and fundamental laws of the land."[7] However, the seminal civil rights decisions of this era redressed some of the most egregious instances of state-sponsored racism. In so doing, the Court took its first tentative steps away from *Plessy* and toward *Brown*.

Civil Rights for African Americans in the 1930s: The Constitutional Dream of Equality and the Daily Reality of Degradation

Two examples suffice to demonstrate the wide gap that existed during the Hughes Court era between the constitutional promise of equal treatment under the law and the daily reality of racial discrimination faced by even the most influential and powerful African Americans.

Segregation and the Congressman: "It didn't make a damn bit of difference who I was." [8]

The first incident involved the then highest ranking African-American public official in the United States—Arthur W. Mitchell of Chicago, the sole African-American member of the United States House of Representatives. On April 20, 1937, Congressman Mitchell boarded a Pullman car in Chicago with a first-class ticket to Hot Springs, Arkansas. When the train left Memphis, the conductor told him that he could no longer ride in the first-class section. Later, Mitchell testified, "I thought it might do some good for me to tell him who I was. I said, 'I am Mr. Mitchell, serving in the Congress of the United States.' He said it didn't make a damn bit of difference who I was, that as long as I was a nigger I couldn't ride in that car."[9] The conductor then warned Mitchell that he had "better get out of that car, and had better be gone when he came back."[10]

The conductor's unmuted order forced Mitchell to decide whether he should retreat to the decrepit African-American coach, which had no running water or working toilet, or whether he should challenge the conductor's policy by refusing to move.

Mitchell testified:

> [F]or a moment, I decided that I wouldn't go, that I would let them put me in jail down there and see how the thing would finally come out. But I happened to think that I was in Arkansas, and sometimes they don't keep

them in jail for trial down there, but they take them out and lynch them after they put them in jail; so I thought maybe I had better not; being the only negro in Congress, that I had better not be lynched on that trip.[11]

The conductor's behavior was in clear violation of a 1914 Supreme Court ruling that the denial of first-class accommodations on trains to African Americans violated the Fourteenth Amendment.[12] In 1937, however, Mitchell was aware that even an African-American congressman ran the risk of being lynched in Arkansas for demanding his well-established legal rights.

In 1941, the Supreme Court declared that the railroad's treatment of Mitchell violated his rights under the Interstate Commerce Act.[13] Because of further litigation after the Supreme Court's remand, however, Mitchell did not settle with the railroad until late 1945.[14] Despite the humiliation he had endured, and the time and expense of litigating his case before an administrative agency and the state and federal courts, Mitchell received in settlement the sum of $1,250, which he split with his attorney.[15]

Race Discrimination at the Citadel of Justice

The second example of racial discrimination in the 1930s occurred at the citadel of justice in this country, the United States Supreme Court. Although it is difficult to document the Court's discriminatory practices, reputable African-American lawyers who practiced in the 1930s have related that African Americans were occasionally discriminated against in the Supreme Court's cafeteria.

Judge Lois Forer, a respected Philadelphia jurist, stated that, as a young lawyer in Washington in the late 1930s, she often used the Supreme Court library for her research.[16] On one occasion, while standing in the line at the Supreme Court's cafeteria, she stood next to an African-American lawyer who had an argument scheduled before the Court. A manager came over to the lawyer and told him he could not be served. An observer, who Judge Forer believes was a law clerk, rushed out of the cafeteria and returned with Justice Louis Brandeis. The Justice approached the manager and said, "If this man is not served, I will leave the Supreme Court." After this unexpected intervention, the cafeteria manager seated the African-American lawyer at a table in the corner, and placed a screen around him.[17]

In July of 1990, I discussed the history of segregation at the Court cafeteria with Justice Thurgood Marshall. Justice Marshall reported that he had been told that in the late 1930s, when Thomas E. Waggaman was marshal of the Court, a number of incidents demonstrated that Waggaman had only contempt for African Americans.[18] According to what Justice Marshall had been told, Waggaman was so concerned that African Americans were using the Supreme Court cafeteria that he complained to Chief Justice Hughes. Hughes instructed Waggaman to go outside the building and look at the portals of the Supreme Court, which are emblazoned with the words "Equal Justice Under Law." The Chief Justice added that if after reading these words Waggaman did not understand what the policy of the Supreme Court should be, he would be replaced. From that date onward, there reportedly were no further attempts made to exclude African Americans from the Court's cafeteria.[19]

The *Mitchell* case and the segregation at the Supreme Court exemplify two realities facing African Americans in 1930s America: first, the grudging recognition by the courts that African Americans were entitled to the most basic rights of citizenship; and, second, the wearying legal battles that African Americans were forced to fight to secure those fundamental rights.

"The Prejudices Which Judges Share with Their Fellow-Men": Politics, Race, and the Hughes Court's Views on Civil Rights

The Supreme Court proclaims to be a non-political institution, and most justices strive to be objective, dispassionate, and "neutral" in their decision making. However, Justice Holmes's oft-quoted observation about the prejudice of judges applies with particular force to the Supreme Court's civil rights jurisprudence.

> The life of the law has not been logic: it has been experience. The felt necessities of the time, the prevalent moral and political theories, intuitions of public policy, avowed or unconscious, *even the prejudices which judges share with their fellow-men,* have had a good deal more to do than the syllogism in determining the rules by which men should be governed.[20]

Indisputably, political and sociological developments in this country and throughout the world profoundly influenced the Hughes Court's civil rights decisions. In the first third of this century, several factors combined to undermine the post-Reconstruction philosophy of white supremacy underlying the *Plessy* doctrine. Millions of African Americans had fled the stifling poverty and racial oppression of the Deep South to seek better lives in northern and midwestern cities. As they gained economic and political power, these urban pioneers became increasingly strident in their opposition to discrimination and state-imposed racial segregation. African Americans and some whites were struck by the hypocrisy of America's self-proclaimed international mission in World War I to "make the world safe for democracy" while African Americans were denied the most basic rights of citizenship at home. Finally, after decades of experience with the "separate but equal" doctrine, no reasonable American could any longer deny that the disproportionate allocation of resources in the separate schools, separate public accommodations, and separate public transport for African Americans was vastly, unmistakably *unequal.*[21]

The "prejudices which judges share with their fellow-men" affected how the members of the Hughes Court viewed these developments and shaped their vision of the Court's role in redressing human rights abuses of African Americans. The wide divergence of racial views among the justices is perhaps best illustrated by comparing the judicial careers of two jurists. One man emerged as one of the Court's fairly consistent supporters of racial justice. The other remained trapped by the bigotry and petty pretenses of his upbringing and became an increasingly lonely and bitter dissenter as the Court turned away from *Plessy* to emphasize equality of treatment as a higher value than racial segregation.

The Gulf Between Two Justices

CHARLES EVANS HUGHES

In an era when most judges shared, or at least implicitly accepted, the white supremacist principles at the foundation of Jim Crow legislation, Chief Justice Hughes held relatively progressive racial views. After Hughes's death, John Lord O'Brian recalled:

> Racial problems were always a matter of serious private concern to him and remained so even in the final years following his retirement from public life. . . . As early as 1908, he declared that "with respect to white and black, conditions which promote the *wholesome feeling of personal honor* and *individual worth* are alone the conditions which will secure lasting benefits for our society and the solution of the grave problems which confront it."[22]

The son of an abolitionist minister, Hughes served two terms as a progressive, reform-minded governor of New York before his appointment to the Supreme Court in 1910. He resigned from the Court in 1916 to mount an unsuccessful presidential campaign against Woodrow Wilson. From 1920 to 1925, Hughes served as Secretary of State under President Harding. In 1930, President Hoover appointed Hughes as Chief Justice of the Supreme Court, where he served until his retirement in 1941.

In two opinions, written in his first years on the Court, Hughes demonstrated his practice of redressing specific civil rights violations, without emphasizing the pervasive racism that gave rise to the abuses. In *Bailey v. Alabama*,[23] Hughes's majority opinion reversed, on Thirteenth Amendment grounds, the conviction of an African-American laborer found guilty of breaking a one-year employment contract.[24] Despite clear evidence that the Alabama statute at issue was designed to keep indigent, primarily African-American, farm-workers permanently indebted to white farm-owners,[25] Hughes began his decision by "dismiss[ing] from consideration the fact that plaintiff in error is a black man."[26] He continued: "No question of a sectional character is presented, and we may view the legislation in the same manner as if it had been enacted in New York or in Idaho."[27]

Hughes may be fairly criticized for downplaying the racial aspects of this case. However, in so doing, he undoubtedly held together a majority of a Court that was decidedly unsympathetic to legal claims by African Americans.[28] Hughes also articulated the important point that the Reconstruction Amendments' guarantees protected *all* Americans, and thus that civil rights was not a peculiarly African-American issue. "Opportunities for coercion and oppression, in varying circumstances, exist in all parts of the Union," Hughes wrote, "and the citizens of all the States are interested in the maintenance of the constitutional guarantees, the consideration of which is here involved."[29]

In *McCabe v. Atchison Topeka & Santa Fe Railway*,[30] five African-American Oklahomans sued to enjoin the state from enforcing a state law that permitted railroad companies to deny African Americans access to first-class railcars. In his opinion for the Court, Hughes reaffirmed *Plessy's* holding that the Fourteenth Amendment allowed Oklahoma "to require separate, but equal, accommodations for the two races."[31] However, he then destroyed the state's argument that the denial of first-class services to African-American passengers was justified by the legislature's finding that " 'there was no substantial demand for Pullman car and dining car service for persons of the African race.' "[32] Hughes wrote:

> This argument with respect to volume of traffic seems to us to be without merit. It makes the constitutional right depend upon the number of persons who may be discriminated against, whereas the essence of the constitutional right is that it is a personal one. Whether or not particular facilities shall be provided may doubtless be conditioned upon there being a reasonable demand therefor, but, if facilities are provided, substantial equality of treatment of persons traveling under like conditions cannot be refused.[33]

Ironically, this ringing endorsement of the Fourteenth Amendment's guarantee of equal treatment had no effect on the appellants in *McCabe*. Hughes concluded his opinion by holding that the appellants were not entitled to injunctive relief, as they had not demonstrated that they had been actually injured by the statute.[34]

JAMES C. MCREYNOLDS

In contrast, the Supreme Court tenure of James C. McReynolds, perhaps the most bigoted justice to sit on the Supreme Court in this century,[35] is an exam-

ple of the disastrous consequences of a President's ill-considered Supreme
Court appointment. Born in 1862 in Elkton, Kentucky, McReynolds rose to
prominence as a conservative and puritanical antitrust attorney during the
Theodore Roosevelt and Taft administrations. In 1913, Woodrow Wilson
named McReynolds as his Attorney General, where McReynolds's bad tem-
per and poor judgment in the handling of several politically sensitive matters
made his tenure "brief and disastrous."[36] In 1914, Wilson rid himself of this
cantankerous and controversial cabinet member by appointing him to the Supreme Court.

McReynolds did not reform himself during his judicial career. It was
with just a touch of hyperbole that Harold Laski remarked that "McReynolds
and the theory of a beneficent deity are quite incompatible."[37] The Justice
was intolerably rude to his colleagues, acidly sarcastic to the attorneys who
appeared before him, and generally reactionary in his conduct and judicial
opinions. Hughes's predecessor as Chief Justice, William Howard Taft, observed that McReynolds was "selfish to the last degree" and "fuller of prejudice than any man I have ever known."[38] Anecdotes about his racist, anti-
Semitic, and sexist conduct are legion. In 1938, Charles Hamilton Houston,
a brilliant African-American lawyer with the NAACP and a former member
of the *Harvard Law Review*, argued a landmark desegregation case before the
Supreme Court. During Houston's oral argument, McReynolds turned his
back on the attorney and stared at the back wall of the courtroom.[39] He once
referred to Howard University, a historically African-American institution in
Washington, D.C., as a "nigger university."[40] He repeatedly snubbed Justices
Brandeis and Cardozo because of their Jewish faith.[41]

A stalwart opponent of New Deal economic reforms, McReynolds also
vociferously resisted the Court's growing liberalism in civil rights cases. His
bitter dissents, often joined by his reactionary colleague from Minnesota, Justice Pierce Butler, railed against the Court's decisions that remedied racial
discrimination in jury selection,[42] criminal trials,[43] the electoral process,[44]
and schools.[45]

The Hughes Court's Diminution of the Inferiority Precept Under Law

The Criminal Justice Process

A series of criminal cases in the 1930s gave the Supreme Court a stark education about the injustices that African Americans faced in the American criminal justice system. The justices were not yet prepared to question the legal
basis of racial segregation, but these cases forced them to address the openly

racist and unfair treatment of African-American defendants in southern courts. In so doing, the Supreme Court accelerated a trend it had begun with decisions in *Frank v. Mangum*[46] and *Moore v. Dempsey*,[47] cases applying the Fourteenth Amendment's Due Process Clause to require the states to conduct fair criminal proceedings.[48]

The Hughes Court's landmark criminal justice cases were dramatic proof that in the criminal justice field the "separate but equal" concept of *Plessy* was not working in accordance with the rationale of equality that the Court had articulated in 1896. In *Plessy*, counsel had argued that separation of facilities on an intrastate train "stamp[ed] the colored race with a badge of inferiority."[49] The Supreme Court responded, "[i]f this be so, it is not by reason of anything found in the act, but solely because the colored race chooses to put that construction upon it."[50] In contrast, the Hughes Court's criminal justice cases demonstrated that courts treated African-American criminal defendants far more harshly than their white counterparts, and that this harsher treatment was not a figment of African Americans' imagination. These cases demonstrated that in many areas of the country the treatment of African Americans was both separate and *un*equal. In observing the extraordinarily disparate treatment African-American criminal defendants received in the courts, the justices undoubtedly must have recognized that a political system that permitted such gross racial discrimination even within its halls of justice would probably have similar inequities in its segregated schools, universities, and public facilities, and in other aspects of its public and private culture.

The Supreme Court's new direction in criminal justice matters became apparent shortly after Hughes became Chief Justice in 1930. The Court reversed the conviction of an African-American defendant sentenced to death for the murder of a white policeman.[51] The District of Columbia trial judge had refused to permit the defense to question prospective jurors about their racial prejudices.[52] In his opinion, Hughes remarked that "[n]o surer way could be devised to bring the processes of justice into disrepute" than to "permit it to be thought that persons entertaining a disqualifying prejudice were allowed to serve as jurors."[53]

In the famous Scottsboro cases, the Court reviewed the trials of several African-American youths, ages thirteen to nineteen, who were charged with raping two white girls in a freight car in Alabama.[54] The defendants were indicted, tried, convicted, and sentenced to death within two and a half weeks of the incident.[55] The trial judge did not name a lawyer for the defendants until the morning of trial.[56] Each defendant's trial lasted no more than a single day.[57] All were conducted after white protesters had swarmed into the small town of Scottsboro, Alabama.[58] Hundreds of militia were stationed around the courthouse.[59] The Supreme Court called the trial's setting a "community

. . . of great hostility."[60] The scene could more appropriately be character-ized as a hysterical lynch mob environment.

In *Powell v. Alabama*,[61] the first of three opinions involving the Scottsb-oro defendants,[62] the Court reversed the condemned African-American youths' convictions.[63] To build consensus in this highly politicized case, Chief Justice Hughes assigned the majority opinion to the conservative Justice George Sutherland of Utah.[64] Sutherland's carefully crafted opinion docu-mented the "atmosphere of tense, hostile and excited public sentiment"[65] that surrounded the Scottsboro trial and the trial court's rush to convict the unrep-resented, poorly educated, and frightened young defendants.

In its landmark ruling, the Court held that due process required state trial courts to appoint attorneys for indigent defendants in death penalty cases.[66] In a marked departure from the dry, abstract language that characterized most of the Court's previous civil rights decisions, Sutherland's opinion was clearly animated by the evidence of oppressively racist conditions that almost leapt from the trial record. Sutherland stated:

> [I]n the light of the facts outlined in the opinion—the ignorance and illiter-acy of the defendants, their youth, the circumstances of public hostility, the imprisonment and the close surveillance of the defendants by the military forces, the fact that their friends and families were all in other states and communication with them necessarily difficult, and above all that they stood in deadly peril of their lives—we think the failure of the trial court to give them reasonable time and opportunity to secure counsel was a clear denial of due process.[67]

Although the principles of fundamental fairness underlying the Due Process Clause mandated this holding, the stark racial injustice of the Scottsboro trial moved a majority of the Court to reach this result long before they might otherwise have done so.

In *Norris v. Alabama*,[68] the second Scottsboro decision, Chief Justice Hughes held, for a unanimous Court,[69] that the systematic exclusion of all African-American citizens of Jackson County, Alabama, from the jury rolls violated the Equal Protection Clause.[70] This case is remarkable not for its holding, which essentially reinforced a longstanding constitutional doctrine,[71] but because of the Court's readiness to examine the discriminatory application of a facially neutral jury selection system. In words that would later haunt those who attempted to hide racist motives behind the veil of "objective" factfinding, Hughes stated that the Supreme Court must determine not only whether a federal right has been denied "in express terms," but also whether it has been denied "in substance and effect."[72] He added: "If this requires an examination of evidence, that examination must be made. Otherwise, re-

view by this Court would fail of its purpose in safeguarding constitutional
rights."[73]

Unfortunately, as federal courts have continued to combat the most blatant forms of racial discrimination in jury selection, legislatures, prosecutors,
and jury commissioners have developed an imaginative array of devices to
bar African Americans and other minorities from the jury box. Sadly, recent
cases show that the American criminal justice system is still some distance
from its constitutional objective of color-blind jury selection.[74]

Anyone searching for a particularly egregious civil rights violation in
American history is well advised to begin reviewing the reported Mississippi
cases.[75] *Brown v. Mississippi*[76] is one example. In 1934, three impoverished
and "ignorant" African Americans in Kempner County, Mississippi, were suspected of murdering a white man. A deputy sheriff and several of his white
cronies brutalized the defendants with some of the most extreme torture ever
revealed in a reported American case. One defendant, Yank Ellington, so
enraged a mob of twenty white men with his professions of innocence that
they whipped him and twice hung him from a tree before finally releasing
him to return home in agony.[77] Two days later, the deputy again seized Ellington and took him to jail by a circuitous route that led into the State of
Alabama.[78] While in Alabama, the deputy again severely whipped the defendant until he "agreed to confess to such a statement as the deputy would
dictate, . . . after which he was delivered to jail."[79]

The same deputy then arrested two other African-American men, Ed
Brown and Henry Shields. One night, the deputy, the jailer, and several other
white men made the defendants strip. The two men were then "laid over
chairs and their backs were cut to pieces with a leather strap with buckles on
it."[80] They were repeatedly whipped and told that the whipping would continue until they admitted "in every matter of detail" a confession "in the exact
form and contents as desired by the mob."[81] During a two-day trial, the rope
burns on Ellington's neck were clearly visible,[82] and the deputy sheriff and
others freely admitted to beating all three defendants.[83] The deputy testified
that Ellington's whipping by the mob was "[n]ot too much for a negro; not as
much as I would have done if it was left to me."[84] Despite the clear evidence
that the defendants' pretrial statements were coerced, the trial court denied
the defendants' motion to suppress the "confessions."[85] The three men were
convicted and sentenced to death.[86] The aggressive young attorney prosecuting the case was John Stennis, and he did not deny the severe police brutality.
This case was one of the first steps in a political career that would later lead
Stennis into becoming an "esteemed" member of the United States Senate.[87]

Over a strident dissent from two judges,[88] the Mississippi Supreme Court disregarded the defense attorney's protest that the defendants' coerced confessions were invalid and inherently unreliable.[89]

In an appeal argued by former Mississippi governor Earl Brewer and partially financed by the NAACP,[90] the United States Supreme Court set aside the convictions and death sentences as a violation of due process. Writing for a unanimous Court, Chief Justice Hughes stated that although a state could adopt criminal procedures "in accordance with its own conceptions of policy," it could not institute a "trial by ordeal."[91] In language that bristled with outrage, Hughes continued:

> The rack and torture chamber may not be substituted for the witness stand. The State may not permit an accused to be hurried to conviction under mob domination—where the whole proceeding is but a mask—without supplying corrective process. . . . It would be difficult to conceive of methods more revolting to the sense of justice than those taken to procure the confessions of these petitioners, and the use of the confessions thus obtained as the basis for conviction and sentence was a clear denial of due process.[92]

In 1940, the Supreme Court reaffirmed the principle, announced in *Brown v. Mississippi,* that involuntary confessions were inadmissible. In *Chambers v. Florida,*[93] several "ignorant young colored tenant farmers"[94] were imprisoned, held incommunicado, beaten, threatened, and questioned almost continuously by the police until they finally "confessed."[95]

In a unanimous opinion written by Justice Hugo Black, the Supreme Court reversed the convictions, finding that the police coercion rendered the defendants' confessions invalid. "We are not impressed," Justice Black wrote, "by the argument that law enforcement methods such as those under review are necessary to uphold our laws. The Constitution proscribes such lawless means irrespective of the end."[96] The opinion of Justice Black was of great significance because it was one of his first decisions on the Court. Critics attacked Black's nomination because of his previous membership in the Ku Klux Klan, but he made his judicial philosophy clear in *Chambers,* where he wrote that "courts stand . . . as havens of refuge for those who might otherwise suffer because they are helpless, weak, outnumbered, or . . . are non-conforming victims of prejudice and public excitement."[97] Until quite recently, the Court firmly adhered to the principle enunciated in *Brown* and *Chambers* that coerced confessions have absolutely no place in criminal trials.[98]

A little known in forma pauperis case also shows the Hughes Court's growing sensitivity to the plight of African Americans in southern courts. In *White v. Texas,*[99] an African-American defendant sought review of his state conviction for raping a white woman. The Supreme Court originally denied White's poorly written certiorari petition.[100] However, Chief Justice Hughes was persuaded by White's rehearing petition that the Court might have acted too hastily. He sent for the state court record, which revealed that the Texas Rangers had coerced White's confession by third-degree methods. The Court summarily reversed the conviction[101] and denied the state's rehearing petition in a scathing opinion by Justice Black.[102]

In the midst of the retrial, White was shot and killed by the husband of the alleged victim. White's murderer was acquitted after the district attorney told the jury that the suppression of the coerced confession had forced the husband to take the law into his own hands.[103] According to Hughes's biographer, "[s]uch lawlessness in the name of law was sufficient to keep Hughes vigilant in examining the in forma [pauperis] cases."[104] At the present time, when the Supreme Court is restricting its review of in forma pauperis matters,[105] the Court's experience in White v. Texas bears remembering.

The Hughes Court's criminal decisions mark the feeble beginnings of a criminal justice jurisprudence that ultimately would curb the most severe abuses against African Americans and other citizens by police, jailers, district attorneys, and judges.

Education

During Chief Justice Hughes's tenure, lawsuits challenging the exclusion of African Americans from public graduate schools spelled the beginning of the end of school segregation. NAACP attorneys such as Charles Hamilton Houston,[106] Houston's cousin, William Henry Hastie,[107] and Houston's student, Thurgood Marshall, orchestrated the legal attack.[108]

In 1935, Lloyd L. Gaines, a twenty-five-year-old Missouri citizen, graduated from Lincoln University, the state's segregated African-American university. Gaines applied for admission to the University of Missouri Law School, the only state-supported law school in Missouri. Although a qualified applicant, he was denied admission solely because he was African-American. The registrar acknowledged that the University of Missouri admitted white students from other states, Asian-American students, foreign students—in fact, everyone except "students of African descent."[109]

The Missouri Supreme Court unanimously held that the State had satisfied its Fourteenth Amendment obligation to Gaines by offering to subsidize his schooling in the law schools of Illinois, Iowa, Kansas, or Nebraska, none of which excluded African Americans.[110] The court downplayed the fact that these schools were as much as 300 to 400 miles from Gaines's St. Louis home, stating that the necessity to travel great distances to attend an out-of-state school was "but an incident to any classification for school purposes and furnishes no substantial ground for complaint."[111]

Charles Hamilton Houston argued the *Gaines* appeal on November 9, 1938.[112] In an opinion for the majority in *Missouri ex rel. Gaines v. Canada,*[113] Chief Justice Hughes brushed aside the parties' extensive comparison of the legal training at the University of Missouri and at out-of-state schools stating the comparison was "beside the point."[114] According to the Court:

> The question here is not of a duty of the State to supply legal training, or of the quality of the training which it does supply, but of its duty when it provides such training to furnish it to the residents of the State upon the basis of an equality of right. By the operation of the laws of Missouri a privilege has been created for white law students which is denied to negroes by reason of their race. . . . That is a denial of the equality of legal right to the enjoyment of the privilege which the State has set up, and the provision for the payment of tuition fees in another State does not remove the discrimination.[115]

In response to Missouri's assertion that the "limited demand in Missouri for the legal education of negroes" justified the discrimination in favor of whites, the Court stated that Gaines's right was a "personal one." The Court stated that Lloyd Gaines

> as an individual . . . was entitled to the equal protection of the laws, and the State was bound to furnish him within its borders facilities for legal education substantially equal to those which the State there afforded for persons of the white race, whether or not other negroes sought the same opportunity.[116]

Gaines was the first Supreme Court decision to invalidate a state's school-segregation practices. The Court did not explicitly question the *Plessy v. Ferguson* "separate but equal" doctrine and, in fact, noted that the state could constitutionally furnish equal facilities in separate schools for African Americans and whites.[117] However, *Gaines* sounded the death knell of state-sanctioned racial segregation, for it seriously eroded two important legal foundations of *Plessy*'s aberrant reading of the Equal Protection Clause.

First, the *Gaines* opinion showed that the Court would no longer automatically defer to the state's "discretion" to adopt "reasonable" regulations to segregate the races in public schools. For the first time in a segregation case, the United States Supreme Court refused to defer to states' authority to regulate schools and actually scrutinized the *content* of the state's segregation plan.

Second, the logic, if not the language, of *Gaines* undermined the peculiar notion of "equality" which was at the heart of the "separate but equal" doctrine. Following *Plessy*, the Fourteenth Amendment guarantee of equal protection for all races took on a make-believe quality, as the Court strained to uphold state action with clearly racist motives and undeniably discriminatory effects.[118] *Gaines* was the first sign that the Court would no longer give "equality" such a tortured definition. The Court imposed a duty on the state to provide equal educational opportunities for African-American students without regard to the number of African Americans who were in a position to take advantage of those opportunities, and without regard to the availability of those opportunities in other states. Although the Court limited the *Gaines* holding to situations in which African Americans were legally excluded from state-supported professional schools, *Gaines* could not logically be confined to these facts. Because the Court read the principle of *actual* equality of opportunity into the Constitution, it was inevitable that some day the Court would have to face the reality that *all* forms of *de jure* racial segregation inevitably diminish the quality of services and opportunities available to African Americans.

By cutting back on the Court's deferential standard of review and moving toward an equal protection test of *actual* equality, the decision in *Gaines* paved the way for the ultimate victory in *Brown v. Board of Education.*

The Right to Vote

In the decades after the Civil War, the "respectable" leaders of the white power structure in the South did more than the terrorists of the Ku Klux Klan to bar African Americans from the voting booth. Describing his state's experience in a speech to its Constitutional Convention of 1890, Judge Chrisman of Lincoln County, Mississippi, said: "[I]t is no secret that there has not been a full vote and a fair count in Mississippi since 1875."[119] He stressed that "we have been preserving the ascendancy of the white people by revolutionary methods. In plain words, we have been stuffing ballot boxes, permitting perjury and here and there in the State carrying the elections by fraud and violence until the whole machinery for elections was about to rot down."[120]

In varying degrees of intensity, the discrimination against African-American voters persisted throughout the South. The Hughes Court had a mixed record in protecting African Americans' right to vote under the Fifteenth Amendment. The Court showed a willingness to remedy the most direct state-imposed obstacles to African-American voting, but stopped far short of redressing indirect, but equally effective methods of disfranchising African Americans.

The most significant barrier was the exclusion of African-American voters from the Democratic primary elections. In the essentially one-party southern states, the winner of the Democratic primary almost invariably won the later general elections. Thus, states could deny African Americans any meaningful role in the electoral process by the simple expedient of declaring the all-white primary elections the activities of "private" political parties.

After the Supreme Court's 1927 decision invalidating a Texas law that flatly prohibited African Americans from voting in the state's Democratic primary,[121] the Texas legislature enacted an "emergency" statute that permitted the party's executive committee "to prescribe the qualifications of its own members and . . . in its own way determine who shall be qualified to vote or otherwise participate in such political party."[122] The Democratic Executive Committee promptly restricted participation in the party's primary to "white Democrats."[123] In *Nixon v. Condon*,[124] the Court, in an opinion by Justice Benjamin Cardozo, struck down the state's attempt to circumvent the Court's prior ruling, finding that the state had unconstitutionally empowered the Texas Democratic party to "discriminate invidiously between white citizens and black. The Fourteenth Amendment, adopted as it was with special solicitude for the equal protection of members of the Negro race, lays a duty upon the court to level by its judgment these barriers of color."[125]

Despite Cardozo's ringing rhetoric, the Court's enthusiasm for demolishing voting barriers to African Americans soon faltered. After *Nixon v. Condon*, the Texas Democratic party passed a resolution at a party convention restricting membership to qualified "white citizens."[126] The Court unanimously upheld this method of disfranchising African Americans, blithely concluding in *Grovey v. Townsend* that the Fourteenth and Fifteenth Amendments did not prohibit a private political party from barring African Americans if the state did not directly authorize or compel this policy.[127] Thus, the Court accepted the hypocritical fiction that so long as African Americans were afforded a meaningless right to vote in the general election, they could constitutionally be banned from the critical primary election.[128] As one commentator aptly observed, after *Grovey*, "the southern states remained at liberty to render the Fifteenth Amendment hollow by allowing the dominant political party to exclude blacks from the only election that mattered."[129]

The Hughes Court had a mixed record in combating other types of bias against African-American voters. In *Lane v. Wilson*,[130] the Court struck down Oklahoma's patently discriminatory voter registration statute, which essentially disfranchised the state's black citizens. However, this victory was muted by the Court's prior decision in *Breedlove v. Suttles*,[131] which upheld a poll tax, a device which disproportionately disfranchised African-American voters.[132] It was not until the enactment of the Twenty-fourth Amendment that this decision's effect on federal elections was reversed.

On balance, it must be acknowledged that the Supreme Court under Hughes failed to vindicate African Americans' constitutionally guaranteed right to vote. Although the Court was willing to strike down the most blatant forms of voter discrimination, it lacked the will to address the South's increasingly sophisticated means of denying African Americans this most precious right of citizenship.

The Hughes Court in Retrospect

The poets and the writers of the 1920s and 1930s often conveyed the cruelties and the disparities that confronted African Americans more accurately and passionately than was possible in the dry, distilled language of Supreme Court decisions. For example, in his moving introduction to the profound sociological study *Black Metropolis*,[133] Richard Wright in 1945 gave voice to the anger and frustration felt by many of the victims of racism in America. Wright wrote:

> What has America done to people who could sing out in limpid verse to make them snarl about being "pressed to the wall" and dealing "one death-blow"? Is this the result of a three-hundred-year policy of "knowing niggers and what's good for 'em"? Is this the salvation which Christian missionaries have brought to the "heathen from Africa"? That there is something wrong here only fools would deny.[134]

He concluded:

> White America has reduced Negro life in our great cities to a level of experience of so crude and brutal a quality that one could say of it in the words of Vachel Lindsay's *The Leaden-Eyed* that:
> "It is not that they starve, but that they starve so dreamlessly,
> It is not that they sow, but that they seldom reap,
> It is not that they serve, but they have no gods to serve,
> It is not that they die, but that they die like sheep."[135]

Of course the Supreme Court did not and could not significantly deter much of the despair and cruelty which Richard Wright described. But nevertheless, in halting, tentative steps, the Supreme Court in the 1930s began to turn away from *Plessy*—and *Plessy*'s inherent reliance on the precept of black inferiority—in a series of decisions that implicitly recognized that the separate treatment afforded African Americans in the nation's judicial, educational, and political systems was inherently, unmistakably *unequal* and unfair.

During the Hughes Court era, civil rights lawyers began the arduous task of removing some of the most treacherous roadblocks on the "road to freedom."[136] In the following decades, other Supreme Court cases brought down still more barriers to equality in the areas of public education and facilities, employment, housing, criminal procedure, and voting rights.

13

VOTING RIGHTS, PLURALISM, AND POLITICAL POWER

VOTING rights are probably the fundamental rights of citizenship. Three of the most heroic and articulate men in history have deemed voting rights essential. Frederick Douglass proclaimed that the "possession of [the right to vote] is the keystone to the arch of human liberty; and, without that, the whole may at any moment fall to the ground; while, with it, that liberty may stand forever."[1] Justice Thurgood Marshall asserted that voting was "preservative of all rights."[2] Nelson Mandela identified "the right to participate in the making of the laws by which one is governed," as a fundamental principle of "equality before the law."[3]

The precept of black inferiority has guided almost every effort in the last two centuries to deny or hinder African Americans' equal access to the ballot box. The precept drove the efforts to restrict access to voting, and the denial of voting reinforced the precept of inferiority. Denial of the right to participate effectively in the political process has been one of the most effective mechanisms to enforce the precept of inferiority; it has ensured the social and economic subordination of African Americans throughout American history and in many ways even impacts on the present. Over the decades, the patent denial of voting rights to African Americans has been modified to more sophisticated systems of repression that even today can dilute the effectiveness of African Americans in obtaining significant political power.

This chapter describes the evolution of deterrence to effective political participation by African Americans. I focus primarily on Pennsylvania and a few northern states during the antebellum period, and on North Carolina, which has a history of disfranchisement and race-consciousness in politics that is similar to many other southern states, as to the post-Reconstruction era.

"A Page of History"—1832–1992

The Antebellum Period: Pennsylvania and the Northern Responses

The astute nineteenth-century observer Count Alexis de Tocqueville investigated the absence of African Americans from the political process in northern states. In 1832, he wrote of his surprise that African Americans could not vote even in an area of the North with strong abolitionist sentiment. Tocqueville related:

> I said one day to an inhabitant of Pennsylvania: "Be so good as to explain to me how it happens that in a state founded by Quakers, and celebrated for its toleration, free blacks are not allowed to exercise civil rights. They pay taxes: is it not fair that they should vote?"
>
> "You insult us," replied my informant, "if you imagine that our legislators could have committed so gross an act of injustice and intolerance."
>
> "Then the blacks possess the right of voting in this country?"
>
> "Without a doubt."
>
> "How come it, then, that at the polling-booth this morning I did not perceive a single Negro?"
>
> "That is not the fault of the law. The Negroes have an undisputed right of voting, but they voluntarily abstain from making their appearance."
>
> "A very pretty piece of modesty on their part," rejoined I.
>
> "Why the truth is that they are not disinclined to vote, but they are afraid of being mistreated: in this country the law is sometimes unable to maintain its authority without the support of the majority. But in this case the majority entertains very strong prejudices against the blacks, and the magistrates are unable to protect them in the exercise of their legal rights."
>
> "Then the majority claims the right not only of making the laws, but of breaking the laws it has made?"[4]

Tocqueville's query to the Pennsylvanian about African Americans' voting rights was answered by the Pennsylvania Supreme Court in 1837. In *Hobbs v. Fogg*,[5] the court considered whether African Americans could vote in that state. A free African American, William Fogg, was denied the right to vote because of his race, despite the existence of a Pennsylvania statute granting the franchise to every "freeman."[6] The issue that came before the court, therefore, was whether the term "freemen" included free African Americans. The trial court had charged the jury that the law did not deny free African Americans voting rights.[7] Following this instruction, the jury held that Fogg indeed had the right to vote. On appeal, however, the Pennsylvania Supreme Court disagreed. Asserting notions central to the precept of black inferiority, the court gave its imprimatur to the disempowering of African Americans. It declared:

> [O]ur ancestors settled the province as a community of white men; and the blacks were introduced into it as a race of slaves; whence an inconquerable prejudice of caste, which has come down to our day, insomuch, that a suspicion of taint still has the unjust effect of sinking the subject of it below the common level. Consistently with this prejudice, is it to be credited that parity of rank would be allowed to such a race? Let the question be answered by the statute of 1726, which denominated it an idle and slothful people; which directed the magistrates to bind out free negroes for laziness or vagrancy; . . . This act of 1726, however, remained in force till it was repealed by the emancipating act, of 1780; and it is irrational to believe that the progress of liberal sentiments was so rapid, in the next ten years, as to produce a determination in the convention of 1790, to raise this depressed race to the level of the white one.[8]

Faced with the Pennsylvania Constitution, which did not limit the franchise to white freemen, and confronted with a legislative history during which the word "white" originally modified the word "freeman," but was subsequently struck, the court nonetheless decided that African Americans could not vote. The court suggested implausibly that the word "white" was struck "because it was thought superfluous, or still more probably, because it was feared that respectable men of dark complexion would often be insulted at the polls, by objections to their colour."[9] Thus, the court concluded, the provision entitling "every freeman" the right to vote did not include African Americans.

Not satisfied with the victory against African Americans as reached by the Pennsylvania Supreme Court in *Hobbs*, Pennsylvania whites wanted to preclude forever the possibility that a future court might rescind the *Hobbs* ruling and give African Americans access to the ballot box. Thus, in 1838, the Pennsylvania Constitution was amended to limit the vote to whites.[10] Where the state constitution had previously been silent on the race of eligible voters, legislators inserted the word "white." So, in the land founded by Quakers, white supremacy prevailed and was reinforced by state constitutional authority.

Ironically, just as Pennsylvania had been a leader in the gradual abolition of slavery, and was followed by several northern states,[11] other northern states had similar provisions disfranchising free African Americans. Only Maine, Massachusetts, New Hampshire, Rhode Island, and Vermont gave African Americans the right to vote freely.[12] New York imposed property and residence requirements only on African-American voters.[13] By 1840, some 93 percent of free African Americans in the North lived in areas in which they could not vote on equal terms with whites.[14] African Americans were therefore subordinated politically and economically.

Following the *Dred Scott* case, Senator Stephen Douglas announced the sentiments in accord with the rationale that would preclude African Americans from obtaining political power. He declared:

> I believe this Government was made on the white basis. I believe it was made by white men, for the benefit of white men and their posterity for ever, and I am in favor of confining citizenship to white men, men of European birth and descent, instead of conferring it upon negroes, Indians, and other inferior races. . . .
>
> For thousands of years the negro has been a race upon the earth, and during all that time, in all latitudes and climates, wherever he has wandered or been taken, he has been inferior to the race which he has there met. He belongs to an inferior race, and must always occupy an inferior position.[15]

Abraham Lincoln responded to Douglas in their 1858 debates. Though he disagreed with Douglas's denial of African Americans' natural rights as citizens, such as life and liberty, Lincoln agreed with the precept of black inferiority and white supremacy, asserting:

> I am not, nor ever have been in favor of bringing about in any way the social and political equality of the white and black races—that I am not nor ever have been in favor of making voters or jurors out of negroes, nor of qualifying them to hold office, nor to intermarry with white people; and I will say in addition to this that there is a physical difference between the white and black races which I believe will forever forbid the two races living together on terms of social and political equality. And inasmuch as they cannot so live, while they do remain together, there must be the position of superior and inferior, I am as much as any other man in favor of having the superior position assigned to the white race.[16]

At the time the Civil War was about to begin, it was clear that Lincoln did not intend to eradicate the precept of inferiority from the American legal process.

The Reconstruction Era

Reconstruction marked the first challenge to traditional state discretion to wholly deny the right of African Americans to vote and hold public office. The Reconstruction statutes and constitutional amendments granted African Americans the full panoply of citizenship rights. Nevertheless, during the congressional debates on the proposed Fifteenth Amendment, notions of black inferiority pervaded the discussions. Senator James Doolittle, Democrat from

Wisconsin, stated plainly that "as a general rule with some exceptions, the Africans are incompetent to vote."[17] Democrat Garrett Davis of Kentucky also denied African Americans' capacity to exercise voting rights.[18] Senator Thomas Hendricks of Indiana doubted whether African Americans would "add to the common intelligence of the country when we make them voters."[19] Senator Willard Saulsbury of Delaware invoked even God's design to justify excluding African Americans from the franchise.[20]

While laudatory in intentions and hopes to make the United States a true democracy, the passage of the Fifteenth Amendment did not in practice assure for many African Americans voting rights. Waves of violent assaults, assassinations and acts of intimidation were launched against African Americans who dared exercise their rights. Organizations such as the Ku Klux Klan and the Knights of the White Camelia patrolled the streets displaying weapons they would use to prevent African Americans from voting. African Americans were warned to stay away from the polls and, if they disobeyed, were injured and often killed.[21]

Federal laws meant to enforce African Americans' voting rights, nevertheless, assured some measure of African-American participation in the political process during Reconstruction. In national politics between 1870 and 1903, two African Americans served in the United States Senate and twenty in the House of Representatives.[22] The active and thoughtful participation of African Americans in southern politics, where the majority of African Americans resided, dispelled the myth that African Americans were incompetent to vote or to hold office. Many African-American elected officials performed admirably, giving eloquent speeches on the floor of Congress,[23] fighting for equal rights and privileges for all citizens, exerting their influence to bring about racial equality under law, and otherwise reaffirming that African Americans, if allowed the opportunity, were capable of noble contributions as citizens and statesmen.

But as African Americans gained access to the ballot box and public offices, many whites who were opposed to equality in the electoral process sought to destroy African Americans' gains and aspirations. These whites viewed the political participation of African Americans as a dilution of whites' rights. African Americans threatened their perceived right to control every aspect of government policy making. Whites traditionally had used this hegemony to enact laws and issue decisions that perpetuated the very notion of black inferiority and white superiority. Determined to stem the tide of the black threat, whites demolished the spirit and substance of the Fifteenth Amendment and employed pervasive tactics to strip African Americans of their voting rights.

Ultimately, the national government abdicated its responsibility to protect the rights of African Americans. The withdrawal of federal protection gave white supremacists a free hand at disfranchising African Americans. A commonly used weapon in the disfranchisement effort was the enactment of ostensibly race-neutral suffrage requirements which disproportionately affected African Americans. Such laws were often the product of state constitutional conventions or legislative actions designed specifically to eliminate the African-American vote. Mississippi was a leader in devising elaborate methods to disfranchise African Americans.

> An adult male who would vote after January 1, 1892, was required: to be "duly registered" by state officials at least four months prior to an election; to be a resident of the state for two years and his election district for one year; to have paid all taxes including a "2.00 annual poll tax"; to have committed none of a specified number of crimes; and, most transparently, to read any section of the state constitution or "be able to understand the same when read to him, or give a reasonable interpretation thereof." Lest these measures be struck down by the courts, the framers added two other safeguards: legislative reapportionment to increase white-county representation and an electoral college scheme to insure white control of the governor's office.[24]

Judge Chrisman, of Lincoln County, Mississippi, gave an honest assessment to his state's constitutional convention:

> Sir, it is no secret that there has not been a full vote and a fair count in Mississippi since 1875—that we have been preserving the ascendancy of the white people by revolutionary methods. In plain words, we have been stuffing ballot boxes, permitting perjury and here and there in the State carrying the elections by fraud and violence until the whole machinery for elections was about to rot down.[25]

Enforcing the precept of black inferiority meant subverting the democratic process.[26]

The twentieth-century experience brought further and continued reinforcement of the inferiority precept in denying political influence to African Americans. The following section focuses on the North Carolina voting experience.

Post-Reconstruction North Carolina History

The post-Reconstruction era of racial suppression in voting matters in North Carolina began with the "White Supremacy Campaign" of 1898. Professor H. Leon Prather, Sr.'s description of the violence and intimidation of the 1898 election, at the hands of racist "Red-Shirts," is instructive:

[C]rowds of Red-Shirts were waiting for Governor Russell at Laurinburg on his return from voting in Wilmington. Anticipating that some violence would be inflicted upon him, the train conductor suggested that he ride in the baggage car to avoid personal injury, and the Governor obligingly took a prepared seat among the baggage. When the train stopped at Laurinburg, it was surrounded and boarded by Red-Shirts, shouting: "Where is Russell?" "Where is the Governor?" "Bring him out!" Those outbursts were accompanied by all sorts of vulgar language. There were rumors of threats to assassinate Governor Russell, and a race riot in the state appeared imminent. It was pathetic, indeed, to see a chief executive of a state subjected to such crass humiliation. This incident not only made a mockery out of the two-party tradition, but the democratic process as well.[27]

That the Republican governor was so intimidated by race-mongers that he hid in a baggage car so that his fellow white citizens would not assassinate him serves only to underscore the legitimacy of the fear felt by African Americans were they, against the wishes of the white community, either to exercise their franchise rights or to move into white residential areas.

The Red-Shirts' tactics of violence and intimidation dominated the election of 1898, when "armed with Winchester rifles and shotguns . . . [t]hey stalked about, frightening Republicans, Fusionists, and blacks away from the polls."[28] Two years later, volatile elections again rocked North Carolina and resulted in passage of legislation disfranchising African Americans with the use of literacy tests and poll taxes:

> As in 1898, Red-Shirts with all types of guns could be seen throughout the Black Belt loitering around the polls in riotous manner. To avoid violence, blacks as a body just did not vote. The elections were most gratifying to the Democrats. Aycock won the governorship against his Republican rival, Adams, by a decisive vote of 186,650 to 126,296, the largest majority ever given a gubernatorial candidate. Likewise, the [disfranchisement] amendment was carried. To win the election, intimidation, physical terror, "fraud and rascality have reigned supreme," complained Senator Butler.[29]

After Governor Aycock was inaugurated, he made clear that the state's primary governmental obligation was to disfranchise African Americans to assure white supremacy. The implementation of Aycock's disfranchisement scheme, in 1900, incorporated all means possible to defeat George White, the last African American from North Carolina for over ninety years to serve in the United States Congress, until Eva Clayton and Mel Watt were elected in November 1992.

Congressman White's defeat was part of a pervasive conspiracy throughout the southern United States to keep the colored man "in his place" and to destroy his "manhood-suffrage."[30] White's defeat symbolized the power of governmental, vigilante, and other forces to deny the African American what he had pleaded for: "the same chance for existence."[31]

Governor Aycock of North Carolina was determined, at all costs, to deny African Americans first-class citizenship and to preclude them from the right to participate in the governmental process. In December 1903, Aycock spoke before the North Carolina Society of Baltimore, Maryland, and proclaimed:

> I am inclined to give to you our solution of this problem. It is, first, as far as possible under the Fifteenth Amendment *to disfranchise him*; after that let him alone, quit writing about him; quit talking about him, . . . Let the negro learn once for all that there is unending separation of the races . . . that they cannot intermingle; let the white man determine that no man shall by act or thought or speech cross this line, and the race problem will be at an end.[32]

Governor Aycock set the tone for his successors. Several years later, Governor Locke Craig described and supported a proposed amendment to the North Carolina Constitution under which "the white men of North Carolina shall make and administer *all* the laws."[33] And, in his presentation to the all-white legislature of 1920, Governor Thomas W. Bickett said:

> Candor and my deep friendship for and my abiding interest in the permanent happiness of the negro race compel me to add that it is the settled conviction of the best people in all political parties in the South that it is necessary for the protection, the progress and the happiness of both races *for the government to be run by white people, and it is the unalterable determination of the whites to keep in their own hands the reins of government*.[34]

The explicit racism in government spanned from almost every southern state public official to, at times, the White House. As an example, in 1896 President Grover Cleveland, distraught about a false rumor that an African American had been present at an official White House function, made a frenzied denial: "It so happens that I have never, in my official . . . position, either when sleeping or waking, alive or dead, on my head or on my heels, dined, lunched, or supped, or invited to a wedding reception any colored man, woman, or child."[35]

Seven years after the Supreme Court decided *Plessy v. Ferguson,* incorporating segregation into the Constitution,[36] President Theodore Roosevelt, who was less hostile on the race issue, invited the moderate Booker T. Washington for an informal lunch at the White House.[37] In response, the *Memphis Scimitar* wrote: "The most damnable outrage which has ever been perpetrated by any citizen of the United States was committed yesterday by the President, when he invited a nigger to dine with him at the White House."[38] Senator Benjamin Tillman of South Carolina said: "Now that Roosevelt has eaten with that nigger Washington, we shall have to kill a thousand niggers to get them back to their places."[39] Georgia's governor was sure that "no Southerner can respect any white man who would eat with a negro."[40]

Senator James K. Vardaman of Mississippi, who often used Booker T. Washington as a foil for his racist rhetoric, once commented: "I am just as much opposed to Booker Washington as a voter, with all his Anglo-Saxon reinforcements, . . . as I am to the coconut-headed, chocolate-covered, typical little coon, Andy Dotson, who blacks my shoes every morning. Neither is fit to perform the supreme function of citizenship."[41] Contempt for African-American suffrage was well pronounced in the political arena.[42]

Moreover, even the institution of the Supreme Court was not immune to racist influence:

> [President] Hoover nominated as Justice of the United States Supreme Court John J. Parker of North Carolina, in spite of the fact that Parker had opposed the right of Negroes to vote. We have been told that Parker was willing to repudiate this stand but that the White House refused to let him; at any rate, while Mr. Hoover hastened to explain Parker's labor decisions, he treated his anti-Negro attitude with disdainful silence and despite advice and pleading, insisted upon sending this nomination to the Senate. It was finally defeated by a narrow margin by the influence of the Negro and labor vote and despite every effort of the administration to force it through.[43]

From birth to death, even in defense of the country, innumerable aspects of legitimized racism affected the lives of most African Americans every day. In World War I, African-American soldiers fought abroad and lost their lives in what President Woodrow Wilson proclaimed was the war to make the world "safe for democracy." Yet, at home there was segregation, not democracy. During World War II, thousands of African-American soldiers lost their lives for what President Roosevelt said was the fight for the Four Freedoms. But, at home, many African Americans were denied the Four Freedoms, including the right to vote.

Nearly every achievement was gained only through struggle. For example, consider the experiences of John Hope Franklin, presently the James B. Duke Professor Emeritus at Duke University:

> [John Hope Franklin] has achieved all of [these academic honors] despite having had to cope with the outrageous indignities that can be visited on a black person in our society. When his father, who was an attorney in Indian Territory before it became Oklahoma, moved to Tulsa, the building in which he had acquired a law office was burned down by a white mob, and for months his father had to work out of a tent. As a boy riding on a Jim Crow train in Oklahoma, John Hope and his mother were put off the coach by a white conductor and left stranded in the dust.
>
> When as a graduate student he sought to pursue historical research at

the archives in Raleigh, he was not permitted to sit with white researchers but was shunted off to an isolated chamber. The Library of Congress was still worse . . . [he] could not eat with . . . colleagues at any downtown restaurant, not even at the greasiest People's Drug Store counter. Nor, after having fought a victorious war against fascism, was there a downtown movie a black person could go to, or a downtown hotel at which, in the nation's capital, a black person could stay. That was John Hope's experience as a young scholar.

During this same period, on a train journey in North Carolina from Greensboro to Durham, he was compelled to stand even though there were ample seats in an adjacent coach—for those coach seats were reserved for whites, who sat there grinning at his discomfort. They were Nazi prisoners of war.[44]

The Persistence of Significant Political Racism in North Carolina in the Last Four Decades

Through the mid-twentieth century, voting by African-American North Carolinians was nearly non-existent, as literacy tests prohibited African Americans from exercising their political rights.[45] Although voting slowly increased through the course of the century, by 1948 still only 15 percent of North Carolina's African Americans were registered to vote.[46] Even as courts began to take action against *de jure* segregation, the displacement of African Americans from America's and North Carolina's political life continued. After the North Carolina literacy requirement was eliminated in 1961, North Carolina continued to require voting registrants "of uncertain ability" to read and copy the North Carolina Constitution, a practice that continued for another decade, disproportionately disfranchising African-American citizens.[47]

Beyond the realm of political empowerment, discrimination governed all facets of life including neighborhood development, business development, employment patterns, schooling, and criminal justice. There can be little doubt that such discrimination was able to occur because African Americans were excluded from civic life. Through the 1960s, every significant decision-making agency in the state—public and private—was completely dominated by whites even though their policy decisions had full effect in African-American communities.[48] In fact, North Carolina did not elect its first African-American state legislator until 1968, at a time when it refused to abolish patently discriminatory multimember districts.[49]

THE RETURN OF RACE-BAITING CAMPAIGNS

After the demise of the Jim Crow era, the exclusion of African Americans from the political process took different forms; in particular, racial rhetoric once again inflamed North Carolina politics to divide voters along racial lines. In a 1950 Democratic Party senate primary, Willis Smith took on incumbent Frank Graham, appealing to white voters' racism. Smith supporters distributed leaflets warning: "WHITE PEOPLE WAKE UP! . . . FRANK GRAHAM FAVORS MINGLING OF THE RACES."[50] From that point forward, although direct barriers to voting fell, white North Carolinians increasingly appealed to white prejudice and fear to polarize the electorate and marginalize African Americans and candidates who might protect their interests.

In 1954, supporters of Alton Lennon distributed a false endorsement of rival Ken Scott by an African-American political leader, in order to discredit him. Scott responded with an adamant endorsement of segregated schools.[51] In 1956, two of the three North Carolina representatives who refused to endorse the "Southern Manifesto," which vowed to resist the desegregation order of *Brown v. Board of Education,* were defeated at the hands of segregationist groups.[52]

In 1960, I. Beverly Lake ran for North Carolina governor on a segregationist platform, while his opponent, Terry Sanford, was accused of being "soft" on the race issue.[53] In the 1964 gubernatorial election, Lake again defended segregation, prompting primary rivals to oppose the pending federal civil rights acts. Concurrently, presidential candidate Barry Goldwater, pressing for the support of North Carolina voters, asserted his own opposition to civil rights legislation.[54]

THE AFTERMATH OF THE VOTING RIGHTS ACT

The passage of the Voting Rights Act in 1965 did little to quell racial appeals in North Carolina politics. Although the Act has encouraged African-American voter registration, which between 1960 and 1982 rose in North Carolina from 39.1 to 50.9 percent of the African-American voting-age population,[55] not until the 1991 redistricting has the Act enabled African Americans in North Carolina to choose representatives who would protect their interests.

After passage of the Voting Rights Act of 1965, subtle (and not so subtle) appeals to white racism persisted in North Carolina elections, intimidating African-American voters, punishing candidates for protecting "black" interests or for being African-American, and dividing voters along racial lines.

In 1966, two Democratic congressmen drew fire and were defeated for acceding to federal pressures for desegregation in an election marred by "violent intimidation against African-American families who proposed to register their children in formerly all-white schools."[56] George Wallace's 1968 presidential campaign appealed to voters' fears of court-ordered busing.[57] And, Jesse Helms, in his bid to be Senator in 1972, signaled his racial animus with slogans like "He's one of us."[58]

In the 1960s, if not beyond, the North Carolina legislature continued to dilute African-American political rights with the redistricting process. Time and again the legislature approved gerrymanders to dilute the vote of African Americans living in the well-organized, African-American community of Durham County. In 1965, for example, a proposal to create a "Research Triangle District" of Durham, Wake, and Orange counties was rejected in favor of a gerrymander placing Durham with conservative Forsyth County.[59] This "solution" led to the 16-year-term of L.H. Fountain—a conservative who opposed the civil rights movement, ignoring the interests of Durham County's substantial African-American population.[60]

This district finally was broken up in 1982, after a protracted fight marred by neutral sounding, race-based appeals. But even in Durham County's new district, African Americans fared no better.[61] Although African-American voters represented 40 percent of this district's Democratic party electorate,[62] due to the extreme racial polarization of North Carolina politics, the African-American community was still unable to elect a representative who would support its interests.

In the Democratic primary for that seat, African-American candidate H. M. "Mickey" Michaux—a United States Attorney appointed by President Jimmy Carter—opposed Tim Valentine—a white Democrat, who did not hesitate to appeal to white voters' racist instincts.[63] In an initial primary, Michaux finished first among three candidates, with 44.1 percent of the racially polarized vote, receiving 88.6 percent of the African-American vote, but only 13.9 percent of the white vote.[64] In a runoff between Michaux and Valentine, Valentine emphasized racial themes, warning against "the *well organized bloc vote*" and predicting that Michaux "will again be *busing his supporters* to the polling places in record numbers."[65] In a vote straight along racial lines, Valentine defeated Michaux by a spread of 6 percent and went on to win the general election.[66] Notably, Michaux received 91.5 percent of the African-American vote, but only 13.1 percent of the white vote.[67] Two years later, in a vote similarly split along racial lines, African-American candidate Kenneth Spaulding also lost the district's primary election to Valentine.[68]

As the Michaux race demonstrates, African-American candidates and candidates representing African-American interests have faced an immense barrier in garnering white votes in North Carolina. Due to racial polarization alone, the prospect of winning 30 to 40 percent of the white vote for such candidates has been remote if not inconceivable.[69] Where Michaux had the support of the district's 40 percent African-American voters, he still failed to garner sufficient white votes to win.[70]

In the 1980s and 1990s, race-baiting campaigns, marginalizing African-American voters, have been commonplace. In 1983, advertising supporting

Jesse Helms's bid for governor against Jim Hunt showed Hunt beside Jesse Jackson. As one journalist described, "the primary motive is simply to make the association between Hunt and blacks and to raise fears among whites that Hunt is a captive of black voters."[71] Helms also used a multitude of racially oriented signals in his 1990 bid for re-election to the Senate against an African-American candidate, Harvey Gantt. Gantt had been leading in the polls until the final week of the race when the Helms campaign ran an advertisement showing a white man's hand crumpling a job rejection notice, with a voice-over explaining:

> You needed that job, and you were the best qualified. But they had to give it to a minority because of a racial quota. Is that really fair? Harvey Gantt says it is. Gantt supports Ted Kennedy's racial quota law that makes the color of your skin more important than your qualifications.[72]

This advertisement galvanized white support for Helms, bringing him victory.[73]

More directly, an anonymous leaflet appeared in rural Columbus County in 1990, warning voters of "the Negro Vote" and that "more *Negroes* will vote in this election than ever before."[74] Representative J. Alex McMillan of the 9th District fanned racial fears with a 1990 fund-raising letter that warned of "the potential danger of a sophisticated get-out-the-vote effort among the core Gantt constituency—a constituency that particularly exists in substantial numbers in the most populous part of my district, Mecklenburg County."[75]

In the 1992 presidential campaign, local Republican party advertisements warned that "[i]f Bill Clinton is elected President, Jesse Jackson will be a U.S. Senator."[76] The Republican party engaged in a massive "postcard campaign," mailing postcards to African-American voters to discourage them from voting by threatening prosecution against voters who no longer lived at addresses registered with the Board of Elections.[77]

North Carolina's Racial Politics Disproportionately Harm African Americans

There can be no dispute that race consciousness has been—and continues to be—central to North Carolina politics. Racial appeals in campaigns are serious strategic tactics, designed to bring victory, that minimize the effectiveness of African-American participation in the electoral process. Race consciousness and racial polarization have regularly marginalized African-American voters—intimidating African Americans from voting; fomenting fear among white voters of candidates who may forward interests of African-American citizens; suggesting that African-American candidates are unable to protect the interests of all constituents; and perpetuating animosity and political divisions along racial lines.

Moreover, a mere decade ago, the federal courts found that North Carolina's *de jure* exclusion of African Americans from the voting process—with, among other means, a poll tax, a literacy test, and a prohibition against bullet voting[78]—had contributed to the continued suppression of African-American participation in North Carolina's political process.[79] In 1982, there was approximately a 14 percent disparity between voter registration of white and black age-qualified citizens—66.7 percent of whites were registered as compared with 52.7 percent of African Americans.[80] Although the court expressed a hope that continued registration efforts would overcome the chilling effect of historic discrimination,[81] such efforts have not yet succeeded. The lingering effects of historic discrimination in voting (as well as in myriad other facets of civic life) continue to dilute the political power of African Americans in North Carolina.[82] In fact, a significant disparity in voter registration alone—approximately 6.8 percent—between whites and African Americans still persists, limiting the ability of African Americans in North Carolina to assert their political interests.[83]

The exclusion from North Carolina politics that African Americans have suffered has served only to reinforce the legacy of racial segregation in which many African-American North Carolinians have lived. For example, African-American North Carolinians suffer the harms of poverty, inadequate education and medical care, infant mortality, unemployment, and violent crime more acutely than their white counterparts.[84]

The historical background of this chapter provides evidence of pervasive discrimination and exclusion of African Americans from the political process of North Carolina. It must be remembered, however, that North Carolina may have been less oppressive than some other southern states. Many whites have used means—subtle and blatant—to deny African Americans voting rights and thereby to enforce the precepts of African-American inferiority and African-American powerlessness. The current congressional redistricting controversy during the 1990s has been triggered by a series of United States Supreme Court opinions that, for the 1990s, has been almost as retrogressive as were the Supreme Court's opinions in the 1896 *Plessy v. Ferguson* era.[85] Many will view the 1990s decisions as a re-incorporation of some aspects of the shameful history of white supremacy, a process that was designed to safeguard white control and to exclude African Americans from significant political power.

EPILOGUE

As Published in

THE NATIONAL LAW JOURNAL

June 5, 1995

A. Leon Higginbotham, Jr.

DEAR MR. SPEAKER: AN OPEN LETTER

May 19, 1995

Honorable Newt Gingrich
The Speaker
U.S. House of Representatives
Washington, DC 21515

Dear Speaker Gingrich:

I congratulate you on your election as Speaker of the United States House of Representatives. For now, you are probably the most powerful Speaker this country has known in half a century. Power as great as yours brings terrible responsibilities. Because I care about this country and because I believe you do too, I write to you about your power and your responsibility.

As passed during the 100-day whirlwind session of the House of Representatives, the first draft of the Contract With America weakens the poor, the powerless and minorities. It has frightening implications that remind me of how, in the past, the states' rights doctrines were used to make African-Americans and the poor almost powerless under the dominance of arbitrary state governments.

Because of political spins and distortion, you and your colleagues have often branded the critics of your Contract as irresponsible "liberals," detached from the real America. As Barbra Streisand has said: "I am worried about the name calling, the stereotypical labeling. It was dangerous when Newt Gingrich developed a strategy in the last campaign of pitting President Clinton against so-called 'normal Americans.' The new scapegoats are members of what Gingrich calls the 'Counterculture McGoverniks.' "

183

Liberals are now typecast as abnormal, almost diseased, Americans. George McGovern, the son of a Republican Methodist minister, has been married to the same woman for 51 years. He flew 35 combat missions in World War II. It is absurd that his patriotism is disputed or that he is branded as "counterculture" by a person who never served in the military and whose own family history can hardly be called exemplary.

To deal with those who might seek to besmirch me because of my condemnation of some aspects of your Contract, let me give my personal family history. I am a 67-year-old African-American man. For 29 years, I served my country as a federal judge. I come from modest circumstances. My mother was a domestic, my father a laborer. Like them, I believe in the work ethic and that all able-bodied adults should work when jobs are available and that people should go on welfare only when it is a rational alternative to their plight.

We are not—and never have been—soft on crime, and we are advocates of fair and vigorous law enforcement. We always supported our church and family values. My parents were hard-working people, but the condition of their lives was limited. In their time, most African Americans were treated like second-class citizens, and many poor people, despite their best efforts, could not survive without welfare assistance. These facts have shaped my life and my values and my concern about the poor. I am a survivor of segregation. I have been an architect and a beneficiary of the civil rights movement of the 1950s and 1960s, and a witness to its legacy.

In 1899, the U.S. Supreme Court had a simple case of racial discrimination against blacks in your state of Georgia. *Cumming v. County Board of Education*, 175 U.S. 528 (1899). The Richmond, Ga., school board closed the high school for blacks, claiming they could not afford a high school for 60 blacks and, at the same time, provide an elementary education for 400 black children.

Despite alleged funding problems, the Richmond School Board made certain that *all* white children could obtain a high-school education; they provided a high-school education for all white girls, and they subsidized a high-school education within the county for all white boys. The Supreme Court did not find unconstitutional the invidious discrimination of the Richmond County Board of Education.

In 1915, South Carolina was spending an average of $23.76 on the education of each white child, and $2.91 on that of each black child. As late as 1931, Georgia and five other Southern states (Alabama, Arkansas, Florida and North and South Carolina) spent less than one-third for each black child of what it spent for each white child, and 10 years later, this figure had risen to only 44 percent. At the time of the 1954 decision in *Brown v. Board of*

Education, the South, as a whole, was spending, on the average, 43 percent more a year for a white pupil than it was for a black pupil.

Though, throughout Georgia, there were many public high schools accessible to whites, there was *not even one* public high school for blacks until the 1920s. Thus, perhaps the distant past and the "good old days" were relatively good for many whites who didn't care about excluding their fellow citizens from equal options, but those days were profoundly tragic for blacks and the poor.

And, in many ways, even today we are suffering the consequences of the devastating inequalities that have been imposed by the education system's shortchanging of blacks, generation by generation by generation, in thousands of school districts. I would have hoped that Congress would now be dealing with those past inequities by spending even disproportionate amounts of revenue to aid those who are weak and poor and who have suffered the maximum disadvantages in our society.

All of these *contracts* are permanently filed in the consciousness of this nation. So, there is no need to belabor the point. What all these contracts of the past have in common is that whenever politicians purported to enter into a "Contract With America," it seemed that most often the weak and the powerless were not the beneficiaries of it.

No better example can be found than in your book, *Contract With America.* You devote a whole chapter to your concern to enhance "Fairness for Seniors." However, you have no chapter on enhancing the fairness of entitlements for *children.* You propose letting the states decide their own standards for programs designed to help poor children, such as the school lunch program and aid to families with dependent children.

If the concept of letting states determine the allocation of such vital financial benefits is so sound, then perhaps you and your colleagues should consider turning over the entire Social Security system to the states as well. If your proposed system of block grants is so good for poor children, then our senior citizens should not be deprived of its advantages.

I suspect that you are willing to let the states do as they will with children, but not with senior citizens, because children do not vote and do not have political power, whereas senior citizens vote and have powerful lobbies.

Yet, surely politicians and academicians as informed as you and your colleagues must know, as the American Bar Association and the Children's Defense Fund have reported, that in today's America, our children are at great and grave risk:

- More than 9.4 million children had no health insurance in 1993, an increase of more than 800,000 from 1992.

- The United States has a higher proportion of low-birthweight babies than 31 other countries, including Romania, Greece, Turkey and Portugal.

- The United States ranks 19th among developed countries in infant mortality rates.

- The United States ranks 17th among all nations in the percentage of one-year-olds who are fully immunized against polio—behind Romania, Albania, Greece, North Korea and Pakistan. Our polio immunization rate for children of color ranks us 70th in the world.

- One in four children, or nearly 16 million children, live below the poverty line. In 1994, one in four homeless people was a child under the age of 18.

- 5,379 children and teens were killed by gunfire in 1992—one child every 98 minutes.

- A record level of 14.2 million children relied on food stamps to eat in 1993—up 51 percent since 1989.

I cite these data because of my concern about the welfare of all of America's poor children. I trust that Congress and the public will come to grips with the hard-core fact that there are more poor white children in this country than there are poor black children. Thus, any program that helps the poor benefits all Americans, regardless of their race, religion or national origin. Given these statistics, one then begins to wonder why the 100-day legislative program seems to ignore or victimize children.

Abraham Lincoln closed his first Inaugural Address by stating: "We are not enemies, but friends. We must not be enemies. Though passion may have strained, it must not break our bonds of affection." He prayed that: "The mystic chords of memory . . . will yet swell the chorus of the Union when again touched, as surely they will be, by the better angels of our nature."

In applying Lincoln's words to the challenges of today, in seeking justice for the poor, minorities and women, "we must not be enemies," whether one is white or black or any shade in between, whether one is male or female, whether one is rich or poor, or Republican or Democrat, and we must exemplify the "better angels of our nature."

Yet I fear that some aspects of the recent legislative program have awakened the *worst* forces of our nature and have set them loose. These forces overshadow the lives of the poor, the weak and the powerless and threaten to beat them down, and back to the great miseries of the Great Depression.

If this continues, history will not place you along with your hero Abraham Lincoln. Rather, your place will be with Rutherford B. Hayes, who betrayed blacks in the 1877 Compromise to win 19 electoral votes from the South and Oregon. After Hayes agreed with southern Democrats to withdraw federal protection of former slaves, the chairman of the Kansas Republican State Committee summed up their Faustian pact as follows: "As matters look to me now, I think the policy of the new administration will be to conciliate the white men of the South. Carpetbaggers to the rear, and niggers take care of yourselves."

It seems that in order to win the white-male vote, you and your colleagues have formulated a conciliation policy for white males that says: "Poor people to the rear and minorities take care of yourselves." It may be a successful political formula for the moment, but ultimately, this country will pay a heavy price for those unwise diversions. The weak and the poor will not long tolerate programs that give persons earning $200,000 a year tax breaks, while school lunches, food stamps and other programs for the needy are cut back with block grants that have tens of billions of dollars in cuts.

There is no moral or economic justification for dismantling and replacing federal entitlements with unaccountable state block grants. The retrogression that your Contract has set loose will not only beat down the poor, it will, in time, engulf us all, leaving no safe haven for either the enforcers or the victims of the inequitable Contract With America.

Sincerely,
A. Leon Higginbotham, Jr.

As Published in
THE BOSTON SUNDAY GLOBE
May 19, 1996

A. Leon Higginbotham, Jr.

100 YEARS LATER,
PLESSY V. FERGUSON STILL HURTS

This month is the 100th anniversary of *Plessy v. Ferguson,* one of the most retrogressive "civil rights" decisions ever rendered by the United States Supreme Court.

In 1992, Justices Kennedy, O'Connor and Souter said: "We think *Plessy* was wrong the day it was decided." Other justices, including Chief Justice William H. Rehnquist, seem to agree that the dissent of Justice John Marshall Harlan stated the proper rule of constitutional law. On this anniversary year, this malevolent and significant case and its tragic consequences should be put in perspective.

One hundred years ago, the Court declared that it was constitutionally permissible for the state of Louisiana to require that colored people could be separated from all other groups of people on trains.

In attempting to point out the absurdity of state-imposed racial segregation policies, counsel for the plaintiff Homer Plessy asserted that "the same argument" that would justify racial segregation on railway cars would also make valid any future state statutes that would require "separate cars . . . for people whose hair is of a certain color, or who are aliens, or who belong to certain nationalities."

Counsel was asserting that if it would be impermissible to segregate various groups within the white race—such as separating redheads from blondes, brunettes from bald heads, Irishmen from Italians, Episcopalians from Methodists, Jews from Gentiles, or any other configuration of segregation within the white race—then why would it be permissible to segregate blacks from everyone else?

In 1896, counsel for the plaintiff was asking the same question that Thurgood Marshall, 57 years later, would present to the Supreme Court in the *Brown v. Board of Education* case. In his oral argument, Marshall asked: "Why of all the multitudinous groups of people in this country [do] you have to single out Negroes and give them this separate treatment?"

Because of the racism that *Plessy v. Ferguson* sanctioned and the human tragedies it caused, we must recognize that the 100th year of *Plessy v. Fergu-*

son is NOT a celebratory event; instead it is more like a belated post-mortem, where lawyers, citizens and social scientists now dissect the corpse of racism. Today, we seek to analyze the virus that was unjustifiably implanted into the American legal process 100 years ago by the United States Supreme Court. This disease was the federal legitimization of racism in the post-Reconstruction era that destroyed much of the vitality that had been contemplated and assured by the 13th and 14th Amendments.

For generations, African Americans went to their graves knowing that the words of Langston Hughes were true when he wrote: "There's never been equality for me. Nor freedom in this 'homeland of the free.' "

There is probably no more vivid illustration of the impotence of African Americans during the *Plessy* era than the brief that Plessy's counsel filed. Counsel argued that Plessy, who was seven-eighths white, was deprived of his reputation of being white by the conductor's power to order him to sit in the colored section. Counsel also contended that being considered a white man was property, "which [had] an actual pecuniary value" that could not be taken without due process of law. He further stated:

> How much would it be *worth* to a young man entering upon the practice of law to be regarded as a *white* man rather than a colored one? . . . Nineteen-twentieths of the property of the country is owned by white people. Ninety-nine hundredths of the business opportunities are in the control of white people. . . . Probably most white persons, if given a choice, would prefer death to life in the United States as colored persons. Under these conditions, is it possible to conclude that the reputation of being white is not property? Indeed, is it not the most valuable sort of property, being the master-key that unlocks the golden door of opportunity?

From its inception, and for more than half a century thereafter, the separate but equal doctrine legitimized the segregation and exclusion of blacks in virtually every area of American life, including education, politics, business, employment, religion, health, housing, and transportation. *Plessy* defined what life was like for the vast majority of blacks as recently as the early '60s.

In the last two years, Americans have heard millions of words about what House Speaker Newt Gingrich proclaims is the "Contract With America." I, and other persons of good will, listen to the rhetoric surrounding the Contract With America with considerable skepticism. Why? Because, in Justice Oliver Wendell Holmes's phrase, "a page of history is worth a volume of logic." We know about the bitter consequences of *Plessy*, and the Contract With America sounds much too historically familiar.

It reminds us of how, in the past, states' rights doctrines were used to keep African Americans poor and almost powerless under the dominance of arbitrary state governments.

In Georgia, there were many public high schools accessible to whites, but not even *one* public high school for blacks until the 1920s. In 1915, South Carolina was spending an average of eight times more on the education of each white child than it was on each black child.

As late as 1931, Georgia and five other Southern states spent less than one-third for each black child than for each white child. At the time of the 1954 decision in *Brown v. Board of Education,* the South, as a whole, was spending on the average 43 percent more a year for a white pupil than a black pupil.

Even today, in many ways, we are suffering from the consequences of the devastating inequalities that have been imposed by the education system short-changing blacks generation by generation in thousands of school districts.

In the 1940s, Richard Wright wrote: "White America has reduced Negro life in our great cities to a level of experience of so crude and brutal a quality that one could say of it in the words of Vachel Lindsay's 'The Leaden-Eyed' that:

> *It is not that they starve, but they starve so dreamlessly.*
> *It is not that they sow, but that they seldom reap,*
> *It is not that they serve, but they have no gods to serve,*
> *It is not that they die, but they die like sheep.*

Although not stated with the anger of Richard Wright, even conservatives seem to recognize that *Plessy* was a case wrongly decided. In a tribute to Justice Thurgood Marshall published in the *Stanford Law Review,* Chief Justice Warren Burger wrote:

Measured in historical terms, the progress of the civil rights movement in this country has been agonizingly slow. . . . In 1896, the promises of the Declaration of Independence, the Emancipation Proclamation and the Civil War Amendments were "put on hold" when, in *Plessy v. Ferguson,* the Supreme Court approved the pernicious "separate but equal" doctrine.

In the long run, many more millions of African Americans were denied the benefits of first class citizenship by the seven Supreme Court Justices who wore black robes and wrote the majority's opinion in *Plessy v. Ferguson* than were the systematic injustices caused by hooded vigilantes wearing white sheets and the emblem of the Ku Klux Klan.

I do not raise this 100-year history to further polarize our nation. I acknowledge that there has been significant progress in this nation, but I also start with the perspective of George Santayana, who once said: "Those who cannot remember the past are condemned to repeat it."

As Published in
THE BOSTON SUNDAY GLOBE
June 30, 1996

Cleo Fields and A. Leon Higginbotham, Jr.

THE SUPREME COURT'S REJECTION OF PLURALISM

Racial pluralism and diversity in the U.S. Congress are as essential to a democracy as is rain for crops and air for breathing. Nevertheless, once again, the federal courts have denied African Americans the opportunity to have significant political power in shaping the public policy of Louisiana and in Congress.

Last Monday, the U.S. Supreme Court dismissed as moot *Hays v. Louisiana*, the congressional redistricting case involving the 4th Congressional District of Louisiana, which is represented by Cleo Fields, an African American who has been a member of Congress for more than three years. As the culmination of three years of litigation, the dismissal was merely the tip of an iceberg that was created in 1993 by a Supreme Court decision, *Shaw v. Reno*, which, in a dissent, Justice Byron White described as "both a fiction and a departure from settled equal-protection principles."

From 1878 to 1991, the one constant in Louisiana congressional politics was the triumph of white supremacy. African Americans were excluded from voting by fraud, manipulation, intimidation, violence and even murder. As recently as last January, the federal district court in Louisiana stated: "We in no way wish to understate the gravity of Louisiana's well-documented history of racial discrimination with regard to its voting policies."

In 1991, William J. Jefferson of New Orleans became the first African American from Louisiana to serve in Congress in 113 years. He was joined in 1993 by Rep. Cleo Fields. Therefore, for the first time in 1993, two out of seven members of Congress from Louisiana were African-American in a state where the African-American population exceeds 30 percent. Last week, the Supreme Court's dismissal left in place the boundaries created by the trial court in 1996 that had redrawn the 4th Congressional District with new configurations that decreased the African-American voting population from approximately 55 percent to 27 percent in Field's district. Some months after the district court created its redistricting plan, the Louisiana Legislature adopted the court-ordered plan.

In the recent voting rights cases, the Supreme Court dealt African Americans a blow almost as cruel as when it issued the "separate but equal" doctrine in *Plessy v. Ferguson,* a racial segregation case arising out of Louisiana 100 hundred years ago. At the time, John Marshall Harlan, the lone dissenting justice, stated that the segregation of African Americans from the rest of society was unconstitutional because our "Constitution is color blind, and neither knows nor tolerates classes among citizens. . . . The humblest is the peer of the most powerful."

The ultimate irony is that now conservatives are using the "color blind" jargon of ancient cases and distorting those concepts to restore unmuted white political supremacy to most of the major positions of political power. If the conservatives succeed, neither blacks nor the humble will be the "peer of the most powerful."

The three-judge federal court knowingly precluded pluralism by rejecting Field's district boundaries and creating new congressional districts from which African Americans are highly unlikely to be elected. The "reality" of white bloc voting is such that never in the history of Louisiana has an African American been elected to a statewide position or to a state legislative position where the African-American voting population was not approximately 50 percent. It is precisely with that "reality" in mind that Justice Ruth Bader Ginsburg noted:

> To accommodate the reality of ethnic bonds, legislatures have long drawn voting districts along ethnic lines. Our nation's cities are full of districts identified by their ethnic character—Chinese, Irish, Italian, Jewish, Polish, Russian, for example. . . .
>
> If Chinese-Americans and Russian-Americans may seek and secure group recognition in the delineation of voting districts, then African-Americans should not be dissimilarly treated. Otherwise, in the name of equal protection, we would shut out "the very minority group whose history in the United States gave birth to the Equal Protection Clause."

Everyone seems to be content with blacks as entertainers, dancers and athletes, but is there some discomfort and anxiety when avenues open for African Americans to attain significant political power and to determine the public policy rather than the entertainment policy of this nation?

In 1992, with the help of majority-minority districts, African Americans were elected to Congress from Florida for the first time, and from Alabama, South Carolina, Virginia, and North Carolina for the first time in more than a century.

Their victory may be short-lived. Due to the Supreme Court-imposed defeats in Texas, Florida, Georgia, North Carolina, and Louisiana, the number of African-American and Latino members of Congress might be reduced by nine and a further possible loss of seven seats in other states.

Yet we often wonder, why is it that when there was finally a significant number of African Americans in Congress, the Supreme Court imposed the new and previously unheard of constitutional doctrine in *Shaw v. Reno?* We do not speak out because of any feelings of personal defeat. Rather, we write in sadness for our country because it is a lesser nation without gender, racial and minority pluralism in positions of significant political power.

Even though some may be tempted to emphasize the potential dramatic reduction of African Americans in Congress, we persist in sharing the faith George White expressed in 1901, as the last African American to serve in that body for decades, that "Phoenix-like" we "will rise up some day and come again" as significant forces in Congress.

The greatest irony throughout these events is that if Thurgood Marshall were still on the court, or if his successor was sympathetic to Justice Marshall's views and to those of the four dissenting justices, the pernicious doctrine of *Shaw v. Reno* would never have been born.

Five Supreme Court justices have done to African Americans in Louisiana what no hooded Ku Klux Klan mobs were able to do in this decade—remove an African American from Congress. The federal district court created a new district where David Duke, a former Klan leader, will have a far better chance of election than Cleo Fields.

In addition to the recent gubernatorial race, two other recent major statewide elections have demonstrated that race is still the driving force in Louisiana politics.

In two races—first for the U.S. Senate and then for governor—white supremacist David Duke ran disturbingly successful campaigns based on the resurgence of white supremacy. In both elections, Duke's racist views were well publicized.

In the parishes now included in the new congressional district created by the federal court, when David Duke previously ran for the U.S. Senate and governorship, he won a majority of the votes. He believes that the district court's new congressional district was "tailor-made" for him.

With this sad state of recent events, we sometimes feel like the late Adlai E. Stevenson; the defeats "hurt too much to laugh," and we are "too old to cry."

Cleo Fields is a Democratic U.S. representative from Louisiana. A. Leon Higginbotham, Jr., chief judge emeritus of the U.S. Court of Appeals, is the public service professor of jurisprudence at the Kennedy School of Government at Harvard University and Of Counsel to Paul, Weiss, Rifkind, Wharton & Garrison. He was pro bono publico counsel for Rep. Fields in the recent district court litigation.

APPENDIX: THE TEN
PRECEPTS OF AMERICAN
SLAVERY JURISPRUDENCE

I would formulate the Ten Precepts of American Slavery Jurisprudence as follows:

1. *Inferiority:* Presume, preserve, protect, and defend the ideal of the superiority of whites and the inferiority of blacks.
2. *Property:* Define the slave as the master's property, maximize the master's economic interest, disregard the humanity of the slave except when it serves the master's interest, and deny slaves the fruits of their labor.
3. *Powerlessness:* Keep blacks—whether slave or free—as powerless as possible so that they will be submissive and dependent in every respect, not only to the master but to whites in general. Limit blacks' accessibility to the courts and subject blacks to an inferior system of justice with lesser rights and protections and greater punishments. Utilize violence and the powers of government to assure the submissiveness of blacks.
4. *Racial "Purity":* Always preserve white male sexual dominance. Draw an arbitrary racial line and preserve white racial purity as thus defined. Tolerate sexual relations between white men and black women; punish severely relations between white women and non-white men. As to children who are products of interracial sexual relations, the freedom or enslavement of the black child is determined by the status of the mother.
5. *Manumission and Free Blacks:* Limit and discourage manumission; minimize the number of free blacks in the state. Confine free blacks to a status as close to slavery as possible.

6. *Family:* Recognize no rights of the black family, destroy the unity of
the black family, deny slaves the right of marriage; demean and
degrade black women, black men, black parents, and black children;
and then condemn them for their conduct and state of mind.[1]

7. *Education and Culture:* Deny blacks any education, deny them
knowledge of their culture, and make it a crime to teach those who
are slaves how to read or to write.

8. *Religion:* Recognize no rights of slaves to define and practice their
own religion, to choose their own religious leaders, or to worship
with other blacks. Encourage them to adopt the religion of the white
master, teach them that God who is white will reward the slave who
obeys the commands of his master here on earth. Use religion to
justify the slave's status on earth.

9. *Liberty—Resistance:* Limit blacks' opportunity to resist, bear arms,
rebel, or flee; curtail their freedom of movement, freedom of association, and freedom of expression. Deny blacks the right to vote and
to participate in government.

10. *By Any Means Possible:* Support all measures, including the use of
violence, that maximize the profitability of slavery and that legitimize racism. Oppose, by the use of violence if necessary, all measures that advocate the abolition of slavery or the diminution of
white supremacy.

The Problem of Categorization: Precept, Commandment, or Declaration

For years, I have struggled to discern how the concepts in this framework
should be articulated. Should they be labeled the ten "commandments," "precepts," or a "declaration of non-rights"? When I gave the Du Bois Lectures
at Harvard in 1984 on the legitimization of racism, I formulated these concepts as the Ten Commandments of Slavery. At other times, I have described
these categories as the Ten American Precepts of Racial Villainy, the Declaration of Non-Rights for Blacks, and the Declaration of Dependence for
Blacks.

I originally used "The Ten Commandments of Slavery" because it conveyed a certain moral and human tone. "Thou shalt not kill" expresses a
stronger feeling about the value of life than the statute defining, in rather drab
language, first-degree murder.[2] I chose the word "commandment" to describe
the guiding premises of the slave system, as well as the Scriptural "Thou
shalt" in the formulation of the slavery commandments, because these terms

suggest goals, rules, or preferences designed to be accepted, followed, and implemented as "Gospel truth." Thus, the first commandment read "Thou shalt constantly and unrelentingly advocate the superiority of the white race and the inferiority of blacks. Thou shalt firmly implant in the minds of blacks the feeling of inferiority, and shalt convince both whites and blacks that blacks are innately inferior." In the operation of slavery, judges, legislators, and plantation owners often spoke of slavery as if it were an institution favored by the Almighty Himself and imposed upon blacks as a moral duty.[3] The original formulation of my proposed Ten Commandments of Slavery is presented in an endnote.[4]

After first articulating the concept as a commandment, I later felt that the premises of slavery could be better explained in an ironic way as an explicit repudiation of the Declaration of Independence. As a political document designed to encourage a revolution, the Declaration of Independence was an effort by Thomas Jefferson and others to state some compelling premises or truths that they believed governed, or should govern, mankind. Thus, in the Declaration of Independence, they noted those "self-evident" truths and "certain unalienable Rights" that "all men" had to "Life, Liberty and the pursuit of Happiness." They listed the "long train of abuses and usurpations" that were part of "[t]he history of the present King of Great Britain" and they felt that they were obliged to "let [those] Facts be submitted to a candid world."[5] Jefferson condemned King George in the Declaration of Independence (for whites), and in the Declaration of the Causes and Necessity of Taking Up Arms (for whites).[6] However, equally dramatic documents might have chronicled the repeated injuries and usurpations imposed on blacks by those white colonists demanding liberty from the British. Such a comparison would make King George's "taxation without representation" of the colonists seem quite trivial. One could say of these "revolutionaries," as Samuel Johnson did in response to the 1775 resolution and address of the American Congress: "If slavery be thus fatally contagious, how is it that we hear the loudest yelps for liberty among the drivers of negroes."[7] Finally, Johnson summed up the colonists' arguments as "too foolish for buffoonery [and] too wild for madness."[8]

Any declaration in condemnation of the plight of blacks and particularly of slaves in colonial America would have been a document more dramatic than the Declaration of Independence. Any document that described the cruelty of slavery in America could have been labeled "The Declaration of Dependence for Blacks" or "The Declaration of Non-Rights for Blacks." By whatever terms such a document used, it would have reflected what Jefferson knew—that slavery was a villainy that had no moral justification. In his *Notes on the State of Virginia*, Jefferson described the malevolent consequences of slavery as follows:

The whole commerce between master and slave is a perpetual exercise of
the most boisterous passions, the most unremitting despotism on the one
part, and degrading submissions on the other . . . permitting one half the
citizens thus to trample on the rights of the other, transforms those into
despots, and these into enemies, destroys the morals of the one part, and
the amor patriae of the other.[9]

He then proceeded to ask and answer the security and moral questions:

And can the liberties of a nation be thought secure when we have removed
their only firm basis, a conviction in the minds of the people that these
liberties are of the gift of God? That they are not to be violated but with
his wrath? Indeed I tremble for my country when I reflect that God is just:
that his justice cannot sleep forever: . . . The almighty has no attribute
which can take side with us in such a contest.[10]

With such a commentary, Thomas Jefferson acknowledged the venalness of
the practices that I describe in these volumes. Although he did not speak of
these concepts with the explicitness of my present formulations, he recognized that many of those in power had a common understanding as to how
the slavery system should be run and of the rules of governance that should
be applied against both slaves and free blacks in order to maximize the advantages of slaveholders.

After considerable consultation and experimentation, I decided to call
these explicit and implicit rules of governance the Ten Precepts of American
Slavery Jurisprudence. Over the past decade, among the many scholars I have
consulted and students I have taught, there has been an almost equal division
as to whether the term "precept" as a less value-laden term was preferable
to "commandment" or any of the other categorizations with which I have
experimented. I recognize that "precept" has an overtone of neutrality or even
one of objectivity that partially masks the full magnitude of the cruelty and
injustice spawned in the rules and rationale sanctioning slavery and limiting
the options of free blacks.

Why Ten Precepts?

One might ask if there is any hierarchical significance in the order of the ten
precepts, and why they were cast as ten rather than nine or thirteen or some
other number. I can imagine someone asking whether Precept Five is more
significant than Precept Nine. In my view, the first three precepts on inferiority, property, and powerlessness are the *sine qua non*. Precepts Four to Ten
each exemplify some aspect of at least one of the first three.[11]

The choice of ten, rather than a larger or smaller number, creates a symbolic irony as a contrast to the Ten Commandments of the Judeo-Christian religion. There is an additional tension in likening the ten precepts of slavery to the first ten amendments to the U.S. Constitution, our Bill of Rights. The Bill of Rights exemplifies some of the most noble aspirations of our nation's founders. Yet at the very same time that they were drafting a bill of rights for themselves, many of the "forefathers" exemplified, by their practice and laws, either several or all of the ten precepts I have noted. The phrase "Ten Precepts of American Slavery Jurisprudence" reveals the duality of the conflicting principles that governed American society. From one perspective, the United States was a nation that enacted a bill of rights for whites, and, from another, it was a nation that sanctioned the complete denial of liberty and justice to almost all blacks.

The delineation of these ten categories has not been easy.[12] More than a century ago, Justice Holmes suggested that the law was a seamless web, and he attempted to explain much of the common law under several broad categories in his classic treatise, *The Common Law*. The task of drawing crisp, sharp lines distinguishing one legal concept from another is, however, difficult at best. As Chief Justice Earl Warren pointed out in *Bolling v. Sharpe*,[13] a public school segregation case decided on the same day as *Brown v. Board of Education*, "the concepts of equal protection [in the Fourteenth Amendment] and due process [in the Fifth Amendment], both stemming from our American ideal of fairness, are not mutually exclusive."[14] Just as the Fourteenth Amendment concepts of due process, equal protection, and privileges and immunities are not separate, unconnected concepts, likewise there is also an unavoidable overlap between some of the other precepts of slavery. As Justice Holmes once explained: "I do not think we need trouble ourselves with the thought that my view depends upon differences of degree. The whole law does so as soon as it is civilized."[15]

These precepts are not intended to be like the basic elements of the natural world, where each element has an irreducible and separate atomic structure. The "atomic structure" of a precept cannot be so sharply differentiated. While others might prefer to draw the lines differently, by increasing or reducing the number of precepts, these differences are matters of delineation or degree and do not warrant an assumption that because it is difficult to draw a line, no line can be drawn.

The Interrelationships of the Precepts

For one person to own another, thus allowing the owner to dominate, often with cruelty, the person who is owned, demands a "reason." That reason is supplied primarily by the first three precepts, which express the underlying theoretical, moral, and legal foundations for the denial by whites of the slave's humanity, liberty, dignity, competence, and intelligence. All of the other precepts are exemplifications of some aspect of the first three precepts. The interrelationships of the ten precepts can be put in perspective by focusing on each of the first three precepts briefly.

The First Precept: Inferiority

For centuries, the inferiority of blacks and the superiority of whites provided the justification for European and American enslavement of Africans. One rationale for the inferiority of the African slave was that the African is not human at all. To consider the black slave as a subspecies of man[16] or a person, most often a heathen, who was from a less advanced, oppressed civilization,[17] could justify his enslavement. The whites' "logic" went as follows: The African is different in appearance and manner from us; he must not be human or at least not equally as human as we are; therefore, he is inferior to us and can be enslaved by us, his superiors.[18]

This enslavement was, of course, for the benefit of those in power. Yet, ultimately, many would claim that it was also beneficial to the slaves, as former Chief Judge Ruffin of the North Carolina Supreme Court declared in 1855 to the State Agricultural Society of North Carolina:

> Then let me say once more to you, men of North Carolina, stick to her, and make her what she can and ought to be. For you and your sons she will yield a rich harvest; to some "thirtyfold, some sixtyfold, and some an hundredfold," according to the skill and diligence with which the tillage of the good ground is done.
>
> The nature of the labor employed in our agriculture is the next subject for our consideration. It is a most important element in the cost, amount, and value of production. I very frankly avow the opinion, that our mixed labor of free white men of European origin and of slaves of the African race, is as well adapted to the public and private ends of our agriculture as any other could be—making our cultivation not less thorough, cheap and productive than it would be, if carried on by the whites alone, and far more so than the blacks by themselves would make it; *and, therefore, that it has a beneficial influence on the prosperity of the country, and the physical and moral state of both races, rendering both better and happier than either would be here, without the other.*[19]

The premise of black inferiority and white superiority unifies many of the strands of moral and legal rationale present in the other precepts, which amplify or follow from the first precept. For example, in order to maintain the first precept's assumption of white superiority and black inferiority, whites had to adhere to an ideal of racial purity, enforced by a rigid color line (the fourth precept). The color line applied primarily and most severely against the most vulnerable and least powerful elements of the society: white women, black men, and black women. Whites struck back, sometimes violently, against dissenters.

Free blacks presented a challenge to the validity of the first precept. If free blacks were as inferior to whites as their enslaved brethren, why were they freed and what was to be done with the free blacks? What rights, if any, and responsibilities did these "free" persons of color have? The fifth precept answers those questions by considering all blacks as servile beings, whether legally enslaved or not. The first precept's assumed inferiority of all blacks justified the differentiated meaning of freedom between free blacks and free whites.

The Second Precept: Property

The *property* aspect of slavery, the second precept, is also a unifying theme for all the other precepts. Once it has been justified for men and women to own black human beings as they would any chattel possession, the owners can do whatever they please with their chattel/slaves. In general, property owners have free rein to put their possessions to whatever lawful use they see fit; this same principle applied when the possession in question was a person. Like a pet, or a work horse, the slave was made totally dependent on the whim of the owner. The owner can make all the basic decisions in the slaves' lives: how and when they work; what tasks they will do, will not do, or be allowed to do; how much they will be fed; what "housing" they will be provided; whether they may "marry" and remain with their spouse (sixth precept); and even whether they live or die. The owner can use slaves' "wives," or any slave women, as concubines, or he may sell off slaves' families piecemeal (the fourth and sixth precepts). The owner can dictate the religion (eighth precept) their slaves will outwardly follow,[20] and with whom and when their slaves shall profess that "faith" (eighth precept). Manumission was a property prerogative, although subject to certain public-law limitations, and the owner could thus decide whether slaves were to remain enslaved or were to be set free; and, if freed, under what terms and conditions (fifth precept). Once having assumed absolute dominance, the slave's owner could assert absolute control over the slave's movements and contacts (the ninth precept).

The Third Precept: Powerlessness

The third precept, keeping blacks powerless, whether slave or free, and dependent on the whites in power, was one of the most important aspects of maintaining control of and subordinating blacks. Once rendered powerless, slave families could be broken up at the whim of the master (sixth precept), slaves could be deprived of an education (seventh precept), and have their contact with the rest of the world controlled and circumscribed (ninth precept). In short, together these precepts guaranteed that slaves lost control over their livelihoods and their lives.

The precept of powerlessness is also intertwined with the other two primary precepts on inferiority and property rights. White men could preserve their sexual dominance over both white women and black women (fourth precept). Because of the powerlessness of blacks in protecting themselves and their families, white men could impose the selective rigid color line that wreaked havoc on the black woman and the black family (sixth precept). Lacking freedom of movement (ninth precept) and education (seventh precept), the slave lived at the benevolence and whim of the master. Political powerlessness was one of the defining characteristics of slavery, even for free blacks, and full control over their destinies remained an elusive dream (fifth precept).

Problems of Formulation

I wrestled with the phrasing of these precepts to include as much of the oppression embodied in the law without being so general as to ignore the exceptions within the law. For example, I had to take care in using the terms "blacks" and "slaves" to differentiate between the precepts applied across the board by race and those applied by slave status. Frequently, both race and status are involved, thus the use of the general term "blacks" in some of the precepts. When the terms "slaves" and "free blacks" are used separately, they indicate that only one group faced the deprivations and repressions of that precept. Since these are the Ten Precepts of American Slavery Jurisprudence, of course slave status is the primary focus.[21]

The second precept, disregard of the humanity of slaves, implies some initial consideration of the issue as to whether there was any recognition of the slave's humanity. Given the presumption of inferiority of the first precept, often there was no recognition of the slaves' humanity. But actual conduct during this era displayed some recognition of the slave's humanity by making it a crime to kill a slave under certain, particularly heinous circumstances.

The voice of the early nineteenth century leadership raised additional word-choice problems. Keeping consistency with an alien mind-set while trying to read minds from over a century-and-a-half ago is quite difficult. For example, the third precept includes the phrase "whether free or slave." It is debatable whether many members of the 1820s power structure would significantly differentiate the status of blacks, be they slave or free.

When formulating the sixth precept, on the denial of the right of marriage, I first wrote that blacks were denied this right. Upon reflection, I realized that the precept was not being sufficiently precise. Though all slaves' marriages, with the possible exception of Louisiana's, had no sanction under the law, free blacks were able to marry free blacks; but the marriage of a free black to a slave or a white person was void. The sixth precept concludes with the ironic, white condemnation of blacks' behavior, although it was white culture that bred much of the perceived "immoral" conduct. The causal linkage between the whites' destruction of the black family and white condemnation for the resulting behavior and thought patterns is implied in this precept, although it is unlikely that many 1820s statesmen would have recognized the connection.

The seventh precept's deprivation of culture, especially African culture, to blacks embodies the denial of a unified and untrammeled family (sixth precept), as well as the freedom of association, movement, and religious expression (eighth and ninth precepts). Much of this tragic denial of culture started with the international slave trade. On the shore of western Africa and in the "Middle Passage," slavers would purposely mix the tribal groups of the captured Africans to deprive them of the opportunity to communicate and unite.[22] Involved in the kidnapping and forced passage of millions of slaves for three centuries was the destruction of the Africans' languages, heritage, families, customs, practices, religions, as well as the destinies of the individual Africans. The transformation of African into American slave was completed during the seasoning period, when the African learned English (or the European language of the colony/state where the slave was deposited) and his job, and felt the whip. Deprived of their African cultures, many blacks were compelled to assimilate European and, later, American culture. The facet of the seventh precept covering the denial of education encompasses the denial of public education to free blacks, even where public schooling was available, as well as those laws that forbade teaching slaves how to read and write.

All blacks, whether slave or free, faced restrictions in movement and association (ninth precept), although free blacks did not have restrictions on their ability to resist, rebel, or flee any more than whites did. The restrictions were more direct and severe on slaves and on free blacks in or near the South. Free blacks anywhere in America, however, faced the potential of enslavement or re-enslavement by kidnappers (ninth and tenth precepts).

All ten precepts are interrelated, but the present volume limits its discussion to the first precept so as to give it appropriate consideration. Within the next two years I hope to publish volumes that analyze precepts two through ten and their interrelationship with the first.

The Post-Civil War Impact of the Precepts

It would be a mistake of the highest order to perceive these ten precepts as concepts that perished at the end of the Civil War or upon the passage of the Thirteenth, Fourteenth, and Fifteenth Amendments. While the Thirteenth Amendment abolished slavery, it did not eradicate the racial prejudices within the minds of most white men and women of that era. Although the Fourteenth and Fifteenth Amendments prohibited the states from practicing certain types of racial discrimination, these Amendments and related laws in many instances would be construed and enforced by persons who originally justified slavery on the basis that blacks were inferior. Now with slavery abolished, persons with the same mind-set were designing separate educational and other systems predicated on the same assumption that blacks were inferior. Thus, the black codes enacted immediately after the Civil War by many of the southern states, and some of the post-Reconstruction legislation and judicial decisions, involved the same old poison of racial prejudices poured into new bottles. Even though these bottles carried labels such as "equal protection," "due process," and "privileges and immunities," some of the poison that constituted the slavery precepts was dispensed by the courts and the government as part of the rationale to segregate and discriminate, just as earlier these toxins had been used to enslave. Often the broth of the post-Reconstruction era was indistinguishable from the racist poisons which the courts, legislatures, and others had used to formulate the original ten precepts of slavery.

Most southern plantation owners who constantly implemented the third precept—to keep blacks as powerless as possible during the slavery era—wanted blacks in a similar powerless position in the post-Civil War era. Though the Civil War and these Amendments obviously made a significant change in the rights and options of blacks, the federal courts' interpretation of these Amendments did not place blacks on a plane of full equality either in the operation of the legal process or within the society. Perhaps the more one understands about how the Ten Precepts of American Slavery Jurisprudence were applied in the antebellum period, the better one can identify the implementation, under different labels, of the same or less pernicious racist precepts in the post-Civil War era and, in some cases, even in the present.

The Quest for Universal Human Rights

Writing in 1981, Professor Louis Henkin has observed:

> *Human rights is the idea of our time.* It asserts that every human being, in every society, is entitled to have basic autonomy and freedoms respected and basic needs satisfied. These claims by every individual against his society are designated "rights," presumably in some moral order, perhaps under "natural law." The society has corresponding duties to give effect to these rights through domestic laws and institutions.
>
> *Today, the human rights idea is universal,* accepted by virtually all states and societies regardless of historical, cultural, ideological, economic, or other differences. It is international, the subject of international diplomacy, law, and institutions. It is philosophically respectable, even to opposed philosophical persuasions.
>
> The universalization of human rights is a political fact.[23]

The implementation of human rights as "the idea of our time" has expanded beyond the limitations of the world that Professor Henkin saw in 1981. A decade later, speaking before a joint session of the United States Congress, the newly elected President of the Czechoslovak Socialist Republic, Vaclav Havel, said:

> What does all this [the collapse of the former Soviet Union, the democratization of the former Eastern bloc nations] mean for the world in the long run? This is, I am firmly convinced, a historically irreversible process. . . . But that is still not the most important thing: the main thing is, it seems to me, that these revolutionary changes will enable us to escape from the rather antiquated straitjacket of this bipolar view of the world, and to enter at last into an era of multipolarity. That is, into an era in which all of us—large and small—former slaves and former masters—will be able to create what your great President Lincoln called the family of man.[24]

Some months later, then Deputy President of the African National Congress, Nelson Mandela, also speaking before a joint session of the United States Congress, said:

> To deny any person their human rights is to challenge their very humanity. To impose on them a wretched life of hunger and deprivation is to dehumanise them. But such has been the terrible fate of all black persons in our country under the system of apartheid. . . .

. . . Justice and liberty must be our tool, prosperity and happiness our weapon.[25]

He asserted that:

Our people demand democracy . . . because the citizens assert that equality, liberty and the pursuit of happiness are *fundamental human rights* which are not only inalienable but must, if necessary, be defended with the weapons of war.[26]

There is a nexus between the abolition or the diminution of those precepts as advocated by the slavemasters in power in the American colonial and antebellum periods and the efforts in this decade to advocate universal human rights for all. The more we appreciate the extraordinary injustice of the original precepts, the more persistent we will be in eradicating the vestiges of those precepts in the United States and the equivalent denigration throughout the world. In this volume and the next volumes, I explore eras when human rights for blacks was not the idea of the time, but instead the property rights of white masters, and white domination of blacks comprised the "idea of the time."

I recognize that these ten precepts are strong indictments of the slavemasters in power. Thus, I shall seek to document by precise citations those statutes and cases which, through the "majesty of law," embodied the racist imperatives of the Ten Precepts of American Slavery Jurisprudence. These jurisprudential and statutory examples will be given in the form of quotations from the actual language of the laws and judicial opinions and will demonstrate how these racial values reflected in the precepts were legitimized by the courts and legislatures.

I hope that the exploration of these precepts can cause all of us "to think beyond the substantive rules of law to the function of law, the nature of its influence, the opportunities it offers, the limitations it imposes—as well as to understand the limits of its influence in a society of sovereign nations."[27]

ARTICLES PUBLISHED BY
A. LEON HIGGINBOTHAM, JR.

The Ten Precepts of American Slavery Jurisprudence: Chief Justice Roger Taney's Defense and Justice Thurgood Marshall's Condemnation of the Precept of Black Inferiority, 17 CARDOZO L. REV. (forthcoming 1996).

Rekindling the Spirit of Martin Luther King, Jr. in a Time of Retrenchment and *Martin Luther King's Open Letter to Newt Gingrich*, in REFLECTIONS OF THE DREAM, 1975–1994: TWENTY YEARS CELEBRATING THE LIFE OF DR. MARTIN LUTHER KING, JR. AT THE MASSACHUSETTS INSTITUTE OF TECHNOLOGY 127 & 289 (Clarence G. Williams ed., 1995).

Violence in America: "Contracts," Myths and History, 36 B.C. L. REV. 899 (1995).

Rosa Parks: Foremother and Heroine Teaching Civility and Offering a Vision for a Better Tomorrow, 22 FLA. ST. U. L. REV. 899 (1995).

50 Years of Civil Rights, EBONY, Nov. 1995, at 148.

The Hill-Thomas Hearings—What Took Place and What Happened: White Male Domination, Black Male Domination, and the Denigration of Black Women, in RACE, GENDER, AND POWER IN AMERICA: THE LEGACY OF THE HILL-THOMAS HEARINGS 26 (Anita F. Hill and Emma C. Jordan eds., 1995).

Fundamental Rights and the Constitution: A Heavenly Discourse, in AFRICAN AMERICANS AND THE LIVING CONSTITUTION IN THE TWENTY-FIRST CENTURY 289 (John H. Franklin and Genna R. McNeil eds., 1995).

Opening Argument, in LINN WASHINGTON, BLACK JUDGES ON JUSTICE: PERSPECTIVES FROM THE BENCH 1 (1994).

Introduction to WILLIAM J. BUTLER ET AL., THE NEW SOUTH AFRICA—THE DAWN OF DEMOCRACY: REPORT OF A MISSION ON BEHALF OF THE INTERNATIONAL COM-

MISSION OF JURISTS AND THE AMERICAN ASSOCIATION FOR THE INTERNATIONAL COMMISSION OF JURISTS 5 (1994).

Shaw v. Reno: A Mirage of Good Intentions with Devastating Racial Consequences, 62 FORDHAM L. REV. 1593 (1994) (with Gregory A. Clarick and Marcella David).

Justice Clarence Thomas in Retrospect, 45 HASTINGS L.J. 1405 (1994) (the Mathew O. Tobriner Memorial Lecture).

Looking For God and Racism in All the Wrong Places, 70 DENV. U. L. REV. 191 (1993) (with Aderson B. Francois).

Reflections on the Impact of Charles Hamilton Houston—From a Unique Perspective, 27 NEW ENG. L. REV. 605 (1993).

Seeking Pluralism in Judicial Systems: The American Experience and the South African Challenge, 42 DUKE L.J. 1028 (1993).

"Yearning to Breathe Free": Legal Barriers Against and Options in Favor of Liberty in Antebellum Virginia, 68 N.Y.U. L. REV. 1213 (1993) (with F. Michael Higginbotham).

An Open Letter to Justice Clarence Thomas from a Federal Judicial Colleague, 140 U. PA. L. REV. 1005 (1992).

The "Law Only As An Enemy": The Legitimization of Racial Powerlessness Through the Colonial and Antebellum Criminal Laws of Virginia, 70 N.C. L. REV. 969 (1992) (with Anne F. Jacobs).

The Hughes Court and the Beginning of the End of the "Separate But Equal" Doctrine, 76 MINN. L. REV. 1099 (1992) (with William C. Smith).

An Open Letter to Justice Clarence Thomas from a Federal Judicial Colleague, in RACE-*ING* JUSTICE, *EN*-GENDER*ING* POWER: ESSAYS ON ANITA HILL, CLARENCE THOMAS, AND THE CONSTRUCTION OF SOCIAL REALITY (Toni Morrison ed., 1992).

Seeking Pluralism in Judicial Systems: The American Experience and the South African Challenge, Presentation in South Africa to the Conference on a Constitutional Court for South Africa sponsored by the Constitutional Committee of the African National Congress, the Centre for Applied Legal Studies, University of the Witswatersrand, and the Lawyers' Committee for Civil Rights Under Law (Feb. 1, 1991) (with S. Sandile Ngcobo).

A Tribute to Justice Thurgood Marshall, 105 HARV. L. REV. 55 (1991).

"Rather Than the Free": Free Blacks in Colonial and Antebellum Virginia, 26 HARV. C.R.—C.L. L. REV. 17 (1991) (with Greer C. Bosworth).

Racism in American and South African Courts: Similarities and Differences, 65 N.Y.U. L. REV. 479 (1990).

De Jure Housing Segregation in the United States and South Africa: The Difficult Pursuit for Racial Justice, U. ILL. L. REV. 763 (1990) (with F. Michael Higginbotham & S. Sandile Ngcobo).

45 Years in Law and Civil Rights, EBONY, Nov. 1990, at 80.

Civil Rights in the Federal Courts: A Racial Perspective, in THE FEDERAL COURTS: YESTERDAY, TODAY & TOMORROW 15 (1990).

The Dream with Its Back Against the Wall, YALE L. REP., Spring 1990, at 34.

Race, Sex, Education and Missouri Jurisprudence: Shelley v. Kraemer in a Historical Perspective, 67 WASH. U. L.Q. 673 (1989).

Racial Purity and Interracial Sex in the Law of Colonial and Antebellum Virginia, 77 GEO. L.J. 1967 (1989) (with Barbara K. Kopytoff).

Property First, Humanity Second: The Recognition of the Slave's Human Nature in Virginia Civil Law, 50 OHIO ST. L.J. 511 (1989) (with Barbara K. Kopytoff).

Federal Jurisdiction: The Essential Guarantor of Human Rights, in THE FEDERAL APPELLATE JUDICIARY IN THE TWENTY-FIRST CENTURY 57 (Cynthia Harrison and Russell R. Wheeler eds., 1989).

Racial Justice and the Priorities of American Leadership, in SOCIAL CLASS AND DEMOCRATIC LEADERSHIP: ESSAYS IN HONOR OF E. DIGBY BALTZELL 276 (Harold J. Bershady ed., 1989) (with Laura B. Farmelo).

The Life of the Law: Values, Commitment, and Craftsmanship, 100 HARV. L. REV. 795 (1987) (part of *Essays Commemorating the 100th Anniversary of the* Harvard Law Review).

The Persistent Struggle: From Racial Injustice to Human Rights for All—An American View, The Pennsylvania-Ibadan Exchange Lecture, delivered at the University of Ibadan, Nigeria (March 1985).

West Virginia's Racial Heritage: Not Always Free, 86 W. VA. L. REV. 3 (1983).

Foreword to GENNA R. MCNEIL, GROUNDWORK: CHARLES HAMILTON HOUSTON AND THE STRUGGLE FOR CIVIL RIGHTS at xv (1983).

Foreword to GERALDINE R. SEGAL, BLACKS IN THE LAW: PHILADELPHIA AND THE NATION at xiii (1983).

210 Articles Published

The Summit of Black Lawyers in America: New Goals for the Next Decade, NAT'L B. ASS'N MAG., Summer 1983.

Race, Values and Priorities, 3 J. PUB. & INT'L AFF. 115 (1983).

Judge William Henry Hastie—One Who Changed the Immutable, 24 HOW. L.J. 259 (1981) (annual William Henry Hastie Lecture).

Foreword to ROLES OF THE BLACK LAWYER: A SYMPOSIUM, 7 BLACK L.J. 1 (1981).

I Probably Would Have Been a Slave . . . , ALMANAC (U. Pa.), Nov. 29, 1979.

Is Slavery Relevant to Corrections Today?, 41 CORRECTIONS TODAY 8 (1979).

The Relevance of Slavery: Race and the American Legal Process, 54 NOTRE DAME L. REV. 171 (1978).

Race in American Law, in AMERICAN LAW: THE THIRD CENTURY 45 (Bernard Schwartz ed., 1976).

The Priority of Human Rights in Court Reform, Remarks at the Nat'l Conf. on the Causes of Popular Dissatisfaction with the Admin. of Justice, in St. Paul, Minn. (Apr. 8, 1976), *reprinted in* 70 F.R.D. 134 (1976) and 15 THE JUDGE'S JOURNAL 34 (1976).

Cobblestones or Diamonds?, YALE L. REP., Winter 1975–76, at 5.

From Racism to Affirmative Action—Will Universities Span the Gap?, 4 BLACK L.J. 230 (1975).

The Impact of the Declaration of Independence?, 82 THE CRISIS (Winter 1975).

To the Scale and Standing of Men, 60 J. NEGRO HIST. 347 (1975).

Book Review, 122 U. PA. L. REV. 1044 (1974) (reviewing DERRICK A. BELL, JR., RACE, RACISM AND AMERICAN LAW (1973)).

Racism and the Early American Legal Process, 1619–1896, 407 ANNALS AM. ACAD. POL. & SOC. SCI. 1 (1973).

"American Education and an Open Society: So Many Deeds Cry Out to Be Done!," *in* THE AMERICAN COLLEGE TESTING PROGRAM, MONOGRAPH NO. 9, COLLEGE/ CAREER CHOICE: RIGHT STUDENT, RIGHT TIME, RIGHT PLACE 53 (1972) (proceedings of the 1972 ACT Invitational Conf., Iowa City, Iowa).

A Dream Deferred, in 18 CRIME & DELINQUENCY 30 (1972).

Racism and the American Legal Process: Many Deeds Cry Out to Be Done, PROGRESS IN AFRICA AND AMERICA, SCHOLARS AND STATESMEN LECTURE SERIES, No. 3, Dillard University, New Orleans, La., 1971–72.

Channel Change Through Law—Reason, 2 S. TEX. L.J. 180 (1971).

Effective Use of Modern Technology, in JUSTICE IN THE STATES (William F. Swindler ed., 1971).

The Black Prisoner: America's Caged Canary, in VIOLENCE: A CRISIS OF AMERICAN CONFIDENCE 103 (Hugh Davis Graham ed., 1971).

As if Bound with Them, 12 THE HOURGLASS (Ctr. for Interfaith Studies, Lincoln University) Fall 1971, at 4.

What Kind of Vaccine?, 143 AM. J. PHARMACY 77 (1971).

From Presidential Fact Finding Commissions to Justice for Blacks—Can We Bridge the Gap?, THE PURSUIT OF A CULTURE AND HUMAN DIGNITY, SCHOLARS/STATESMEN LECTURE SERIES, No. 2, Dillard University, New Orleans, La., 1970–71.

From the Outside Looking In: Is Yesterday's Racism Relevant to Today's Corrections?, in LAW ENFORCEMENT ASSISTANCE ADMIN., U.S. DEP'T OF JUSTICE, OUTSIDE LOOKING IN at 1 (Apr. 1, 1970).

Law Enforcement and Justice, in NATIONAL URBAN PROBLEMS 106 (Harry B. Yoshpe & F.R. Burdette eds., 1970).

Trial Backlog and Computer Analysis, 44 F.R.D. 104 (1968).

Dream of Freedom, 13 J. HUM. REL. 166 (1965).

From Riot Study Commissions to Justice in the Ghetto—Will We Bridge the Gap?, in SOCIAL UNREST, CRIME & DELINQUENCY (1965).

Defense Argument in Support of Probation in a Difficult and Highly Publicized Morals Case, TRIAL LAW. GUIDE, Feb. 1963, at 67.

Contributor to the following publications:

• REPORT OF THE WHITE HOUSE CONFERENCE "TO FULFILL THESE RIGHTS" (1966) (final report of the Conference).

• FINAL REPORT OF THE NATIONAL COMMISSION ON REFORM OF FEDERAL CRIMINAL LAWS: A PROPOSED NEW FEDERAL CRIMINAL CODE (1971) (final report of the Brown Commission).

- NATIONAL COMMITTEE ON THE CAUSES AND PREVENTION OF VIOLENCE, TO IN-SURE' DOMESTIC TRANQUILITY, TO ESTABLISH JUSTICE (1969) (final report of the Commission).

- FINAL REPORT OF THE COMMISSION TO CONSIDER STANDARDS FOR ADMISSION TO PRACTICE IN THE FEDERAL COURTS TO THE JUDICIAL CONFERENCE OF THE UNITED STATES, *reprinted in* 83 F.R.D. 215 (1979) (final report of the Devitt Committee).

Notes

INTRODUCTION

1. JAMES BALDWIN, *Stranger in the Village*, in THE PRICE OF THE TICKET 85 (1985).
2. President Abraham Lincoln, The Gettysburg Address (Nov. 19, 1863), *in* 1 DOC-UMENTS OF AMERICAN HISTORY 428, 428 (Henry S. Commager & Milton Cantor eds., 10th ed. 1988).
3. BALDWIN, *supra* note 1, at 85.
4. WILLIAM W. HENING, STATUTES AT LARGE OF VIRGINIA (1671).
5. WILLIAM GOODELL, THE AMERICAN SLAVE CODE 36 (reprint ed. 1968) (1853).
6. 1 THE RECORDS OF THE FEDERAL CONVENTION OF 1787, at 561 (Max Farrand ed., 1911). Paterson was a slaveholder and "was no abolitionist and . . . lack[ed] . . . any burning desire to free blacks from their chains . . . ." *See* JOHN E. O'CONNOR, WILLIAM PATERSON; LAWYER AND STATESMAN, 1745–1806, at 129, 212 (1979).
7. 1 THE RECORDS OF THE FEDERAL CONVENTION OF 1787, *supra* note 6, at 208. Gerry made this statement in a "voice dripping with sarcasm" because slaves "counted for representation in Congress without being accorded their human rights . . . ." *See* GEORGE A. BILLIAS, ELBRIDGE GERRY: FOUNDING FATHER AND RE-PUBLICAN STATESMAN 168, 242 (1976).
8. A. LEON HIGGINBOTHAM, JR., IN THE MATTER OF COLOR: RACE AND THE AMER-ICAN LEGAL PROCESS: THE COLONIAL PERIOD (1978).
9. W.E.B. DU BOIS, THE SOULS OF BLACK FOLK 23 (Fawcett Publications 1967) (1903).
10. Warren E. Burger, *Tribute to the Honorable Thurgood Marshall*, 44 STAN. L. REV. 1227, 1227 (1992) (emphasis added) (footnotes omitted).
11. *Id.*
12. *Id.*
13. Christopher Quinn, *Police Seek Woman's Killer; The Driver Gave the Gunman His Wallet, the Gun Fired and the Driver's Wife Screamed, Witnesses Said*, OR-LANDO SENTINEL, Apr. 18, 1995, at C3.
14. Tom Leithauser, *Husband Charged in Wife's Slaying; Detectives Said an Orange County Man and an Alleged Accomplice Staged a Robbery Before the Fatal Shooting*, ORLANDO SENTINEL, July 28, 1995, at C1.

15. *Accused Gunman Is Freed; Husband Remains Charged*, ORLANDO SENTINEL, Oct. 26, 1995, at D3.

16. *Murder Suspect's Brother Jailed on Tampering Charge*, ORLANDO SENTINEL, Aug. 29, 1995, at C3.

17. Rick Bragg, *Mother of 'Carjacked' Boys Held in Their Deaths; Police Say Woman Admits to Killings as Bodies of 2 Children Are Found Inside Her Car*, N.Y. TIMES, Nov. 4, 1994, at A1.

18. *Id.* at A30 (quoting Interview with Susan Smith, *This Morning* (CBS television broadcast, Nov. 3, 1994)).

19. Michele Parent, *Happy Façade Hid Smith's Secret Life*, NEWSDAY (Long Island), Nov. 6, 1994, at A3.

20. *See* Rick Bragg, *Mother in South Carolina Guilty of Murder in Drowning of 2 Sons*, N.Y. TIMES, July 23, 1995, § 1, at 1.

21. *See* Rick Bragg, *Carolina Jury Rejects Execution for Woman Who Drowned Sons*, N.Y. TIMES, July 29, 1995, § 1, at 1.

22. Ellis Henican, *Black Guy Sketched Yet Again*, N.Y. NEWSDAY, Nov. 6, 1994, at A3.

23. John T. McQuiston, *Woman Says Police Forced Her To Deny Holdup Report*, N.Y. TIMES, Feb. 21, 1994, at B4.

24. Henican, *supra* note 22, at A3.

25. McQuiston, *supra* note 23, at B4.

26. Alexander C. Kafka, *The Holdup That Wasn't; Woman Admits False Report of ATM Robbery*, NEWSDAY (Long Island), May 25, 1994, at 23.

27. Joe Mahoney, *History of Abuse Helped Unravel Student's Story; Police Believe Kendra Gillis Was Frequently Attacked by Her Father*, TIMES UNION (Albany), Dec. 10, 1994, at B1. *See also* Mike Hurewitz, *When Race Enters a Dubious Report Society's Prejudices and Stereotypes Can Often Victimize the Innocent*, TIMES UNION (Albany), Dec. 9, 1994, at A1 (discussing false racial allegations today, as exemplified by the Kendra Gillis and other incidents).

28. Mahoney, *supra* note 27, at B1.

29. Joe Mahoney, *Assault Victim's Mother Speaks Out*, TIMES UNION (Albany), Dec. 14, 1994, at B3.

30. The assault charge against David Gillis was adjourned in contemplation of dismissal. Joe Mahoney, *UAlbany Assault Case Adjourned in Court*, TIMES UNION (Albany), May 4, 1995, at A1.

    For comments on the racial implications of the Kendra Gillis case, *see* Alice P. Green, *Blame and the Black Man*, TIMES UNION (Albany), Jan. 15, 1995, at E1; Virgil H. Hodges, *The News Media Too Often Casts Suspicion on All African-Americans (Letter to the Editor)*, TIMES UNION (Albany), Dec. 21, 1994, at A18.

31. Marc Carey, *Teens Charged in Robbery They Blamed on Black Man*, TIMES UNION (Albany), Dec. 21, 1994, at B1.

32. *Police Arrest Husband in Wife's Stabbing; Compared to Stuart Case*, UPI, Apr. 27, 1992, *available in* LEXIS, Nexis Library, UPI File.

33. *Man Convicted in Killing He Accused Blacks of Committing*, N.Y. TIMES, Aug. 16, 1992, at 29.

34. Sally Jacobs & Diego Ribadeneira, *No Wallet, So Killer Opened Fire*, BOSTON GLOBE, Oct. 26, 1989, Metro/Region, at 1.

    The baby was delivered by Caesarean section eight weeks early, *see id.*, but died seventeen days later. *See* Renee Graham, *Stuart Dies in Jump Off Tobin Bridge After Police Are Told He Killed His Wife; Image Proved Unjust; The Stuart Murder Case*, BOSTON GLOBE, Jan 5, 1990, Metro/Region, at 1.

35. Chris Reidy & Doris S. Wong, *A Tearful Stuart Admits His Guilt, Gets 3 to 5 Years*, BOSTON GLOBE, Nov. 3, 1992, National/Foreign, at 1.
   Matthew Stuart pled guilty to charges of conspiracy to commit insurance fraud and obstruction of justice. He was sentenced to three to five years in prison. *Id.*

36. *Id.*

37. *Charles Stuart's Brother Denied Parole*, UPI, Apr. 19, 1994, *available in* LEXIS, Nexis Library, UPI File; Leonard Greene, *Raise Panel Cozy with Legislature; Stuart Brother Urges Mom To Release Chuck's Story; Vote Keeps Seas Rocky for Hub NAACP Chapter*, BOSTON HERALD, Dec. 2, 1994, at 4. *See also* Reidy & Wong, *supra* note 35, at 1.

38. BESSIE SMITH, *Standin' in the Rain*, on BESSIE SMITH ORIGINAL JAZZ PERFORMANCES 1925–1933 (Nimbus Records 1987).

39. THOMAS JEFFERSON, NOTES ON THE STATE OF VIRGINIA 156 (Harper and Row 1964) (1787) (emphasis added).

40. PHILIP S. FONER, 2 THE LIFE AND WRITINGS OF FREDERICK DOUGLASS 189 (1950).

41. The term "self-evident lie" was used by Abraham Lincoln in a letter to Hon. George Robertson in 1855. *See* JOHN G. NICOLAY & JOHN HAY, 1 ABRAHAM LINCOLN: A HISTORY 390–91 (1890) (emphasis added). Originally, Senator John Pettit of Indiana in his "forcible declaration . . . upon the floor of the United State Senate . . . [called] The Declaration of Independence . . . a 'self-evident lie' . . . ." *See* 3 THE COLLECTED WORKS OF ABRAHAM LINCOLN 301–02 (Roy P. Basler ed., 1953); 2 *id.* at 275, 283.

42. *See* GUNNAR MYRDAL, AN AMERICAN DILEMMA xlv–lix (1944).

43. U.S. BUREAU OF THE CENSUS, STATISTICAL ABSTRACT OF THE UNITED STATES: 1995, at 472 (1995). *See* THE BLACK COMMUNITY CRUSADE FOR CHILDREN, CHILDREN'S DEFENSE FUND, A BLACK COMMUNITY CRUSADE AND COVENANT FOR PROTECTING CHILDREN 60 (1995).

44. 60 U.S. (19 How.) 393 (1857).

45. *Dred Scott*, 60 U.S. at 407.

46. 163 U.S. 537 (1896).

47. 305 U.S. 337 (1938).

48. *See generally* THE ROAD TO BROWN (California Newsreel 1989) (documenting the legal history leading up to *Brown v. Board of Education*).

49. 347 U.S. 483 (1954).

50. 2 THE CONSTITUTION AND THE SUPREME COURT: A DOCUMENTARY HISTORY 266 (Louis H. Pollak ed., 1966).

51. 509 U.S. ____, 113 S. Ct. 2816 (1993). *See* Chapter Thirteen for a discussion of the congressional redistricting cases.

52. *Compare* Planned Parenthood of Southeastern Pa. v. Casey, 505 U.S. 833, 863 (1992) (plurality opinion) ("[W]e think *Plessy* was wrong the day it was decided.").

53. *See* CARL T. ROWAN, DREAM MAKERS, DREAM BREAKERS: THE WORLD OF JUSTICE THURGOOD MARSHALL 453–54 (1993).

54. *Id.*

55. ROBERT FROST, *Stopping by Woods on a Snowy Evening, in* COLLECTED POEMS OF ROBERT FROST 275, 275 (Halcyon House ed. 1939).

CHAPTER ONE

1. Even earlier, in my senior thesis at Antioch College in 1948–49, I attempted to explore the use of American law to perpetuate racial abuse and racial discrimination. I argued, despite the skepticism of my thesis adviser, that comprehensive federal fair employment practice laws should be enacted and were constitutionally permissible.

2. WEBSTER'S THIRD NEW INTERNATIONAL DICTIONARY OF THE ENGLISH LANGUAGE 1783 (1993) (emphasis added). As Judge Aldisert points out, in the broad sense of the term, precept can include moral principles and social policies that may be used as a justification for the creation of a rule of law in a judicial decision. Memorandum from Judge Ruggero J. Aldisert to A. Leon Higginbotham, Jr. on April 10, 1992 (on file with the author) [hereinafter Aldisert Memorandum]. *See also* RUGGERO J. ALDISERT, THE JUDICIAL PROCESS (1st ed. 1976, 2d ed. 1996).

3. *See* Aldisert Memorandum, *supra* note 2.

4. The legitimization of inferiority by the law was accomplished through the persistence of the Ten Precepts of American Slavery Jurisprudence. The term legal precepts would be what Roscoe Pound described as:

> The body of authoritative materials, and the authoritative gradation of the materials, wherein judges are to find the grounds for decision, counselors the basis for assured prediction as to course of the decision, and individuals reasonable guidance toward conducting themselves in accordance with the demands of the social order.

Roscoe Pound, *Hierarchy of Sources and Forms in Different Systems of Law,* 7 TUL. L. REV. 475-76 (1933).

The Ten Precepts of American Slavery Jurisprudence likewise guided the "grounds for decisions" for judges, the "assured prediction[s]" of counselors and, most of all, gave "guidance" to individuals as the American system proceeded to treat African Americans differently. These precepts were legitimized through the courts and the legal process and concretized racial injustice in the hearts of men "in accordance with the demands of the social order." *Id.*

5. Holmes's often-quoted insight bears repeating in full:

> The life of the law has not been logic: it has been experience. The felt necessities of the time, the prevalent moral and political theories, intuitions of public policy, avowed or unconscious, *even the prejudices which judges share with their fellow-men,* have had a good deal more to do than the syllogism in determining the rules by which men should be governed.

OLIVER W. HOLMES, THE COMMON LAW 1 (1881) (emphasis added).

6. ORLANDO PATTERSON, SLAVERY AND SOCIAL DEATH: A COMPARATIVE STUDY at vii (1982).

7. *See* A. LEON HIGGINBOTHAM, JR., IN THE MATTER OF COLOR: RACE AND THE

AMERICAN LEGAL PROCESS: THE COLONIAL PERIOD 19–60 (1978) [hereinafter IN THE MATTER OF COLOR]; A. Leon Higginbotham, Jr. & Greer C. Bosworth, *"Rather Than the Free": Free Blacks in Colonial & Antebellum Virginia*, 26 HARV. C.R.-C.L. L. REV. 20 (1991) (footnote omitted).

8. "Many persons who were originally residents of Virginia subsequently migrated to other states. As an example, Henry Clay was taught by Virginia's first professor of law George Wyeth, who had also taught Thomas Jefferson and John Marshall. Clay moved to Kentucky in 1797 and later was a member and speaker of the U.S. House of Representatives, and was an influential person on issues related to slavery and colonization of blacks during the antebellum period." Higginbotham & Bosworth, *supra* note 6, at 20 n.13 (citing CLEMENT EATON, HENRY CLAY AND THE ART OF AMERICAN POLITICS 6–7, 118, 164 (1957); GLYNDON G. VAN DEUSEN, THE LIFE OF HENRY CLAY 8–15, 18–19 (1937); HENRY CLAY, THE LIFE AND SPEECHES OF THE HONORABLE HENRY CLAY (Daniel Mallory ed., Hartford, Conn., Silas Andrus & Son 1853)).

9. 1 CHARLES WARREN, THE SUPREME COURT IN UNITED STATES HISTORY 2 (rev. ed. 1926).

10. Leroy Fibre Co. v. Chicago, Milwaukee & St. Paul Ry. Co., 232 U.S. 340, 354 (1914) (Holmes, J., concurring).

11. *See generally* Higginbotham & Bosworth, *supra* note 6, at 17 (documenting the application of the precepts of inferiority and powerlessness during slavery); A. Leon Higginbotham, Jr. & Anne F. Jacobs, *The "Law Only As An Enemy": The Legitimization of Racial Powerlessness Through the Colonial and Antebellum Criminal Laws of Virginia*, 70 N.C. L. REV. 969 (1992) (examining the precept of powerlessness); A. Leon Higginbotham, Jr. et al., *De Jure Housing Segregation in the United States and South Africa: The Difficult Pursuit for Racial Justice*, 1990 U. ILL. L. REV. 763, 820–24 (discussing the slavery precepts' reincarnation during legalized segregation).

12. However, there is some question as to the status of blacks from the time when they first arrived in Virginia in 1619 to 1669. *See* IN THE MATTER OF COLOR, *supra* note 6, at 19–32.

13. *See* Drew G. Faust, *Introduction* to THE IDEOLOGY OF SLAVERY: PROSLAVERY THOUGHT IN THE ANTEBELLUM SOUTH, 1830–1860, at 1–20 (Drew G. Faust ed., 1981) (discussing historiography of pro-slavery ideology). *See also generally* WINTHROP D. JORDAN, WHITE OVER BLACK: AMERICAN ATTITUDES TOWARD THE NEGRO, 1550–1812 (1968); SLAVERY DEFENDED: THE VIEWS OF THE OLD SOUTH (Eric L. McKitrick ed., 1963); LARRY E. TISE, PROSLAVERY: A HISTORY OF THE DEFENSE OF SLAVERY IN AMERICA, 1701–1840 (1987).

14. Faust, *supra* note 12, at 4 (emphasis added).

15. *See* IN THE MATTER OF COLOR, *supra* note 6, at 82–98, 267–69, 292–310 (quoting, at 310, FREDERICK DOUGLASS, LIFE AND TIMES OF FREDERICK DOUGLASS 509 (Hartford, Park Publishing Co. 1881)).

16. Two scholars in the mid-1800s identified some concepts that I have incorporated in my Ten Precepts of Slavery. *See generally* JOHN C. HURD, THE LAW OF FREEDOM AND BONDAGE IN THE UNITED STATES (Boston, Little, Brown & Co. 1858); GEORGE M. STROUD, A SKETCH OF THE LAWS RELATING TO SLAVERY IN THE SEVERAL STATES OF THE UNITED STATES OF AMERICA (Negro Universities Press reprint ed. 1968) (1856).

17. *See generally* WE, THE OTHER PEOPLE: ALTERNATIVE DECLARATIONS OF INDE-PENDENCE BY LABOR GROUPS, FARMERS, WOMAN'S RIGHTS ADVOCATES, SOCIAL-ISTS, AND BLACKS, 1829–1975 (Philip S. Foner ed., 1976) (emphasis added).

CHAPTER TWO

1. 60 U.S. (19 How.) 393, 407 (1857) (emphasis added).
2. *See generally* W.E.B. DU BOIS, THE SOULS OF BLACK FOLK 7–15 (reprint ed. Alfred A. Knopf 1993) (1903) (discussing the historical and continued social degradation of African Americans and the struggle for self-realization).
3. *See, e.g.,* DERRICK BELL, FACES AT THE BOTTOM OF THE WELL: THE PERMA-NENCE OF RACISM 3–5 (1992). Bell states:

   [T]he fact of slavery refuses to fade, along with the deeply embedded personal attitudes and public policy assumptions that supported it for so long. . . . Despite undeniable progress for many, no African Americans are insulated from incidents of racial discrimination. Our careers, even our lives, are threatened because of our color.

   Id. at 3.
4. *See, e.g.,* SHELBY STEELE, THE CONTENT OF OUR CHARACTER: A NEW VISION OF RACE IN AMERICA 15–16 (Harper Perennial 1991) (1990).
5. ALEXIS DE TOCQUEVILLE, DEMOCRACY IN AMERICA 10 (Henry Reeve trans., New York, George Dearborn & Co., 3d ed. 1838) (1835).
6. DU BOIS, *supra* note 2, at 16.
7. 347 U.S. 483 (1954).
8. ARGUMENT: THE ORAL ARGUMENT BEFORE THE SUPREME COURT IN BROWN V. BOARD OF EDUCATION OF TOPEKA, 1952–55, at 239 (Leon Friedman ed., 1969) (emphasis added).
9. Brown v. Board of Educ. (Brown I), 347 U.S. 483, 494 (1954).
10. Thomas Jefferson found blacks to be inferior to whites in body and in mind. He wrote:

    Besides those of colour, figure, and hair, there are other physical distinctions proving a difference of race. . . . They [blacks] secrete less by the kidneys, and more by the glands of the skin, which gives them a very strong and disagreeable odour. . . . They seem to require less sleep. A black after hard labour through the day, will be induced by the slightest amusements to sit up till midnight, or later, though knowing he must be out with the first dawn of the morning. They are at least as brave, and more adventuresome. But this may perhaps proceed from a want of forethought, which prevents their seeing a danger till it be present. . . . They are more ardent after their female: but love seems with them to be more an eager desire, than a tender delicate mixture of sentiment and sensation. Their griefs are transient. . . . In general, their existence appears to participate more of sensation than reflection.

    THOMAS JEFFERSON, NOTES ON THE STATE OF VIRGINIA 145–46 (Boston, Lilly and Wait 1832) (1787).
11. *See, e.g.,* BERNARD C. STEINER, LIFE OF ROGER BROOKE TANEY: CHIEF JUSTICE OF THE UNITED STATES SUPREME COURT 522–42 (1922) (documenting the praise Chief Justice Taney received, especially from the bar, after his death, and the

minor criticisms of him as a supporter of slavery). *See also* DON E. FEHREN-
BACHER, THE DRED SCOTT CASE: ITS SIGNIFICANCE IN AMERICAN LAW AND POL-
ITICS 587–90 (1978) (discussing scholarly works defending Taney's opinion).
More than two decades after *Brown*, Chief Justice Taney has, erroneously in
my view, been termed a "great" jurist. In 1977, a group of one hundred scholars
evaluated the first one hundred justices on the Supreme Court. Chief Justice Taney
was one of twelve justices categorized as "great." *See* ALBERT P. BLAUSTEIN &
ROY M. MERSKY, THE FIRST ONE HUNDRED JUSTICES 37–40 (1978).

Chief Justice Taney, writing in 1857 for a majority of the Supreme Court, in
response to the question whether slaves were to be included among "We the People" of the Constitution, concluded:

> In the opinion of the court, the legislation and histories of the times, and
> the language used in the Declaration of Independence, show, that neither the
> class of persons who had been imported as slaves, nor their descendants,
> whether they had become free or not, were then acknowledged as a part of the
> people, nor intended to be included in the general words used in that memora-
> ble instrument.
>
> They had for more than a century before been regarded as beings of an
> inferior order, and altogether unfit to associate with the white race, either in
> social or political relations; and so far inferior, that they had no rights which
> the white man was bound to respect; and that the negro might justly and law-
> fully be reduced to slavery for his benefit. He was bought and sold, and treated
> as an ordinary article of merchandise and traffic, whenever a profit could be
> made by it. This opinion was at that time fixed and universal in the civilized
> portion of the white race. It was regarded as an axiom in morals as well as in
> politics, which no one thought of disputing, or supposed to be open to dispute;
> and men in every grade and position in society daily and habitually acted upon
> it in their private pursuits, as well as in matters of public concern, without
> doubting for a moment the correctness of this opinion.

Dred Scott v. Sandford, 60 U.S. (19 How.) 393, 407 (1857).

12. As Toni Morrison writes in her brilliant meditation on race and American literature:

> Race has become metaphorical—a way of referring to and disguising forces,
> events, classes, and expressions of social decay and economic division far more
> threatening to the body politic than biological "race" ever was. Expensively
> kept, economically unsound, a spurious and useless political asset in election
> campaigns, racism is as healthy today as it was during the Enlightenment. It
> seems it has a utility far beyond economy, beyond the sequestering of classes
> from one another, and has assumed a metaphorical life so completely embedded
> in daily discourse that it is perhaps more necessary and more on display than
> ever before.

TONI MORRISON, PLAYING IN THE DARK: WHITENESS AND THE LITERARY IMAGI-
NATION 63 (1992).

13. *See infra* Chapter Three.

14. *See* U.S. CONST. amend. XIII.

15. A. LEON HIGGINBOTHAM, JR., IN THE MATTER OF COLOR: RACE AND THE AMER-
ICAN LEGAL PROCESS: THE COLONIAL PERIOD 29 (1978) [hereinafter IN THE MAT-
TER OF COLOR].

16. *Id.* at 27–29.
17. *Id.* at 31.
18. ERIC WILLIAMS, CAPITALISM & SLAVERY 7 (1944).
19. WINTHROP D. JORDAN, WHITE OVER BLACK: AMERICAN ATTITUDES TOWARD THE NEGRO, 1550–1812, at 7 (1968).
20. In any case, as Winthrop Jordan has pointed out, it may very well be that we will forever lack sufficient evidence from that period to definitively settle the questions of the causes of slavery in America:

> [T]he details of this process [i.e., the reduction of Africans to slavery in America] can never be completely reconstructed; there is simply not enough evidence (and very little chance of more to come) to show precisely when and how and why Negroes came to be treated so differently from white men, though there is just enough to make historians differ as to its meaning. . . . That those early years were crucial ones is obvious, for it was then that the cycle of Negro debasement began; once the Negro became fully the slave it is not hard to see why white men looked down upon him. Yet precisely because understanding the dynamics of these early years is so important to understanding the centuries which followed, it is necessary to bear with the less than satisfactory data and to attempt to reconstruct the course of debasement undergone by Negroes in seventeenth-century America.

Id. at 44–45.
21. BELL, *supra* note 3, at epigraph.
22. RICHARD WRIGHT, 12 MILLION BLACK VOICES 146 (1941).
23. RALPH ELLISON, *What America Would Be Like Without Blacks, in* THE COLLECTED ESSAYS OF RALPH ELLISON 582–83 (John F. Callahan ed., 1995).
24. JAMES BALDWIN, *In Search of a Majority, in* THE PRICE OF THE TICKET: COLLECTED NONFICTION, 1948–1985, at 229, 232 (1985) (emphasis in original).
25. MORRISON, *supra* note 12, at 52.
26. IN THE MATTER OF COLOR, *supra* note 15, at 22 (citing 1 HELEN T. CATTERALL, JUDICIAL CASES CONCERNING AMERICAN SLAVERY AND THE NEGRO 53–54 (Negro University Press reprint ed. 1968) (1926)).
27. CARL T. ROWAN, DREAM MAKERS, DREAM BREAKERS: THE WORLD OF JUSTICE THURGOOD MARSHALL 10 (1993) (quoting Sen. James Henry Hammond) (emphasis added).
28. *See generally* A. Leon Higginbotham, Jr. & Greer C. Bosworth, *"Rather Than the Free": Free Blacks in Colonial and Antebellum Virginia,* 26 Harv. C.R.-C.L. L. REV. 17 (1991).
29. *See generally* A. Leon Higginbotham, Jr. & Barbara K. Kopytoff, *Racial Purity and Interracial Sex in the Law of Colonial and Antebellum Virginia,* 77 GEO. L.J. 1967 (1989) (discussing the development of racial purity laws and their legal and social significance).
30. There are several constitutional provisions that explicitly or implicitly recognize slavery. Historian William Wiecek lists among them the following:

    1. Article I, section 2: the "three-fifths" clause, apportioning representatives in the House by counting all free persons and three-fifths of the slaves. *See* U.S. CONST. art. I, § 2;
    2. Article I, section 2, and Article I, section 9: direct taxes (including capitations) are to be apportioned among the state in the same manner as that for appor-

tioning representatives, to prevent Congress from imposing taxes per slave, to encourage emancipation. *See* U.S. CONST. art. I, §§ 2, 9;

3. Article I, section 8: allows Congress to call up states' militias to suppress insurrections, including slave uprisings. *See* U.S. CONST. art. I, § 8;

4. Article I, section 9: 1808 was established as the earliest date for Congress to abolish the international slave trade to the United States. *See* U.S. CONST. art. I, § 9;

5. Article I, section 9, and Article I, section 10: prohibits the federal government and the states from taxing exports (including the products generated by slave labor). *See* U.S. CONST. art. I, §§ 9, 10;

6. Article IV, section 2: prohibits states from emancipating fugitive slaves, who would be returned to the master on demand. *See* U.S. CONST. art. IV, § 2;

7. Article IV, section 4: requires the federal government to protect states against domestic violence, including slave insurrections. *See* U.S. CONST. art. IV, § 4;

8. Article V: made unamendable the provisions of Article I, section 9 (concerning the slave trade and direct taxes). *See* U.S. CONST. art. V.

Wiecek also notes that:

Later opponents and supporters of slavery found other clauses relevant in ways not foreseen by the framers, among them the clauses requiring the federal government to guarantee to the states republican forms of government (Article IV, section 4), giving Congress full legislative power over the federal district (Article I, section 8), and giving Congress power to admit new states and make "Regulations" for the territories (Article IV, section 3, clauses 1 and 2.)

WILLIAM M. WIECEK, THE SOURCES OF ANTISLAVERY CONSTITUTIONALISM IN AMERICA, 1760–1848, at 62–63 (1977).

In addition to the above, I would also include:

1. Article I, section 8: provides Congress with the power to make laws to implement several enumerated powers of the Government of the United States. *See* U.S. CONST. art. I, § 8.

2. Article II, section 2: asserts President's role as Commander in Chief of the armed forces, which was the source of power relied upon by Abraham Lincoln in issuing the Emancipation Proclamation. *See* U.S. CONST. art. II, § 2.

31. *See infra* Chapter Six, Part A.

32. 60 U.S. (19 How.) 393 (1857).

33. *See* DON E. FEHRENBACHER, SLAVERY, LAW, AND POLITICS: THE DRED SCOTT CASE IN HISTORICAL PERSPECTIVE 289–94 (1981). Fehrenbacher argues that: "[*Dred Scott*] was a conspicuous and perhaps integral part of a configuration of events and conditions that did produce enough changes of allegiance to make a political revolution and enough intensity of feeling to make that revolution violent." *Id.* at 294.

34. 163 U.S. 537 (1896).

35. BENJAMIN N. CARDOZO, THE NATURE OF THE JUDICIAL PROCESS 103 (1921).

36. 347 U.S. 483 (1954).

37. Anonymous, *Evicted: A Russian Jew's Story (Again)*, HARPER'S MAGAZINE, June 1991, at 17, 19.

38. *See generally* MITCHELL DUNEIER, SLIM'S TABLE: RACE, RESPECTABILITY, AND

MASCULINITY 157–62 (1992); A. Leon Higginbotham & Aderson B. François, *Looking For God and Racism in All the Wrong Places*, 70 DENV. U. L. REV. 191 (1993).

CHAPTER THREE

1. *See* A. LEON HIGGINBOTHAM, JR., IN THE MATTER OF COLOR: RACE & THE AMERICAN LEGAL PROCESS: THE COLONIAL PERIOD 20 (1978) [hereinafter IN THE MATTER OF COLOR].
2. ALDEN T. VAUGHAN, *Blacks in Virginia: A Note on the First Decade*, 29 WM. & MARY Q. 469, 470 (1972).
3. *Id.*
4. IN THE MATTER OF COLOR, *supra* note 1, at 21–22 (citing Oscar Handlin & Mary F. Handlin, *Origin of the Southern Labor System*, 7 WM. & MARY Q. 199, 202–03 (1950) ("almost everyone, even tenants and laborers, bore some sort of servile obligation")).
5. Paul C. Palmer, *Servant into Slave: The Evolution of the Legal Status of the Negro Laborer in Colonial Virginia*, 65 S. ATLANTIC Q. 355, 356 (1966).
6. *See* IN THE MATTER OF COLOR, *supra* note 1, at 20–22.
7. *Id.* at 393; ABBOT E. SMITH, COLONISTS IN BONDAGE: WHITE SERVITUDE AND CONVICT LABOR IN AMERICA 1607–1776, at 16–21 (1947).
8. IN THE MATTER OF COLOR, *supra* note 1, at 54–55.
9. *See, e.g., id.* at 28.
10. *See, e.g., id.* at 20. It should be noted that many indentured servants did not come to America voluntarily. Some were kidnapped, and others were falsely accused of crimes by conspiring shipowners and judicial authorities, who profited from the selling of indentured servants. *Id.* at 393–95.
11. WINTHROP D. JORDAN, WHITE OVER BLACK: AMERICAN ATTITUDES TOWARD THE NEGRO, 1550–1812, at 7 (1968).
12. *See* IN THE MATTER OF COLOR, *supra* note 1, at 21–22, 58.
13. 1 JUDICIAL CASES CONCERNING AMERICAN SLAVERY AND THE NEGRO 76 (Helen T. Catterall ed., 1926) [hereinafter Catterall] (citing MINUTES OF THE COUNCIL AND GENERAL COURT OF COLONIAL VIRGINIA 33 (H.R. McIlwaine ed., 2d ed. 1979) (1924) [hereinafter McIlwaine]) (footnote omitted).
14. McIlwaine, *supra* note 13, at 33–35.
    Since *Tuchinge* is the first case discussed, it is appropriate here to set out my approach to evaluating colonial cases. During colonial times judicial opinions tended to be very brief. There is much that we do not know (and may never know) about the complete facts of these cases. The interpretation of the cases in this work draws upon many sources in order to give shape and meaning to the precept of black inferiority. As such, this work takes a more creative approach in interpreting colonial cases by focusing more on what the courts do not say (and their probable reasons for not saying it) than on what they do say. Obviously, this mode of interpretation would not be appropriate for modern cases where courts almost always lay out the background facts and the judicial rationale in their decisions. But it is perfectly appropriate for colonial cases where more often than not one has to "read between the lines" to truly understand the rationale for the holding of the court. After all, it is not possible to understand, for example, how the United States Constitution promoted

the institution of slavery by focusing solely on what the Framers wrote. One must also focus on what the Framers did not write about African Americans in the Constitution (and their reasons for not writing it) in order to understand the relationship between the Constitution and slavery.

15. LERONE BENNETT, JR., BEFORE THE MAYFLOWER: A HISTORY OF BLACK AMERICA 45 (5th ed. 1982).

16. McIlwaine, *supra* note 13, at 479.

17. *Id.* at 477.

18. *Id.*

19. The property rights issue may be viewed in a different way if a system of hereditary slavery had definitely been in place in 1640 Virginia. There exists no conclusive evidence that by 1640 Virginia had already established a system of chattel slavery. Had such system been in place, the woman servant could have possibly been considered more valuable pregnant than not because her child at birth would have belonged to Lieutenant Sheppard. The use of the term "servant" does not negate the possibility that this woman was a slave. IN THE MATTER OF COLOR, *supra* note 1, at 24.

20. Even if, as a servant, she was coerced by Sweat to engage in sexual intercourse, in the context of the precept of black inferiority, the law always assumed that the choice was hers. If the choice had not been hers, the law would have had no cause to punish her.

21. McIlwaine, *supra* note 13, at 477.

22. *Id.*

23. *Id.*

24. *Id.*

25. *Id.*

26. *Id.*

27. *See* IN THE MATTER OF COLOR, *supra* note 1, at 20–21.

28. McIlwaine, *supra* note 13, at 477 (emphasis added).

29. *See also* 1 Catterall, *supra* note 13, at 76–78.

30. *See* IN THE MATTER OF COLOR, *supra* note 1, at 32–60.

31. WILLIAM GOODELL, THE AMERICAN SLAVE CODE 36 (New York, American and Foreign Anti-Slavery Society 3d ed. 1853).

32. THOMAS JEFFERSON, NOTES ON THE STATE OF VIRGINIA 150 (Boston, Lily and Wait 1832) (1787).

CHAPTER FOUR

1. MINUTES OF THE COUNCIL AND GENERAL COURT OF COLONIAL VIRGINIA 33 (H.R. McIlwaine ed., 2d ed. 1979) (1924).

2. *Id.*

3. *Id.* at 477.

4. *See* A. LEON HIGGINBOTHAM, JR., IN THE MATTER OF COLOR: RACE & THE AMERICAN LEGAL PROCESS: THE COLONIAL PERIOD 32 (1978) [hereinafter IN THE MATTER OF COLOR]. "The first legislative enactment making reference to blacks was the statute of 1639," twenty years after blacks first arrived in Virginia. *Id.* Another twenty years passed before the Virginia legislature made direct reference to blacks as slaves within its enactments. *Id.* at 33–34.

5. *See* FREDERICK DOUGLASS, LIFE AND TIMES OF FREDERICK DOUGLASS 150 (reprint rev. ed. 1962) (1892).
6. BENJAMIN N. CARDOZO, THE NATURE OF THE JUDICIAL PROCESS 133–34 (1921).
7. JAMES BALDWIN, THE EVIDENCE OF THINGS NOT SEEN 31 (1985).
8. IN THE MATTER OF COLOR, *supra* note 4, at 32–57.
9. *Id.* at 38.
10. *Id.* at 50–57.
11. *Id.* at 32–51.
12. *See* JOHN H. FRANKLIN & ALFRED A. MOSS, JR., FROM SLAVERY TO FREEDOM: A HISTORY OF AFRICAN AMERICANS 124 (7th ed. 1994).
13. *See, e.g., id. See* IN THE MATTER OF COLOR, *supra* note 4 (describing the evolution of slave codes in the colonial period).
14. *See* IN THE MATTER OF COLOR, *supra* note 4, at 36.
15. *Id.* at 55.
16. BELL HOOKS, YEARNING 52–53 (1991).
17. IN THE MATTER OF COLOR, *supra* note 4, at 58.
18. *See id.* at 36–38, 40–47. *See generally* A. Leon Higginbotham, Jr. & Barbara K. Kopytoff, *Racial Purity and Interracial Sex in the Law of Colonial and Antebellum Virginia*, 77 GEO. L.J. 1967 (1989).
19. WINTHROP D. JORDAN, WHITE OVER BLACK: AMERICAN ATTITUDES TOWARD THE NEGRO, 1550–1812, at 24–28, 32–40 (1968).
20. IN THE MATTER OF COLOR, *supra* note 4, at 44.
21. *See id.* at 36–37.
22. TONI MORRISON, PLAYING IN THE DARK: WHITENESS AND THE LITERARY IMAGINATION 34–35 (1992).
23. *Id.* at 34.
24. *Id.* at 35.
25. THOMAS JEFFERSON, NOTES ON THE STATE OF VIRGINIA 150 (Richmond, Va., J.W. Randolph 1853) (1787).
26. CORNEL WEST, RACE MATTERS 85 (1993).
27. JAMES BALDWIN, *White Racism or World Community?, in* THE PRICE OF THE TICKET: COLLECTED NONFICTION, 1948–1985, at 435–36 (1985).
28. IN THE MATTER OF COLOR, *supra* note 4, at 43.
29. *See* MARY F. BERRY & JOHN W. BLASSINGAME, LONG MEMORY: THE BLACK EXPERIENCE IN AMERICA 118 (1982).
30. IN THE MATTER OF COLOR, *supra* note 4, at 45.
31. *Id.*
32. JUNE P. GUILD, BLACK LAWS OF VIRGINIA: A SUMMARY OF THE LEGISLATIVE ACTS OF VIRGINIA CONCERNING NEGROES FROM EARLIEST TIMES TO THE PRESENT 52–53 (Negro Universities Press 1969) (1936).
33. 1 HELEN T. CATTERALL, JUDICIAL CASES CONCERNING AMERICAN SLAVES AND THE NEGRO 89–90 (Negro Universities Press reprint ed. 1968).
34. *Id.* at 90.
35. *See generally* A. Leon Higginbotham, Jr., & Greer C. Bosworth, *"Rather Than the Free": Free Blacks in Colonial and Antebellum Virginia*, 26 HARV. C.R.-C.L. L. REV. 17 (1991).
36. MORRISON, *supra* note 22, at 63.
37. *See* Higginbotham & Kopytoff, *supra* note 18. Other aspects of an individual's

heritage might, of course, determine important legal rights (for example, whether his mother was a slave or freewoman, or whether his mother was an unwed indentured white servant or a free white woman). *See* Act XII, 2 Laws of Va. 170, 170 (Hening 1823) (enacted 1662) (whether children bound or free depends solely on condition of mother); Act C, 2 Laws of Va. 114, 114–15 (Hening 1823) (enacted 1661) (birth of bastard child by servant extends term of indenture or subject servant to fine).

38. But *see* Jordan, *American Chiaroscuro: The Status and Definition of Mulattoes in the British Colonies,* 19 WM. & MARY Q. 183, 186 (1962) [hereinafter Jordan, *American Chiaroscuro*] (finding no evidence of higher social position for mulattoes in the mainland colonies). An explicit statement that Negroes and mulattoes were the same in the eyes of the law did not occur until 1860. Then, in a statute defining "mulatto," the legislators said, "the word 'negro' in any other section of this, or in any future statute, shall be construed to mean mulatto as well as negro." Va. Code ch. 103, § 9 (1860).

39. Jordan, *American Chiaroscuro, supra* note 38, at 185.

40. *Id.* North Carolina was the other.

41. *Id.*

42. Ch. IV, 3 Laws of Va. 250, 251 (Hening 1823) (enacted 1705). Although the term "mulatto" was not defined by law until 1705, we find it used as early as March 12, 1655, when the record refers to a "Mulatto held to be a slave and appeal taken." McIlwaine, *supra* note 1, at 504.

43. Ch. IV, 3 Laws of Va. 250, 251 (Hening 1823) (enacted 1705). This statute defines "mulatto" for purposes of holding office only. It could have been defined differently for other purposes, but there was no other statutory definition until 1785. As we shall see below, however, the courts did not apply the strict statutory definition.

44. *Id.* at 252. Presumably the other ancestors would all be white.

45. After the Civil War, a single term, "colored," was often used for both Negroes and mulattos in legal writing.

46. The favored treatment of Indians was still present in 1924 as indicated by an act of the Virginia legislature that made it unlawful for a white person to marry anyone but another white. A white was defined as someone with "no trace whatsoever of any blood other than Caucasian" or someone with no admixture of blood other than white and a small proportion of American Indian, 1924 Va. Acts ch. 371, § 5, at 535. This provision was the so-called "Pocahontas exception," designed to protect descendants of John Rolfe and Pocahontas, who were by then considered part of the white race. However, John Rolfe could not, in 1924, have married Pocahontas. Under the most likely interpretation of the statute, he would have been limited to whites or those who were no more than ¹/₁₆ American Indian. Wadlington, *The Loving Case: Virginia's Anti-Miscegenation Statute in Historical Perspective,* 52 VA L. REV. 1189, 1202–03 (1966).

47. The statute was entitled "An Act declaring what persons shall be deemed mulattoes," and it stated:

> [E]very person whose grandfathers or grandmothers any one is, or shall have been a negro, although all his other progenitors, except that descending from the negro, shall have been white persons, shall be deemed a mulatto; and so every person who shall have one-fourth part or more of negro blood; shall, in like manner, be deemed a mulatto.

Ch. LXXVIII, 12 Laws of Va. 184, 184 (Hening 1823) (enacted 1785; effective 1787).

48. In an 1877 case, McPherson v. Commonwealth, 69 Va. (28 Gratt.) 292, Judge Moncure declared that Rowena McPherson could marry a white man because "less than one-fourth of her blood is negro blood. If it be but one drop less, she is not a negro." *Id.* at 292. Negro in this context meant both Negro and mulatto, as they comprised one legal category.

49. Ch. LXXVIII, 12 Laws of Va. 184 (Hening 1823) (enacted 1785, effective 1787). In this statute, persons of mixed Indian and white ancestry are no longer classified mulattoes, but they appear as mulattoes again in the same statutes drawing racial boundary lines starting in 1866. Ch. 17, § 1, 1865–1866 Va. Acts 84. A person who has one-fourth or more of Indian blood is an Indian, if he is not "colored."

50. J. Johnston at 193–94.

51. *Id.* at 193.

52. *Id.* at 194.

53. Ch. 357, § 49, 1910 Va. Acts 581.

54. Ch. 371, § 5, 1924 Va. Acts 534–35; Ch. 85, 1930 Va. Acts 96–97. After the Civil War there was a shift from the use of the term "mulatto" to "colored" in the statutes, the latter term comprising the former categories of Negro and mulatto. Ch. 17, § 1, 1865-1866 Va. Acts 84.

55. "Mustee" was a term used in Georgia and the Carolinas to describe a person who was part Indian, "usually Indian-Negro but occasionally Indian-white." JORDAN, *supra* note 19, at 168–69.

56. THE COLONIAL RECORDS OF THE STATE OF GEORGIA, 659 (Chandler, comp. 1904–16), *quoted in* Jordan, *American Chiaroscuro, supra* note 38, at 187.

57. *Id.* No one was actually naturalized under the statute. Note that Georgia was not willing to give Negroes the full rights and privileges of whites, nor were they willing to give naturalized mulattoes or mustees political power. It was "a begrudging kind of citizenship" that was extended by the legislature. *Id.*

58. Ch. 17, § 1, 1865–66 Va. Acts 84.

59. Ch. 371, § 5, 1924 Va. Acts 534–35. All of the acts setting out racial definitions, with the exception of the 1924 "Act to Preserve [white] Racial Integrity" defined "mulatto" or "colored" rather than"white." White is defined by implication. In the 1924 act, "white" is given an explicit definition for the first time in the statute which sets out whom whites could marry. It is the most restrictive of racial definitions. It defines a white person as one "who has no trace whatsoever of any blood other than Caucasian; but persons who have [only] one-sixteenth or less of the blood of the American Indian . . . shall be deemed to be white persons." Ch. 371, 1924 Va. Acts 535. The 1930 statute defining as colored anyone "in whom there is ascertainable any Negro blood" is only slightly less restrictive. Ch. 85, 1930 Va. Acts 97.

60. 45 Va. (4 Gratt.) 210 (1847).

61. *Id.* at 210.

62. *Id.* at 210–11.

63. *Id.* at 210 (emphasis omitted).

64. In Chaney v. Saunders, 17 Va. (3 Munf.) 621 (1811), the plaintiff tried to introduce the deposition of a man who the defense claimed was one-fourth Negro. *Id.* at 622. A number of witnesses were called by both sides on the issue of the

deponent's race. The trial court ruled in favor of the defendant and would not allow the deposition to be read. *Id.* The district court reversed the ruling, but the Supreme Court of Appeals reversed again, on the ground that the trial court was better able to judge the credibility of the witnesses. *Id.* The Supreme Court called the evidence "extremely contradictory." *Id.*

65. *See* 20th-century Virginia statutes defining white and "colored" persons.
66. JAMES BALDWIN, *The Fire Next Time, in* THE PRICE OF THE TICKET 376 (1988).
67. WEST, *supra* note 26, at 83.
68. IN THE MATTER OF COLOR, *supra* note 4, at 44 (omission in original).
69. *Id.* at 46.
70. *Id.*
71. Wallace Turner, *Rusk's Daughter, 18, Is Wed to Negro,* N.Y. TIMES, Sept. 22, 1967, at 1.
72. *See* 1 CATTERALL, *supra* note 33, at 55 & n.14 (describing the development of this pattern). Catterall explains:

> Butts v. Penny, 3 Keble 785, in 1677, is the first reported English case which enunciates this doctrine, but it was not new. In Maryland, in 1664, the lower house desired the upper house "to draw up an Act obligeing negros to serve *durante vita* [.] . . for the prevencion of the dammage Masters of such Slaves may susteyne by such Slaves pretending to be Christned And soe pleade the lawe of England." I Md. Arch. 526. Such "lawe of England" must have been in force in 1612, for "John Phillip A negro," who was "sworn and exam" in the General Court of Virginia in 1624, was qualified as a free man and Christian to give testimony, because he had been "Christened in England 12 years since."

Id. at 55 n.14. *See also* IN THE MATTER OF COLOR, *supra* note 4, at 21, 36–38.
73. 1 CATTERALL, *supra* note 33, at 57.
74. FREDERICK L. OLMSTED, A JOURNEY IN THE SEABOARD SLAVE STATES, WITH REMARKS ON THEIR ECONOMY 118–19 (New York, Dix & Edwards 1856).
75. IN THE MATTER OF COLOR, *supra* note 4, at 36–37 (emphasis in original).
76. *See* GUILD, *supra* note 32, at 44.
77. *Id.* at 46.
78. IN THE MATTER OF COLOR, *supra* note 4, at 53.
79. *Id.* at 36 (first change in original) (second omission in original).
80. *Id.* at 55.
81. *Id.* at 35.
82. *Id.* at 34–35.
83. THOMAS JEFFERSON, NOTES ON THE STATE OF VIRGINIA, at 143 (William Peden ed., 1954) (1787) (emphasis added).

CHAPTER FIVE

1. DOCUMENTS OF AMERICAN HISTORY 37 (Henry S. Commager ed., 8th ed. 1968).
2. *Id.*
3. James Otis, *The Rights of the British Colonies Asserted and Proved, in* 1 PAMPHLETS OF THE AMERICAN REVOLUTION, 1750–1776, at 408, 439 (Bernard Bailyn ed., 1965) [hereinafter Bailyn].
4. 1 PHILIP S. FONER, THE LIFE AND WRITINGS OF FREDERICK DOUGLASS 28 (1950).
5. *Id.* at 28–29. *See also* A. LEON HIGGINBOTHAM, JR., IN THE MATTER OF COLOR:

RACE & THE AMERICAN LEGAL PROCESS: THE COLONIAL PERIOD 380–83 (1978) [hereinafter IN THE MATTER OF COLOR].

6. 1 FONER, *supra* note 4, at 28–29. Of course, Jefferson's proposal to abolish slavery was not motivated only out of concern for the slaves. Rather, at the time Jefferson believed slavery had a corrupting influence on American morality and American society. So immediately following emancipation, Jefferson would have colonized them away from the United States. THOMAS JEFFERSON, NOTES ON THE STATE OF VIRGINIA 149, 173–75 (Richmond, Va., J.W. Randolph 1853) (1787).

7. 1 FONER, *supra* note 4, at 28.

8. HARRIET B. STOWE, UNCLE TOM'S CABIN at V (NAL Penguin Inc. 1981) (1852).

9. *Id.*

10. *Id.*

11. 2 FONER, *supra* note 4, at 226.

12. EDGAR J. MCMANUS, BLACK BONDAGE IN THE NORTH 180 (1973).

13. FREDERICK L. OLMSTED, A JOURNEY IN THE SEABOARD SLAVE STATES, WITH REMARKS ON THEIR ECONOMY 17–18 (New York, Dix & Edwards 1856).

14. 2 FONER, *supra* note 4, at 437.

15. 2 *id.* at 48–54.

16. 1 *id.* at 40.

17. 1 *id.*

18. 1 *id.*

19. 1 *id.* at 44–45.

20. 2 *id.* at 50.

21. 2 *id.* at 51 & n.7.

22. 1 *id.* at 40–41. Garrison stated:

> If we were a political party, the struggle for places of power and emolument would render our motives suspect, even if it did not prove too strong a temptation to our integrity. If we were a distinct party, every member of it must vote for its candidates, however he might disagree with them on other points of public policy. Experience seems to show that under a free government, there cannot be at one time, more than two powerful political parties.

1 *id.* at 41.

23. 2 *id.* at 58–59.

24. 2 *id.* at 59 (emphasis added).

25. *See generally* HONORÉ DE BALZAC, THE WORKS OF HONORÉ DE BALZAC (1901); CHARLES DICKENS, CHARLES DICKENS COMPLETE WORKS (1880).

26. 1 FONER, *supra* note 4, at 33.

27. DON E. FEHRENBACHER, THE DRED SCOTT CASE: ITS SIGNIFICANCE IN AMERICAN LAW AND POLITICS 117, 118–19 (1978).

28. 60 U.S. (19 How.) 393 (1857).

29. FEHRENBACHER, *supra* note 27, at 337.

30. *Id.* at 240.

31. *Id.* at 239–40.

32. *Id.* at 240.

33. *Id.* at 244.

34. *Id.*

35. *Id.*

36. *Id.* at 244–45.
37. *Id.* at 245–46.
38. *Id.* at 247.
39. *Id.*
40. *Id.* at 247–48.
41. *Id.* at 248.
42. *Id.* at 249.
43. *Id.*
44. *Id.*
45. *Id.* at 250.
46. *Id.*
47. *Id.* at 250–51.
48. *See id.* at 253.
49. *See id.* at 252–53.
50. *Id.* at 252.
51. *Id.*
52. *Id.*
53. *Id.* at 253–54.
54. *Id.* at 254.
55. *Id.*
56. *Id.* at 255.
57. *Id.* at 256.
58. *Id.* at 257.
59. *Id.* at 264.
60. *Id.*
61. *Id.* at 265.
62. *Id.* at 270.
63. *Id.* at 282, 288.
64. *Id.* at 293.
65. *Id.* at 302.
66. Dred Scott v. Sandford, 60 U.S. (19 How.) 393, 403 (1857).
67. *Id.* at 404–05.
68. *Id.*
69. *Id.* at 407 (emphasis added).
70. *Id.* at 410.
71. *Id.* at 411.
72. *Id.* at 416–17.
73. *Id.* at 405.
74. *Id.* at 426.
75. *Id.* at 409.
76. *Id.* at 407.
77. *Id.* at 410.
78. *Id.* at 409.
79. *Id.* at 420.
80. *Id.* at 410.
81. *Id.* at 416.
82. *Id.* at 419.
83. *Id.* at 409.

84. 3 CHARLES WARREN, THE SUPREME COURT IN UNITED STATES HISTORY 31 (1922) (citation omitted). Other northern papers denounced the decision as an affront to moral decency and as a threat to the nation. *See id.* at 31–34. Still other northern newspapers supported the decision. *See id.* at 31–35.
85. FEHRENBACHER, *supra* note 27, at 418.
86. *Id.* at 427.
87. *Id.* at 428.
88. *Id.*
89. Abraham Lincoln, Address on the Dred Scott Decision at Springfield, Illinois (June 26, 1857), *in* FAMOUS SPEECHES: ABRAHAM LINCOLN 14, 17 (Peter Pauper Press ed. 1935).
90. *Id.* at 32.
91. *Id.* at 30–32.
92. *Id.* at 24.
93. *Id.* at 29.

CHAPTER SIX

1. JOHN Q. ADAMS, ARGUMENT OF JOHN QUINCY ADAMS BEFORE THE SUPREME COURT OF THE UNITED STATES IN THE CASE OF THE UNITED STATES, APPELLANTS, VS. CINQUE, AND OTHERS, AFRICANS 39 (New York, S.W. Benedict 1841) (emphasis added). *See also* 2 CHARLES WARREN, THE SUPREME COURT IN UNITED STATES HISTORY 73–76 (rev. ed. 1937) (emphasis added).
2. Dred Scott v. Sandford, 60 U.S. (19 How.) 393, 537 (1857) (McLean, J., dissenting).
3. 2 THE RECORDS OF THE FEDERAL CONVENTION OF 1787, at 370 (Max Farrand ed., rev. ed. 1966) [hereinafter Farrand].
4. U.S. CONST. art. I, § 2, cl. 3 (emphasis added).
5. U.S. CONST. art. I, § 9, cl. 1 (emphasis added).
6. U.S. CONST. art. IV, § 2, cl. 3 (emphasis added).
7. U.S. CONST. art. V. For a discussion of these and other constitutional provisions that accommodated slavery, see *supra* Notes for Chapter Two, n. 30.
8. 3 Farrand, *supra* note 3, at 210.
9. 3 *id.*
10. 3 *id.* (emphasis in original).
11. 3 *id.* at 376 (emphasis added) (citation omitted).
12. 3 *id.* at 436–37 (emphasis in original).
13. 2 JOSEPH STORY, COMMENTARIES ON THE CONSTITUTION OF THE UNITED STATES 659 (Boston, Little, Brown, & Co. 5th ed. 1891).
14. *See* 2 Farrand, *supra* note 3, at 370–71.
15. GUNNAR MYRDAL, AN AMERICAN DILEMMA: THE NEGRO PROBLEM AND MODERN DEMOCRACY 86 (20th anniversary ed. 1962) (quoting Kelly Miller, *Government and the Negro*, ANNALS ACAD. POL. & SOC. SCI., Nov. 1928, at 99).
16. Charles A. Miller, *Constitutional Law and the Rhetoric of Race, in* LAW IN AMERICAN HISTORY 147, 155 (Donald Fleming & Bernard Bailyn eds., 1971).
17. 2 Farrand, *supra* note 3, at 642 (quoting Benjamin Franklin).
18. 1 PHILIP S. FONER, THE LIFE AND WRITINGS OF FREDERICK DOUGLASS 362 (1950) (quoting Frederick Douglass).

19. WILLIAM L. GARRISON, SELECTIONS FROM THE WRITINGS AND SPEECHES OF WILLIAM LLOYD GARRISON 140 (Boston, R.F. Wallcut 1852).

20. To reach this calculation, I counted the members who signed the Constitution (not including William Jackson, the Secretary, and George Washington, President). To this, I added those who "declined giving it the sanction of their names"— Mr. Randolph, Mr. Mason and Mr. Gerry. 2 Farrand, *supra* note 3, at 648–49, 663–65.

21. 2 *id.* at 642 (emphasis added).

22. 2 *id.* at 645 (citation omitted).

23. JAMES M. BECK, THE CONSTITUTION IN THE UNITED STATES: YESTERDAY, TODAY—AND TOMORROW? 52 (1924) (quoting Alexis de Tocqueville).

24. THOMAS JEFFERSON, NOTES ON THE STATE OF VIRGINIA 163 (William Peden ed., University of North Carolina Press 1955) (1787).

25. PHILIP S. FONER, HISTORY OF BLACK AMERICANS: FROM AFRICA TO THE EMERGENCE OF THE COTTON KINGDOM 409 (1975).

26. 2 FONER, *supra* note 18, at 118 (quoting Frederick Douglass).

27. 1 *id.* at 362.

28. GARRISON, *supra* note 19, at 308, 311, 314.

29. Garrison further argued:

> The Union that can be perpetuated only by enslaving a portion of the people is 'a covenant with death, and an agreement with hell,' and destined to be broken in pieces as a potter's vessel. When judgment is laid to the line, and righteousness to the plummet, the hail shall sweep away the refuge of lies, and the waters shall overflow the hiding-place. The Republic that depends for its stability on making war against the government of God and the rights of man, though it exalt itself as the eagle, and set its nest among the stars, shall be cast into the bottomless deep, and the loss of it shall be a gain to the world.
>
> There must be no compromise with slavery—none whatever. Nothing is gained, every thing is lost, by subordinating principle to expediency. The spir[i]t of freedom must be inexorable in its demand for the instant release of all who are sighing in bondage, nor abate one jot or tittle of its righteous claims. By one remorseless grasp, the rights of humanity have been taken away; and by one strong blow, the iron hand of usurpation must be made to relinquish its hold. The apologist for oppression becomes himself the oppressor. To palliate crime is to be guilty of its perpetration. To ask for a postponement of the case, till a more convenient season, is to call for a suspension of the moral law, and to assume that it is right to do wrong, under present circumstances. Talk not of other questions to be settled, of other interests to be secured, of other objects to be attained, before the slave can have his fetters broken. Nothing can take precedence of the question of liberty. No interest is so momentous as that which involves 'the life of the soul;' no object so glorious as the restoration of a man to himself. It is idle to talk of human concerns, where there are not human beings. Slavery annihilates manhood, and puts down in its crimson ledger as chattels personal, those who are created in the image of God. Hence, it tramples under foot whatever pertains to human safety, human prosperity, human happiness. Hence, too, its overthrow is the primary object to be sought, in order to secure private advantage and promote the public weal.

Id. at 140–41.

30. 12 Stat. 1268 (1863) (emphasis added).

31. *Id.*

32. *Id.* at 1269.
33. *Id.* For further discussion of the Emancipation Proclamation and its limitations, see A. Leon Higginbotham, Jr., *West Virginia's Racial Heritage: Not Always Free,* 86 W. VA. L. REV. 3, 23 (1983).
34. GARRISON, *supra* note 19, at 140.
35. U.S. CONST. amend. XIII.
36. The answer may be found in the black codes. Each of the southern states between 1865 and 1866 enacted a set of laws known as "black codes" that were designed to regulate the lives of the southern African-American population. These black codes were principally aimed at maintaining the inferior and subordinate status of the newly freed African Americans, especially through regulation of labor relations. *See generally* THEODORE B. WILSON, THE BLACK CODES OF THE SOUTH (1965) (describing the black codes and providing excerpts of several states' versions).
37. 83 U.S. (16 Wall.) 36 (1873).
38. *Id.* at 70.
39. *Id.*
40. *See* ERIC FONER, RECONSTRUCTION: AMERICA'S UNFINISHED REVOLUTION, 1863–1877, at 118–19, 243–47, 250–51, 257–59 (1st Perennial Library ed. 1989).
41. Civil Rights Act of 1866, ch. 31, 14 Stat. 27 (emphasis added).
42. *Id.* at § 1.
43. 60 U.S. (19 How.) 393 (1857).
44. *Id.* at 407. *See also supra* Chapter Five.
45. Civil Rights Act of 1866, § 1.
46. *Id.*
47. *Id.* at §§ 2–3.
48. *Id.* at § 3.
49. *Id.*
50. 27 F. Cas. 785 (C.C.D. Ky. 1866) (No. 16,151). See also statement of Ida B. Wells Barnett. Linda T. Wynn, *Ida B. Wells Barnett, in* NOTABLE BLACK AMERICAN WOMEN 1232, 1233 (Jessie C. Smith ed., 1992). In May 1884, Ida B. Wells Barnett was evicted from the ladies' car in Tennessee. *See* her comment in the photo gallery.
51. *Id.*
52. KY. REV. STAT. ch. 107, § 1 (Stanton 1867) (emphasis added).
53. ROBERT J. KACZOROWSKI, THE POLITICS OF JUDICIAL INTERPRETATION: THE FEDERAL COURTS, DEPARTMENT OF JUSTICE AND CIVIL RIGHTS, 1866–1876, at 9 (1985).
54. *Rhodes,* 27 F. Cas. at 787.
55. *Id.* (emphasis added).
56. KACZOROWSKI, *supra* note 53, at 9.
57. *Cf.* Cooley v. Board of Wardens, 53 U.S. (12 How.) 299, 315 (1851) ("[T]his contemporaneous construction of the Constitution since acted on with such uniformity in a matter of much public interest and importance, is entitled to great weight, in determining whether such a law is repugnant to the Constitution."); Edwards' Lessee v. Darby, 25 U.S. (12 Wheat.) 206, 210 (1827).
58. *Rhodes,* 27 F. Cas. at 788.
59. *Id.* at 794.

60. *Id.* at 787.
61. 80 U.S. (13 Wall.) 581 (1872).
62. KACZOROWSKI, *supra* note 53, at 135.
63. *Blyew,* 80 U.S. (13 Wall.) at 585.
64. *Id.* at 584–85.
65. *Id.* at 585.
66. *Id.*
67. *Id.* at 583–84; KACZOROWSKI, *supra* note 53, at 135.
68. KACZOROWSKI, *supra* note 53, at 140.
69. Civil Rights Act of 1866, § 3.
70. *Blyew,* 80 U.S. (13 Wall.) at 591–93.
71. *See United States v. Rhodes,* 27 F. Cas. 785, 786–88 (C.C.D. Ky. 1866) (No. 16, 151). *See also* KACZOROWSKI, *supra* note 53, at 12.
72. *Blyew,* 80 U.S. (13 Wall.) at 595.

CHAPTER SEVEN

1. LOREN MILLER, THE PETITIONERS: THE STORY OF THE SUPREME COURT OF THE UNITED STATES AND THE NEGRO 100 (1966).
2. 27 F. Cas. 785, 794 (1866) (C.C.D. Ky. 1866) (No. 16,151).
3. *Id.*
4. MILLER, *supra* note 1, at 100.
5. *Id.* (change in original) (emphasis in original).
6. *Id.* at 100–101.
7. *Id.* at 101 (emphasis added) (omissions in original).
8. 347 U.S. 483 (1954).
9. ARGUMENT: THE ORAL ARGUMENT BEFORE THE SUPREME COURT IN BROWN V. BOARD OF EDUCATION OF TOPEKA, 1952–55, at 239–40 (Leon Friedman ed., 1969) (emphasis added) [hereinafter ARGUMENT].
10. 83 U.S. (16 Wall.) 36, 71 (1873) (emphasis added).
11. William Gillette, *John Campbell, in* 2 THE JUSTICES OF THE UNITED STATES SUPREME COURT, 1789–1969: THEIR LIVES AND MAJOR OPINIONS 936–38 (Leon Friedman & Fred L. Israel eds., 1969).
12. *Id.* at 937–38.
13. *See* PROCEEDINGS OF THE BENCH AND BAR OF THE SUPREME COURT OF THE UNITED STATES: IN MEMORIAM: MATTHEW H. CARPENTER (Washington, D.C., 1881).
14. *See* GOVERNMENT PRINTING OFFICE, CONGRESSIONAL DIRECTORY: 43RD CONGRESS 67 (1874) (listing Carpenter as an elected senator from Wisconsin).
15. *Slaughter-House Cases,* 83 U.S. (16 Wall.) at 39. Purportedly passed to "*protect the health of the City of New Orleans,*" *id.* at 38 (emphasis added), the statute required construction of one "GRAND SLAUGHTER-HOUSE" with sufficient capacity to slaughter 500 animals per day, *id.* at 40. After construction of the new corporation's facilities, all other stock landings and slaughterhouses were required to close, *id.* at 41, but the new statutorily created slaughterhouse corporation was required to permit any person to slaughter animals, that have been certified by an inspector as fit for human food, in the new facilities and there was a statutorily set fee that was to be imposed for each animal slaughtered, *id.* at 41,

42. Furthermore, there was a required inspection of all animals intended to be slaughtered by an officer appointed by the governor of Louisiana. *Id.* at 41. When the cases came before the Supreme Court of Louisiana, the court had decided them in favor of the slaughterhouse company. *See id.* at 57.

16. *Id.* at 66.

17. *Id.*

18. It should be noted from the outset of this discussion, however, that in terms of slavery jurisprudence and future decisions that affected African Americans, it was the *dissenting* opinion of Justice Joseph Bradley in the *Slaughter-House Cases* which seemed to recognize the greater significance and vitality of the Thirteenth, Fourteenth, and Fifteenth Amendments.

It should also be mentioned that Justice Bradley's views on these matters apparently changed in the interim between the *Slaughter-House Cases* and the *Civil Rights Cases* of 1883. One scholar cites Bradley's participation in the Electoral Commission examining the disputed returns following the 1876 presidential election and his later " 'difficult task' of reconciling the Constitution with the political mandate of the compromise of 1877" as causing his changed stance regarding the national protection of African Americans' rights. *See* John A. Scott, *Justice Bradley's Evolving Concept of the Fourteenth Amendment from the* Slaughterhouse Cases *to the* Civil Rights Cases, 25 RUTGERS L. REV. 552, 565–69 (1971).

Despite Justice Bradley's initial view that the Reconstruction Amendments provided national rights for African Americans, Bradley nevertheless displayed even then a limited vision of universal human rights. In *Bradwell v. Illinois*, 83 U.S. (16 Wall.) 130 (1872), Bradley rejected the claim of Myra Bradwell, a woman who sought to become a lawyer. Bradley asserted that there was: "a wide difference in the respective spheres and destinies of man and woman. Man is, or should be, woman's protector and defender. The natural and proper timidity and delicacy which belongs to the female sex evidently unfits it for many of the occupations of civil life." *Id.* at 560 (quoting 83 U.S. (16 Wall.) at 141).

19. *Slaughter-House Cases*, 83 U.S. (16 Wall.) at 71–72 (emphasis added).

20. *Id.* at 70.

21. *Id.*

22. *Id.* at 70–71.

23. ARGUMENT, *supra* note 9, at 239.

24. MILLER, *supra* note 1, at 103–04 (quoting Sen. Jacob Howard of Michigan) (emphasis added) (change in original).

25. *Slaughter-House Cases*, 83 U.S. (16 Wall.) at 68–69.

26. *Id.* at 69.

27. 84 U.S. (17 Wall.) 445 (1873).

28. *Id.* at 452–53.

29. *Id.*

30. 163 U.S. 537 (1896).

31. 84 U.S. (17 Wall.) at 445, 452.

32. *Id.* at 447, 452–53.

33. 80 U.S. (13 Wall.) 581 (1872). *See supra* Chapter Six.

34. *Slaughter-House Cases*, 83 U.S. (16 Wall.) 36, 71–72, 73–80 (1873). *See also* LOREN MILLER, THE PETITIONERS, chapter 7 (1966).

35. ROBERT J. KACZOROWSKI, THE POLITICS OF JUDICIAL INTERPRETATION: THE FEDERAL COURTS, DEPARTMENT OF JUSTICE AND CIVIL RIGHTS, 1866–1876, at 175 (1985).
36. *Id.*
37. *Id.* at 176.
38. *Id.* at 176–77; United States v. Cruikshank, 92 U.S. 542, 544–45 (1876).
39. KACZOROWSKI, *supra* note 35, at 177–78.
40. *Id.* at 178.
41. *Id.* at 179.
42. *Id.*
43. *Id.* at 183.
44. *Id.* at 184.
45. United States v. Cruikshank, 92 U.S. 542, 553–54 (1876).
46. Watts v. Indiana, 338 U.S. 49, 52 (1949) (citing Taft, C.J., Bailey v. Drexel Furniture Co., 259 U.S. 20, 37 (1922) (Child Labor Tax Case)).
47. On the same day they decided *Cruikshank*, the Supreme Court in *United States v. Reese*, 92 U.S. 214 (1875), voided two sections of the Enforcement Act of 1870 as beyond congressional powers to enforce the Fifteenth Amendment. *Id.* at 220–22. The case involved an indictment under the Act "against two of the inspectors of a municipal election in the State of Kentucky, for refusing to receive and count at such election the vote of William Garner," an African American. *Id.* at 215.
48. KACZOROWSKI, *supra* note 35, at 217.
49. *Id.*
50. ERIC FONER, RECONSTRUCTION: AMERICA'S UNFINISHED REVOLUTION, 1863–1877, at 581 (1988) (quoting the Kansas Republican state committee chairman).
51. *See, e.g.,* United States v. Cruikshank, 92 U.S. 542 (1876).
52. C. VANN WOODWARD, REUNION AND REACTION: THE COMPROMISE OF 1877 AND THE END OF RECONSTRUCTION 17–21 (1951).
53. *Id.* at 17.
54. *Id.* at 8.
55. RAYFORD W. LOGAN, THE BETRAYAL OF THE NEGRO: FROM RUTHERFORD B. HAYES TO WOODROW WILSON 24 (enlarged ed. 1965).
56. *Id.* at 25 (quoting Rutherford B. Hayes).
57. *Id.* at 25–26.
58. *Id.* at 26 (quoting 1 CHARLES R. WILLIAMS, THE LIFE OF RUTHERFORD BIRCHARD HAYES 488–89 (1928) (omission in original).
59. *Id.* at 23.
60. *Id.* at 26. *See also* WOODWARD, *supra* note 52, at 3–9 (1951).
61. LOGAN, *supra* note 55, at 27 (quoting Rutherford B. Hayes) (emphasis in original) (change in original).
62. FONER, *supra* note 50, at 582 (quoting Henry Adams).
63. *Id.* (quoting African-American Southerner).
64. JOHN H. FRANKLIN & ALFRED A. MOSS, JR., FROM SLAVERY TO FREEDOM: A HISTORY OF AFRICAN AMERICANS 254 (7th ed. 1994).
65. *Id.*
66. *Id.*
67. FONER, *supra* note 50, at 581 (quoting the Kansas Republican state committee chairman).

CHAPTER EIGHT

1. 43 CONG. REC. app. at 3 (1874) (speech of Rep. Hiram P. Bell).
2. Abolitionist Frederick Douglass described his pre-Civil War experiences:

   My treatment in the use of public conveyances about these times was extremely rough, . . . there was a mean, dirty, and uncomfortable car set apart for colored travelers called the Jim Crow car. Regarding this as the fruit of slaveholding prejudice and being determined to fight the spirit of slavery wherever I might find it, I resolved to avoid this car, though it sometimes required some courage to do so. . . . I . . . sometimes was soundly beaten by conductor and brakemen. On one occasion six of these 'fellows of the baser sort,' under the direction of the conductor, set out to eject me from my seat. As usual, I had purchased a first-class ticket and paid the required sum for it, and on the requirement of the conductor to leave, refused to do so. . . . They . . . found me much attached to my seat, and in removing me I tore away two or three of the surrounding ones, on which I held a firm grasp, and did the car no service in some other respects. . . . The result was that Stephen A. Chase, superintendent of the road, ordered all passenger trains to pass through Lynn, where I then lived, without stopping.

   JOHN W. BLASSINGAME, FREDERICK DOUGLASS: THE CLARION VOICE 23 (1976) (quoting Frederick Douglass).
3. Senator Sumner had a distinguished record as an abolitionist and civil rights advocate. In 1856, he was attacked on the floor of the Senate by Rep. Preston S. Brooks of South Carolina for espousing antislavery remarks. Rep. Brooks repeatedly beat Senator Sumner about the head with a cane until he fell unconscious on the floor. It took him two-and-a-half years to recover sufficiently to return to the Senate. See MOORFIELD STOREY, CHARLES SUMNER 138–49, 170 (1900).

   By the time the Civil Rights Act was passed, Senator Sumner had died. See id. at 430 (noting Sumner's death in 1874).
4. 43 CONG. REC. 977–78 (1875) (statement of Rep. James Blount).
5. 43 CONG. REC. app. at 4 (1875) (speech of Rep. John M. Glover).
6. 43 CONG. REC. app. at 3 (1874) (speech of Rep. Hiram P. Bell).
7. 43 CONG. REC. 3451 (1874) (statement of Sen. Frederick T. Frelinghuysen) (emphasis in original).
8. 43 CONG. REC. 940 (1875) (statement of Rep. Benjamin Butler).
9. Id. at 944–45 (statement of Rep. John R. Lynch) (emphasis in original). Rep. Lynch's statement also included the following:

   That the passage of this bill can in any manner affect the social status of any one seems to me to be absurd and ridiculous. I have never believed for a moment that social equality could be brought about even between persons of the same race. I have always believed that social distinctions existed among white people the same as among colored people. But those who contend that the passage of this bill will have a tendency to bring about social equality between the races virtually and substantially admit that there are no social distinctions among white people whatever, but that all white persons, regardless of their moral character, are the social equals of each other; for if by conferring upon colored people the same rights and privileges that are now exercised and enjoyed by whites indiscriminately will result in bringing about social equality between the races, then the same process of reasoning must necessarily bring us to the conclusion that there are no social distinctions among whites, because all white persons, regardless of their social standing, are permitted to enjoy these rights. See then how unreasonable, unjust, and false is the assertion that social equality is involved in this legislation. I cannot believe that gentlemen on the other side of the House mean what they say when they admit as they do, that the immoral, the ignorants and the degraded of their own race are the social equals of themselve[s], and their families. If they do, then I can only assure them that they do not put as high an estimate upon their own social standing as respectable and intelligent colored people place upon theirs; for there are hundreds and thousands of white people of both sexes whom I know to be the social inferiors of respectable and intelligent colored people. I can then assure that portion of my democratic friends on the other side of the House whom I regard as my social inferiors that if at any time I should meet any one of you at a hotel and occupy a seat at the same table with you, or the same seat in a car with you, do not think that I have thereby accepted you as my social equal. Not at all. But if any one should attempt to discriminate against you for no other reason than because you are identified with a particular race or religious sect, I would regard it as an outrage; as a violation of the principles of republicanism; and I would be in favor of protecting you in the exercise and enjoyment of your rights by suitable and appropriate legislation.

Id. at 944.

10. Civil Rights Act of 1875, § 1, ch. 114, 18 Stat. 335 (1875).

11. *Id.* at § 2.

12. 1 ALEXIS DE TOCQUEVILLE, DEMOCRACY IN AMERICA 330 (H. Reeve trans., 1961) (1835) (quoted in Davis v. Bandemer, 478 U.S. 109, 143 (1986) (Burger, C.J., concurring in judgment)).

13. *See* Record, United States v. Stanley (C.C.D. Ka. 1876) (No. 1568, United States Supreme Court); Record, United States v. Nichols (C.C.W.D. Mo. 1877) (No. 1334, United States Supreme Court) (reported as Transcripts of Record in the United States Supreme Court).

14. *See* Record, United States v. Ryan (C.C.D. Cal. 1876) (No. 248, United States Supreme Court); Record, United States v. Singleton (C.C.S.D.N.Y. 1880) (No. 196, United States Supreme Court) (reported as Transcripts of Record in the United States Supreme Court).

15. *See* Record, Robinson v. Memphis & Charleston R.R. Co. (C.C.W.D. Tenn. 1880) (No. 2611, United States Supreme Court) (reported as Transcript of Record in the United States Supreme Court) [hereinafter Robinson].

16. *See id.*

17. The question "Ain't I a Woman?" was asked by Sojourner Truth, a legendary abolitionist, while speaking at the 1851 Woman's Rights Convention in Akron, Ohio. *See* BLACK WOMEN IN NINETEENTH-CENTURY AMERICAN LIFE: THEIR WORDS, THEIR THOUGHTS, THEIR FEELINGS 235–36 (Bert James Loewenberg & Ruth Bogin eds., 1976).

18. This is the same issue that many scholars of African-American women have been exploring in their research into the history of that status as it developed during and as a consequence of slavery. *See, e.g.,* Evelyn B. Higginbotham, *Beyond the Sound of Silence: Afro-American Women in History,* 1 GENDER & HIST. 50 (1989).

19. State of Missouri v. Celia, 2 Index to Court Cases of Callaway County, File No.

4,496, at 13 (1855) [hereinafter Celia]. The Clerk of Callaway County paginated solely the front of each page. Thus, citation to page numbers may include either the front or the back of that page.

20. *Id.* at 33.

21. The deceased's daughter, Virginia Wainscott, testified as such. *See id.* at 34.

22. *Id.* (testimony of Virginia Wainscott).

23. At the time of Celia's trial in 1855, and for some twenty-six years following, the testimony of witnesses was summarized by the Clerk of the Court. Thus the accuracy of the reporting depended wholly upon the ability, diligence, and integrity of the Clerk. Not until about 1881 did word-by-word (shorthand) reporting of testimony become the practice. *See* Hugh P. Williamson, *The State Against Celia, a Slave,* 8 Midwest J. 409 n.3 (1956).

24. *See Celia, supra* note 19, at 34 (testimony of Virginia Wainscott).

25. *Id.* at 33 (testimony of Colonel Jones at the inquest).

26. *Id.*

27. *Id.*

28. *Id. See also id.* at 21 (sworn affidavit of Celia).

29. *Id.* at 19 (Celia's inquest testimony), 33, 34 (testimony of Harvey Newsom, son of the deceased and testimony of "Coffee" Wainscott, 11-year-old grandson of the deceased).

30. Indeed, all of her counsel's requests for jury instructions to that effect were refused:

> [Requested Instruction No. 10.] An attempt to compel a woman to be defiled by using force, menace, or duress is a felony within the meaning of the fourth section of the second [article] concerning crimes & punishments in Missouri statutes for 1845.
> [Requested Instruction No. 11.] The using of a slave to be by him defiled, is using force, menace, and duress, within the meaning of the 29 section of the 2nd article of Missouri statute for 1845 concerning crimes and punishments.
> [Requested Instruction No. 12.] The words any woman in the first clause of the 29th section, of second article of laws of Missouri for 1845, concerning crimes & punishments, *embrace slave women, as well as free white women.*

> *Id.* at 12–13 (emphasis added).

31. Missouri statutes were explicit in protecting women from attempts to ravish, rape, or defile. *See* Mo. Rev. Stat. ch. 47, § 29 (1845) ("Every person who shall take any woman, unlawfully, against her will, with intent to compel her by force, menace or duress . . . to defile [her] upon conviction thereof shall be punished by imprisonment . . . ."); Mo. Rev. Stat. ch. 47, § 4 (1845) ("Homicide shall be deemed justifiable when committed by any person [who is] resisting [attempts] to commit any felony upon . . . her."). A "justifiable homicide" is not a crime even though a person intentionally kills another person.

 When the Missouri legislature intended to limit the privileges of blacks or expose them to harsher penalties, it used the express terms "negro," "slave," and "mulatto." Similarly, when it intended to protect only white females, it used the language "white female." For example, in section 31 of the criminal code, the legislature, in an attempt to deter relationships between black males and white females, noted with specificity that it was a crime for any negro or mulatto to attempt to commit a rape on a white female, or to marry or defile a white female. The statute read:

If any *negro* or *mulatto* shall either, *First* commit, or attempt to commit a rape on a *white female*, as hereinbefore declared; or *Second*, By force, menace, or duress, compel, or attempt to compel any *white* female to marry him, or any *negro* or *mulatto* to be defiled by him or another *negro* or *mulatto*; or, *Third*, Marry or defile, or attempt to defile any *white female*, who shall have been compelled thereto by force, menace or duress, employed or used by him or any other; or, *Fourth*, Take away any *white female* under the age of eighteen years, as specified in the last preceding section, for the purpose of prostitution, concubinage, or marriage with him, or any other *negro* or *mulatto*, he shall on conviction, instead of the punishment declared in the preceding section, be sentenced to castration, to be performed under the direction of the sheriff, by some skillful person, and the expense shall be adjusted, taxed and paid as other costs.

Mo. Rev. Stat. ch. 47, § 31 (1845) (emphasis added).
  The failure to limit section 29 to white females suggests that the legislature meant to criminalize the rape of "any woman." The concept of *ejusdem generis* supports my hypothesis as to how the Missouri statutes should be construed. *See* Norman J. Singer, Statutes and Statutory Construction § 47.17 (5th ed. 1992).

32. *Celia, supra* note 19, at 14 (emphasis added).
33. *Id.*
34. One of the ironies is that the master's estate was denied a profit from Celia's rape. Despite the court's "mercy" in delaying execution until the birth of the child, the record reflects that a Doctor Carter delivered Celia's child, who was born dead. The bill of costs lists "Medical attendance of prisoner during sickness & delivering her of dead child by Dr. Carter allowed by court." *Id.* at 1.
35. Professor Williamson estimates her date of death to be December 13, on which date she was taken from the prison to the gallows and there "hanged until she died." *See* Williamson, *supra* note 23, at 420. If this date is correct, she was hanged one day before the Supreme Court of Missouri acted on the petition by her counsel "that an order might be made staying the execution of the [s]entence of the Court until the appeal might be heard in the Supreme Court at the next term thereof in January next, at Jefferson City." *Celia, supra* note 19, at 4.
36. Williamson, *supra* note 23, at 408 (1956).
37. 43 Cong. Rec. 944 (1875).
38. Robinson, *supra* note 15, at 1, 2, 4.
39. *Id.* at 2.
40. *Id.* at 8.
41. *Id.*
42. *Id.*
43. *Id.* at 4.
44. It should be noted that apparently the conductor, when he testified, called Mrs. Robinson "girl" for, on cross-examination, the Robinsons' attorney asked the conductor why he had done so. The conductor replied that it was not a "term of opprobrium," but was "customary in this country to call young colored women girls, and I did it from force of habit." He followed up this statement by concluding, "I do not think every colored woman wanting in virtue, and I want you to know that."

Id. at 9.

45. *Id.*
46. *Id.* at 13. Among the other instructions given to the jury were:

> If ill founded, her remedy is not under this statute, but in some other form of
> action, unless you further find that it was because she was supposed to be a
> colored prostitute that she was excluded, and that the same treatment would not
> have been applied to a white woman similarly suspected, in which case the
> statute would be violated. *Id.*
> There is no presumption of law or fact that a colored woman travelling with a
> white man is a prostitute, and he her paramour. Yet if you find as a matter of
> fact, the conductor did believe they were improperly associated, and therefore
> improper characters, and for that belief excluded them, the defendant is not
> liable.

Id. at 14.
    I conclude, however, it is unlikely that such discretion would have been
given to exclude white women travelling with white men.
47. The court refused to give the following proposed jury instructions, submitted by
    the plaintiffs, the Robinsons:

> [Requested Instruction] No. 1. If you believe that the plaintiff Sallie J. Rob-
> inson was excluded from the ladies' car because she was a colored woman,
> travelling with a white man, and that the conductor believed she was such
> colored woman, and believed that she was travellng with a white man, it fur-
> nishes no ground for such exclusion, as there is no law to prevent a white man
> and a colored woman travelling together, and such exclusion would simply be
> an exclusion on account of race, there being no presumption of law that when-
> ever a white man and a colored woman travel together there exists any improper
> relations between them.

Id. at 14–15.

> [Requested Instruction] No. 5. It is no sufficient reason to impute a want of
> virtue to a woman of African descent that she is travelling in company with a
> white man on the cars of a railroad. And the defendant's conductor was not
> justified in suspecting or concluding from the fact that the plaintiff Sallie J. was
> a colored woman, and the supposition (even taking it to be true) that Joseph C.
> Robinson was a white man, and the circumstances that the two were travelling
> together, that the plaintiff Sallie J. was a woman without virtue, or that im-
> proper relations existed between her and the said Joseph C. and if the jury find
> from the evidence that the defendant's conductor did entertain the suspicion
> that improper relations existed between the said Sallie J. and the said Joseph
> C., and that such suspicion was based on the circumstance that he believed the
> one to be of African descent and the other to be white, then such suspicion was
> no sufficient reason in law for excluding the said Sallie J. from the lady's car
> of the defendant's train; and if the jury find from the evidence that the conduc-
> tor excluded her from such car because of the said suspicion, then the jury will
> find for the plaintiffs.

Id. at 16.
    These proposed instructions capture the assumption of the conductor, prem-
ised on notions of presumptions of black inferiority.
48. *Id.* at 13.

49. There were instructions to the contrary. The court stated that "[t]he carrier . . . may . . . temporarily exclude persons on a mere suspicion." *Id.* But again, it must be asked, on what basis would the conductor suspect white women?

I am not unmindful of the possibility that the conductor may actually have sought to exclude prostitutes, African-American or white, evenhandedly. At trial, the conductor was asked whether he had ever excluded a white woman traveling with a white man "on account of suspicion as to her character." The conductor responded that he had done so several times, gave one example, and said that the woman turned out to be a prostitute. *Id.* at 9.

50. *Id.* at 19.

51. Evelyn B. Higginbotham, *African-American Women's History and the Metalanguage of Race, in* REVISING THE WORD AND THE WORLD: ESSAYS IN FEMINIST LITERARY CRITICISM 91, 101 (VeVe A. Clark et al. eds., 1993).

52. Earl M. Maltz, *The Civil Rights Act and the* Civil Rights Cases: *Congress, Court, and the Constitution,* 44 FLA. L. REV. 605, 618 (1992). Maltz notes: "The basis of this difference was the view that while a common carrier may be private in form, it performs a public function and thus for many purposes should be considered an arm of the state." *Id.*

53. New Jersey Steam Navigation Co. v. Merchants' Bank, 47 U.S. (6 How.) 344, 382 (1848) (cited in Maltz, *supra* note 52, at 618).

54. The Civil Rights Cases, 109 U.S. 3, 11 (1883) (emphasis added).

55. *Id.* at 3.

56. *Id.* at 24–25.

57. The Civil Rights Cases, 109 U.S. at 25.

58. *Id.* at 26–62 (Harlan, J., dissenting).

The dissenting opinion of Justice John Harlan brilliantly exposed the hypocrisy of the Court's findings regarding the federal government's power to *protect* African Americans. Under slavery, Justice Harlan noted, the Court had no trouble upholding the Fugitive Slave Law of 1793 or the Fugitive Slave Act of 1850 protecting *slaveowners' property rights* through the return of runaway slaves. *Id.* at 28–30 (Harlan, J., dissenting) (citing Prigg v. Pennsylvania, 41 U.S. (16 Pet.) 539 (1842); Ableman v. Booth, 62 U.S. (21 How.) 506 (1859)). Justice Harlan thus affirmed the federal power to secure civil rights now found in the Constitution because of the dramatic legal changes wrought by the Civil War and Reconstruction.

59. *Id.*

60. *Id.* Apparently, more important to the Court than the status of the defendants was the racial status of the plaintiffs, whose rights were to be secured by the Civil Rights Act. I draw this conclusion by comparing Justice Bradley's comments in the *Civil Rights Cases* with his earlier position. In previous cases Justice Bradley was a staunch advocate for a broad application of the Thirteenth and Fourteenth Amendments to protect African Americans as well as whites. For example, in the *Slaughter-House Cases* in 1873, a case involving white butchers, he dissented from the majority opinion, which he believed unduly restricted the national rights of citizenship contained in the Reconstruction amendments, writing: "if a man be denied full equality before the law, he is denied one of the essential rights of citizenship as a citizen of the United States." 83 U.S. (17 Wall.) 36, 113 (Bradley, J., dissenting). Given this broad reading, one would think that when African

Americans—the very group the amendments had been primarily designed to protect—urged their protection following denials of their "full equality before the
law," Justice Bradley would have held firm to his earlier view that this unequal
treatment denied African Americans their citizenship rights. But by this time—
following the political retreat ending Reconstruction—Bradley was apparently unwilling to fight to repudiate the precept of black inferiority in the area of public
accommodations.

One scholar cites Bradley's participation in the Electoral Commission examining the disputed returns following the 1876 presidential election and his later
" 'difficult task' of reconciling the Constitution with the political mandate of the
compromise of 1877" as causing his changed stance regarding the national protection of African Americans' rights. *See* John A. Scott, *Justice Bradley's Evolving
Concept of the Fourteenth Amendment from the* Slaughterhouse Cases *to the* Civil
Rights Cases, 25 RUTGERS L. REV. 552, 565–69 (1971). *See also* Arthur Kinoy,
The Constitutional Right of Negro Freedom, 21 RUTGERS L. REV. 387, 396
(1967) ("The Bradley Court, reflecting the profound changes which had occurred
in the nation in the immediate years following the fateful decisions of 1877, faced
the immensely difficult task of constructing a legal rationale which could justify
the conclusion already reached by the new national political majority.")

61. *Id.* at 45–47 (Harlan, J., dissenting).
62. *Id.* at 48 (Harlan, J., dissenting).

CHAPTER NINE

1. 505 U.S. 833, 863, 112 S. Ct. 2791, 2813 (1992) (plurality opinion) (noting, in
   abortion rights decision, that "[w]hile we think *Plessy* was wrong the day it was
   decided, . . . we must also recognize that the Plessy Court's explanation for its
   decision was so clearly at odds with the facts apparent to the Court in 1954 that
   the decision to reexamine *Plessy* was on this ground alone not only justified but
   required").
2. Plessy v. Ferguson, 163 U.S. 537, 541 (1896).
3. 347 U.S. 483 (1954).
4. Theoretically, *Brown* could be read as a constitutional doctrine applicable solely
   to public education. But after its issuance the Court held in a variety of cases that
   the Fourteenth Amendment prohibits state-imposed racial discrimination in other
   areas. *See, e.g.,* Schiro v. Bynum, 375 U.S. 395 (1964) (per curiam) (ordinance
   requiring segregation in municipal auditorium); Johnson v. Virginia, 373 U.S. 61
   (1963) (per curiam) (courtroom seating); Turner v. City of Memphis, 369 U.S.
   350 (1962) (per curiam) (administrative regulation requiring segregation in airport
   restaurant); State Athletic Comm'n v. Dorsey, 359 U.S. 533 (1959) (per curiam)
   (statute prohibiting integrated athletic contests); New Orleans City Park Dev.
   Ass'n v. Detiege, 358 U.S. 54 (1958) (per curiam) (public parks and golf course);
   Gayle v. Browder, 352 U.S. 903 (1956) (per curiam) (statute requiring segregation on buses); Holmes v. City of Atlanta, 350 U.S. 879 (1955) (per curiam)
   (municipal golf courses); Mayor of Baltimore v. Dawson, 350 U.S. 877 (1955)
   (per curiam) (public beaches and bathhouses); Muir v. Louisville Park Theatrical
   Ass'n, 347 U.S. 971 (1954) (per curiam) (city lease of park facilities), *cited in* 2
   THOMAS I. EMERSON ET AL., POLITICAL AND CIVIL RIGHTS IN THE UNITED
   STATES 1249 (Student ed. 1967).

5. *Plessy*, 163 U.S. at 541, 542–43, 549.
6. Brief for Plaintiff in Error at 8, Plessy v. Ferguson, 163 U.S. 537 (1896) (No. 210) (emphasis added).
7. *Id.* at 9.
8. LA. CONST. of 1868, arts. I, XIII, CXXXV. *See also* Louis Harlan, *Desegregation in New Orleans Public Schools During Reconstruction*, 67 AM. HIST. REV. 663–75 (1962); Keith W. Medley, *The Sad Story of How 'Separate But Equal' Was Born*, SMITHSONIAN, Feb. 1994, at 105.
9. Act of Feb. 23, 1869, No. 38, §§ 1–2, 1869 La. Acts 37, declared unconstitutional in Hall v. De Cuir, 95 U.S. 485 (1877). *See* Paul A. Kunkel, *Modifications in Louisiana Legal Status Under Louisiana Constitutions, 1812–1957*, 44 J. OF NEGRO HIST. 1, 13 & nn. 65–66 (1959).
10. JOHN W. BLASSINGAME, BLACK NEW ORLEANS, 1860–1880, at 183 (1973).
11. *Id.*
12. *Id.* at 184.
13. Act of Apr. 19, 1873, No. 84, 1873 La. Acts 156, 156–57 *cited in* Kunkel, *supra* note 9, at 14.
14. *See* Act of July 10, 1890, No. 111, 1890 La. Acts 152, 152–54.
15. *Id.* at § 1, 1890 La. Acts at 153. The statute required railway officers to assign passengers to the appropriate compartments. *Id.* at § 2, 1890 La. Acts at 153. The law set fines and terms of imprisonment for violations of the requirements by passengers or railway officers. *Id.* at §§ 2–3, 1890 La. Acts at 153.
16. *Id.* at § 3, 1890 La. Acts at 153.
17. *Cf.* JOHN DUGARD, HUMAN RIGHTS AND THE SOUTH AFRICAN LEGAL ORDER 73 (1978) (noting analogous exception to South African apartheid policies, which allowed migrant laborers to enter a "white area" to further whites' agricultural and industrial interests).
18. Brief for Plaintiff in Error at 19, *Plessy* (No. 210).
    Another lesson of the statute and its exception is that racists always want the option to implement their venal policies without causing themselves any significant inconvenience.
19. Plessy v. Ferguson, 163 U.S. 537, 538 (1896).
20. *Id.* at 538–39.
21. JACK BASS, UNLIKELY HEROES: THE DRAMATIC STORY OF THE SOUTHERN JUDGES WHO TRANSLATED THE SUPREME COURT'S BROWN DECISION INTO A REVOLUTION FOR EQUALITY 16 (1982).
22. John Minor Wisdom, Plessy Rides Again, George Abel Dreyfous Lecture on Civil Liberties, Tulane Law School (April 18, 1972), at 10–11.
23. *Id.* at 11–12.
24. *Id.* at 12–13.
25. Plessy v. Ferguson, 163 U.S. 537, 538 (1896).
26. *Id.* at 539–40.
27. Brief for Plaintiff in Error at 57–58, *Plessy* (No. 210).
28. *Id.* at 549.
29. *Id.* at 542–43.
30. *Id.* at 543.
31. *Id.* at 551.
32. 59 Mass. (5 Cush.) 198 (1850).
33. 60 U.S. (19 How.) 393 (1857).

34. *Id.* at 407.
35. 55 Pa. 209 (1867).
36. *Id.* at 213.
37. Brief for Plaintiff in Error at 56, *Plessy* (No. 210).
38. Plessy v. Ferguson, 163 U.S. 537, 550 (1896).
39. *Id.*
40. *Id.* at 551.
41. *Id.* at 557 (Harlan, J. dissenting).
42. *See id.* at 549. *See also* Cheryl I. Harris, *Whiteness as Property*, 106 HARV. L. REV. 1707 (1993).
43. *Plessy*, 163 U.S. at 552 (citations omitted).
44. *Id.* at 559 (Harlan, J., dissenting).
45. *Id.*
46. *Id.*
47. *Id.*
48. *See* ROBERT J. KACZOROWSKI, THE POLITICS OF JUDICIAL INTERPRETATION: THE FEDERAL COURTS, DEPARTMENT OF JUSTICE AND CIVIL RIGHTS, 1866–1876, at 8 & n.12, 18–19 (1985); Stephen J. Riegel, *The Persistent Career of Jim Crow: Lower Federal Courts and the "Separate But Equal" Doctrine, 1865–1896*, 28 AM. J. LEGAL HIST. 17, 20–21 (1984).
49. One comprehensive survey cites more than fifty pre-*Brown* school cases in which the courts or counsel relied on the segregation doctrine of *Plessy*. These cases concern issues ranging from the physical, aesthetic condition of the facility to the more qualitative, substantive considerations of the curriculum and faculty. *See* Robert A. Leflar & Wylie H. Davis, *Segregation in the Public Schools—1953*, 67 HARV. L. REV. 377, 430–35 (1954).
50. It matters not whether one views *Plessy* as merely a ratification of legal and social developments throughout the nation in the years following the Civil War or, as I do, as a signal event in the jurisprudence of American race relations; from the day the decision was delivered in 1896, it should not have escaped public attention and critical legal scrutiny. *Plessy* was, after all, a decision of the United States Supreme Court, and it was accompanied by perhaps the most forceful and prescient dissenting opinion a justice has ever filed. *Plessy* addressed a topic of widespread concern to both blacks and whites and elevated the separate but equal doctrine to the status of supreme law of the land. To state my thesis bluntly, it should have been noticed in the premier law review of that time—*Harvard Law Review*. Yet, the editors of the *Harvard Law Review* did not even comment upon the 1896 *Plessy* decision when it was rendered. Ironically, the *Review* did note two other decisions handed down by the Supreme Court on the day that *Plessy* was decided, both of which also happened to involve trains. *Hennington v. Georgia*, 163 U.S. 299 (1896), upheld state laws forbidding freight trains to run on Sunday; *Illinois Central Railroad v. Illinois*, 163 U.S. 142 (1896), struck down a state law requiring passenger trains to stop at county seats. In the eyes of the editors of the *Harvard Law Review*, two state laws regulating train operation were apparently of greater legal significance than legislation imposing second-class citizenship on blacks. *See Recent Cases*, 10 HARV. L. REV. 379, 380 (1897).

Harvard, to be sure, was not alone in its lack of response to *Plessy*. "Except for indignation expressed in some black newspapers, the American public was largely silent." Riegel, *supra* note 48, at 17, 39 n.93 (noting the extensive and regular *New York Times* coverage of public accommodation cases in the 30 years preceding *Plessy*).

51. *See supra* Chapter Five.
52. Justice Brewer did not hear the argument or participate in the decision of this case. *Plessy*, 163 U.S. at 564.
53. DERRICK A. BELL, JR., RACE, RACISM AND AMERICAN LAW 452 (1973) (citing ANTHONY LEWIS, THE SCHOOL DESEGREGATION CASES, PORTRAIT OF A DECADE 17 (1965)).
54. 448 U.S. 448, 522–23 (1980) (Stewart, J., dissenting, joined by Rehnquist, J.).
55. William B. Reynolds, *Individualism v. Group Rights, The Legacy of* Brown, 93 YALE L.J. 995, 1000 (1984).
56. 505 U.S. 833, 863, 112 S. Ct. 2791, 2813 (1992) (plurality opinion).
57. 347 U.S. 483 (1954).
58. 305 U.S. 337 (1938).
59. 339 U.S. 629 (1950).
60. 339 U.S. 637 (1950).
61. *See, e.g.,* A. Leon Higginbotham, Jr., *Foreword* to GENNA R. MCNEIL, GROUNDWORK: CHARLES HAMILTON HOUSTON AND THE STRUGGLE FOR CIVIL RIGHTS xvi (1983) (noting "Even the false rumor that a black had been present at an official White House function was sufficient to drive President Cleveland into a frenzy, and thus he responded: 'It so happens that I have never in my official position, either when sleeping or waking, alive or dead, on my head or my heels, dined, lunched, supped, or invited to a wedding reception, any colored man, woman, or child.' ")

CHAPTER TEN

1. Brief for Defendant in Error, at 7, 12, Buchanan v. Warley, 245 U.S. 60 (1917) (No. 33). The brief by the City of Louisville for defendant in error, as well as the supplemental and reply brief for defendant in error on rehearing, also intimated that the NAACP counsel arguing the case, Moorfield Storey, advocated interracial marriage, but not for himself. *Id.* at 12; Supplemental and Reply Brief for Defendant in Error on Rehearing at 142–44, Buchanan v. Warley, 245 U.S. 60 (1917) (No. 33).
   This chapter substantially relies on the research and analysis in A. Leon Higginbotham, Jr., et al., *De Jure Housing Segregation in the United States and South Africa: The Difficult Pursuit for Racial Justice,* 1990 U. ILL. L. REV. 763. I would also like to thank Professor Mitchell Duneier for his assistance in the preparation of this chapter.
2. I have lumped together the entire time period from 1865 to the 1990s as the fourth stage in the development of the precept of inferiority. I recognize that some historians may prefer to partition this fourth stage into shorter spans of time. They may prefer a more traditional delineation as such: (1) the Reconstruction era, approximately 1865 to 1876; (2) the nadir of post-Reconstruction, 1877 to 1912 or 1916 (or even 1877 to the 1930s); (3) the "Road to *Brown*," 1938 to 1954; (4) the twentieth-century civil rights revolution, starting with *Brown v. Board of Education* as the major catalyst in a chain of events that escalated through the Kennedy-Johnson-Carter and, to some extent, the Nixon-Ford eras; and (5) the decline of racial civil rights during the Reagan-Bush era. I explore racial civil rights issues and decisions during the Clinton administration elsewhere.

The finer time-line distinctions that historians often use to analyze the legal process are not essential. For my purposes it is not necessary to summarize the extensive present historical scholarship on all of these eras, from 1866 to the 1990s. Instead, my more limited purpose is to describe some of the continuation of legal events after the Civil War that sometimes involved at least the partial repudiation of the slavery jurisprudential precept of inferiority and the other significant events that sometimes involved legal efforts to sanction, reinstate, or implement the slavery jurisprudential precept of racial inferiority.

The implementation of the inferiority precept still has effects in the modern day. *See* Gary Orfield, *Separate Societies: Have the Kerner Warnings Come True?* in QUIET RIOTS: RACE AND POVERTY IN THE UNITED STATES 100–122 (Fred R. Harris and Roger W. Wilkins eds., 1988); GARY ORFIELD & CAROLE ASHKINAZE, THE CLOSING DOOR: CONSERVATIVE POLICY AND BLACK OPPORTUNITY (1991). *See also* DOUGLAS S. MASSEY & NANCY A. DENTON, AMERICAN APARTHEID: SEGREGATION AND THE MAKING OF THE UNDERCLASS (1993); Thomas F. Pettigrew, *Racial Change and Social Policy*, ANNALS AM. ACAD. POL. & SOC. SCI. 114–31 (1979).

3. Of course, there was pervasive discrimination in northern courts as well. *See* DERRICK BELL, RACE, RACISM AND AMERICAN LAW 368–71, 475–81 (2d ed. 1980); A. Leon Higginbotham, Jr., *Racism in American and South African Courts: Similarities and Differences*, 65 N.Y.U. L. REV. 479, 495 n.49 (1990). However, the northern legislative discrimination was less pervasive.

4. 123 Ky. 209, 94 S.W. 623 (1906).

5. *Id.* at 213, 94 S.W. at 625.

6. *Id.*

7. W.E.B. DU BOIS, THE PHILADELPHIA NEGRO (Schocken Books 1967) (1899).

8. MASSEY & DENTON, *supra* note 2, at 20–21.

9. The classic studies on racial discrimination in housing include: KENNETH B. CLARK, DARK GHETTO (1965); ST. CLAIR DRAKE & HORACE R. CAYTON, BLACK METROPOLIS: A STUDY OF NEGRO LIFE IN A NORTHERN CITY (1945); LUIGI LAURENTI, PROPERTY VALUES AND RACE (1961); STANLEY LIEBERSON, ETHNIC PATTERNS IN AMERICAN CITIES (1963); W. MENDELSON, DISCRIMINATION (1962); THOMAS F. PETTIGREW, A PROFILE OF THE NEGRO AMERICAN (1964); ROBERT C. WEAVER, THE NEGRO GHETTO (1948); ROBERT C. WEAVER, THE URBAN COMPLEX: HUMAN VALUES IN URBAN LIFE (1964).

10. Prior to 1910, San Francisco had passed a residential segregation ordinance that required all Chinese inhabitants to move from whatever area they lived in to a designated section of the city. However, the ordinance was invalidated on what appeared to be both equal protection and due process grounds. *In re* Lee Sing, 43 F. 359 (N.D. Cal. 1890). In holding that the statute was void, the circuit court reasoned that the statute was "discriminating against Chinese as unequal in its operation as between them and all others but also involved an arbitrary confiscation of property without any process of law." *Id.* at 361. In concluding its opinion, the court added "that this ordinance is a direct violation of, not only the express provisions of the constitution of the United States, in several particulars, [and that it] . . . is so obvious, that I shall not waste more time, or words in discussing the matter." *Id.*; *see also* Warren B. Hunting, *The Constitutionality of Race Distinctions and the Baltimore Negro Segregation Ordinances*, 11 COLUM. L. REV. 24, 25 (1911).

11. `See Hunting, *supra* note 10; Garrett Power, *Apartheid Baltimore Style: The Residential Segregation Ordinances of 1910–1913*, 42 MD. L. REV. 289, 310 (1983).

12. *See* M. Foerenbach, THE LEGAL AND SOCIAL ORIGINS OF RESIDENTIAL SEGREGATION: AN EXAMINATION OF RESIDENTIAL SEGREGATION ORDINANCES IN RICHMOND AND BALTIMORE—1910–1917, at 5–6 (1984) (unpublished manuscript); Benno C. Schmidt, *Principle and Prejudice: The Supreme Court and Race in the Progressive Era. Part 1: The Heyday of Jim Crow*, 82 COLUM. L. REV. 444, 523–24 (1982).

13. Baltimore, Md., Ordinance 692 (May 15, 1911). Two prior ordinances, Ordinance 610 of December 19, 1910, and Ordinance 654 of April 7, 1911, had been nominally revised. *See* Power, *supra* note 11, at 300–305.

14. *See* Power, *supra* note 11, at 298–300.

15. *See* Petition to the Mayor and City Council, Baltimore City Archives, Mahool Files, File 406 (July 5, 1910).

16. *See* W. Ashbie Hawkins, *A Year of Segregation in Baltimore*, 3 Crisis 27, 28 (1911); Power, *supra* note 11, at 298–300.

17. *See* Hawkins, *supra* note 17, at 28; Power, *supra* note 11, at 298–300.

18. Petition to the Mayor and City Council, Baltimore City Archives, Mahool Files, File 406 (July 5, 1910).

19. *See* Baltimore, Md., Ordinance 610 (Dec. 19, 1910). This ordinance did not last long. In its first legal challenge, the ordinance was found to be technically flawed and thus void as drawn. No specific reference was made, but the flaw is presumed to be a defect in the ordinance's title. Section 221 of the City Charter provided: "Every ordinance enacted by the City shall embrace but one subject which shall be described in the title." The ordinance's title was "an ordinance for preserving order, securing property values and promoting the great interests and insuring the good government of Baltimore City." Thus, not only did the title contain several subjects, but none of the subjects involved racial segregation of housing. However, the court did not examine the merits of the ordinance. *See* Hawkins, *supra* note 17, at 29. The second Baltimore ordinance lasted even less time. Within the month, the City Council had repealed the legislation due to another technical flaw. *See* Power, *supra* note 11, at 305.

20. Baltimore, Md., Ordinance 692 (May 15, 1911).

21. The ordinance's inapplication to mixed blocks was a direct result of complaints about the first ordinance from real estate brokers and white property owners located in integrated neighborhoods. *See* Power, *supra* note 11, at 302.

22. Baltimore, Md., Ordinance 692 (May 15, 1911).

23. *Id.*

24. State v. Gurry, 3 Baltimore City Ct. 262 (1913); *see also* Hawkins, *supra* note 17, at 28–30.

25. *Gurry*, 3 Baltimore City Ct. at 263.

26. *Id.*

27. State v. Gurry, 88 A. 546 (1913).

28. *Id.* at 548.

29. *Id.* at 552–53.

30. *Id.* The court's finding applied equally to blacks and whites although, in practice, very few blacks owned property on all white blocks.

31. *Id.* at 552.

32. *Id.* at 552–53.

33. *Id.* at 561.
34. *Id.* at 552.
35. For an illuminating empirical and theoretical discussion of the concepts of public sphere and multiple sites, see EVELYN B. HIGGINBOTHAM, RIGHTEOUS DISCONTENT: THE WOMEN'S MOVEMENT IN THE BLACK BAPTIST CHURCH, 1880–1920 (1993). Higginbotham focuses on the church as a multiple site for activities which have no outlet elsewhere, and it follows from her analysis that the public sphere in a segregated society becomes restricted along a variety of dimensions. Thus, Drake and Cayton write, "[Segregation] results in a pattern of relations which reduces to a minimum any neighborly contacts, school contacts, or chance meetings in stores, taverns, and movie houses between Negroes and whites of approximately the same socio-economic status." *See* DRAKE & CAYTON, *supra* note 9, at 195.
36. In an earlier draft memorandum, Professor Mitchell Duneier in 1993 explained this concept as follows:

> The hospitality of a constellation of neighboring homes is the hospitality of brotherhood. The domestic ritual involved in living in close proximity and being neighborly affirms and gives rise to distinctions between "us" and "them": those who are part of the domestic sphere and those who are not. The notion that "charity begins at home" powerfully calls forth the association in Western culture of "us" and "home." Indeed, when St. Paul speaks of the Gentiles, he contrasts their former outcast and alienated condition with the privileges of membership in God's family or household. Those we call neighbors are therefore those with whom we share a fundamental dignity. We think of those who congregate on our block, not as inferiors but, with the mind set of St. Paul, as members of the human family. These are the persons who we might invite inside on some occasions to "break bread."

37. *Gurry,* 88 A. at 548, 551.
38. In an earlier draft memorandum, Professor Mitchell Duneier in 1993 explained this concept as follows:

> One of the reasons it is difficult for any dominant society to accept an alien inferior body into its neighborhood is that "home" is a refuge to which we do not admit those who will do us harm. By contrast, when blacks are permitted to live among whites, the latter's acknowledgment of the black man's legitimate participation in that public sphere symbolizes a recognition of ontological safety and security that previously seemed impossible in the black man's proximity.

39. 245 U.S. 60, 81 (1917).
40. *Id.* at 79 (emphasis added).
41. *Id.* at 81.
42. *Id.* at 81–82.
43. *Id.* at 61. Brief for defendant in Error at 80, Buchanan v. Warley, 245 U.S. 60 (1917) (No. 33).
44. *Id.* at 72.
45. For example, Moorfield Storey's comment after the decision was not pure hyperbole. He said, "I cannot help thinking it is the most important decision that has been made since the *Dred Scott* case and happily this time it is the right way." *See* Power, *supra* note 11, at 313–14; Schmidt, *supra* note 12, at 508. Storey was not the only person moved by the Buchanan decision. *The Nation* called it a

"momentous decision." 105 NATION 526 (1917). The *New York Age,* a black newspaper, said it increased blacks' confidence in the Constitution and proved "that the instrument devised by the fathers of the Republic has not yet become a 'scrap of paper.' " *See The Negro's Right of Residence,* 55 LITERARY DIG. 17, 18 (Nov. 24, 1917). The *Survey* wrote in anticipation of the decision that *Buchanan* involved more than the 42,000 blacks living in Louisville, but that it "may in fact determine if the negro is to be segregated in the United States." 33 SURVEY 32 (1914). For other responses from the African-American press, see *The Negro's Right of Residence, supra;* Power, *supra* note 11, at 313–14; Roger L. Rice, *Residential Segregation by Law, 1910–1917,* 34 J. S. HIST. 179, 195–96 (1968); Schmidt, *supra,* at 508–09.

46. *See* George D. Hott, *Constitutionality of Municipal Zoning and Segregation Ordinances,* 33 W. VA. L.Q. 332, 348–49 (1927).

47. *See* Schmidt, *supra* note 12, at 522.

48. Restrictive covenants were used in numerous neighborhoods throughout the country to effectively keep blacks from moving in. *See* Isaac N. Groner & David M. Helfeld, *Race Discrimination in Housing,* 57 YALE L.J. 426 (1948).

49. GUNNAR MYRDAL, AN AMERICAN DILEMMA: THE NEGRO PROBLEM AND MODERN DEMOCRACY (1944).

50. "In 1910 there were no communities in which Negroes were over 61 per cent of the population. More than two-thirds of the Negroes lived in areas less than 50 per cent Negro, and a third lived in areas less than 10 per cent Negro. By 1920, 87 per cent of the Negroes lived in areas over half Negro in composition. A decade later 90 per cent were in districts of 50 per cent or more Negro concentration. Almost two-thirds (63.0 per cent) lived where the concentration was from 90 to 99 per cent Negro!" DRAKE & CAYTON, *supra* note 9, at 176 n.*.

Drake and Cayton regarded as so significant the role of the courts in institutionalizing black residential inferiority that they devoted a portion of their analysis to Hansberry v. Lee, 311 U.S. 32 (1940). It is clear that Drake and Cayton regard the courts as fundamental to the process by which the ghettos were created. *See* DRAKE & CAYTON, *supra* note 9, at 186.

51. 334 U.S. 1 (1948).

52. *See* MASSEY & DENTON, *supra* note 2, at 12.

53. *Id.* at 145.

54. *Id.* at 12.

55. STUDS TERKEL, RACE: HOW BLACKS AND WHITES THINK AND FEEL ABOUT THE AMERICAN OBSESSION 334 (1992) (overview of Kenneth B. Clark).

56. JOHN S. ADAMS, HOUSING AMERICA IN THE 1980s, at 105–11 (1987).

57. The "equalitarian" concept was taken from the title and substance of Judge William Hastie's 1973 seminal article on civil rights. *See* William H. Hastie, *Toward an Equalitarian Legal Order, 1930–1950,* 407 ANNALS AM. ACAD. POL. & SOC. SCI. 18 (May 1973).

58. In 20 of the 21 jurisdictions in which the issue arose, courts upheld the enforcement of racially restrictive covenants. ROBERT C. WEAVER, *supra* note 9; Groner & Helfeld, *supra* note 48, at 446–47.

59. *See* Schmidt, *supra* note 12, at 521–24.

CHAPTER ELEVEN

1. RAYFORD W. LOGAN, THE BETRAYAL OF THE NEGRO 9–10 (1965) (emphasis in original) (quoting Frederick Douglass). The material in this chapter substantially based on A. Leon Higginbotham, Jr., *Racism in American and South African Courts: Similarities and Differences*, 65 N.Y.U. L. REV. 479 (1990). These notes include the state reporter citations along with the regional citations in order to help those who wish to research the individual states' criminal justice systems.
2. *See generally* CORNEL WEST, RACE MATTERS (1993).
3. U.S. CONST. pmbl. (emphasis added).
4. *See* West, *supra* note 2.
5. *See, e.g.*, DERRICK BELL, RACE, RACISM AND AMERICAN LAW 33 (2D ED. 1980).
6. CHARLES LAWRENCE III, *The Id, the Ego, and Equal Protection: Reckoning with Unconscious Racism*, 39 STAN. L. REV. 317, 329 (1987).
7. *Id.* at 363.
8. *Id.* at 330, 351.
9. *Id.* at 333–34, 341, 352.
10. *Id.* at 352, 357, 367.
11. *Id.* at 370, 372.
12. *Id.* at 322, 326.
13. CHARLES WARREN, THE SUPREME COURT IN UNITED STATES HISTORY 2 (1923):

    The Court is not an organism disassociated from the conditions and history of the times in which it exists. It does not formulate and deliver its opinions in a legal vacuum. Its Judges are not abstract and impersonal oracles, but are men whose views are necessarily, though by no conscious intent, affected by inheritance, education and environment and by the impact of history past and present.

    Oliver Wendell Holmes shared this perception:

    The life of the law has not been logic: it has been experience. The felt necessities of the time, the prevalent moral and political theories, intuitions of public policy, avowed or unconscious, *even the prejudices which judges share with their fellow-men* . . . .

    OLIVER W. HOLMES, THE COMMON LAW 1 (1881) (emphasis added).
14. Letter from Anthony Amsterdam, Professor, New York University School of Law, to A. Leon Higginbotham, Jr. 4 (Oct. 10, 1989).
15. For discussion of the American culture of racism and reflections on the significance of the trial and acquittal of the white officers who beat Rodney King, see A. Leon Higginbotham, Jr. & Aderson B. François, *Looking for God and Racism in All the Wrong Places*, 70 DENV. U. L. REV. 191 (1993).
16. JACK BASS, UNLIKELY HEROES: THE DRAMATIC STORY OF THE SOUTHERN JUDGES WHO TRANSLATED THE SUPREME COURT'S *BROWN* DECISION INTO A REVOLUTION FOR EQUALITY 13 (1981). It is purely coincidental that the mural appears in a federal rather than a state courthouse. It captures the essence of what I discuss in this chapter regarding symptoms and symbols of racism in the state judicial process.
17. Murray v. State, 202 Miss. 849, 33 So. 2d 291 (1948).
18. *Id.* at 857, 33 So. 2d at 292.

19. *Id.*
20. 373 U.S. 61 (1963).
21. *Id.* at 62.
22. *Id.*
23. *Id.* (citations omitted).
24. *See* Charles Lawrence, *supra* note 6, at 350 (1987).
25. *See* State v. Cox, 244 La. 1087, 1108, 156 So. 2d 448, 456 (1963), *rev'd*, 379 U.S. 536 (1965).
26. *Id.* (citations omitted).
27. The United States Supreme Court, in a landmark decision, reversed Cox's conviction on First Amendment grounds but did not discuss the question of segregation in the courtroom. *See* State v. Cox, 379 U.S. 536 (1965).
28. Plummer v. Casey, 148 F. Supp. 326 (S.D. Tex. 1955), *aff'd*, 240 F.2d 922 (5th Cir. 1956), *cert. denied*, 353 U.S. 924 (1957).
29. *Id.* at 329.
30. For an analysis of the application of the equal protection doctrine to facilities owned and operated by the state, but leased to private parties, see Burton v. Wilmington Parking Auth., 365 U.S. 715 (1961).
31. Dawley v. Norfolk, 159 F. Supp. 642 (E.D. Va. 1958), *aff'd*, 260 F.2d 647 (4th Cir. 1958), *cert. denied*, 359 U.S. 935 (1959).
32. *Id.* at 644.
33. *Id.* at 645. The judge thereafter declined to consider the claim as presented by the pleadings because it "is exclusively one cognizable by the state courts." *Id.*
34. 163 U.S. 537, 544 (1896) ("Laws permitting, and even requiring, . . . separation [of African Americans and whites] in places where they are liable to be brought into contact do not necessarily imply the inferiority of either race to the other. . . .").
35. Brown v. Board of Educ., 347 U.S. 483, 494 (1954).
36. Charles Black, *The Lawfulness of the Segregation Decisions*, 69 YALE L.J. 421, 424–26 (1960) (emphasis added).
37. *Ex parte* Mary Hamilton, 275 Ala. 574, 574, 156 So. 2d 926, 929 (1963), *rev'd*, 376 U.S. 650 (1964). For an acknowledgment that the use of first names for African Americans was part of the southern caste system, see Black, *supra* note 36, at 425.
38. *See* Petitioner's Brief at 2, Hamilton v. Alabama, 376 U.S. 650 (1964) (No. 793).
39. *Hamilton*, 275 Ala. at 574–75, 156 So. 2d at 926.
40. *Id.*
41. *Id.*, 156 So. 2d at 927.
42. 350 U.S. 422 (1956).
43. The Supreme Court ruled that, since he had been granted immunity, he had to testify because it was "every man's duty to give testimony before a duly constituted tribunal unless he invokes some valid legal exemption in withholding it." *Hamilton*, 175 Ala. at 575, 156 So. 2d at 927 (quoting *Ullmann*, 350 U.S. at 439).
44. *Id.*, 156 So. 2d at 927.
45. Hamilton v. Alabama, 376 U.S. 650 (1964).
46. Constance Baker Motley, the distinguished civil rights lawyer and former Chief Judge of the United States District Court for the Southern District of New York,

recalls being subjected to similar indignities. "Often a southern judge would refer to the men attorneys as Mister, but would make a point of calling me 'Connie', since traditionally black women in the South were called only by their first name." KAREN B. MORELLO, THE INVISIBLE BAR: THE WOMAN LAWYER IN AMERICA, 1683 TO THE PRESENT 161 (1986). (White women in the South are traditionally referred to as "Miz First Name," a practice that separates them out from the most respectful, white male appellation, "Mr. Last Name," and poor whites, referred to as "poor white trash" or "crackers," have also been denied dignity in public settings.)

47. 652 F.2d 427 (5th Cir. 1981), cert. denied, 455 U.S. 944 (1982). See Tom Wicker, Worthy of Contempt, N.Y. TIMES, Mar. 27, 1979, at A25 (an editorial describing the effects of the contempt citation on Farmer's ability to argue subsequent death penalty appeals).

48. Farmer, 652 F.2d at 430.

49. Id. at 435.

50. Id. (emphasis in original).

51. Id.

52. Likewise, judges who are sympathetic to the cause might use the standing doctrine liberally to enhance the ability of individuals to challenge discriminatory practices. See Steven L. Winter, The Metaphor of Standing and the Problem of Self-Governance, 40 STAN. L. REV. 1371, 1418–52 (1988).

53. The cases are replete with instances of prosecutors continually referring to the race of the witness or defendant. Although these references often have a clearly racist message, I have chosen, due to sheer volume, not to review those cases here.

54. 73 So. 791 (Miss. 1917).

55. Id. at 791.

56. Id.

57. Id.

58. Id. at 792.

59. Id. at 791.

60. Tannehill v. State, 159 Ala. 51, 52, 48 So. 662, 662 (1909).

61. Id. For a similar result, also from this time period in Alabama, see Perdue v. State, 17 Ala. App. 500, 86 So. 158 (1920). There, the Alabama Court of Appeals reversed a conviction in which the trial court overruled the defendant's objections to the following statement by the prosecutor: "Yes gentlemen of the jury, you know the Negro, and you know that even when one gets into trouble the others all come in and swear lies to get him out." Id. at 501, 86 So. at 158.

62. Simmons v. State, 14 Ala. App. 103, 104, 71 So. 979, 979 (1916).

63. Id.

64. Allison v. State, 157 Tex. Crim. 200, 201, 248 S.W.2d 147, 147 (1952).

65. Id., 248 S.W.2d at 148.

66. Id. (emphasis in original).

67. People v. Richardson, 49 Ill. App. 3d 170, 172–73, 363 N.E.2d 924, 926 (1977).

68. Id. at 173–74, 363 N.E.2d at 927.

69. Johnson v. State, 59 Tex. Crim. 11, 11, 127 S.W. 559, 559 (1910).

70. Id.

71. *Id.* at 12–13, 127 S.W. at 559–60.
72. State v. Lee, 116 La. 607, 615, 40 So. 914, 917 (1906).
73. *Id.*
74. 18 Ala. App. 618, 92 So. 909 (1922).
75. *Id.*
76. *Id.* at 617–18, 92 So. at 910.
77. 22 Ala. App. 74, 112 So. 177 (1927).
78. *Id.* at 74–75, 112 So. at 177.
79. *See, e.g.*, Brown v. Mississippi, 297 U.S. 278 (1935); Chambers v. Florida, 309 U.S. 227 (1939).
80. S. v. Augustine, 1980 (1) S.A. 503, 506 (A.D.) (quotation translated from Afrikaans).
81. While I cannot address it here, prosecutors have used similar stereotypes against other racial minorities as well. *See, e.g.*, People v. Reyes, 133 Cal. App. 574, 577, 24 P.2d 531, 532 (1933) (In murder trial with a Mexican American defendant, the prosecutor told the jury: "Mexicans are peculiar, they are a stoical race. They can face death unflinchingly, the average Mexican can, and perhaps that is why they can take other lives unflinchingly and quite calmly."). The appellate court affirmed the conviction, stating that the defendant was convicted after a "full, fair, and impartial trial." *Id.* at 578, 24 P.2d at 532.
82. Kelly v. Stone, 514 F.2d 18, 19 (9th Cir. 1975) (on appeal from district court's denial of a writ of habeas corpus on grounds of prosecutorial misconduct).
83. *Id.*
84. People v. Lurry, 77 Ill. App. 3d 108, 113–14, 395 N.E.2d 1234, 1237–38 (1979).
85. *Id.* at 114, 315 N.E.2d at 1238.
86. Reed v. State, 232 Miss. 432, 434, 99 So.2d 455, 456 (1958).
87. *Id.* (stating that "[t]he jury had the duty and right to evaluate [the principal witness's] testimony and other evidence independently of the emotional factor of racial prejudice being injected into the case by the State's attorney").
88. Herrin v. State, 201 Miss. 595, 602, 29 So. 2d 452, 453 (1947).
89. *Id.*, 29 So. 2d at 454.
90. People v. Jones, 205 Cal. App. 2d 460, 466, 23 Cal. Rptr. 418, 422 (1962).
91. *Id.*
92. Brown v. State, 50 Tex. Crim. 79, 95 S.W. 126 (1906).
93. *Id.* at 83, 95 S.W. at 128.
94. *See* Susan Estrich, Real Rape 20–26, 82–83 (1987) (distinguishing rape from other violent crimes).
95. *See* Bell, *supra* note 5, at 68; Joel Kovel, White Racism: A Psychohistory 67–71 (1970).
96. George M. Fredrickson: The Black Image in the White Mind: The Debate on Afro-American Character and Destiny, 1817–1914, at 271–82 (1971); Ralph Ginzburg, One Hundred Years of Lynchings (1988); Allen D. Grimshaw, Racial Violence in the United States (1969); Kovel, *supra* note 95, at 67–71 (1970); N.A.A.C.P., Thirty Years of Lynching in the United States, 1889–1918, at 8 (W.L. Katz ed., 1969); Claude H. Nolan, The Negro's Image in the South 46–50 (1967); John G. Van Deusen, The Black Man in White America 154–58 (1944); Ida B. Wells-Barnett, On

LYNCHINGS: SOUTHERN HORRORS; A RED RECORD; MOB RULE IN NEW OR-
LEANS 1 (1969); WALTER F. WHITE, ROPE AND FAGGOT: A BIBLIOGRAPHY OF
JUDGE LYNCH (1969); ROBERT L. ZANGRANDO, THE N.A.A.C.P. CRUSADE
AGAINST LYNCHING, 1909–1950, at 3 (1980).

97. *See, e.g.,* McClesky v. Kemp, 481 U.S. 279, 328–35 (1987) (Brennan, J.,
dissenting); Furman v. Georgia, 408 U.S. 238, 250–251 (1972), *reh'g denied,*
409 U.S. 902 (1972). *See also* Marvin E. Wolfgang & Marc Riedel, *Rape, Race
and the Death Penalty in Georgia,* 45 AM. J. OF ORTHOPSYCHIATRY 658 (1975);
Rupert C. Koeninger, *Capital Punishment in Texas, 1924–1968,* 15 CRIME &
DELIN. Q. 132, 141 (1969).

98. Weems v. State, 236 Ala. 261, 263, 182 So. 3, 4 (1938).

99. *Id.*

100. *Id.,* 182 So. at 4–5.

101. Garner v. State, 120 Miss. 744, 83 So. 83, 83 (1919).

102. *Id.* at 751, 83 So. at 83.

103. *Id.* at 751, 83 So. at 84.

104. 165 Ark. 284, 264 S.W. 856 (1924).

105. *Id.* at 289, 264 S.W. at 857.

106. *Id.*

107. Taylor v. State, 50 Tex. Crim. 560, 561, 100 S.W. 393, 393 (1907).

108. *Id.,* 100 S.W. at 394.

109. Roby v. State, 147 Miss. 575, 575, 113 So. 185, 185 (1927).

110. *Id.,* 113 So. at 186.

111. 199 Ala. 411, 74 So. 454 (1917).

112. *Id.* at 412, 74 So. at 454.

113. For a discussion of these early efforts by one of their participants, see Derrick
Bell, *Foreword: The Civil Rights Chronicles,* 99 HARV. L. REV. 4, 13 & n.33
(1985). *See also* Mari J. Matsuda, *Looking to the Bottom: Critical Legal Studies
and Reparations,* 22 HARV. C.R.-C.L. L. REV. 323, 357 n.140 (1987) (noting
that initial demand in what became Montgomery bus boycott was for courteous
treatment on buses).

114. 88 Miss. 257, 40 So. 545 (1906).

115. *Id.* at 259, 40 So. at 545–46.

116. 21 Ala. App. 234, 109 So. 189 (1926).

117. *Id.* at 236, 109 So. at 190.

118. *Id.*

119. *Id.* at 237, 109 So. at 190–91. Even white, purported scholars have referred to
African Americans as pickaninnies. *See* W. CLEON SKOUSEN, THE MAKING
OF AMERICA: THE SUBSTANCE AND MEANING OF THE CONSTITUTION 733
(1985). For a critique of these scholars, see A. Leon Higginbotham, Jr., *The
Bicentennial of the Constitution: A Racial Perspective,* 22 STAN. L. REV. 8
(1987).

Former Arizona Governor Evan Meecham created a furor when he said that
he did not believe that the term "pickaninny" was offensive, and that in his day
black people referred to their own children as pickaninnies. E.J. Montini, *To
Slur with Love: Meecham Must Know Something That Blacks Don't,* ARIZ. RE-
PUBLIC, Mar. 26, 1987, at A2. Columnist E.J. Montini responded to the governor's comment:

I spoke to a black man here and . . . never in his life have his parents referred to him as a pickaninny.

Then it struck me. What about *my* family?

I can't remember a single tender moment when my father or mother called me a "wop" or "dago." Not once.

My parents say they're old fashioned people with old fashioned values—like the governor. But not once did they express their affection for me through one of the many quaint ethnic slurs available to them.

Not once did I hear, "Hi Eddie, my little guinea."

So I investigated further. Not one of the Mexican-Americans I talked to was referred to by his parents as a "spic" or "wetback."

None of the Jewish mothers called her offspring "kikes" or "hymies" or even "Jew-boys."

None of the Polish parents I know referred to their children as "polacks." Including a family I know whose given name was Pollack.

Based on this overwhelming evidence, it's obvious that family values in America have collapsed and why a person like Gov. Meecham wants to return us to the good old days, an era when white men were "men" and black men were "boys." It was less confusing then, a time when black boys were pickaninnies, and all the little spics and wops and kikes knew their place.

Id.

120. 125 Miss. 140, 87 So. 487 (1921).
121. *Id.* at 151–52, 87 So. at 488.
122. *Id.* at 150–51, 87 So. at 488.
123. 136 Fla. 23, 186 So. 230 (1939).
124. *Id.* at 25–26, 186 So. at 230–31.
125. William v. State, 25 Ala. App. 342, 343, 146 So. 422, 423 (1933).
126. *Id.* at 343–44, 146 So. at 423.
127. *Id.* at 344, 146 So. at 423–24.
128. For an equally overt appeal to prejudice, and an example of how prejudice was a direct attempt to dominate African Americans, see Blocker v. State, 112 Tex. Crim. 275, 16 S.W.2d 253 (1929). In that case, the prosecutor explained the victim's assault on defendant, an African-American man, as "an effort on his part to keep this negro in his place, and Southern gentlemen will not condemn him for it." *Id.* at 278, 16 S.W.2d at 254. The prosecutor also stated: "I have lived in this country all my life and I do not have to tell twelve Southern men what to do in this case." *Id.* The trial judge instructed the jury to disregard the first comment. The appellate court reversed, stating that the prosecutor's argument "constituted a veiled and covert appeal to race prejudice." *Id.*

A Mississippi case from the same period also bluntly espoused notions based on the notion that the criminal law's purpose was to keep African Americans who fought their domination in their place. In Collins v. State, 100 Miss. 435, 56 So. 527 (1911), an African-American defendant was convicted of murdering an African-American man where the prosecutor made the following comments to the jury: "This bad nigger killed a good nigger. The dead nigger was a white man's nigger, and these bad niggers like to kill that kind. The only way you can break up this pistol toting among these niggers is to have a necktie party." *Id.* at 440, 56 So. at 528. The trial judge apparently did not instruct the jury to disregard this statement. The appellate court reversed the conviction, noting that "the appellant may be a bad negro, and a very undesirable member of society, yet he is entitled to go before the jury of the land untrammeled by voluntary epithets, the occasion for which is not shown justified by this record." *Id.* As in the cases discussed in the section above, without appellate supervision, the criminal law could be used to reinforce the power structure that supported the domination of African Americans.

129. 195 Tenn. 94, 257 S.W.2d 6 (1953).

130. *Id.* at 98, 257 S.W.2d at 8.

131. Even though it reversed the conviction, the Tennessee Supreme Court's opinion displayed a racist, patronizing attitude: "Our judges, court officials, and jurors, are uniformly white men. The white race is dominant and the Negroes are, in a sense, our wards." *Id.* at 99, 257 S.W.2d at 9 (quoting Roland v. State, 137 Tenn. 663, 665, 194 S.W. 1097, 1097 (1917)). The prosecutor rebuked whites for appearing as character witnesses for African-American defendants.

132. 481 F.2d 152 (2d Cir. 1973).

133. *See* People v. Haynes, 33 A.D.2d 893, 308 N.Y.S.2d 316 (1969).

134. *McKendrick*, 481 F.2d at 155.

135. *See id.* at 154–55. The Second Circuit commented in detail on all of the prosecutor's racist remarks, noting that their cumulative effect was to admonish the all-white jury to think of African Americans as a group separate from and foreign to themselves. *See id.* at 155 n.3.

136. 45 Tex. Crim. 574, 78 S.W. 514 (1904).

137. *Id.* at 575, 78 S.W. at 516.

138. *Id.* at 577, 78 S.W. at 516.

139. *Id.*

140. 233 Ala. 202, 172 So. 344 (1936).

141. *Id.* at 203, 172 So. at 344.

142. *Id.*

143. *Id.*, 172 So. at 345.

144. State v. Miles, 199 Mo. 530, 533, 98 S.W. 25, 31 (1906).

145. Adams v. State, 86 Tex. Crim. 422, 423, 216 S.W. 863, 864 (1919).

146. Green v. State, 105 P.2d 795, 797 (Okla. Ct. App. 1940).

147. State v. Hubbard, 165 Kan. 406, 408, 195 P.2d 604, 605 (1948).

148. People v. Curry, 97 Cal. App. 2d 537, 551, 218 P.2d 153, 161 (1950).

149. Quarles v. Commonwealth, 245 S.W.2d 947, 949 (Ky. Ct. App. 1951).

150. Thornton v. State, 451 S.W.2d 898, 903 (Tex. Crim. App. 1970).

151. Thornton v. Beto, 470 F.2d 657, 658 (5th Cir. 1972), *cert. denied,* 411 U.S. 920 (1973).

152. Hilson v. State, 96 Tex. Crim. 550, 551, 258 S.W. 826 (1924).

153. *In re* Stevens, 31 Cal. 3d 403, 645 P.2d 99, 183 Cal. Rptr. 48 (1982). *Cf.* Phillips v. Joint Legislative Comm., 637 F.2d 1014 (5th Cir. 1981) (holding that evidence of racist comments by a judge, from the bench and in published opinions, as well as statistics concerning high reversal rate in civil rights cases heard by the judge, were insufficient to require recusal in a case where there was no evidence of bias against any particular parties to the suit in question); John Leubsdorf, *Theories of Judging and Judge Disqualification,* 62 N.Y.U. L. Rev. 237, 256, 258–60 (1987).

154. *Stevens,* 31 Cal. 3d at 404, 645 P.2d at 99, 183 Cal. Rptr. at 48 (Kaus, J., concurring).

155. *Id.*
156. *Id.*, 645 P.2d at 100, 183 Cal. Rptr. at 49.
157. *Id.*, 645 P.2d at 99, 183 Cal. Rptr. at 48. The judge's racist comments were by no means reserved for African Americans, however. During his tenure, the judge referred to Hispanics as "cute little tamales," "Taco Bell," "spic," and "bean." *Id.* at 405, 645 P.2d at 100, 183 Cal. Rptr. at 49. On one occasion, the judge said that a Hispanic attorney who changed his position on a settlement was "acting like a Mexican jumping bean." *Id.*
158. *Id.* at 405–06, 645 P.2d at 100–101, 183 Cal. Rptr. at 48.
159. *Id.* at 404, 645 P.2d at 99, 183 Cal. Rptr. at 48.
160. *Id.*
161. Black, *supra* note 36, at 425.
162. 268 N.C. 320, 150 S.E.2d 481 (1966).
163. *Id.* at 324, 150 S.E.2d at 484.
164. *Id.*
165. *Id.* at 325, 150 S.E.2d at 484–85.
166. 283 F.2d 465 (8th Cir. 1960).
167. *Id.* at 467.

CHAPTER TWELVE

1. 163 U.S. 537, 560 (1896) (Harlan, J., dissenting).
  This chapter is substantially taken from A. Leon Higginbotham, Jr. & William C. Smith, *The Hughes Court and the Beginning of the End of the "Separate But Equal" Doctrine*, 76 MINN. L. REV. 1099 (1992).
2. For background issues on racism and the law, see DERRICK A. BELL, JR., AND WE ARE NOT SAVED: THE ELUSIVE QUEST FOR RACIAL JUSTICE (1987); DERRICK A. BELL, JR., RACE, RACISM AND AMERICAN LAW (2d ed. 1980) [hereinafter RACE LAW]; MARY F. BERRY, BLACK RESISTANCE, WHITE LAW (1971); MARY F. BERRY & JOHN W. BLASSINGAME, LONG MEMORY: THE BLACK EXPERIENCE IN AMERICA (1982); JOHN H. FRANKLIN & ALFRED A. MOSS, JR., FROM SLAVERY TO FREEDOM: A HISTORY OF NEGRO AMERICANS (7th ed. 1994); JACK GREENBERG, CASES AND MATERIALS ON JUDICIAL PROCESS AND SOCIAL CHANGE: CONSTITUTIONAL LITIGATION 1–237 (1977); JACK GREENBERG, RACE RELATIONS AND AMERICAN LAW (1959); A. LEON HIGGINBOTHAM, JR., IN THE MATTER OF COLOR: RACE AND THE AMERICAN LEGAL PROCESS: THE COLONIAL PERIOD (1978); RICHARD KLUGER, SIMPLE JUSTICE (1975); GENNA R. MCNEIL, GROUNDWORK: CHARLES HAMILTON HOUSTON AND THE STRUGGLE FOR CIVIL RIGHTS (1983); LOREN MILLER, THE PETITIONERS: THE STORY OF THE SUPREME COURT OF THE UNITED STATES AND THE NEGRO (1966); GUNNAR MYRDAL, AN AMERICAN DILEMMA: THE NEGRO PROBLEM AND MODERN DEMOCRACY (20th anniversary ed. 1962); CARTER G. WOODSON & CHARLES H. WESLEY, THE NEGRO IN OUR HISTORY (12th ed. 1972); C. VANN WOODWARD, THE STRANGE CAREER OF JIM CROW (3d rev. ed. 1974); Evelyn B. Higginbotham, *Beyond the Sound of Silence: Afro-American Women's History*, 1 GENDER AND HIST. 50 (1989); Evelyn B. Higginbotham, *In Politics To Stay: Black Women Leaders and Party Politics in the 1920's*, in LOUISE A. TILLEY & PATRICIA GURIN, WOMEN, CHANGE AND POLITICS (1989); Evelyn B. Higginbotham, *African-American Women's History and the Metalanguage of Race*, SIGNS, Winter 1992.

3. *See, e.g.*, HOWARD BALL, THE WARREN COURT'S CONCEPTIONS OF DEMOCRACY: AN EVALUATION OF THE SUPREME COURT'S APPORTIONMENT DECISIONS (1971); L. BRENT BOZELL, THE WARREN REVOLUTION: REFLECTIONS ON THE CONSENSUS SOCIETY (1966); ARCHIBALD COX, THE WARREN COURT: CONSTITUTIONAL DECISION AS AN INSTRUMENT OF REFORM (1968); JOHN P. FRANK, THE WARREN COURT (1964); BERNARD SCHWARTZ AND STEPHAN LESHER, INSIDE THE WARREN COURT (1983); THE WARREN COURT: A CRITICAL ANALYSIS (Richard H. Salyer et al. eds., 1969).

4. *See, e.g.*, THE BURGER YEARS: RIGHTS AND WRONGS IN THE SUPREME COURT, 1969–1986 (Herman Schwartz ed., 1987); NANCY MAVEETY, REPRESENTATION RIGHTS AND THE BURGER YEARS (1991); NEITHER CONSERVATIVE NOR LIBERAL: THE BURGER COURT ON CIVIL RIGHTS AND CIVIL LIBERTIES (Francis G. Lee ed., 1983).

5. *See, e.g.*, STANLEY H. FRIEDELBAUM, THE REHNQUIST COURT IN PURSUIT OF JUDICIAL CONSERVATISM (1994); DAVID G. SAVAGE, TURNING RIGHT: THE MAKING OF THE REHNQUIST SUPREME COURT (1992).

6. 347 U.S. 483 (1954).

7. RAYFORD W. LOGAN, THE BETRAYAL OF THE NEGRO 9–10 (1965) (emphasis in original) (quoting Frederick Douglass).

8. Record from the United States Supreme Court at 79, Mitchell v. United States Interstate Commerce Comm'n, 313 U.S. 80 (1941) (No. 577) (reprinting the testimony of Arthur W. Mitchell before the Interstate Commerce Comm'n, Mitchell v. Chicago, R.I. & Pac. Ry., 229 I.C.C. 703 (1938) (No. 27844)).

9. *Id.*

10. *Id.*

11. *Id.*

12. McCabe v. Atchison, T. & S.F. Ry., 235 U.S. 151, 161–62 (1914) (stating that "if he [the African-American traveler] is denied by a common carrier . . . a facility or convenience in the course of his journey which under substantially the same circumstances is furnished to another traveler, he may properly complain that his constitutional privilege has been invaded").

13. Mitchell v. United States Interstate Commerce Comm'n, 313 U.S. 80, 97 (1941). The Court concluded that "the discrimination shown was palpably unjust and forbidden by the Act." *Id.*

    Since its adoption in 1887, the Interstate Commerce Act has prohibited unreasonable discrimination by common carriers. Act of Feb. 4, 1887, ch. 104, § 3, 42 Stat. 379, 380 (current version codified at 49 U.S.C. § 10731(b) (1988)). As originally enacted, the Act made it unlawful for interstate carriers "to subject any . . . person . . . to any undue or unreasonable prejudice or disadvantage in any respect whatsoever." *Id.* Long before *Mitchell*, the Interstate Commerce Commission recognized that this language prohibited discrimination between white and black passengers. *See, e.g.*, Edwards v. Nashville, C. & St. L. Ry., 12 I.C.C. 247, 249 (1907) (holding that the failure to provide African-American first-class ticket passengers with equal facilities violated § 3); Heard v. Georgia R.R., 1 I.C.C. 428, 435 (1888) (same); Councill v. Western & Atl. R.R., 1 I.C.C. 339, 347 (1887) (holding that the forcible removal of African-American passenger from a first-class compartment violated § 3 since the passenger had paid first-class fare).

14. *See* Stipulation for Dismissal and Order, Mitchell v. Lowden, No. 37-C-5529 (Cook County Cir. Ct. Nov. 5, 1945).
15. *See* CATHERINE A. BARNES, JOURNEY FROM JIM CROW: THE DESEGREGATION OF SOUTHERN TRANSIT 215 n.26 (1983).
16. Interview with the Honorable Louis G. Forer, Retired Judge of the Court of Common Pleas, in Philadelphia, Pa. (July 23, 1991).
17. *Id.*
18. Telephone conversation with Justice Thurgood Marshall, United States Supreme Court (July 13, 1990).
19. There continued to be incidents in the 1930s and 1940s that showed that the Supreme Court justices were susceptible to the prejudices of their times. Hugo Black's biographer noted that before the Court's historic 1954 decision in *Brown*, the issue of racial segregation

> had been cropping up in the court's own institutional life in one way or another over the past decade and a half. In 1939, because of segregated seating arrangements, what was to have been a private recital of Marian Anderson in Constitution Hall became a public concert at Lincoln Memorial wherein invitations to the Supreme Court produced *one* acceptance. In 1947, a household controversy—whether the black Supreme Court messengers should attend the law clerks' and secretaries' Christmas party—took almost an hour's debate at the weekly judicial conference before being settled by an affirmative 6–2 vote.

> GERALD T. DUNNE, HUGO BLACK AND THE JUDICIAL REVOLUTION 304 (1976) (emphasis added).

> It is interesting to note that no Supreme Court justice selected an African American as a law clerk until the 1948 Term, when William T. Coleman, Jr., clerked for Felix Frankfurter. *Id.* at 287.

20. OLIVER W. HOLMES, THE COMMON LAW 1 (1881) (emphasis added).
21. Professor Bell described the gross disparity of public education in the South before *Brown:*

> In 1915, South Carolina was spending an average of $23.76 on the education of each white child and $2.91 on that of each black child. As late as 1931, six Southern states (Alabama, Arkansas, Florida, Georgia, and North and South Carolina) spent less than a third as much for black children as for whites, and ten years later this figure had risen to only 44 percent. At the time of the 1954 decision in Brown v. Board of Education, the South as a whole was spending on the average $165 a year for a white pupil, and $115 for a black.

> DERRICK A. BELL, JR., RACE, RACISM AND AMERICAN LAW 452 (1973) (citations omitted).

> For a penetrating analysis of the inequality of segregated public education in one of the supposedly enlightened border states before *Brown*, see Parker v. University of Delaware, 75 A.2d 225, 230 (1950) (Del. Ch. 1950).

22. Remarks of John Lord O'Brian, *in* PROCEEDINGS OF THE BAR AND OFFICERS OF THE SUPREME COURT OF THE UNITED STATES, IN MEMORY OF CHARLES EVANS HUGHES 48 (1950) (quoting Justice Hughes).

> In a September 1, 1948, condolence letter, Walter White, the Secretary of the NAACP, wrote: "Thirty years ago [Hughes's] voice was raised at Carnegie Hall against lynchings and other denials of basic human and constitutional rights

to American Negroes and other minorities. Today's concerns with civil liberties are due to the vision and courage of others like him. We are grateful for his leadership." *Id.* at 104.

23. 219 U.S. 219 (1911). For a discussion of *Bailey* and the other peonage cases, see Benno Schmidt, Jr., *Principle and Prejudice: The Supreme Court and Race in the Progressive Era: The Peonage Cases,* 82 COLUM. L. REV. 646 (1982).

24. 219 U.S. at 245.

25. The United States, as amicus curiae, noted that "[t]he statute hits especially, as was intended, negro laborers on farms and plantations. Every reported case under the statute is that of a farm laborer. The maximum penalty fixed by the statute, $300, also makes it peculiarly applicable to this class of laborers." *Id.* at 222–38. *See* Schmidt, *supra* note 23, at 680–81.

26. 219 U.S. at 231.

27. *Id.*

28. *See* Schmidt, *supra* note 23, at 681–82 (discussing Justice Harlan's decision to appoint Justice Hughes to write the majority opinion in *Bailey*).

29. 219 U.S. at 231.

30. 235 U.S. 151 (1914). For an analysis of the Supreme Court's decision in *McCabe,* see Benno Schmidt, Jr., *Principle and Prejudice: The Supreme Court and Race in the Progressive Era: The Heyday of Jim Crow,* 82 COLUM. L. REV. 444, 485–94 (1982). Professor Schmidt notes that Justices White, Holmes, Lamar, and McReynolds "concurred only in the affirmance, thereby disassociating themselves from Hughes' opinion." *Id.* at 488. Professor Schmidt cites a fascinating memorandum from Hughes to Justice Holmes, which indicates that Holmes believed that the Oklahoma law should have been construed to permit "separate but equal," not partitioned, luxury cars for African Americans and whites. *Id.* Hughes concluded his message to his colleague by stating: "I don't see that it is a case calling for 'logical exactness' in enforcing equal rights but rather as it seems to me it is a bald, wholly unjustified, discrimination against a passenger wholly on account of race." *Id.* at 490.

31. *Id.* at 160.

32. *Id.* at 161 (quoting the brief of counsel for the railway company).

33. *Id.*

34. *Id.* at 162–64.

35. *See* Randall Kennedy, *Race Relations Law and the Tradition of Celebration,* 86 COLUM. L. REV. 1622, 1641 (1986). As Professor Kennedy observes, McReynolds's white supremacist allegiances became more pronounced as the Hughes Court began showing more concern for the legal rights of African Americans. *Id.*

36. David Burner, *James C. McReynolds,* in THE JUSTICES OF THE UNITED STATES SUPREME COURT 1789–1969: THEIR LIVES AND MAJOR OPINIONS 2023, 2026 (LEON FRIEDMAN AND FRED L. ISRAEL EDS., 1969).

37. *Id.* at 2024 (quoting Laski).

38. ALPHEUS T. MASON, WILLIAM HOWARD TAFT: CHIEF JUSTICE 215 (1964) (quoting Taft).

39. Videotaped interview with the Honorable Robert Carter, District Judge, U.S. District Court for the Southern District of New York (Aug. 1987) (discussing Judge Carter's observation of the argument in Missouri *ex rel.* Gaines v. Canada, 305 U.S. 337 (1938)).

40. In his autobiography, Justice William O. Douglas described how McReynolds received a rare, but well-deserved, comeuppance when he made a disparaging comment about Howard University.

> One day McReynolds went to the barbershop in the Court. Gates, the black barber, put the sheet around his neck and over his lap, and as he was pinning it behind him McReynolds said, "Gates, tell me, where is this nigger university in Washington, D.C.?" Gates removed the white cloth from McReynolds, walked around and faced him, and said in a very calm and dignified manner, "Mr. Justice, I am shocked that any Justice would call a Negro a nigger. There is a Negro college in Washington, D.C. Its name is Howard University and we are very proud of it." McReynolds muttered some kind of an apology and Gates resumed his work in silence.

WILLIAM O. DOUGLAS, THE COURT YEARS: 1939–1975, at 14–15 (1980).

McReynolds, who died in 1946, never saw the most famous graduate of Howard University's law school, Thurgood Marshall, argue the *Brown* case in 1953 and 1954, and become the first African-American Supreme Court justice in 1967.

41. *See* Burner, *supra* note 36, at 2023. In 1922, McReynolds turned down an invitation by Chief Justice Taft to accompany him and other justices to a ceremonial visit to Philadelphia. He explained to the Chief Justice: "As you know, I am not always to be found when there is a Hebrew abroad. Therefore, my 'inability' to attend must not surprise you." MASON, *supra* note 38, at 216–17. In 1924, McReynolds refused to take his place next to Brandeis for the official Court photograph, forcing the cancellation of the photographic session. *Id.* at 217.

McReynolds remained hostile to these two Jewish justices throughout their tenure on the Court. He refused to attend Cardozo's funeral services in 1938 or to sign the Court's letter of regret about the resignation of Brandeis in 1939. LEONARD BAKER, BRANDEIS AND FRANKFURTER 357, 370 (1984).

42. Aldridge v. United States, 283 U.S. 308, 315 (1931) (McReynolds, J., dissenting). In a seething dissent, typical of his writings on racial matters, Justice McReynolds ignored the daily reality of race relations in the District of Columbia, observing that "[n]othing is revealed by the record which tends to show that any juror entertained prejudice which might have impaired his ability fairly to pass upon the issues." 283 U.S. at 317. He concluded by scolding his colleagues for increasing the difficulty of law enforcement "by excessive theorizing or by magnifying what in practice is not really important." *Id.* at 318.

43. Powell v. Alabama, 287 U.S. 45, 73 (1932) (Butler, J., dissenting). McReynolds joined Butler's dissent, which ignored the overwhelming evidence of injustice, blandly concluding "[t]he record wholly fails to reveal that petitioners have been deprived of any right guaranteed by the Federal Constitution." 287 U.S. at 77.

44. Nixon v. Condon, 286 U.S. 73, 89 (1932) (McReynolds, J., dissenting). The majority decision overturned a Texas law which permitted the state Democratic party to prohibit African Americans from voting in its primary elections. 286 U.S. at 89. McReynolds did not dispute the petitioner's contention that Texas was "overwhelmingly Democratic and nomination by the primaries of that party is equivalent to an election." *Id.* at 91. However, he saw no constitutional difficulties in the exclusion of African Americans from the Democratic primary, noting that "[p]olitical parties are fruits of voluntary action. Where there is no unlawful

purpose, citizens may create them at will and limit their membership as seems wise." *Id.* at 104.

45. Missouri *ex rel.* Gaines v. Canada, 305 U.S. 337 (1938) (McReynolds, J., dissenting). The *Gaines* Court held that Missouri's refusal to admit a qualified African-American applicant to the state's only public law school violated the Fourteenth Amendment. 305 U.S. at 337. In his vitriolic dissent, McReynolds castigated his colleagues for their failure to defer to Missouri's longstanding view "that the best interest of her people demands separation of whites and negroes in schools." *Id.* at 353. McReynolds believed that under the majority decision, Missouri could either "abandon her law school and thereby disadvantage her white citizens without improving petitioner's opportunities for legal instruction or she may break down the settled practice concerning separate schools and thereby, as indicated by experience, *damnify both races.*" *Id.* (emphasis added).

46. 237 U.S. 309 (1915). Although denying relief to the petitioner, the Court held that if a state "supplying no corrective process, carries into execution a judgment of death or imprisonment based upon a verdict thus produced by mob domination, the State deprives the accused of his life or liberty without due process of law." *Id.* at 335.

47. 261 U.S. 861 (1923). The petitioners in *Moore* were sentenced to death by an Arkansas court for killing a white man during a race riot sparked by an attack on a group of African Americans assembled in a church. *Id.* at 87. The defendants were saved from lynching only through the presence of federal troops. *Id.* at 88. African-American witnesses were tortured and whipped to provide incriminating testimony, and African Americans were systematically excluded from the grand and petit juries in the case. *Id.* at 89. The court-appointed defense counsel did not consult with their clients before trial; did not request a continuance, change of venue, or separate trials; failed to challenge any prospective jurors; called no witnesses; and did not put the defendants on the stand. *Id.* After a 45-minute trial and five minutes of jury deliberation, the defendants were sentenced to death. *Id.*

Faced with this massive, undeniable evidence of a gross miscarriage of justice, the Supreme Court held that if a state criminal proceeding is

> a mask,—that counsel, jury, and judge were swept to the fatal end by an irresistible wave of public passion, and that the State Courts failed to correct the wrong, neither perfection in the machinery for correction nor the possibility that the trial court and counsel saw no other way of avoiding an immediate outbreak of the mob can prevent this Court from securing to the petitioners their constitutional rights.

Id. at 91.

48. *See* RICHARD C. CORTNER, A "SCOTTSBORO" CASE IN MISSISSIPPI: THE SUPREME COURT AND BROWN V. MISSISSIPPI 116–20 (1986).

49. Plessy v. Ferguson, 163 U.S. 537, 551 (1896).

50. *Id.*

51. Aldridge v. U.S., 283 U.S. 308, 315 (1931).

52. *Id.* at 310.

53. *Id.* at 315.

54. For a description of the facts and conditions surrounding the trials, see Powell v. Alabama, 287 U.S. 45, 49–53 (1932).

55. *Id.*
56. *Id.* at 56.
57. *Id.* at 50.
58. *Id.* at 51.
59. *Id.*
60. *Id.*
61. 287 U.S. 45 (1932).
62. The two opinions were Norris v. Alabama, 294 U.S. 587 (1935), and Patterson v. Alabama, 294 U.S. 600 (1935).
63. 287 U.S. at 73.
64. *See* 2 MERLO J. PUSEY, CHARLES EVANS HUGHES 724 (1951).
65. 287 U.S. at 51.
66. *Id.* at 71.
67. *Id.*
68. 294 U.S. 587 (1935).
69. Justice McReynolds did not participate in this decision. *Id.* at 599.
70. *Id.*
71. *See* Strauder v. West Virginia, 100 U.S. 303, 310 (1880) (invalidating a West Virginia statute which restricted jury service to "white male persons").
72. 294 U.S. at 590.
73. *Id.* In Patterson v. Alabama, 294 U.S. 600 (1935), the third and final Scottsboro decision, another Scottsboro defendant challenged the systematic exclusion of African Americans from jury duty in Jackson County, Alabama. The Alabama Supreme Court refused to consider the substance of his appeal because of the untimely filing of his bill of exceptions. *Id.* at 602. Noting that the Alabama Supreme Court decided *Norris* and *Patterson* on the same day, Chief Justice Hughes remanded the case to the state court to allow it to reconsider what would ordinarily be deemed a non-federal and non-reviewable question of state procedure. *Id.* at 606–7. Because of the "exceptional features of the present case," *id.* at 605, involving a challenge to the now discredited jury selection scheme of Jackson County, Chief Justice Hughes concluded that "the state court should have an opportunity to examine its powers in the light of the situation which has now developed," *id.* at 607.

One of Hughes's biographers later observed: "The basic motivating consideration in [the *Patterson*] opinion was the awful contemplation that for a technical defect in procedure a human being might be sent to his death. With a little ingenuity in reasoning, the technical requirements of the law were subordinated to the ends of justice." SAMUEL HENDEL, CHARLES EVANS HUGHES AND THE SUPREME COURT 161 (1951).

After *Norris*, the Hughes Court re-emphasized on two occasions the constitutional rule against racial discrimination in jury selection. *See* Pierre v. Louisiana, 306 U.S. 354 (1939); Hale v. Kentucky, 303 U.S. 613 (1938) (per curiam).
74. Recent cases reveal an imaginative array of methods used to limit African-American participation in juries. *See, e.g.*, Batson v. Kentucky, 476 U.S. 79, 83 (1986) (African Americans excluded through peremptory challenges); Swain v. Alabama, 380 U.S. 202, 209–22 (1965) (African Americans excluded through peremptory challenges); Avery v. Georgia, 345 U.S. 559, 560–61 (1953) (jurors selected by means of racially coded tickets); Hill v. Texas, 316 U.S. 400, 402

(1942) (jury commissioners selected jurors from among their personal acquaintances); Labat v. Bennett, 365 F.2d 698, 713 (5th Cir. 1966) (exclusion of hourly wage earners), cert. denied, 386 U.S. 991 (1967); Rabinowitz v. United States, 366 F.2d 34, 40 (5th Cir. 1966) (African Americans excluded through a system of panel selection in which "respectable" citizens were asked to recommend others for jury duty); U.S. ex rel. Goldsby v. Harpole, 263 F.2d 71, 77–78 (5th Cir. 1959) (jury lists drawn from voter registration lists, from which African Americans were excluded), cert. denied, 361 U.S. 838 (1959). See also LAWRENCE D. RICE, THE NEGRO IN TEXAS: 1874–1900, at 255–57 (1971) (African Americans excluded through subjective eligibility criteria for jury duty, jury commissioner discretion, literacy qualifications). See generally, JACK BASS, UNLIKELY HEROES: THE DRAMATIC STORY OF THE SOUTHERN JUDGES WHO TRANSLATED THE SUPREME COURT'S BROWN DECISION INTO A REVOLUTION FOR EQUALITY 278–85 (1981) (discussing race discrimination in jury selection in the Fifth Circuit during the 1950s and 1960s); RACE LAW, supra note 2, at 235–77 (2d ed. 1980).

As Justice Marshall noted in his Batson concurrence, an instruction handbook used by the Dallas, Texas, prosecutor's office in the 1970s, "explicitly advised prosecutors that they conduct jury selection so as to eliminate 'any member of a minority group.' " 476 U.S. at 104. An earlier jury-selection guide used by those same prosecutors phrased this advice more bluntly: "Do not take Jews, Negroes, Dagos, Mexicans, or a member of any minority race on a jury, no matter how rich or well educated." Id. at 104 n.3 (citation omitted).

In Clark v. City of Bridgeport, 645 F. Supp. 890 (D. Conn. 1986), the city attorney candidly admitted that he struck eight of eight African-American venirepersons on purely racial grounds. When asked to justify his peremptory challenges, he stated:

> [I]f I had a choice between a white juror and a black juror under the facts of these cases, I'm going to take a white juror. That's what I'm saying. . . .
> [W]hy should I put my city and my defendants at the mercy of the people in my opinion who make the most civil rights claims, at least in my experience.

Id. at 894.

Recently, in Edmonson v. Leesville Concrete Co., 500 U.S. 614 (1991), the Supreme Court ruled that the Constitution forbade the use of peremptory challenges to exclude African Americans in civil cases. Writing for the Court, Justice Kennedy pointed out that "[b]y enforcing a discriminatory peremptory challenge, [a] court 'has not only made itself a party to the [biased act], but has elected to place its power, property and prestige behind the alleged discrimination.' " 500 U.S. at 624 (quoting Burton v. Wilmington Parking Auth., 365 U.S. 715, 725 (1961)).

The Supreme Court has recently also emphasized that racially motivated peremptory challenges are not a peculiarly African-American concern, holding in Powers v. Ohio, 499 U.S. 400 (1991), that a white criminal defendant may challenge the discriminatory exclusion of African-American citizens from a jury. Id. at 416.

75. Theodore G. Bilbo, who was elected as Mississippi's governor in 1915 and 1927, and who served as its U.S. senator from 1935 to 1947, exemplified the starkly racist nature of Mississippi politics during the Hughes era. Bilbo strenuously opposed federal anti-lynching legislation in the late 1930s, stating:

[T]he underlying motive of the Ethiopian who has inspired this proposed legislation . . . and desires its enactment into law with a zeal and a frenzy equal if not paramount to the lust and lasciviousness of the rape fiend in his diabolical effort to despoil the womanhood of the Caucasian race, is to realize the consummation of his dream . . . to become socially and politically equal to the white man."

CORTNER, *supra* note 48, at 48 (citation omitted).

Bilbo followed the racist tradition of his predecessor, Governor James K. Vardaman, who joined the chorus of outrage by southern politicians when President Theodore Roosevelt had lunch with the moderate black leader Booker T. Washington. Vardaman wrote:

It is said that men follow the bent of their geniuses, and that prenatal influences are often potent in shaping thoughts and ideas in after life. Probably old lady Roosevelt, during the period of gestation, was frightened by a dog, and that fact may account for the qualities of the male pup that are so prominent in Teddy. I would not do either an injustice, but am disposed to apologize to the dog for mentioning it.

MILLER, *supra* note 2, at 206–07.

As a Senator, Vardaman continued to use Booker T. Washington as a foil for his racist rhetoric, stating: "I am just as much opposed to Booker Washington as a voter, with all his Anglo-Saxon reenforcements, as I am to the coconut-headed, chocolate-covered, typical little coon, Andy Dotson, who blacks my shoes every morning. Neither is fit to perform the supreme function of citizenship."

1 HARVARD SITKOFF, A NEW DEAL FOR BLACKS: THE EMERGENCE OF CIVIL RIGHTS AS A NATIONAL ISSUE: THE DEPRESSION DECADE 8 (1978) (citation omitted).

76. 297 U.S. 278 (1936).
77. *Id.* at 281.
78. *Id.* at 281–82.
79. *Id.* at 282.
80. *Id.*
81. *Id.*
82. *Id.* at 281.
83. *Id.* at 284–85. T.H. Nicholson, the marshal of Scooba, Mississippi, testified that defendants Ed Brown and Henry Shields "had been whipped some" at the time of their initial confessions. Record from the United States Supreme Court at 102, Brown v. Mississippi, 297 U.S. 278 (1936) (reporting the record of the trial court).

E.L. Gilbert, another witness for the State, also stated that Shields and Brown were whipped during their interrogations. Gilbert admitted participating in the beating of Brown, stating: "We told him any time he wanted to talk, we would let him up, and he got up." *Id.* at 106.

Kemper County Deputy Sheriff Cliff Dial acknowledged that he was present when a mob of twenty men whipped and tried to hang Ellington, *id.* at 111–12, but that he interceded to save Ellington because he "didn't want any of the negroes beat up." *Id.* at 108. However, Dial's concern for the defendant's well-being was mercurial. He admitted that after Shields and Brown had professed their innocence, three days later, he and his companions "kind of warmed them a little," until they finally confessed. *Id.* at 113. Dial also testified that he "strapped Yank [Ellington] a little bit" during the trip into Alabama, and that Ellington also confessed after this treatment. *Id.* at 114.

84. Record at 112, *Brown* (No. 301).
85. 297 U.S. at 279.
86. *Id.*
87. In 1985, a flattering profile of Stennis in the *New York Times* characterized the senior senator from Mississippi as "the undisputed patriarch of the Senate, a teacher to younger members and a conscience for the entire institution." Steven V. Roberts, *Wisdom in Judgment, 38 Years in the Making*, N.Y. TIMES, Nov. 4, 1985, at B10. However, the same article mentioned that Stennis established his reputation in his first year in the Senate by being selected to lead a floor debate against a civil rights bill, "an unusual honor for a junior legislator." *Id.* It was not until 1982 that Stennis " 'reluctantly' cast his first vote for a civil rights bill, one extending the Voting Rights Act." Marjorie Hunter, *Profile: John C. Stennis; Plowing a Straight Line to the End of the Row*, N.Y. TIMES, Nov. 6, 1987, at A18.
88. A dissent by Mississippi Supreme Court Justice Virgil Alexis Griffith, joined by Justice William D. Anderson, described the torture of the three *Brown* defendants in gruesome detail. Justice Griffith concluded his dissenting opinion with an unusually explicit invitation to the U.S. Supreme Court to reverse his colleagues' majority opinion, stating:

> If this judgment be affirmed by the federal Supreme Court, it will be first in the history of that court wherein there was allowed to stand a conviction based solely upon testimony coerced by the barbarities of executive officers of the state, known to the prosecuting officers of the state as having been so coerced, when the testimony was introduced, and fully shown in all its nakedness to the trial judge before he closed the case and submitted it to the jury, and when all this is not only undisputed, but is expressly and openly admitted.

Brown v. State, 161 So. 465, 472 (Miss. 1935) (Griffith, J., dissenting).
The strength and eloquence of Griffith's dissent was of incalculable value in publicizing the *Brown* case and in persuading the U.S. Supreme Court to review the Mississippi decision. CORTNER, *supra* note 48, at 81–86. Chief Justice Hughes quoted Griffith's dissent at length in his factual summary, agreeing with his state court colleague that the trial transcript "reads more like pages torn from some medieval account, than a record made within the confines of a modern civilization which aspires to an enlightened constitutional government." 297 U.S. at 282 (quoting 161 So. at 470 (Griffith, J., dissenting)).
89. 161 So. at 465. Ironically, on the same day that the Mississippi Supreme Court announced its decision in *Brown*, the United States Senate was consumed by a bitter and ultimately successful filibuster to defeat an anti-lynching bill. *Filibuster Balks Efforts To Speed Roosevelt Bills*, N.Y. TIMES, April 30, 1935, at A1.
90. *See* CORTNER, *supra* note 48, at 89–106.
91. 297 U.S. at 285.
92. *Id.* at 285–86.
93. 309 U.S. 227 (1940).

A contemporary account gives some sense of the atmosphere surrounding the issuance of the *Chambers* decision.

> The court's unanimous and extended opinion was based on the constitutional "due process" clause in the Fourteenth Amendment, passed after the Civil War to protect the newly granted rights of Negroes from arbitrary State judicial action.
>
> It was handed down on the anniversary of the birth of Abraham Lincoln, who was chiefly responsible in obtaining the basis of these rights for the liberated and enfranchised Negro race, and it was voiced eloquently by Justice Black, who admitted, after his nomination to the high bench, that he had once been a member of the Ku Klux Klan.
>
> The drama of the occasion, due to the date of the opinion, the background of the justice rendering it, the defense of constitutional principles and the broad overtones of the court's denunciation of the exercise of dictatorial power by any government, was not lost upon the audience which crowded the great marble court chamber.

Frederick R. Barkley, *High Court Saves 4 Doomed Negroes*, N.Y. TIMES, Feb. 13, 1940, at A1.

94. 309 U.S. at 238.
95. *Id.* at 238–40.
96. 309 U.S. at 240–41.
97. *Id.* at 241.
98. In Arizona v. Fulminante, 499 U.S. 279 (1991), a bitterly divided Court held that the admission of an involuntary confession was subject to the harmless error rule of Chapman v. California, 386 U.S. 18 (1967). Justice Byron White, writing for the four dissenters, stated that "permitting a coerced confession to be part of the evidence on which a jury is free to base its verdict of guilty is inconsistent with the thesis that ours is not an inquisitorial system of criminal justice." 499 U.S. at 293–94 (White, J., dissenting) (citing Chambers v. Florida, 309 U.S. 227, 235–38 (1940)).

For an excellent analysis of the *Fulminante* decision, see Charles J. Ogletree, Arizona v. Fulminante: *The Harm of Applying Harmless Error to Coerced Confessions*, 105 HARV. L. REV. 152 (1991).
99. 309 U.S. 631 (1940) (per curiam).
100. White v. Texas, 308 U.S. 608 (1939).
101. 309 U.S. at 631.
102. White v. Texas, 310 U.S. 608 (1939) (denying the State's petition for rehearing).
103. Edwin McElwain, *The Business of the Supreme Court as Conducted by Chief Justice Hughes*, 63 HARV. L. REV. 5, 25–26 (1949).
104. PUSEY, *supra* note 64, at 727.
105. *See In re* Demos, 500 U.S. 16 (1991) (denying certiorari petition by prolific pro se litigant and denying leave to proceed in forma pauperis in all *future* petitions of extraordinary relief); *In re* Sindram, 498 U.S. 177 (1991) (denying motion by pro se litigant to proceed in forma pauperis on current or future petitions for extraordinary relief); *In re* McDonald, 489 U.S. 180 (1989) (same). *See also* In re Amendment to Rule 39, 500 U.S. 13 (1991) (amending Rule 39 of the Su-

preme Court Rules to allow denial of leave to proceed with "frivolous" or "malicious" in forma pauperis proceedings).

In his dissent in *Demos*, Justice Marshall, joined by Justices Blackmun and Stevens, wrote:

> In closing its doors today to another indigent litigant, the Court moves ever closer to the day when it leaves an indigent litigant with a meritorious claim out in the cold. And with each barrier that it places in the way of indigent litigants, and with each instance that it castigates such litigants for having "abused the system," the Court can only reinforce in the hearts and minds of our society's less fortunate members the unsettling message that their pleas are not welcome here.

500 U.S. at 19 (Marshall, J., dissenting) (citation omitted).

106. *See* McNeil, *supra* note 2, at 13, 52–53, 132–36.

107. *See* Gilbert Ware, William Hastie: Grace Under Pressure 29, 85–86, 95–96 (1984).

108. *See* A. Leon Higginbotham, Jr., *An Open Letter to Justice Clarence Thomas from a Federal Judicial Colleague,* 140 U. Pa. L. Rev. 1005, 1012–15 (1992); A. Leon Higginbotham, Jr., *Tribute to Justice Thurgood Marshall,* 105 Harv. L. Rev. 55 (1991).

For thoughtful collections of articles on Justice Marshall, see also *Tributes,* 101 Yale L.J. 1 (1991); *A Tribute to Justice Thurgood Marshall,* 6 Harv. BlackLetter J. 1 (1989); *Tribute to Justice Thurgood Marshall,* 40 Md. L. Rev. 390 (1981).

109. *See* State *ex rel.* Gaines v. Canada, 113 S.W.2d 783, 785 (Mo. 1937), *rev'd,* 305 U.S. 337 (1938).

110. *Id.* at 790.

111. *Id.* at 789. The Missouri Supreme Court reiterated its earlier determination that racial segregation was justified on the basis of "natural race peculiarities" and "practical results":

> There are differences in races, and between individuals of the same race, not created by human laws, some of which can never be eradicated. These differences create different social relations, recognized by all well-organized governments. If we cast aside chimerical theories and look to practical results, it seems to us it must be conceded that separate schools for colored children is a regulation to their great advantage.

Id. at 788 (quoting Lehew v. Brummel, 15 S.W. 765, 766 (Mo. 1890).

112. *See* McNeil, *supra* note 2, at 143–45, 149–50.

113. 305 U.S. 337 (1938).

114. *Id.* at 349.

115. *Id.* at 349–50.

116. *Id.* at 351.

117. *Id.* at 344.

118. Thus, grossly inequitable practices such as the closing of a county's only African-American high school, Cumming v. Richmond County Board of Education, 175 U.S. 528 (1899), a state's prohibition of integrated *private* schools, Berea College v. Kentucky, 211 U.S. 45 (1908), and the exclusion of all nonwhites from white schools in a dual school system, Gong Lum v. Rice, 275

U.S. 78 (1927), were found to satisfy the state's obligation to provide equal
protection to its citizens.

119. Burke Marshall, Federalism and Civil Rights 13–14 (1964) (quoting
Judge Chrisman).

120. *Id.*

121. Nixon v. Herndon, 273 U.S. 536 (1927).

122. *See* Nixon v. Condon, 286 U.S. 73, 82 (1932).

123. *Id.*

124. 286 U.S. 73 (1932).

125. *Id.* at 89 (citations omitted).

126. Grovey v. Townsend, 295 U.S. 45, 47 (1935), *overruled by* Smith v. Allwright,
321 U.S. 649 (1944).

127. 295 U.S. 45 (1935).

128. In 1944, the Supreme Court overruled *Grovey* in Smith v. Allwright, 321 U.S.
649 (1944), finally recognizing that the Democratic party's discrimination
against African-American voters violated the Fifteenth Amendment's guarantee
of the right to vote to all races.

129. David P. Currie, *The Constitution in the Supreme Court: Civil Rights and Liberties, 1930–1941*, 1987 Duke L.J. 800, 808 (footnote omitted).

130. 307 U.S. 268 (1939).

131. 302 U.S. 277 (1937), *overruled by* Harper v. Virginia State Bd. of Elections,
383 U.S. 663 (1966).

132. In *Breedlove*, the Court upheld a poll tax of one dollar levied against every
Georgia inhabitant between the ages of 21 and 60, except blind and female
residents who did not register to vote. *Id.* at 279–80. Georgians were not allowed to vote in any elections unless the tax was paid. *Id.* at 280.

For a further discussion of the use of the poll tax to disfranchise minorities
and lower income citizens, see 2 Thomas I. Emerson et al., Political and
Civil Rights in the United States 1120–34 (student ed. 1967); President's
Comm. On Civil Rights, To Secure These Rights: The Report of the
President's Committee on Civil Rights 38–39 (1947); Note, *Disenfranchise-
ment by Means of the Poll Tax*, 53 Harv. L. Rev. 645, 645–52 (1940); Note,
Negro Disenfranchisement—A Challenge to the Constitution, 47 Colum. L.
Rev. 76, 92–94 (1947). *See also* Harper v. Virginia State Bd. of Elections, 383
U.S. 663, 668 (1966) (striking down a Virginia poll tax for state elections and
noting "[w]ealth, like race, creed, or color, is not germane to one's ability to
participate intelligently in the electoral process"); United States v. Dogan, 314
F.2d 767, 768, 774 (5th Cir. 1963) (finding impermissible racial discrimination
in a county sheriff's refusal to accept poll taxes offered by African-American citizens).

133. Richard Wright, *Introduction* to St. Claire Drake & Horace R. Cayton,
Black Metropolis: A Study of Negro Life in a Northern City (1945).

134. *Id.* at xxxiv. Wright took the quoted words from "a new and strange cry from
another Negro, Claude McKay, [who] in his sonnet, *If We Must Die*, . . . seems
to snarl through a sob." *Id.* at xxxiii. McKay's sonnet goes:

If we must die—oh, let us nobly die,
     So that our precious blood may not be shed
In vain; then even the monsters we defy

Shall be constrained to honor us though dead!
Oh, kinsmen! We must meet the common foe;
Though far outnumbered, let us still be brave,
And for their thousand blows deal one death-blow!
What though before us lies the open grave?
Like men we'll face the murderous, cowardly pack
Pressed to the wall, dying, but—fighting back!

Id. at xxxiv (quoting portions of McKay's sonnet as published in ANTHOLOGY OF AMERICAN NEGRO LITERATURE 203–04 (V.F. Calverton ed., 1929)).

135. *Id.*

136. Speaking to the Association of the Bar of the City of New York on April 21, 1965, Martin Luther King said: "[T]he *road to freedom* is now a highway because lawyers throughout the land, yesterday and today, have helped clear the obstructions, have helped eliminate road blocks, helped by the selfless, courageous espousal of difficult and unpopular causes." Martin Luther King, Jr., *The Civil Rights Struggle in the United States Today*, 20 THE RECORD OF THE ASS'N OF THE BAR OF THE CITY OF NEW YORK No. 5, at 5, 6 (1965) (emphasis added).

CHAPTER THIRTEEN

1. 3 PHILIP S. FONER, THE LIFE AND WRITINGS OF FREDERICK DOUGLASS 420 (1952).

2. Mobile v. Bolden, 446 U.S. 53, 113, 115 (1980) (Marshall, J., dissenting) (quoting Yick Wo v. Hopkins, 118 U.S. 356, 370 (1886); Reynolds v. Sims, 377 U.S. 533, 561–62 (1964)).

3. NELSON MANDELA, 'Black Man in a White Court': First Court Statement, 1962, *in* THE STRUGGLE IS MY LIFE 133, 135 (Second Pathfinder 1990).

4. ALEXIS DE TOCQUEVILLE, 1 DEMOCRACY IN AMERICA 261 (Anchor Books ed. 1969) (1835) (quoted in DERRICK BELL, RACE, RACISM AND AMERICAN LAW § 4.2 (180) (3rd ed. 1992).

5. 6 Watts (Pa.) 553 (1837).

6. The provision stated: "[E]very *freeman* of the full age of twenty-one years, having resided in this state for a space of one whole year before the day of election, and paid taxes during that time, shall enjoy the rights of an elector." Hobbs v. Fogg, 6 Watts (Pa.) at 559 (emphasis in original).

7. *Id.* at 554.

8. *Id.* at 558–59.

9. *Id.* at 559.

10. PA. CONST. of 1838, art. III, § 1 (cited in DERRICK BELL, RACE, RACISM AND AMERICAN LAW 180 (1992).

11. *See* A. LEON HIGGINBOTHAM, JR., IN THE MATTER OF COLOR: RACE AND THE AMERICAN LEGAL PROCESS: THE COLONIAL PERIOD 267–310 (1978).

12. *See* BERNARD GROFMAN ET AL., MINORITY REPRESENTATION AND THE QUEST FOR VOTING EQUALITY 4 n.1 (1992).

13. BELL, *supra* note 10, at 181 (1992).

14. *Id.*

15. ROBERT J. JOHANNSEN, THE LINCOLN-DOUGLAS DEBATES OF 1858, at 45–46 (1965) (quoting Sen. Stephen Douglas speech of August 21, 1858).

16. HAROLD HOLZER, THE LINCOLN-DOUGLAS DEBATES 245 (1993) (quoting Sen. Stephen Douglas) (speech of Oct. 7, 1858).

17. CONG. GLOBE, 40th Cong., 3rd Sess. 1010 (1869) (statement of Sen. James Doolittle).

18. *Id.* at 1630 (statement of Sen. Garrett Davis).

19. *Id.* at 989 (statement of Sen. Thomas Hendricks).

20. *Id.* at 1299 (statement of Sen. William Saulsbury).

21. BELL, *supra* note 10, at 183.

22. *See* A. Leon Higginbotham, Jr. et al., Shaw v. Reno: *A Mirage of Good Intentions with Devastating Racial Consequences*, 62 FORDHAM L. REV. 1593, 1648–49 (Appendix A) (1994) (listing African Americans in the U.S. Congress, 1870–1993).

23. *See, e.g.*, CONG. REC., 43rd Cong., 2d Sess. 944 (1875) (statement of Rep. John R. Lynch) (supporting passage of the Civil Rights Act of 1875).

24. NEIL R. MCMILLEN, DARK JOURNEY: BLACK MISSISSIPPIANS IN THE AGE OF JIM CROW (1990).

25. BURKE MARSHALL, FEDERALISM AND CIVIL RIGHTS 13 (1964) (quoting Judge Chrisman).

26. Other southern states followed Mississippi's lead. In 1900, North Carolina adopted a poll tax, as well as literacy and property requirements. BELL, *supra* note 10, at 186 n.6. Georgia adopted these requirements and the "grandfather clause" in 1908. *Id.* at 187 n.6. Thus, African Americans gained significant political rights during Reconstruction, but these were short-lived.

27. H. Leon Prather, Sr., *The Red Shirt Movement in North Carolina 1898–1900*, 62 J. NEGRO HIST. 174, 179 (1977) (citation omitted).

   The remainder of this chapter is substantially taken from Higginbotham, et al., *supra* note 22, at 1605–17.

28. *Id.*

29. *Id.* at 182.

30. 34 CONG. REC. 1635–38 (1901).

31. *Id.* at 1638.

32. Charles B. Aycock, *Speech Before the North Carolina Society, Baltimore* (Dec. 18, 1903), *in* THE NORTH CAROLINA EXPERIENCE: AN INTERPRETIVE AND DOCUMENTARY HISTORY 415 (Lindley S. Butler & Alan D. Watson eds., 1984) (emphasis added). Governor Aycock stressed his supposed "regard" for African Americans:

   These things are not said in enmity to the negro but in regard for him. He constitutes one third of the population of my State: he has always been my personal friend; as a lawyer I have often defended him, and as Governor I have frequently protected him. But there flows in my veins the blood of the dominant race; that race that has conquered the earth and seeks out the mysteries of the heights and depths. If manifest destiny leads to the seizure of Panama, it is certain that it likewise leads to the dominance of the Caucasian. When the negro recognizes this fact we shall have peace and good will between the races.

   Id.

33. Locke Craig, Campaign Speech on the Suffrage Amendment, *in* MEMOIRS AND SPEECHES OF LOCKE CRAIG: GOVERNOR OF NORTH CAROLINA, 1913–1917, at 34 (May F. Jones ed., 1923) (emphasis added). He further explained:

This one section will wipe out the negro vote in North Carolina. Of the 120,000 negro voters it will disfranchise 110,000 of them, practically all of them. It will be good-bye to all negro office holders, and all those who base their hope of office on the negro vote. . . . There is only one kind of a white man in North Carolina that will be disfranchised, and that is the white man who . . . denies his race and his color . . . and swears that he is a negro or the son of a negro, or the grandson of a negro, and that white man will be disfranchised.

Id. at 36–38.

34. Thomas W. Bickett, Message to the General Assembly of 1920, *in* PUBLIC LETTERS AND PAPERS OF THOMAS WALTER BICKETT, GOVERNOR OF NORTH CAROLINA, 1917–1921, at 292 (R.B. House ed. 1923) (emphasis added).

35. GEORGE SINKLER, THE RACIAL ATTITUDES OF AMERICAN PRESIDENTS: FROM ABRAHAM LINCOLN TO THEODORE ROOSEVELT 227 (1971) (emphasis omitted).

36. *See supra* Chapter Eight.

37. *See* WILLIAM A. SINCLAIR, THE AFTERMATH OF SLAVERY 187–96 (2d ed. 1905).

38. *Id.* at 187.

39. *Id.*

40. *Id.* at 188. Not to be outdone by others in racist rhetoric, James K. Vardaman, then governor of Mississippi, wrote in his newspaper:

It is said that men follow the bent of their geniuses, and that prenatal influences are often potent in shaping thoughts and ideas in after life. Probably old lady Roosevelt, during the period of gestation, was frightened by a dog, and the fact may account for the qualities of the male pup that are so prominent in Teddy. I would not do either an injustice, but am disposed to apologize to the dog for mentioning it.

Id. at 196.

41. 1 HARVARD SITKOFF, A NEW DEAL FOR BLACKS: THE EMERGENCE OF CIVIL RIGHTS AS A NATIONAL ISSUE 8 (1978) (citation omitted). *See also* David L. Lewis, W.E.B. DU BOIS: BIOGRAPHY OF A RACE 1868–1919, at 257–61 (1993) (describing white rejection of Washington's conciliatory efforts).

42. African Americans had few allies. Even the woman's suffrage movement placed great reliance on the argument that the votes of white women would serve to dilute the "adverse" impact of black male suffrage mandated by the Fifteenth Amendment. Suffragists Elizabeth Cady Stanton and Susan B. Anthony "opened the way to . . . bigotry" in their influential National Suffrage Association. ELEANOR FLEXNER, CENTURY OF STRUGGLE: THE WOMAN'S RIGHTS MOVEMENT IN THE UNITED STATES 316 (rev. ed. 1975). Indeed, the National Board of that organization issued a statement noting that "granting suffrage to women who can read and write and pay taxes *would insure white supremacy without resorting to any methods of doubtful constitutionality.*" *Id.* at 317 (citation omitted); *see also* WILLIAM H. CHAFE, THE AMERICAN WOMAN 15 (1972). The Equal Suffrage League of Raleigh, North Carolina—a chapter of the National American Woman's Suffrage Association—was particularly strident in its calls for woman's suffrage, limited through the application of literacy tests to white women, to ensure white domination. *See* Glenda E. Gilmore, Gender and Jim Crow: Women and the Politics of White Supremacy in North Carolina, 1896–1920, at 439–47 (1993) (Ph.D. dissertation, University of North Carolina, Chapel Hill) (forthcoming UNC Press).

43. W.E.B. Du Bois, *Herbert Hoover,* THE CRISIS 39 (Nov. 1932), *reprinted in* 2 WRITINGS IN PERIODICALS EDITED BY W.E.B. DU BOIS 675 (1983) (Herbert Aptheker ed., 1983).

44. William E. Leuchtenburg, *Tribute: John Hope Franklin,* 42 DUKE L.J. 1022, 1023–24 (1993).

45. *See* Gingles v. Edmisten, 590 F. Supp. 345, 360 (E.D.N.C. 1984), *modified sub nom.* Thornburg v. Gingles, 478 U.S. 30 (1986). From 1900 through 1919, African Americans also were prohibited from voting, as North Carolina enforced a voting poll tax. *See* JOHN V. ORTH, THE NORTH CAROLINA STATE CONSTITUTION: A REFERENCE GUIDE 119 (1993).

46. *See* J. Morgan Kousser, After 120 Years: Redistricting in North Carolina 30–31 (Mar. 22, 1994) (submitted as sworn testimony in Shaw v. Hunt, No. 92–202-CIV-5-BR (E.D.N.C.)).

47. *Gingles,* 590 F. Supp. at 359 (quoting Bazemore v. Bertie County Bd. of Elections, 119 S.E. 2d 637 (N.C. 1961)).

48. *See* Alex Willingham, Report on Certain Questions Involving Race and North Carolina Congressional Redistricting with Reference to the 1990 Round 5–6 (Mar. 22, 1994) (submitted as sworn testimony in Shaw v. Hunt, No. 92–202-CIV-5-BR (E.D.N.C.)).

49. *See* Kousser, *supra* note 46, at 21–22.

50. *See* Higginbotham, et al., *supra* note 22, at 1597 (reproduction).

 Willis Smith ran against and defeated Dr. Frank Graham, a distinguished educator and former president of the University of North Carolina. *See* JULIAN M. PLEASANTS & AUGUSTUS M. BURNS III, FRANK PORTER GRAHAM AND THE 1950 SENATE RACE IN NORTH CAROLINA (1990); *see also* SAMUEL LUBELL, THE FUTURE OF AMERICAN POLITICS 106–17 (3d ed. 1965). Jesse Helms, who was a campaign worker for Smith, was later elected to the United States Senate, using racist, though more subtle, campaign literature. *See* KATHLEEN H. JAMIESON, DIRTY POLITICS 80 (1992).

51. *See* Harry L. Watson, Race and Politics in North Carolina, 1865–1994, at 13 (submitted as sworn testimony in Shaw v. Hunt, 92–202-CIV-5-BR (E.D.N.C.)); *see also Alton Lennon Forces Flood State with 'Phony' Race Issue Leaflet,* RALEIGH NEWS & OBSERVER, May 28, 1954, at 1. The fact that a supposed endorsement by a black leader proved such an effective tool for discrediting Scott is striking evidence of white voters' hostility to black candidates and black issues, an attitude that still prevails.

52. *See* Watson, *supra* note 51, at 13.

53. *See id.* at 14.

54. *See id.* at 14–15.

55. *See id.* at 15.

56. *Id.* at 16.

57. In an ad placed in the *Charlotte News* by the Wallace Campaign, a school bus was pictured with the text:

 If you're wondering why more and more millions of your fellow Americans are turning to Governor Wallace: Follow, as your children are bused. All across town. Governor Wallace as President will let you and your local schools decide what is best for your children.

CHARLOTTE NEWS, Oct. 29, 1968, at 5C.

58. *See* Watson, *supra* note 51, at 17.

59. *See id.* at 23–24.

60. *See id.*

61. *See* Kousser, *supra* note 46, at 36–41; James M. O'Reilly, A Report Prepared for *Shaw v. Hunt* 4–5 (Mar. 22, 1994) (submitted as sworn testimony in Shaw v. Hunt, 92–202-CIV-5-BR (E.D.N.C.)).

62. *See* O'Reilly, *supra* note 61, at 5–6.

63. *See* Kousser, *supra* note 46, at 48.

64. *See id.* at 49.

65. Watson, *supra* note 51, at 25–26; *see also* Kousser, *supra* note 46, at 50.

66. *See* Watson, *supra* note 51, at 26.

67. *See* Kousser, *supra* note 46, at 50.

68. *See id.* at 53–54.

69. *See* O'Reilly, *supra* note 61, at 2.

70. Moreover, as J. Morgan Kousser demonstrates, the ability to elect a black representative is not merely symbolic. *See* Kousser, *supra* note 46, at 20. Black representatives more effectively and consistently present and protect the chosen interests of their black constituency. *See id.* at 20–23. This is neither surprising nor disturbing. Due to their unique history and state-enforced inequality in America, blacks tend to hold attitudes divergent from those of whites on the issues of most import to them, including race relations, remedies for discrimination, and other areas of civil rights policy. *See id.* at 24–27.

71. Watson, *supra* note 51, at 18.

72. Jamieson, *supra* note 50, at 97.

73. *See id.* at 99–100. The "white hands" commercial was not an isolated incident of the Helms campaign playing to racial fears and animus. The Helms campaign featured numerous advertisements highlighting Democratic Party Chairman Ron Brown, an African American, as well as advertisements featuring Gantt's black campaign manager. *See* Watson, *supra* note 51, at 20.

74. Watson, *supra* note 51, at 21.

75. *Id.* at 26.

76. *Id.* at 21.

77. *See* Affidavit of Representative Mel Watt, ¶8 (sworn to Mar. 23, 1994) (submitted as evidence in Shaw v. Hunt, No. 92–202-CIV-5-BR (E.D.N.C.); Affidavit of Charles E. Johnson, ¶¶8–13 (sworn to Mar. 18, 1994) (submitted as evidence in Shaw v. Hunt, No. 92–202-CIV-5-BR (E.D.N.C.)).

78. Bullet voting is a practice designed to maximize a group's voting strength in at-large voting schemes. In at-large districts—where multiple seats are filled in a single election—voters may cast one vote for as many candidates as there are seats available. Thus if there are five seats available each voter may cast a vote for any five candidates running. With bullet voting, voters decline to cast all of their votes—choosing instead to vote only for their "target" candidate—thereby avoiding the dilution of their vote that would accompany voting for a full slate. When done in concert, and particularly where racial bloc voting occurs, bullet voting provides gains to the "target" candidate relative to other candidates, and therefore increases the likelihood of minority representation.

79. *See* Gingles v. Edmisten, 590 F. Supp. 345, 359–60 (E.D.N.C. 1984), *modified sub nom.* Thornburg v. Gingles, 478 U.S. 30, 38–39 (1986).
80. *See Gingles,* 590 F. Supp. at 360. In North Carolina, 70.8% of voting-age whites are registered, while only 64% of voting age blacks are registered. *See* Jerry T. Jennings, U.S. Dep't of Commerce, Voting and Registration in the Election of November 1992, at 27 (on file with the *Fordham Law Review*).
81. *See Gingles,* 590 F. Supp. at 361.
82. *See* Willingham, *supra* note 48, at 30–31.
83. *See* Jennings, *supra* note 80, at 27.
84. *See* Willingham, *supra* note 48, at 28–30.
85. *See* Higginbotham et al., *supra* note 22, at 1603 & n. 43–45, 1643–47.

APPENDIX

1. *See generally* Margaret A. Burnham, *An Impossible Marriage: Slave Law and Family Law,* 5 LAW & INEQ. J. 187 (1987); A. Leon Higginbotham, Jr., *Race, Sex, Education and Missouri Jurisprudence: Shelly v. Kraemer in a Historical Perspective,* 67 WASH. U. L. Q. 673, 688–96 (1989).
2. For example, "A criminal homicide constitutes murder of the first degree when it is committed by an intentional killing." 18 PA. CONS. STAT. ANN. § 2502(a) (1983).
3. In a later volume I will develop the interaction of legal and religious elites in promulgating the biblical sanction for black bondage. *See* A. Leon Higginbotham, Jr., *Denial of Slaves' Religious Freedom* (unpublished manuscript on the Eighth Precept of American Slavery, on file with author). A number of scholars have traced the development of attempts to offer spiritual sanction for slavery. *See, e.g.,* C. ERIC LINCOLN, RACE, RELIGION, AND THE CONTINUING AMERICAN DILEMMA 23–59 (1984); ALBERT J. RABOTEAU, SLAVE RELIGION: THE "INVISIBLE INSTITUTION" IN THE ANTEBELLUM SOUTH 96–210 (1978); Elizabeth Fox-Genovese & Eugene D. Genovese, *The Divine Sanction of Social Order: Religious Foundations of the Southern Slaveholders' World View,* 55 J. AM. ACAD. RELIGION 211 (1987).

   Raboteau notes that "the duty of Christian slaves" was invoked as a part of African enslavement by King Charles II of England. Raboteau also notes, however, the deep reluctance of the earliest colonial slaveholders to act upon this sense of mission, thereby exposing the economic imperative which underlay the colonial planters' actions. *See* RABOTEAU, *supra,* at 97–109. Slaveowners feared the subversive potential of Christianity, but legislative actions in Maryland and in Virginia removed doubts that the Christian baptism of Africans would prohibit slave status. *See id.* at 99. With the assistance of such laws, the mass conversion of slaves which occurred during the Great Awakening of 1740 marked the beginning of the aggressive appropriation of Christianity as a means of maximizing slave obedience and economic profitability. *See* LINCOLN, *supra,* at 46; RABOTEAU, *supra,* at 128–50.

   Fox-Genovese and Genovese note that these attempts to formulate a divine sanction for slaveholding would form the core of pro-slavery ideology in the nineteenth century. Fox-Genovese & Genovese, *supra,* at 211–29.

4. *The Ten Commandments of Slavery:*

1. "Thou shalt constantly and unrelentingly advocate the superiority of the white race and the inferiority of blacks." [Thou shalt firmly implant in the minds of blacks the feeling of inferiority, and shalt convince both whites and blacks that blacks are innately inferior.]
2. "Thou shalt generally disregard the *humanity* of the slave, and shalt treat the slave as a sub-human non-person and preserve at all cost the slave's status as the master's *property*."
3. "Thou shalt keep blacks—whether slave or free—as powerless as possible so that they will be submissive and dependent in every respect, not only to the master, but to whites in general."
4. "Thou shalt destroy the unity of the black family, deny blacks the right of marriage, and demean and degrade black parents to the psychological detriment of their children."
5. "Thou shalt deprive blacks of any freedom of movement, freedom of association, and any opportunity to resist, rebel or flee."
6. "Thou shalt deny to blacks any education and thou shalt make it a crime to teach slaves to read or to write."
7. "Thou shalt deny slaves the opportunity to worship with other blacks, to define and practice their own religion and to choose their own religious leaders." [But thou shalt encourage them to adopt the religion of the white master, teaching that god is white and that he rewards the slave who obeys the commands of his white master here on earth.]
8. "Thou shalt always preserve white racial purity, white male sexual dominance and a rigid color line." [In practice white racial purity and white male sexual dominance means a rigid color line only as to black males and white females. To enforce this commandment, thou shalt prohibit and prosecute any intimate interracial relationships between black males and white females, even if thou must impose harsh measures against any white woman who dares to have an intimate association with a black male, and thou shall discourage any white male from legitimizing his intimate relationships with a black female.]
9. "Thou shalt seek to have blacks among thy midst as slaves, to be hostile to free blacks, to limit manumission, and to relegate free blacks to a status as near as possible to slavery." [Thou shalt force blacks who do become free to leave your midst.]
10. "Thou shalt promulgate any doctrine from any source whatsoever which aids in perpetuating slavery and legitimizing the view that blacks are inferior, so long as that doctrine makes slavery maximally profitable and keeps blacks in the position of perpetual subordination to whites." [Thou shalt also retaliate with vengeance against all who dare to believe that slavery should be abolished or that blacks are not inherently inferior.]

Alternative Commandments:

11. "Thou shalt support any practice or doctrine from any source whatsoever that maximizes the profitability of slavery and legitimizes racism."
12. "Thou shalt also retaliate with vengeance, including the use of violence, against all who dare to believe that slavery should be abolished or that blacks are not inherently inferior."

5. THE DECLARATION OF INDEPENDENCE para. 2 (U.S. 1776).

6. Completed in 1776, the Declaration was composed by a committee consisting of John Adams, Benjamin Franklin, Thomas Jefferson, Robert Livingston, and Roger Sherman, although the final draft appeared to be the work of Jefferson. *See* DOCUMENTS OF AMERICAN HISTORY 100 (Henry S. Commager ed., 1973).

7. Samuel Johnson, *Taxation N. Tyranny; an answer to the Resolutions and Address of the American Congress, in* POLITICAL WRITINGS, VOL. X OF THE YALE EDITION OF THE WORKS OF SAMUEL JOHNSON 454 (Donald J. Greene ed., 1977).

8. *Id.*

9. THOMAS JEFFERSON, NOTES ON THE STATE OF VIRGINIA 169–70 (1832) (1787).

10. *Id.* at 170–71.

11. Analytically it may have been easier to limit my categorization to the first three precepts. But because of the bulk of materials that would be required under each of the three precepts and because institutions such as the family, education, and religion have unique histories, for purposes of the volumes it was easier to expand the number to ten.

12. The difficulty is similar to an attempt to reduce the law of contracts, torts, or evidence to ten basic concepts that permeate all of the cases and statutory law in those areas. Nevertheless, every author of a major legal treatise, by using chapter headings, in some way reduces the innumerable forests of cases and laws to specific categories.

13. 347 U.S. 497, 499 (1954).

14. *Id.* at 499.

15. LeRoy Fibre Co. v. Chicago, Milwaukee & St. Paul Ry., 232 U.S. 340, 354 (1914) (Holmes, J., concurring).

16. For example, Dr. Samuel Cartwright claimed that blacks were a different species of man, designated as Prognathous. *See* SLAVERY DEFENDED: THE VIEWS OF THE OLD SOUTH 139–47 (Eric L. McKitrick ed., 1963) (comparing blacks' anatomy to that of monkeys).

17. South Carolina Senator John C. Calhoun appealed to the "facts" of the condition of blacks in Africa before slavery:

> Never before has the black race of Central Africa, from the dawn of history to the present day, attained a condition so civilized and so improved, not only physically, but morally and intellectually [while as slaves]. It [the black race] came among us in a low, degraded, and savage condition, and in the course of a few generations it has grown up under the fostering care of our institutions, reviled as they have been, to its present comparatively civilized condition. This, with the rapid increase of numbers, is conclusive proof of the general happiness of the race, in spite of all the exaggerated tales to the contrary.

Id. at 13 (reprinting speech before the U.S. Senate, Feb. 6, 1837).

Benjamin Quarles has noted that Europeans seemingly found existing slavery and intertribal warfare in Africa as means for their enslavement of Africans. BENJAMIN QUARLES, THE NEGRO IN THE MAKING OF AMERICA 21 (rev. ed. 1969). Slave trader William Snelgrave justified, to slaves during a mutiny on his slaver, his enslavement and transport of the slaves by saying "they had forfeited their Freedom before I bought them, either by Crimes or by being taken in War," noting also that "they seemed to be convinced of their Fault." DANIEL P. MANNIX & MALCOLM COWLEY, BLACK CARGOES: A HISTORY OF THE ATLANTIC SLAVE TRADE, 1518–1865, at 109–10 (1962).

18. *See* WINTHROP D. JORDAN, WHITE OVER BLACK: AMERICAN ATTITUDES TOWARD THE NEGRO, 1550–1812, at 234–65 (1968).

19. 4 *The Papers of Thomas Ruffin in* 8 PUBLICATIONS OF THE NORTH CAROLINA HISTORICAL COMMISSION 329 (1920) (emphasis added).

20. Despite his intentions, the master could not always dominate the slave's internal beliefs about the master's construction of Christianity.

21. Another word-choice problem arose in the first precept. I had before me the choice of "advocate," "presume," "enforce," and "preserve, protect and defend." "Preserve, protect and defend" was chosen because of its constitutional ring; the phrase is from the Oath of Office of the President of the United States. The oath reads: "I do solemnly swear (or affirm) that I will faithfully execute the Office of President of the United States, and will to the best of my Ability, preserve, protect and defend the Constitution of the United States." U.S. CONST., art. II, § 1, cl. 8. Other federal officials, and all state officials, must swear only to support the Constitution. U.S. CONST., art. VI, cl. 3. *Cf.* 5 U.S.C. § 3331 (1977) (reciting the United States Civil Service or uniformed services oath to "support and defend the Constitution").

    At least one state has modeled its oath of office to the presidential model. S.C. CONST. art. III, § 26. *See also* CONFEDERATE CONST. art. II, § 1, cl. 10 (cited in CHARLES R. LEE, JR., THE CONFEDERATE CONSTITUTIONS app. at 186, 189–90 (1963)) (copying U.S. Constitution's oath, save using "Confederate States"). *Cf., e.g.,* VA. CONST. art. II, § 7; N.C. CONST. art. III, § 4; TENN. CONST. art. I, § 4; W. VA. CONST. art. IV, § 5; WISC. CONST. art. IV, § 28.

22. *See* MANNIX & COWLEY, *supra* note 17, at 108–11 (discussing slaveship mutinies at port and precautions taken against them).

23. Louis Henkin, *Introduction* to THE INTERNATIONAL BILL OF RIGHTS: THE COVE-NANT ON CIVIL AND POLITICAL RIGHTS 1 (Louis Henkin ed., 1981) (emphasis added).

24. 136 CONG. REC. H393 (daily ed. Feb. 21, 1990).

25. 136 CONG. REC. H4136–37 (daily ed. June 26, 1990).

26. *Id.* at H4136 (emphasis added).

27. LOUIS HENKIN, HOW NATIONS BEHAVE: LAW AND FOREIGN POLICY 4–5 (2d ed. 1979).

INDEX

Abolition, xxviii, 16–17, 25, 53–61, 72, 128, 171; and Thirteenth Amendment, 5, 30, 68, 71, 192; early movement for, 53–57; self-interest of whites, 55; and civil rights, 56; by resistance, 56–58; by moral suasion, 57; motives of, 58–59; African-Americans' perception of, 58–60; and Native Americans, 59; and precept of inferiority, 59–61

Accusations, false. *See* Allegations, false

Adams, Henry (African American, from Louisiana), 93

Adams, John Quincy, 68–69, 230n1

Adams, John S., 249n56

Adams, Lionel, 112

Affirmative action, viii, ix

African-American, as term: in author's terminology, ix–x

African Americans: as Congressional pages, viii; and affirmative action, viii; as part of "We the People," xxiii, xxviii, xxxii, 65, 82, 127, 218–19n11; arrival in U.S. (1619), xxviii, xxxii, 18–19; and precept of inferiority, 3–4, 11, 29; and *Dred Scott*, 7, 61–67; as objects of hate, 10–15, 50; and social and color ladder, 13–14, 38, 59; and blackness as sin, 19–27; stereotypes of, 31, 41–42, 44–46, 96, 103–105, 129, 130, 132; and Lincoln's view of separation of races, 67; and Reconstruction Amendments, 83–87, 89–90; and election of 1876, 91; semantic distinction of term, 145; and Hughes Court, 159–164. *See also* Inferiority, precept of

African National Congress, x, 193

Alabama, 117–118, 254n113, 259n21; Supreme Court of, 137, 139–140, 144, 148–149; Court of Appeals, 141, 146

Aldisert, Ruggero J., 4, 216n2

Allegations, false, xxv, xxvii

American Anti-Slavery Society, 57. *See also* Abolition

American Bar Association, 185

Amsterdam, Anthony, 131

Ancestry, black, 35–41; and religion, 47–48. *See also* Purity, racial

Anderson, Jesse, xxvii

Anderson, Marian, 259n19

Anderson, William D., 266n88

Antebellum period (1820–1865) 5, 94; 217n7; master and slave and, 25, 34, 42–44; Reconstruction Amendments, 83, 84; plight of freed slaves, 85–86; federal civil-rights enforcement, 89–90; continued repression of African Americans (1876), 91; and public accommodations, 95; treatment of women, 99; and criminal justice system, 128; and the vote, 169–172; and Ten Precepts of American Slavery Jurisprudence, 204, 206

Anthony, Susan B., 272n42

Antidiscrimination laws, post-Civil War, 109–110

Anti-lynching bill (1935), 266n89

Anti-Semitism, 17; and Justice McReynolds, 159, 261n41

Antislavery movement, 53–59. *See also* Abolition

Apartheid, South African, 133

Appellate courts: racist language and, 145–147; importance in deterring court-sanctioned racism, 148. *See also* Courts; Supreme Court, U.S.

Appleton, Nathaniel, 53–54

Aptheker, Herbert, 273n43

TABLE OF CASES

300

CPSIA information can be obtained at www.ICGtesting.com
Printed in the USA
BVOW071045160212

283074BV00001B/2/A